Baloney, Baloney, Baloney!

Baloney, Baloney, Baloney!

A Memoir

R OBERT A LFARO

ISBN 979-8-89316-303-2 (Paperback)
ISBN 979-8-89316-302-5 (Hardback)
ISBN 979-8-89316-304-9 (Ebook)

For my

Children

Grandchildren

Great Grandchildren

The First Years

I was born on a Sunday in 1951 at seven a.m. July 29 of 1951 was not a special day in the world. Not much was going on in our country either. I don't know whether it was a hot day or a cold day, a wet day or a dry day. All I know is that I was born on that day in Dr. Gibson's hospital.

My mother named me Roberto Favela Alfaro. I was called "Bavy" by my parents and my mother's family members. It was the Spanish equivalent of "Baby." By the time I was five, being called "Bavy" was embarrassing. I usually answered to just about any name you could think of during my early years. "Mocoso" was one of my uncle's favorites, meaning "boy with a runny nose," and stuck for about five years.

It was not until I started school that my mother, Pino, insisted that everyone stop calling me "Baby" and start calling me Robert with no *o* on the end. Years later, when I was thirty-five, I found her cleaning out an old desk. She called me aside to show me some old documents. There were old report cards, award certificates, notes from teachers, and one official-looking document.

"Here," she said, handing me a tattered envelope. "I've been meaning to give you this." As I opened it, she continued. "That's your birth certificate. I think you need to keep it."

I looked down at the document and said, "Roberto? My real name is Roberto?"

"Yes, that's your real name."

For thirty-five years, I'd really thought my name was Robert with no *o*. I'd gone through school being called Robert. It was a good thing though, because there was another Hispanic boy about my age who went by the name Roberto. He was born with an oversized head, which made him look oddly strange. The kids made fun, calling him "pumpkin head" behind his back. The power of one letter separated me from such humiliation. I didn't want people getting us confused. I liked being called Robert.

One of my uncles would call me "Heford." I asked him why he called me by that name. He explained, with a mischievous look on his face, that it was in Hereford, Texas, where he thought I was conceived. He just couldn't pronounce it.

"What in the world were my parents doing in Hereford?" I asked. He told me they had been picking cotton. He believed my parents were having sex, and he just put two and two together. "Heford" stuck for about three years.

My mother's maiden name was Favela, and traditionally, Mexican women who married used their last name for a middle name for their children. I was stuck with Favela. Hard to explain to white folks. Favela was later changed to Fabela, and it stuck.

My dad, Chuy, was sixteen years older than my mom. And since he left Sahuayo, Mexico, without any kind of identification, it was hard to determine his exact age. He claimed to have been born on May 25, 1923, but we were never really sure. Mother decided it was a good day for him, so we didn't question it. Besides, who were we to question the adults?

I don't know whether this makes any difference when you are in love with somebody, but in those days, it wasn't unheard of for men to marry much younger women. Seems like it didn't matter to my parents until several years later, when Mom found out that Dad was a jealous, vindictive man. He felt his word was law and nothing else mattered. This would be the long struggle between them, making life at home, at times, a living hell.

Seven kids were born to Chuy and Pino. Being born first was a stroke of luck for me. I was the only child for a year. So for one year, I was pampered, adored, and loved. My mother loved me so. I know because she would tell me often. When my sister Nancy was born a year later, that ended the coddling. And then, children kept coming. Wanda, Jesse, Imelda, Nora, and Waldo. Seven kids! A big family was the norm, and we weren't any different.

I never questioned my name, though at times, I wondered where the name Waldo came from. There were no other Mexican kids named Waldo. *Why are our names similar to Anglo names?* I would ask myself. We grew up with a Mexican father and a Mexican American mother. Why not José, or Juan, or Miguel? My father had such a cultural influence on our upbringing that it was surprising to me that we were given what I considered white names. My mother shared with me, years later, why. She wanted us to be more American than Mexican.

"You live in America. You are American, and you deserve those names," she demanded, as if that made a difference to young children. I didn't get it until I was much older. I'm glad she said more American than Mexican and not more white than brown. Not that I have anything against whites. One or two of them were good friends of mine growing up.

My parents struggled to make ends meet during those first few years of marriage. Mother told me, "The first few years after you were born were quite difficult for us. We lived in a one-bedroom apartment on South Jackson Street. The building, made from adobe, looked like an army barracks. The building housed two other families."

"Did you know them?" I asked.

"No. Your father didn't like to associate with anyone, so he made us keep to ourselves. One room, one door, which your father locked from the outside when he went to work. At the end of the day, upon his return, he would unlock it. Sometimes it was later than sooner. If I had to go to the bathroom, it was in a Folgers coffee can. You know, the big ones."

When I asked her why he locked the door from the outside, she said he didn't want anybody coming to the house while he was gone. Especially her relatives.

"You and I spent a lot of time together during that first year," she said. "You were growing fast and eating more than I expected. Food was scarce, but we survived," she recalled with a sad look.

Those first few years were sorely lacking for us, but we didn't lack love from our mother. Family always came first, so in spite of my father's hatred toward her family, she would not separate us from them. Grandfather and Grandmother were always close by to provide support when needed, which was quite often.

Once, when I was about four years old, my grandparents were having a Sunday gathering at their house. Aunts, uncles, cousins, and tons of kids were there. We seldom attended these functions as a family. And when my mom and we kids went, my dad rarely went with us. The house wasn't very big, but it had more than one room, a wooden floor, four windows, and two doors. There was a kitchen, a bedroom, another bedroom, and a small foyer at the entrance. It had a small backyard with no grass, only dirt. The rooms were small and crowded when everyone was there. Like my mother, some of the older Fabela kids had married and moved on. But when everyone was there, the women stayed inside gossiping while the men lingered outdoors. On that particular day, most of the men were outside deciding what they were going to cook for dinner. I was inside admiring all the different things Grandma and Grandpa had collected over the years—a family Bible, cups and saucers carefully displayed on top of a cabinet, and pictures of Mom alongside a picture of Jesus Christ plastered on the wall.

I noticed an unplugged radio in one of the bedrooms. I tried plugging it in but couldn't get the prongs to go in the socket. So, curiosity getting the better of me, I wanted to know how this wall socket worked. I looked around to see if there was something I could insert into the socket. Luckily, I found a bobby pin—one of those things women use to hold down their hair. I opened the ends enough to fit into the sockets and pushed.

The current shocked and blew me ten feet backward, with the bobby pin burned and molded into my palm. The shock knocked me out. It burned fuses, which cut off all electricity to the house. The electrical box almost caught fire.

I snapped out of consciousness, crying and yelling for my mother. Instantly, my uncle scooped me up off the floor and rushed me outside while the others filled a pan with kerosene. They stuck my hand in the pan and told me to keep it there. As tears ran down my puffy cheeks and slimy boogers ran down my upper lip, I did what I was told.

Every culture has a home remedy that is supposed to cure any ailment. Kerosene for Hispanics, or at least for this group, was the magic medicinal formula that cured it all. I was wailing at the point of screaming obscenities, thinking my hand was going to have to be amputated.

Those watching me didn't say a word. They just kept looking at me until one of the men—could have been my grandfather—let out a smirk, bringing the others to hysterical, unstoppable laughter.

"You're lucky you didn't burn down the house!" he mused. After my crying subsided, I was even more lucky I didn't get an ass-whooping for doing something so stupid.

Curiosity was in my nature.

On another occasion at my grandparents' house, one of my uncles bought a billy goat (a *cabrito*), which always created excitement. The Fabela family was known for their love of cabrito. There was a sense of festivity in the air when families got together and butchered one. Folks brought over beans, tortillas, *fideo*, and *papas* to complement the meat. Jalapeños, cilantro, onion, and *pico de gallo* were frequently a given when having cabrito.

The tradition was carried on by the young kids, like us, who were allowed to stand around as the goat was pulled off the truck, hog-tied, and butchered. My uncle, with a huge butcher knife in hand, grabbed the goat by the horns and cut along the throat as the goat—eyes popping out of his sockets and bleating with fright—eventually succumbed.

We were allowed to watch this! We were too young!

"Get the pots!" yelled my uncle. Then people rushed to get pans and pots. Everyone scrambled to place them under the goat's neck to catch the blood as it gushed and dripped down its neck. After a few minutes, with his tongue hanging out the side of his mouth, the goat stopped moving.

I'd never seen anything like it before. Surprisingly, it really didn't bother me. Nancy, who had no business standing there with the boys in the group, started to throw up and had to be taken inside. I wondered if they were going to give her kerosene to make her feel better.

A hole big enough to cook the goat in was dug into the ground. The goat was hung upside down by its hind legs as the butcher, my uncle Oscar, took the knife and plunged it not far from its testicles, then brought it down toward the neck. The intestines, steaming from the goat's hot innards, were caught in a pan. All sorts of gooey stuff fell into pans. Intestines, heart, lungs, liver, pancreas—it all would become food. Nothing was wasted.

The skin was cut away, starting from the middle of the abdomen and around to the back.

A fire was started in the hole, creating hot, burning coal. Once the hole had enough coal, my grandfather cut the meat off the goat's bones and passed it on to the men, who wrapped it up in wet tow sacks and placed them in the hole. There was no aluminum foil to wrap the meat. Tow sacks did the job just fine. Once all the meat was placed in the ground, more hot coals were added on top.

I kept thinking, *What a stupid idea. The sack is going to burn, ruining all the meat!* But that didn't happen. I learned quite a few things on that day.

Inside the house, the women were preparing the liver, pancreas, lungs, tongue, cheeks, and who knows what else. I didn't stay long enough to see the cooking. I wasn't about to eat any of that stuff. It looked yucky and unappetizing. I bet it tasted yucky too. Nope, it was not for me.

It took several hours for the meat in the hole to be brought up, filling the air with this intoxicating aroma. The women prepared a plate for the men, who took it outside to eat. The children were fed next. I made sure I only got meat cooked from the ground and not anything else.

"Pino, I don't want that stuff there," I said, pointing to different dishes.

"*Come esto,*" she said. ("Here, try this.") Then she put the cooked cabrito next to the beans, rice, and potatoes. As she poured some yuck onto my plate, she turned to the others and said, "*¿Está muy bueno, verdad?*" ("It's good, right?)

"*No, por favor. No quiero,*" I cried. ("Please, Mom, I don't want any.")

She would not hear any of my objections. She just kept placing things on my plate. I'd never had cabrito before. I didn't want to eat what I'd seen being killed. But I had no choice. I took a small piece so my uncle wouldn't get offended and Mom wouldn't chastise me. I took the meat, placed it on a tortilla with pico de gallo, and wrapped it like a burrito. Reluctantly, I took my first bite. I was surprised at how delicious and tasty it was. I went back for more three times around until I could eat no more. This meal was a rarity, and I realized that. To have any kind of meat—other than just tortillas, potatoes, and beans—was special for us. This was big time for the Fabela family. I still don't know what the occasion was. I didn't care. It was special.

The tradition died with me. I would never kill a goat. The eyes popping out of its sockets gave me nightmares for weeks! Although I loved the taste of cabrito, we kids should have never been allowed to see the butchering of any animal for food. It would be weeks before I got a chance to eat meat again. I wasn't cut out to be a vegetarian. I liked meat. It was hard to come by, but when it did, we ate heartily. There were many instances when bologna was the only meat we had for weeks. I had no complaints when it came to bologna.

When the adults were busy doing adult things, I'd snoop around. It didn't matter where I was. Once, I found a spinning top in one of my grandmother's kitchen cabinets. It must have belonged to either Sammy or Fidel, my uncles. It was a pretty bright-blue top. I'd never spun a top before, but I'd seen it done. Around the front of the house, where no one could see, I started playing with it. Wrapping the string around the top, I threw it on the ground. I tried it again, throwing it harder. Not much luck. It would land flat on its side, not spinning like I'd seen before. I tried it again and again, feeling agitated until I finally blurted out, *"Pinche trompo. ¡No vale madre!"* ("F—ing top. It's not worth a mother.") I didn't realize that my grandfather was coming around the corner and heard me. He had a wood saw in his hand. Holding me up by one hand, he swatted me across the ass. I squirmed, trying to get away, but he was holding on tight.

"*No quiero que andes echando maldiciones, chamaco.*" ("I don't ever want to hear you cussing again, boy!") He let go, and I ran crying to Mother, who was too busy to ask what happened. It would be another two years before I mastered the toy. I had a lot of growing up to do first.

It wasn't long before we had to move out of our house. But the new house was not new at all. It was just another one-room house not too far from the barracks. The house was adobe and had a wooden door with a screen. Big time!

It also had a rusty tin roof. When it rained, it leaked. When it was cold outside, we kept warm by standing or sitting close to the gas stove, which was the only heat in the house.

There was an outhouse behind our small home, but it was only used for pooping. We always kept those big Folgers coffee cans just in case someone had to pee during the winter months. My dad had his own can, and he filled that thing to the brim every night. In the morning, I had to pick it up from the sides, since it had no handles, and dump it. I'd walk slowly through the front door, hoping and praying it wouldn't slip from my tiny hands and splash all over my feet. If I got past the door to the outside, I'd pour his pee in the weeds, killing everything it came in contact with.

I did this every morning till one day I asked him, "Why don't we just go outside to pee?" Peeing in a can without having to go outside in the middle of the night was so much easier for Chuy.

He raked his knuckles over my head, saying, "Remember, you have a job too."

I didn't get it, but I knew this was not something I would be doing for a long time. To this day, Folgers coffee is not my favorite.

The outhouse was off-limits for me. I was not allowed anywhere near it until I was four. Mom figured that by that age, I was big enough to go by myself without falling in the hole. The place smelled bad, especially during hot summer days. When I sat to take care of business, half the time, I kept swatting flies with the pages of the Sears and Roebuck catalog, which we kept nearby for wiping our asses. I don't remember using real toilet paper until we moved to a house with a real floor and in-house plumbing. That would be several years later. Back then, it was the catalog or newspaper. They were both stainers. They stained your ass with black print that rubbed off as you wiped. Corn cobs were out of the question, since we didn't eat corn.

When I was four and a half years of age, one of the happiest moments in my young life was opening Christmas presents. I remember asking my parents for an axe and some guns. Yeah. Just a little axe I could take camping. The guns were for hunting down the animals that might try to eat me. There was a *llano*, or empty lot, across the street. It was the perfect place to go camping and hunting because it didn't have any buildings. It had tall weeds that hid me from intruders. It was my very own jungle and my home away from home. I could spend hours in the jungle, pretending to hunt down wild animals.

Christmas came around, and, to my surprise, I didn't get an axe. I got a hatchet! The hatchet came with a little holster. I found a belt, strapped it around my waist, tucked the axe near my hip, grabbed my cowboy hat and shoes, and headed out to the jungle. I managed to cut a few weeds, making an area wide enough to start a fire. I ran back to the house and grabbed some matches, a potato, and a knife.

Mom yelled, "*¡Espérate, chamaco! ¿Dónde vas con esa papa?*" ("Wait, boy! Where are you going with that potato?")

"I'm going to make lunch!" I yelled back, not stopping as I ran out the door. She never questioned the knife or the matches!

I made a small fire in the hole I had cut out with the hatchet. I cut small pieces of sticks and placed them over dry grass. Grabbing the matches out of the box, I lit enough of them to start a fire. It wasn't a big fire, but it was big enough to have set everything around me in a blaze.

Fortunately, that didn't happen. It was a miracle.

Once I had enough embers in the hole, I placed the potato on top. I sat there for what seemed like hours, watching the potato cook, with skin and all. I watched the smoke turn the peeling black. I used the knife to roll the potato around until the entire thing was black with soot. It looked like a roasted, burned rock. When I thought it was done, I stuck my axe back in my hip belt, stabbed the potato with the knife, and ran back across the street with lunch.

Pino made me throw it away, making me promise not to take any more potatoes for my experiments.

"We can't afford to waste food! No more!" she demanded.

I learned fairly early that food was most important—more important than matches or knives. It was not something we played with or wasted. What was surprising to me was that she never questioned where I had started a fire to cook that potato. Or that I had even started a fire! Those were great days.

The Family Grows

By 1957, our family was getting bigger. After Nancy, my sister Wanda came in June of 1954, followed close behind by Jesús (Jesse,) who was born on August 1, 1955.

The house was getting too small for us. Chuy was working odd jobs as a construction worker, and it seemed like things were going well. But if they weren't, I wouldn't have known. I got a hatchet for Christmas. Things must have been good. In the whole scheme of things, we still qualified as poor and couldn't afford a bigger house, so we made do.

Our days were filled with thoughtful play. Pino would sit me down, and we'd listen to the radio. It was all in English, which I didn't understand. But she insisted I listen. There were times when I would pass out with boredom. I mean, I'd fall over into a deep sleep while the radio announcer droned on about who knows what. I felt like she was punishing me. I didn't realize she was trying to learn English by listening to the radio and didn't want to do it alone. If she could do it, then she reckoned I could do it too. Learn English from the radio? Are you kidding me?

In 1957, just about the time I was turning six, my mother registered me for school. There was no kindergarten in the barrio. Everybody started school as a first grader. At least the Mexican kids did.

Butz Elementary School, which was considered the Mexican school, was two blocks away from where we lived. On the first day of school, Mother made sure I got in with a Spanish-speaking teacher because I knew no English. (The damn radio hadn't helped.) She walked me to school that first day, freshly bathed, my hair combed, and sporting new underwear.

I remember the first school picture I took. Pino proudly showed that picture to anyone she came in contact with. I think she wanted to show people what I actually looked like when I was clean. She would comb my hair in two parts, one on each side, with the hair coming together on top. Looking at that picture many years later, she told me it was Dad's idea. I had a small face, with little brown eyes and puffy cheeks. I wasn't fat. I just had big cheeks. She dressed me in black pants, a white shirt, and a bow tie with little pistols on each side of the knot. I looked pretty cute for a Mexican kid! She kept that picture on a stand for many years. She was so proud of it.

Mrs. Falcon, my first-grade teacher, was a nice, matronly lady. She was not a very big person, yet she looked intimidating. She had a soft voice, which alleviated for the students the dread of being left alone with her. She dressed nicely, with her hair in a bun, which made her look so professional and rich. I'd not seen anyone dress that nicely.

When Pino left, she warned, "Don't cry, and don't cause the teacher problems. Learn as much as you can so you can have a good job. *¿Comprendes?*" ("Understand?")

I nodded and said, "*Sí.*" I didn't understand how learning English was going to get me a good job. I didn't want a job. I already had one, according to Chuy. I threw out his piss every morning when I got up. If that was a real job, then I didn't want a job!

Much to my surprise, the year started out great with Mrs. Falcon. She passed out pencils and paper to all the kids. For

19

free! I was getting something tangible. How exciting. I went to school with a Big Chief notebook and one No. 2 pencil. I was ready to learn.

The first few days were all about learning English—those English words you need to survive in the world. We learned to say things like:

"I need to go to the bathroom."

"Where is the bathroom?"

"Please."

"Thank you."

"I want some water. Can I get some water, please?"

"When do we go to the cafeteria?"

That was a hard one because *cafeteria* had too many syllables.

I don't know why I found it so hard to ask to go to the bathroom in English. It just wouldn't come out right. I really tried. It was a difficult thing to remember, yet I needed it almost every day at about the same time. I remember going up to Mrs. Falcon one morning and asking her if I could go to the bathroom. I asked her in the only way I could. In Spanish.

"*¿Puedo ir al baño?*" I looked up at her and pleaded my case by wiggling around, holding my hands close to my crotch.

"Tell me in English," she said, pushing her glasses up her nose.

"*¿Puedo* go *al baño?*"

After a couple of tries, she told me to go back to my seat and try to remember how to say it in English. "Go back and sit down," she demanded, moving away from me as she faced the other students.

I had to go. I had to go bad! But I couldn't bring the words together, and by the time I thought I had it, the pee just flowed out of me. I peed in my pants, sitting in my chair, for crying out loud! Pee ran down my pant legs and onto the floor. How any of the students didn't see this was beyond me.

This would not be the only time. I quickly learned that in order to avoid pissing in my pants, I had to learn to say it in English or hold my pee until we all went to the bathroom together during morning break. I must have pissed in my pants at least once a week.

Some days, my pants were so wet that I didn't leave my chair until school let out. I was the first one out the door at the end of the day unless I pissed my pants. On those days, I would wait until everyone left, then I'd leave, making sure my back was to the wall until I got outside. For some reason, by the end of the day, the front of my pants would dry off, but not the rear. If other students were outside, I'd walk with my back to the wall of bricks until I reached the end of the building. I would then run home. At times, I'd be the last one to leave the building, hoping I would not run into a student or teacher. Once I got home, I'd change my underwear and pants before Chuy got home. Instead of being embarrassed, I was dreadfully frightened the other children would see me with wet pants and laugh. Eventually I got it right.

My first year in school didn't go as well as I'd hoped. I was already beginning to hate it. I was having a very difficult time, especially with the language. Pissing my pants wasn't the only thing that made me mad. I also didn't like learning the alphabet. It didn't make sense to me. *Why all this repetition?* I wondered. *What good will this do for me? Why am I learning this stuff? It's silly.* Other children in class saw me struggling, and I could feel their frustration when it came my turn to put letters together to make words I didn't understand. It took me longer than anyone.

About two blocks from our house on the way to school was a water well that had been filled with dirt. The outer wall, made of rock, was still there. It was about four feet deep. More of a decorative thing, it sat right in a neighbor's front yard. One Friday before a holiday, I was walking to school and noticed the well. I had some work to turn in to Mrs. Falcon, but I hadn't done it. It was too hard, and no one at home could help me. They didn't know enough English.

What if I hide in the well until school lets out? I thought. *Nobody will know. I won't get lectured in front of the other students for not turning in my work. No one will ever know. I can skip school.*

These thoughts ran through my mind as I walked past the well. I convinced myself this might be the perfect way to settle my dilemma. As a first grader, my brain didn't register this action as a bad thing. I just thought I was being smart enough to fool the adults.

I didn't know this was called playing hooky. I also didn't know it was against the law. Apparently, there was some rule called Compulsive Education, which required students to be in attendance a certain number of days of the year. Not knowing about the law, I skipped school. I climbed into the well and hid from students heading to school.

I could see the school playground from my hiding place. I lay down on the cool dirt, pondering just how smart this was. I looked up at the sky and watched the clouds go by. At times, I heard cars driving by and wondered who it might be. I sat cross-legged and drew pictures on the dirt. I didn't know how long I'd been in the well, but it seemed like I had been there all day. Besides, I was running out of things to do in the quiet of the well. I heard children talking loudly, and my curiosity got the better of me. I poked my head over the top. That was when I saw the students running out of the building.

I crawled out of the well, thinking, *Que bueno.* (*Oh, good.*) School was out! I made my way toward my grandmother's house because I knew Pino was going to be there that afternoon. I walked in the house, trying to look like I'd had an exhausting day. I put on my best tired face. I was hungry and thirsty.

When Mom saw me, she asked, "*¿Qué estás haciendo aquí tan temprano?*" ("What are you doing here so early?")

"School is out. I'm hungry!" I said eagerly. She took me by the arm and walked me back to school and straight to Mrs. Falcon's room. What I had seen was not the kids coming home after a long day at school but students running out of the building and racing to the playground. It was morning recess!

I was caught. I pleaded guilty, hoping I would not get in trouble with the law. A beating was one thing, but going to jail was another.

Pino said, "*Espera que venga tu papá. Vas a ver.*" ("Wait till your father gets home. You'll see.") The look she gave me most certainly assured me she was going to tell Chuy. That was going to get me a beating.

It did. I was spanked with a belt several times until I cried out for help from Mom, which never came. I was placed in a corner, on my knees, and told to pray for forgiveness for being bad. If I sat on my heels, Chuy would walk over, swing his boot, catch me on my butt, and lift me up on my knees again. I kneeled for what seemed hours. This was not the only time this would happen. It was just the beginning.

The rest of the year went by without incident. I was learning how to write letters in English on the Big Chief tablet, which Pino checked each evening. I settled down to a routine of daily work. I wanted to impress Mrs. Falcon, who, for some reason, took a liking to me. I was learning phases in English, which I combined with Spanish when I didn't know the correct wording. She was proud of me for trying.

We took a break from Mrs. Falcon every day. Or, rather, she took a break from us when we went to music class. Music was taught by a different teacher. I loved this class. We would sing, dance, and play different instruments. The teacher would strum a guitar and ask us to sing along as she played. We sang songs about Thanksgiving, turkeys, and Pilgrims. The best were

Christmas songs. I learned "Silent Night," "Frosty the Snowman," and "Jingle Bells." I loved music. I couldn't get enough of it.

But just when I was beginning to enjoy schooling, school ended. I was sad to be leaving Mrs. Falcon. On the last day of school, I hugged her. I handed her a note I wrote in all English words: "I love you, Mrs. Falcon."

Awaiting the report card to see if I had made it to the second grade weighed heavily on me. I knew my grades were terrible, so if I didn't pass to the next grade, it was not going to be a surprise for me. It was definitely going to be a surprise to Pino and Chuy. I prayed to the Virgin Mary to guide Mrs. Falcon in making the right decision for me. By some miracle, my prayers were answered. I was going to second grade! When Pino got the report card, she looked at it, then handed it to me.

"What does it say?" she asked.

I looked at it: Reading, C. Math, C-. Writing, B. Attendance, U. Music, B+. Attitude, C. The comment section read, "Robert can do better, but he doesn't try hard enough. He will need to practice his vocabulary every day this summer if he is to succeed in the second grade." The teacher's comments further told of my satisfactory efforts at being a good student. She wrote, "With a little help during the summer, Robert will do better in second grade."

"It says I got three Cs, two Bs, and an S in attendance, which is good," I said. "It says I work hard and am a good student. It says to take it easy this summer because next year will be hard."

I tried really hard to avoid eye contact.

She must have believed me because her next comment was, "*¡Ves! ¡Yo sabía que podías! Te voy a comprar un ice cream. Vamos!*" ("See, I knew you could do it!" I'm going to buy you an ice cream. Let's go!") Mom nodded approvingly and smiled.

Off we went for ice cream. On the way to the store, I thought, *How did I manage to get to second grade?*

It still baffles me.

New Experiences

Sometime before my seventh birthday, we moved to a bigger house. Buildings and apartments made of adobe could be found anywhere in the barrio. My parents were able to find one with two rooms. It was right across the street from Fidel's Grocery Store, a convenience store catering to the Hispanic community. The prices resembled today's convenience store prices. Expensive.

The barracks-style building had an outhouse, which we shared with two old men living in separate rooms. Fidel, the old man who owned the store, rented out these rooms to poor people, and we still qualified as poor. There was no air conditioning, but the adobe kept the house cool in the summer and warm in the winter.

Walking five blocks, we moved our meager belongings in one trip. We didn't own a car at the time. However, it wasn't long before Chuy got his hands on a 1951 pickup truck. He drove that truck back and forth to work without a driver's license.

"How can I get a driver's license when the questions are in English?" he would ask. "If they had the test in Spanish, I would pass it, no *problema*."

Fidel's sat on the corner of Ryan and Texas Streets, a busy intersection during the day, but it was very quiet at night. Right next to the front entrance was a big picture window with his name painted on it in big black letters: "Fidel's Grocery Store." The store was small by today's standards and covered with green stucco on the outside.

Fidel had all sorts of items besides groceries. Very few people bought their groceries there because it was too expensive. He made most of his money selling beer, soft drinks, candy, and ice cream. There were times when Fidel would allow us to buy things on credit, which had to be paid at the end of the week.

It was nighttime when we got word that my dad had crashed into Fidel's picture window while driving drunk. Driving south on Texas Street, he'd missed the turn. He must have been in a drunken stupor when he struck the store head-on.

Someone came knocking on our door, saying, "Chuy just crashed into Fidel's store. Come quick!"

It was late at night. As I rubbed my eyes and tried to focus in the darkness, we ran outside. When my eyes adjusted, I saw the truck. He'd gone right through the big picture window. The truck was stuck halfway inside the store. Broken glass was everywhere, and he was standing there with not a single cut or broken bone.

The police arrived in time to find Fidel cussing and yelling. He was furious, threatening to press charges for all damages. The police, once they got Fidel under control, proceeded to question my dad, who was in no condition to describe what had happened. His not being able to stand without stumbling gave it away. It wasn't long before I saw them driving him off to the county jail.

I don't know what ever became of Fidel's threat, but I do know that Dad had hell trying to get a driver's license after that incident. It would take several tickets and a few more days in jail for driving without a license before he decided to learn just enough to pass the test. Even then, it would take several attempts.

The day after the accident, Pino and I walked to the county jail to see Dad. The judge would not be available for a few more days, so he had to stay locked up.

The Pecos County Jail was not a very big place. It sat at the corner of West Gallagher and Main. The building was intimidating. Made of stone inside and out, it resembled an old haunted house. The sheriff lived in an apartment on the bottom floor of the two-story building. The prisoners were kept upstairs.

When it was time to visit the prisoner, Mom and I walked up a flight of steel stairs. The empty, echoing sounds with each step we took reverberated off the walls. The inside was made of old wrought iron with walls painted light green. As we got to the top of the stairs, I noticed steel bars separating those jailed from the visitors. There were several men in one large room. Other prisoners were kept in separate cells. There wasn't much room to move, so we had to wait until a visitor left before another was let in.

I didn't want to go inside, but Mom was insistent that I see what the jail was like and how the prisoners looked behind bars. I stood with my back against the wall, not wanting to get too close to the bars. Dad walked a few steps toward us. I shook at the sight of him behind those bars.

"Hey, come here," he said, putting his hands through the bars and wanting to hold mine. I couldn't move. I couldn't talk. I was terrified.

"Come here!" he demanded. A few short steps got me to the bars. He smiled and said, "Are you being good?"

What the hell do you mean, "Are you being good"? Look at you! Who's behind bars? I thought.

Mom had brought him a clean shirt, clean pants, and a pack of cigarettes. They talked briefly in a whispered tone. I believe it was so I couldn't hear about the serious trouble he was in for driving drunk, damaging the store, and not having a driver's license.

A few days later, my dad showed up at the house, fired from his job and mad as hell. I was totally surprised we didn't get evicted from Fidel's barracks.

The summer of 1957, we were still living in the adobe barracks and struggling to make ends meet. Dad was out of a job, again. Things were getting pretty uncomfortable as conversations turned into arguments between him and Mom. He did manage to find work, but things around the house were still tense.

While Dad was out working or drinking away the week's earnings, I roamed the hood. About a block down the street, heading south toward the town plaza, was an old schoolhouse that had been abandoned when Butz Elementary was built. This place had been turned into living accommodations for poor people. Some of the classrooms had become apartment-like dwellings, but not all of them. The Rodriguez family lived in two of the rooms, and the others were left empty. With doors missing, walls crumbling, and the place trashed by kids, many wondered how the building was still inhabited. But it had become the perfect place for young boys to play in.

The Rodriguez family was made up of a bunch of boys, some close to my age. I would hang out with them, roaming the old building and trashing old desks and chairs. No one cared. We'd play chase, jump through windows, run in hallways, and dangle from old lumber stacked at least six feet high. It made perfect hiding places. It was a jungle, and we loved to zoom in and out of the crevices between the old boards.

One day, I went early to their place and found the boys outside yelling and screaming. They were between the old schoolhouse and an abandoned building with a narrow passage between the two.

One of them said to me, "*Mira, mira.*" ("Look, look.")

They had two dogs surrounded between the buildings. Using brooms and mops to scoot them together, they watched the dogs with wicked smiles on their faces. It was my first experience seeing dogs doing it. I was stunned.

"What are they doing?" I asked.

"You'll see."

The male dog would jump on the back of the female dog and hump.

"What are they doing?" I asked again.

The boys just laughed and pointed at the dogs. I couldn't take my eyes off them, waiting to see what would happen. Once the male dog entered the female dog, they got stuck. I turned to one of the boys, who was yelling and egging them on.

"What are the dogs doing?"

He ignored me and used the broom to beat the female dog so she would let the male free himself from her. Once the dogs were separated, they surrounded them and had them do the same thing again.

I found this difficult to understand. It wasn't the kind of stuff I could discuss with my parents. The incident left a lasting impression on my seven-year-old brain. There were more questions than answers, which I struggled with for a long time. I didn't ask any more questions for fear the boys would make fun of me. Instead, I watched with intensity and asked why these dogs would go back and do the same thing, knowing full well they were going to get beaten until they separated.

It was weeks before I went back to play with the Rodriguez boys again. When I did, there were several little puppies running around outside. I didn't put two and two together. It would be a long time before I understood.

We must have moved up the poor scale that year because by then, we seemed to be managing. I mean, we were still poor, but there were weeks when, with Dad working a steady job, we didn't struggle as much. The arguments between Mom and Dad were still there but weren't as frightful.

The summer was ending abruptly for me. I needed to get ready for the second grade. However, school was not to start until September, so I had some time to keep playing. The Christmas before, Dad had bought me a BB gun—something I had been asking for. (I can understand an axe for Christmas, but a BB gun? I was six. What did I know about guns?)

"I love it! Can I use it?" I had asked that Christmas morning.

"No," my dad had said. "You can use it when you turn seven. It's too dangerous for you. Leave it in the package. On your next birthday, I'll show you how it works."

That summer, I was chomping at the bit to learn how to shoot the BB gun because I was turning seven.

"It's going to be my birthday," I said to both Mom and Dad. "Are you going to show me how to use the rifle?"

On July 29, 1958, we broke open the BB gun. Dad showed me how to load, cock, aim, and shoot. I would sit outside and shoot at beer bottles, mostly missing my target. But the more I shot, the better I got.

The rule was that I could not use it until both my parents were home. One day, knowing they would not be home until later, I pulled the rifle out from under the bed and went outside. I was shooting beer bottles, the quart size because that was what my dad drank. I had my sister Nancy, who was six, place the bottles—two at a time—and I'd shoot at them from twenty to thirty yards away. (Not very far because the rifle didn't have a lot of power. To break the bottles, I needed to be closer. If not, the BB would just bounce right off.)

Nancy would place the bottles on the ground as I'd cock the rifle. I wasn't very strong, so I would place the barrel on the ground and hold the butt of the rifle to steady it. I'd push the cocking lever down until it clicked. By the time I got all that done, my sister would run like a scared jackrabbit, kicking up dust and dirt with her bare feet. She would run as fast as she could as I took aim and fired. Many a time, she wasn't fast enough, and I almost popped her one in the ass.

I was ready. It was time to take this baby into war.

I took the rifle to show the Rodriguez boys. They had BB guns too. Maybe that's where I got the idea of wanting one. We were talking about hunting wild animals, imagining we were in a jungle.

The oldest boy said, "Let's have a war!" That's what I had been waiting for.

We all jumped up, picking sides. I wanted to be with the older kids, of which two had rifles. But I was outranked. The older three boys were on one side, and the younger three boys on the other. I was with the younger group. We had only my rifle. On the oldest boy's signal, we were to run, take our place among the wooden planks, and start firing. Some would hide inside the windowless rooms of the schoolhouse while others went behind the building.

"It's war!" someone shouted, and the shooting began. The two young kids who did not have a gun were told to use rocks as missiles. The three of us ran outside near the debris, where rocks were abundant. There were no rules, like, "Don't shoot at the face" or "Don't shoot at the head." It was a free-for-all.

Since I couldn't cock the rifle fast enough, I handed it to one of the other boys on my side. I let him shoot while I threw missiles. I don't remember how this war was supposed to end, but I swear, I think it took an hour before we gave up. No one got hurt too seriously. At least there was no blood. Just some red welts around the legs and hands.

I took my BB gun and went home exhausted but smiling because I only had one red welt on my nose. I don't know where it came from. It could have come from my own side. Who knows? It was total chaos. Great time!

The next day, we decided to have another BB gun shootout. The problem was that we were running out of BBs. Where to get some was the discussion for an hour or so.

"We have to go to the store!" someone yelled.

One of the older kids said, "*¡No seas pendejo!*" ("Don't be stupid.") Where do you think we're getting money to buy BBs?"

A Thief

T here wasn't much to downtown Fort Stockton, but we had a Ben Franklin five-and-dime store. It was like present-day Walmart but much smaller. It was on Main Street, across from the First National Bank building. It had everything a kid could ever want.

We managed to scrounge a few pennies between the whole lot of us. The older boys convinced us that we had enough for a bag or two of BBs. The older Rodriguez boy picked one of his brothers and me to go into town to buy ammunition for the next war. I was elated. I was going. No parent permission necessary.

We walked toward the town plaza, passed in front of St. Joseph Church, made the sign of the cross, then headed up the road toward town. Halfway there, we passed a gated tunnel used to direct rainwater from the city toward what used to be called Comanche Springs. Back in the day, Comanche Springs flowed from the ground into a pool-sized pond where families went swimming on hot summer days. Not all families, just white ones.

By the time we were headed to the store, the springs were dry. I wanted to know where this tunnel led to. So we opened the gate and crawled through the tunnel on our hands and knees. We crawled for what seemed an eternity, eventually coming to a lighted area. Suddenly, I saw the older boy stand up. The lighted section was big enough for us to stand upright. I looked up to see a metal grate covering the hole. We were standing in a manhole used to drain rainwater from the street and into Comanche Pool. I could see cars going over the grate. We were under the street right in front of the school district offices. As we counted cars and trucks as they passed over the grate, the older Rodriguez boy dared us to put our fingers through the holes.

"Let's see who can put their fingers outside the grate," he said.

"I'm not gonna do it. What if the cars crush my fingers?" I stuttered, alarmed at the suggestion. He egged us on, calling us crybabies.

"You guys are scared. Only cry babies are scared." Look, see? I'm not afraid," he said nervously, placing his fingers out of the grating. "You're just a bunch of crybabies!"

We heard the rumbling of a truck coming before we saw it go over the gate, and he pulled his hand and fingers back just in time. The truck rolled over the grate, and he started laughing. We all tried it once, and when we'd had enough of counting cars going over us, we started back to the tunnel entrance.

The entire episode scared me.

We passed the old hotel that had served as a busy gathering place for businessmen in its heyday. Now it was mostly abandoned, with the exception of the downstairs. It housed a local bar called Cowboys' Place, which was run by a tall, old white man who always wore a cowboy hat. This used to be one of my dad's favorite hangouts. The place was run down. It had been built using large gray stone blocks, which made it look like one of those buildings you see in Batman movies. The windows were covered with foil paper or plain old newspaper. Some of the rooms in the hotel had curtains with broken window blinds. I never saw anyone going in or out of the hotel, so I assumed no one lived there.

The rest of this massive building was abandoned, just like every other store on that street. The downtown was no more than three or four blocks long, with a furniture store, a department store, a bank, and a Ben Franklin's, all surrounded by a few smaller shops.

We finally made our way to Ben Franklin's. We walked the aisles, looking around for the BBs. The store was huge in the eyes of a seven-year-old. I'd never been inside the store. I was mesmerized by the number of different toys. All sorts of items cost very little money—money we didn't have. There were two workers there—the manager and a lady who stood by the cash register, checking people out. There weren't more than four or five people in the store when we went in, so we just wandered aimlessly up and down the aisles until we found the BBs.

"We have enough money to buy two five-cent packages," the older boy said, looking puzzled.

"But these don't have very many BBs," I replied, concerned we had made a trip for very little. We stood, counting our pennies. We barely had enough. This was not going to cut it.

The smaller Rodriguez blurted out, "Look at these!"

Next to the little sacks were rolls stacked three deep. They looked like penny wrappers and contained many more BBs. We could tell just by holding them in our hands. The wrappers were heavy. The price showed it would cost more than what we had.

Luis, the older boy, looked over his shoulder, then back at us. "We'll look out for the manager, and you take one of the rolled packages," he said to me. "Put it in your pocket, then come back to the counter and pay for the two small packages."

"Where are you going to be?" I asked.

"Right over there. We'll keep the lady busy. Don't worry about the manager."

It didn't seem like a hard thing to do. I knew I was stealing, but we needed the ammo to continue the war. I took the first roll and put it in my pocket, then walked away. It was too easy. I walked toward the end of the aisle and walked back toward the BBs. I took four more rolled packs and felt the weight of the BBs pushing down on my pants. I started walking toward the door, following the two boys. I never went to the counter to pay for the two small packages. I put them back, thinking I had enough.

I had made it out the door when I heard the manager yell, "Stop!"

Holding my pants up by one of the belt loops, I froze. The weight of the BBs was causing my pants to slide down the back of my butt, exposing my underwear. I just started walking faster, holding on to my belt loops.

The manager caught me by the shirt collar, yanked me up, and started pulling BB rolls out of my pockets, yelling, "What do you have? What did you take? Is this all you took? Don't you ever come back into my store and try this again!"

Once he had emptied my pockets, he kicked me in the ass, sending me flying out into the street. "Don't ever come back! You hear?"

His yelling faded once I turned the corner, with my little legs moving faster than I'd ever moved before. The boys had disappeared, leaving me to show myself back home. I cried for the next few blocks, realizing how stupid I'd been to think I could get away with stealing. I rubbed my butt where the man had kicked me. I'd been caught doing something wrong. If my mother ever found out, it would devastate her.

I walked slowly, making my way back the same way I had come. I told myself that I would never go back to Ben Franklin's again. I was ruined. I was a criminal. That was my first encounter with crime.

It would not be my last.

St. Joseph Church

B oth my parents had been raised Catholic. But didn't become regular churchgoers until we kids were old enough to behave while the priest dictated the Sunday lecture.

Early on, about the year I turned six, my parents discussed the idea of me being confirmed. I didn't know what confirmation was, so I didn't let it bother me. I could barely make the sign of the cross, and now they were talking about something called confirmation. I'd been to church a few times but not enough to fully understand what being a Catholic meant.

One bright, sunny Sunday morning, Mom woke me up early.

"You need to take a bath," she said, pouring hot water into a tub situated in the kitchen, close to the stove. I never took baths on Sundays, so I wondered, still half asleep, why she was so interested in me bathing.

She said proudly, "*Hoy, te vamos a confirmer.*" ("Today you are getting confirmed.")

It sounded threatening.

"What's that? I asked, fumbling with my clothes as she prepared the bathwater.

"It's a thing the Church does for little children so they can get closer to Jesus," she articulated.

That's all she said. All sorts of images popped into my head. Was I going to be put on a cross like the man I'd seen in church? The man my parents called Jesús? Why did this happen at church? Was it going to hurt? If I was going to be nailed to a cross, I knew it was going to hurt. All these thoughts circled around in my brain. I was expecting the worst.

"I don't want to go to the church," I cried as she scrubbed the dirt and filth from my body.

"It's going to be fine. You need to do this if Jesus is going to accept you into Heaven."

"I don't want to go to Heaven. I want to stay here!" I demanded, shedding the first of many tears.

I got dressed—or she dressed me—in some new clothes. Looking at myself in brand-spanking-new black pants and a white shirt, I had no choice but to submit. I stopped crying, taking pleasure in my new clothing.

"See how nice you look?" my mom said.

"Mom, why is this necessary?" I asked.

"Because the Church wants all children to be confirmed. This way, you'll be close to God."

I could not believe this was happening to me. I argued. But the more I argued, the more determined she was to see me go.

A big, nice car pulled up to our house and honked. Chuy hollered from the other room, where he was getting dressed. "My compadre is here! We have to go!"

Mom combed my hair the way she usually did—two parts on each side of the head, culminating on top. She took me by the hand and walked me outside. Chuy came out of the house looking clean, shaven, and well-dressed.

"I don't want to go," I pleaded.

"Be quiet and get in the car," he demanded, giving me that look he used when we misbehaved. I could tell my resistance was not in my best interest. The man he'd called compadre was also well-dressed. He was a tall man my dad called Hernandez. He had a box wrapped in white paper with a yellow ribbon around it.

"This is for you," he said, handing me the box.

"You can't open it until we get done at church," insisted Chuy.

"I don't want it," I said. "I just want to stay with Mom."

Chuy grabbed me by the arm and pushed me into the car, quickly shutting the door behind me. I started to cry, looking at Mom, who just stood there as these two men were kidnapping me and taking me to the man on the cross. She smiled and waved as if I was going to a party. Did she not understand I feared being nailed to a cross? Who would do this to young children? I didn't stop crying even though Chuy kept telling me to shut up. He was trying to be nice about it, but I wasn't falling for it.

The car pulled up in front of St. Joseph Catholic Church—a large, intimidating place painted white with a cross sitting high above the steeple. Several cars were already there. We were the last to arrive.

"Come on," Chuy told me as he opened the door.

"I don't want to go," I said, still wailing like I was the sacrificial child before God and everybody.

Typically, the ritual of confirmation happens when a member of the Catholic Church reaches at least thirteen or fourteen years of age. In many cases, parents can decide they want it done earlier. Apparently, my parents felt it was time for me to go through the ritual. Not an exorcism but a ritual. Very different. The rite of confirmation states:

... by the sacrament of Confirmation, [the baptized] are more perfectly bound to the Church and are enriched with a special strength of the Holy Spirit. Hence, they are, as true witnesses of

Christ, more strictly obliged to spread and defend the faith by word and deed.

Try explaining that to a young Catholic and see where it gets you. Adults have a hard time understanding the message. Can you imagine a six-year-old? Regardless, as Catholics, we are bound by the teachings of the Church. And it states that parents must confirm their children.

The actual rite is nothing more than a church service, which takes about an hour. Then the children are brought up to the altar with a parent and a sponsor—in this case, Mr. Hernandez, who would be my godfather—as the priest makes the sign of the cross with holy oil on the child's forehead. Now, if someone had explained that to me, maybe my hysteria would not have been so outrageous.

I was being pulled out of the car as I grabbed anything I could hold on to. I was determined not to go inside. Chuy pulled me, shook me, and told me to stand still while he straightened out my shirt.

As soon as he turned around to go inside, I jumped on the opportunity to flee the scene. A perfect time to escape. I slid under the car, keeping just far enough from grabbing hands.

That didn't work. I was dragged out, shaken again, and literally shoved into the church. Chuy wiped my nose with his handkerchief and told me to stop crying, or he was going to spank me.

I sat quietly, hoping I would not be the first to be killed.

The nightmare was over within an hour. I had survived, thanks to Jesus, to whom I gave thanks for letting me see another day. We filed out of the church, parents and children alike, smiling and laughing. I was just itching to get in the car and open that box.

"What's this?" I asked, holding up the small book I removed from the box.

"It's a Bible," stated the Hernandez man.

"What's it for?" I asked him.

"It's for you to use when you come to church. It's your own personal Bible. Every kid gets one when they're confirmed."

I thought it was going to be a toy of some sort. Instead, I got a book. Little did I know, I would lean on that Bible more often than I ever expected growing up. Mr. Hernandez brought me a Christmas present every year until I got to high school. I never saw him but on Christmas Day. As long as he brought me presents, I considered him a great godfather.

There were pleasant times when Dad would relent and allow us to visit Mom's parents. We visited them every so often, especially on Sundays after being dragged to church. Since that awful, excruciating experience I'd endured earlier, I couldn't figure out why church was so important to Hispanics. My grandparents were very religious, always preaching to us about being good Catholics.

Grandmother would say, "Praying to Jesus Christ will help you be a good Christian." She taught me how to pray. In Spanish. "Put your hands together like this," she would say, entwining her fingers together. "Now, you kneel, like this. Now say what I say."

I would mimic her, saying things like, "Please forgive me for my sins," and "Bless my family and help me be a good boy." Or something like that. All this praying would eventually come in handy as I grew older.

It wasn't long after confirmation that I had to attend something called catechism. I had to go every Wednesday after school. Apparently, St Joseph's had classes for children whose parents wanted them to make their first Communion—another one of those things I didn't quite understand. I was a child who had no interest in making my first Communion, but I didn't have a choice.

St. Joseph's was small and built in the shape of a cross. I bet the place didn't hold more than a hundred people. The front door faced Main Street. As you entered the long walkway, which led to the altar where Jesus hung, long benches on either side accommodated churchgoers. Toward the front, the walls split left and right, depicting a cross. The altar stood higher than the rest of the place, giving the priest a good view of his parishioners.

At the center of the altar stood a huge table made of some kind of fancy stone with white cloths hanging from all sides. Behind this table was an exceptionally large cross with Jesus Christ hanging from his hands and feet, held up by huge nails. His head, hanging close to his chest, showed the agony he must have suffered. His long brown hair hung down to his shoulders. A brown beard adorned his face. His closed eyes gave the impression he was asleep. It was a sad but solemn crucifix that would remain in my memory forever.

I, along with about twenty other children my age, took a seat close to the front of the church for our first catechism class. Two nuns appeared out of nowhere, giving us instructions on how to sit. One was pretty and young, the other was old and looked mean.

"This is a place of worship," the older one said. "You must be quiet. As you walk in, you make the sign of the cross. Bend your knee, like this. Put your hands together, like this, and walk slowly."

All instructions were in Spanish. The nuns separated the boys from the girls during these catechism classes, and the boys got Sister Theresa, the older, mean nun, for our teacher. She would scold us if we didn't get the prayers right. Our Father and Hail Mary were the two top prayers everyone had to learn.

After a few weeks of continuous repetition, we could recite these with very few mistakes. It was boring and uninteresting. Even though the nuns tried to explain what these prayers meant, we didn't—or at least I didn't—understand how they related to us. There were a couple of other prayers we had to recite and memorize as part of passing this class, but they had little status in the prayer hierarchy. Sister Theresa wouldn't punish us as harshly if we got those wrong.

We would kneel while the *madrecita*, or Sister Theresa, walked back and forth in front of the pew with a ruler in her hand. In an effort to intimidate us, she would slap her hand with the ruler, as if this gesture would make us memorize the prayers faster.

"Say it again! This time, say it slowly so I can hear the words," she would say, holding the ruler above her head. I could feel her urge to hit someone.

After several months of reciting prayers and listening to Sister Theresa explain parts of the Bible, we were ready to make our first Communion.

How could I have passed catechism? To this day, I'm still trying to figure that out.

My first Communion was a much better event than confirmation. On that day, both my father and mother took me to church. I looked like a gentleman leading a ceremonial party. We kids were lined up in alphabetical order, making me first in line. I had on new black pants, no belt, a white shirt, and old shoes that my dad spent an hour trying to shine so they wouldn't look so old. All the boys were dressed the same, and the girls wore their fancy dresses in bright colors and ribbons in their hair.

We went through the church service. Then, about halfway through Mass, the priest, Father Frankie, called us up front. We recited the Our Father and a Hail Mary. Then he blessed us as we took the host, a round piece of bread that tasted like cardboard. I got to eat Jesus Christ through a round, dry cracker that got stuck on the roof of my mouth. I hacked out loud to get it to unstick. It was the hardest thing to recover from.

We stood, facing the parishioners. They clapped with smiling faces as they looked at their children with utmost pride. After the end of the service, we walked out of the church, following the priest. I could see my father and mother beaming. I was proud of myself. I was on my way to becoming a good Catholic.

For a time, some of us went to church every Sunday. I liked the idea of being there in my Sunday best even though it was always the same thing. Whether Chuy was hungover from the night before determined if we walked or rode. Sunday service ended with a good meal for lunch. Sometimes.

Religion was part of our life growing up. Understanding the significance of prayer helped me. There would be many times when I relied on prayer to help me get through some tough situations. When I felt the world crumbling in on me, I would take time to ask God for assistance. At times, faith would guide me. When that failed, I fell back on good old common sense.

I still pray. I might not go to church as often as I used to, but I still make the sign of the cross and thank God for the day.

The Crime

C huy had run the one vehicle we had into Fidel's picture window, totaling it out. So we walked everywhere after that. We just didn't have the money to afford a used car, let alone a new one. Dad was still working on getting his license and paying off court fines for running into Fidel's store. I didn't mind walking if I didn't have to carry any of my siblings.

One bright Saturday morning, we headed out to my grandparents' house, which was a short distance from where we lived. I asked Mom if I could take my BB gun. I wanted to show it to my uncles—Fidel and Samuel. They were the youngest of the thirteen kids my grandmother gave birth to. Fidel was a year younger than me, and Samuel was two years younger. Because Dad still resented the Fabela clan, he refused to let us refer to any of my mother's siblings as our aunts or uncles. He wanted us to call them by their first names.

He insisted, "*Esos no son tíos o tías.*" (They are not your aunts or uncles.")

Fidel, Sam, and I had a lot in common. We were like brothers. Since we were close in age, we played well together. We got in trouble together. We hung out as much as we could. Sam was the follower, while Fidel and I set the rules. Fidel was the one who would think things out before doing anything, and

Sam would just do it. I liked going to their house even though my father despised most of them. Mostly behind their backs.

I took the BB gun that day and proudly showed it off to the two. Outside, I showed them how it worked. Fidel had some toy soldiers, those tiny green ones, which we lined up along the street.

"This is how you cock it. Be careful the handle doesn't come smashing down on your fingers. It hurts a lot," I told them.

Samuel asked if he could shoot it. I looked at Fidel, who was standing a few feet away from us, waiting for some sign of approval before I handed the rifle to Sam. I thought he was too young to shoot. Fidel looked concerned, so I told Sam, "No."

He wanted to shoot, and I wouldn't release it to him. With both of us holding on to the rifle, we started pulling back and forth, not wanting to let go. We didn't realize the rifle was cocked. Then, somehow, it went off. It struck Fidel in the stomach, and he fell to the ground, crying like a baby.

"You shot him!" I cried, taking the rifle away from Sam's hands.

"No, it was you," he said, pointing at me.

"Well, then you shouldn't have pulled the trigger!" I yelled.

"I'm going to tell!"

"Shut up! You shot him!" I yelled back.

This whole time, Fidel was writhing on the ground, holding his stomach and crying as if it was his last day on Earth. Surprisingly, despite all the yelling and screaming going on between us, no adult came out to see what the problem was. After a few minutes, we moved toward Fidel, who was lying on the ground, crouched like a baby. We tried to console him by telling him he was going to be alright. I didn't know how seriously he was hurt, but from the look of things, I wasn't too concerned. I was more worried about what the adults would say.

Sam and I pulled Fidel's hands off his stomach and pushed his shirt up. He had a small red welt next to his belly button, but no blood. We sighed a breath of relief. Knowing he was not mortally wounded, I grabbed the rifle and ran home. Then I waited until my parents got back, knowing full well I was going to get a beating.

I got a beating. A good one. After the ass-whooping, I was placed in the corner, on my knees, and told to pray for forgiveness. If I slumped down on my heels, the Dad kick came flying at my ass. Those kicks always straightened me out! But only until the next time opportunity came knocking.

It was still summer, but it was fast coming to an end. I was back at Grandmother's house after a brief absence following the shooting of Fidel. We sat around talking and trying to come up with some game to play. I hadn't brought the BB gun this time for fear I'd get another beating.

Not far from Grandmother's house, heading west on West Gallagher Street and maybe a couple of blocks down, was a small neighborhood store owned by Doña Lucia. She was an old gray-haired woman who was blessed with a permanent frown on her face—the kind that says, "I don't trust you." When we'd walk into the store, she would not take her eyes off us. She was making sure we didn't steal anything from her. She looked at us as if we were criminals.

Her house was small to begin with, but she used the front room as the store. It appeared quite crowded with all the stuff she had on shelves. The rest of the house, where she actually lived, was separated from the store by a doorway covered with a curtain that she moved aside when customers came in. When someone opened the screen door, a bell let out a ring, telling her she had customers.

Most customers bought a few last-minute items from her. Cokes, candy, bread, milk, ice cream, and all those things kids love could be found there. She also carried some adult things, like soap, detergent, cigarettes, matches, and the like. No alcohol. Besides that, she carried some luncheon meat she kept in a windowed refrigerator. There were two aisles of shelves packed with canned goods, but the best part were the jars of candies sitting atop the counter.

These jars contained a variety of colorful candy that cost a penny each. It was hard to decide which to buy. If we stood too long, she would just grab some, put them in a bag, and hand them to us. She hated waiting on dumb kids. There were times when I'd save up five pennies to buy my favorite candy— a candy bar made of white gooey stuff with sprinkles of crushed peanuts. It was called the Big Hunk. I would chew off a chunk and savor the delicious sweetness for several minutes. It lasted longer than any other candy. If I was careful, it would last me half a day. That was, if I didn't run into Fidel or Sammy.

That morning, as Sam, Fidel, and I were sitting around the house, just waiting to find something interesting to do, I saw the Gandy's milk truck pull up in front of Doña Lucia's store. Gandy's milk truck delivered milk, ice cream, and eggs every Wednesday.

"Let's get some ice cream from the truck! Richard doesn't lock the door when he delivers stuff," I said.

"Let's do it! I'll watch the store, and the two of you get the ice cream," snickered Sam in a mischievous way.

Fidel and I quickly walked toward the truck. As soon as the delivery man went inside with his load of goods for Doña Lucia, we climbed up on the bumper, opened the refrigerator door, and walked inside. There were stacks of ice cream boxes! I grabbed a box of ice cream sandwiches and handed it to Fidel, who immediately bounced off the truck and ran back to the house.

I turned to leave, hoping Richard would not come out before I jumped. In that instant, I noticed a slab of bologna on one of the shelves.

"Bologna," I whispered. My eyes brightened. My mouth watered. *That slab of bologna would last a lifetime*, I thought.

I grabbed the big roll of bologna and noticed it was heavier than I had expected. I lifted it with both hands, but the red wrapper made it difficult to carry. I managed to jump out of the truck as Richard was coming out. He walked in front of the truck, and I slipped out the back, leaving the door open. Running as fast as a seven-year-old could run—huffing, puffing, and still holding on to the roll of bologna—I made my getaway.

Sam, Fidel, and I hid in an old green car that was sitting on blocks right outside my grandparents' house. It was used for storing old junk. We crawled into the back seat, sweating. We looked at each other, smiling and admiring our catch.

We started with the ice cream. We each had four to five ice cream sandwiches. It didn't take long for us to polish those off. Our bellies full, we sat in the car, arguing.

"You should have taken more!" exclaimed Sammy.

"Yeah! We could have done it. We could have taken six boxes if we wanted to," I agreed.

"We're lucky we weren't caught, you idiots," said Fidel, giving us a disgusted look.

"What are you complaining about? You ate the ice cream, didn't you?" I said.

"Yeah, but you could have gotten caught," Fidel said. "Then what? We all go to jail?"

The conversation went on like this for a few minutes until I remembered the roll of bologna.

"Hey, we got the bologna," I said. "I love bologna. We can eat that too!"

I definitely wanted some. Meat was a delicacy for all of us. But we couldn't take it inside for Grandma to see. She'd give us the third degree. So we had to eat it outside.

The bologna was still cool to the touch, and it looked tasty. Like a vampire looking at a neck, I held it up and licked the wrapper. I needed some. I wanted some. This was the prize, not the ice cream.

"It looks big. We can't eat all this," claimed Fidel, not wanting to touch it.

"We need a knife. We also need bread. Maybe some tortillas. Does Grandma have some?" I asked.

Sam went into the house. A few minutes later, he came back with a butcher's knife and a gallon of water. No bread. No tortillas. We cut big pieces—not slices, but big chunks—and ate. We used our filthy hands like real cavemen.

"I've got a big belly," I said, then howled with laughter. I held up my shirt so they could see me protruding my stomach to make it look big.

"No, mine is bigger," Sam said, laughing and showing us his belly.

"I don't feel so good," cried Fidel with a look of despair. He, too, was holding up his shirt. His stomach looked big.

We kept eating. Once we had our fill, we stashed the remaining piece of the roll and crawled out of the car, laughing and smiling. We'd eaten half that roll of bologna. We drank half a gallon of water, taking big gulps to get the bologna down. It wasn't long before we all needed to take a piss. I could feel the pressure building up. I was going to blow.

"Let's see who can pee the most. We will count, and the one closest to a hundred wins!" Sammy yelled, eager for some competition.

Fidel went first, and before he started peeing, he drank more water.

"One, two, three, four," we counted. He got to thirty.

Sam went next. He drank the last of the water and started peeing. He got to thirty-four.

I had to win this game, so I went to the outside water faucet and filled up the gallon jug. I drank and drank and drank until I felt like I was going to explode. I started peeing, but I only got to twenty-eight.

"You counted too slow!" I should've won that game," I protested, zipping up my pants.

"Fidel wins! He beat you," Sammy said.

"You guys counted too slow. Let's do it again," I replied.

I didn't feel good. I felt my bladder was still full. I needed to pee some more. And I could hear my belly sloshing as I walked.

I tried to tell my uncles that I didn't feel good. But before I could get out the word *good*, I started barfing up bologna, water, and ice cream all over Grandfather's green car.

As soon as Sammy saw me, he started retching. He slumped over, holding on to the bumper, and let it all out. He was farting and barfing at the same time.

This made Fidel sick. As soon as I stopped vomiting, Fidel started.

It was horrible. All three of us, farting and barfing. We walked away from all the vomit, pretending it wasn't ours. The green car had different shades of red slime sliding down the doors.

"I don't want the rest of the bologna," I said.

We threw it away. I felt like we had just buried a dear friend. I walked back home, my stomach still sloshing from all the water I had drank.

There were times when there was very little to eat at home, and at those times, I would remember the bologna we threw away. What a waste. We never said anything about the theft to anyone. That would remain a best buds secret forever.

More English?

S ummer was almost over. I dreaded having to go back to
school after a long, hot summer playing with friends and
family. But in some ways, I was nervously excited at the
same time. As I looked forward to a great beginning, I wanted
to be around kids other than my own siblings.

I turned seven in July of 1958 and was a bit tall for my age. I
imagined being the tallest person in second grade, and although
second grade seemed intimidating, I somehow knew it would be
different.

I hadn't practiced any English all summer. How could I? In
the barrio, all we spoke was Spanish. Seldom did we venture
too far from home, which would require me to translate for
Mom and Dad. Even so, most of the people who worked at
local stores spoke Spanish. Why would we speak anything other
than Spanish?

As the first day of school grew near, I was getting nervous.
I felt like second grade was going to be too difficult, based on
what little I'd learned in first. Other kids would make fun of my
broken English, and it scared me to no end. If I was going to
survive second grade, I had to start the year off with a goal. So
I thought long and hard. What goal could I set for myself that
was reachable? I didn't want to be disappointed if I didn't get

there. But at the same time, I couldn't set it so low that I'd reach it in a few days. No, the goal had to be realistic. I tossed around the idea of hunkering down with English on one hand, and not getting paddled on the other. The paddling I got in first grade should have taught me a lesson: get the work done!

A few days before school, I started speaking English as if I knew what I was saying.

"Give me un baso de agua."

"Voy al bathroom."

"My name is Robert." (That one I could recite fairly well.)

"Vamos to the playground." (That was a hard one, since *playground* was a long word.)

"You sound like a gringo!" Nancy said when she heard me practicing.

"No, I don't!" I said, chasing her around the house and threatening to beat her up.

At the tender age of six, Nancy would make fun of me. How she knew better English than me was puzzling. She had a knack for words. I just couldn't figure out how she did it until I saw her mimicking what people said on TV.

Hmmm, I thought. *Why didn't I think of that?*

I finally settled on my goal: I would not be spanked this year by any teacher. The memory of being spanked too many times in first grade made me sweat. At that time, it was customary to discipline children with corporal punishment. Almost every teacher had a paddle. Any who didn't have one knew that the teacher next door did. I didn't think twice about getting whipped when I did something wrong. I just didn't like it! I got enough beatings at home for things I thought were not worth the effort Dad put out. He was the disciplinarian at home. Mom just threatened.

The year before, in September of 1956, Imelda, the third girl, had been born. This brought the total to five children, thus making it even harder to afford much even though Chuy was working a steady job. I don't know what he was doing at the time, but he must have been working steadily for at least a year. (It wasn't permanent.) We weren't rich, but we had enough food besides just beans. Whenever Dad came home from one of his drunken nights, Mom would search his pants pockets and claim all the loose change she could find before he woke up. I don't care how drunk he was, he always remembered the dollars he had in his wallet. But he never remembered how much change he'd had.

In anticipation of Nancy and me going to school, she managed to accumulate enough nickels, dimes, and quarters to place some cheap clothes on layaway at Gibson's, the local discount store on Dickenson Boulevard. Their layaway plan allowed customers to select whatever they wanted but couldn't pay for right away. The store would place it in the back somewhere with the customer's name on it until it was paid for in full. It only took a couple of dollars to place something on layaway. Mom would pay a little at a time until the bill was paid off. Until then, we waited with anticipation to finally wear or use what had been set aside for weeks, even months.

Mother bought Nancy and me some new clothes that way for our first day of school. I got one pair of pants and a shirt, while Nancy got two dresses and shoes.

"Why does she get so much new stuff?" I cried. "Why can't I have some new shoes too?"

"This is her first time at school, and she needs to look pretty," Mom responded.

"But I need shoes! The ones I have don't fit right." Pleading or throwing a tantrum didn't help. That only got me a *chancla*, or a shoe in the ass.

Holding hands, the three of us walked to school—Mom, Nancy, and me. One of my aunts babysat the other kids until

Mom got back. She insisted on making sure I got to school and didn't get any crazy ideas about ditching again. Nancy was chatty. She was excited to finally be going to school.

"Would you please stop talking? You're making me nervous," I said to my sister.

"You're nervous because you can't say a complete sentence in English," she retorted.

"Yes I can."

"No you can't."

Mom demanded, "*Ya bastante. No quiero que estén arguyendo.*" ("Enough, I don't want the two of you arguing.")

Even though I wasn't a stellar student, I still found school boring. I don't remember my second-grade teacher's name, but I do remember that she was a mathematician, or she liked math better than anything else. She insisted we recite numbers up to one hundred. We had to write them down too. We'd spend most of the morning working with numbers—adding, subtracting, dividing, and multiplying. Dividing was hard for me. So were adding and subtracting. Come to think of it, I had a hard time with multiplying as well!

It was in second grade when I first heard the word *homework*. I ran home the first day of school and complained to Mom about the teacher.

"You need to take me out of that teacher's room and put me somewhere else," I said.

"Why?"

"Because she said we have to do homework." I explained that we had to work at school, and now we had to work at home! "How can they do that?" I cried. "It's not fair! I can't go play with my friends after school because I have to do homework. I don't want to do homework."

"You have to do what the teacher says." Mom immediately stopped my complaining by putting her hand out in front of my face. "You need to know your numbers, and you can't learn them all if you don't practice at home. Don't worry, I'll help you," she politely answered, looking at me with a sincere face.

Counting and memorizing the multiplication tables didn't require too much English, so she would sit with me by candlelight at the kitchen table, and we would write down the numbers up to one hundred. It didn't take long for me to figure it out, and I was writing to two hundred all on my own. Homework was easy.

"You are so smart," Mom would say. "You are going to be the best student in all the school!"

I would smile with delight. It was at times like these, when she complimented me, that I felt I could do anything.

I learned to balance regular schoolwork with activities that didn't require me to just sit at a desk and recite numbers, letters, or words. There were other things that interested me more. I loved gym and recess. Of course, I liked the cafeteria more than anything.

The ladies in the kitchen were good cooks. Butz had a real kitchen, where meals were cooked daily. The smell of the cooking permeated the entire school, making my stomach grumble. I could smell the cooking from far away, and it smelled wonderful. I'd stop listening to the teacher as I tried to make out what we were having for lunch that day. There was a menu, but it was in English. And I didn't care. I wanted to eat something other than tortillas, beans, and rice. I loved cafeteria time. Sometimes better than recess!

My favorite was the peach cobbler! Mmm. Mmm. It was the best. I hadn't known such a thing existed until I got to school! Peach cobbler day was like a holiday. I'd trade anything on my plate for an extra helping of peach cobbler.

Eating in the cafeteria introduced me to so many different foods—some that I had never tasted or even heard of. I grew up mostly on potatoes, beans, fideo, and tortillas. This was all we ate on a regular basis. Meat was a rarity. If we had enough money to buy meat, it was usually bologna. My dad loved bologna. He would come up with creative ideas for what to cook with it. I didn't mind bologna by itself on a piece of bread. I could eat that all day. Many a time, that was all we had. But our meals were mostly made of eggs. Sometimes he would throw in some potatoes with onions, green peppers, and cilantro, mixing it all up to make a Mexican omelet. Other times, he would cook it, put it on a tortilla dripping with butter, and make me salivate like Pavlov's dog.

On special occasions, the cafeteria workers would prepare turkey and dressing with all the trimmings. I could be dying of typhoid fever or some dangerous, catastrophic illness, but I always found the strength to convince my parents I was healthy enough to go to school if I knew turkey was being served. Turkey and dressing were cooked right before we let out for the Thanksgiving holiday. If we were lucky, it was also prepared as a Christmas treat. The gravy was so good, and I really loved it. My tastebuds just loved those delicious offerings.

"Can you put some more gravy on my turkey? Can you put more gravy on my potatoes?" I would ask the servers with a smile wider than the Rio Grande. The servers were all women. All big in size. But it didn't take long to identify the right person to ask. That person was Ms. Martinez. She was older and fatter than the others, but she had kind eyes. She was a puffy woman with a big smile and a tender heart. Ms. Martinez was also the only one who was nice to kids. Seeing her first thing in the morning for breakfast was a joy. She was always smiling and singing some song I'd never heard of. If we ate all our food—which we all did all the time except when they served green beans—she would beam. She was a happy lady who would give us extra gravy or extra mashed potatoes when the manager was not looking. The manager was a white woman who never spoke to kids.

The time after cafeteria, which was reading time, was the most difficult for me. I had a very hard time staying awake, so I dreaded it with a passion. I was not a reader. I wasn't even a near reader. Or a close reader. I had a very difficult time pronouncing words on the page, much less reading an entire sentence. The words were not big, but I just couldn't focus. Many times, I would fall asleep, only to be awakened by the teacher banging a ruler on the desk right next to my ear. I would jump, sit straight up, wipe snot and spit from my face, and pretend like I was paying attention.

"Robert. It's your turn. Read the next sentence," the teacher said one day as she stood over me with the ruler in her hand. I pretended to know which sentence she was talking about.

"Here! Right here," she demanded, pointing to the sentence with the ruler.

"T ... h ... e." I took a deep breath. "C ... aaaa ... t. Rrr ... aaaa ... n." It was excruciating! It was embarrassing. My fellow students waited impatiently, and after a few seconds, they shouted, "It's *CAT*!"

The letter sounds were getting mixed up in my Spanish-speaking brain. Putting letters together to make words seemed nearly impossible. I would continue to struggle for the rest of my educational career.

If I stayed awake for reading, making eye contact with the teacher was a no-no. If I did, she would think I wanted to be next. So I kept my head down and tried to follow along, bored with it all.

To compensate for my lack of reading ability, I learned to fake illness.

"Can I go to the nurse?" I'd ask the teacher as I held my stomach in a manner that suggested vomit was on its way. It worked the first few times. At one point, being really sick with a temperature and a continually running nose, I asked to see the nurse. A cold, cough, and everything that came with it suggested illness.

"No, sir," the teacher said. "Your turn is coming up. You have to read for me."

I had to read in front of all the kids who knew I was a bad reader.

"Ah, ma'am," one of the kids said. "Please let him go to the nurse."

They didn't want the agony of listening to me try to read. Ultimately, the teacher caved and sent me to the nurse, who sent me home. The next day, the teacher read us a story about a boy who cried wolf. I'll never forget that story. It was meant for me.

Toward the middle of the year, my confidence in my ability to learn made my teacher realize I wasn't a dummy. I could learn. During this time, I was picking up enough English to get by. I spoke it with an accent, but so did everybody else. I was so confident that I started talking to a girl in my class.

Chrissy was pretty and always wore nice, clean clothes. She lived behind Butz Elementary and walked to school every day. By herself! I followed her one day, talking some nonsense as we walked across the street to her house. A big pecan tree adorned her front yard. It must have been November because there were pecans on the ground.

"Chrissy, can I have some pecans?" I asked.

"I don't care. Nobody picks them. You can have them." She was sweet.

Looking up, I noticed the bigger pecans were still on the tree. She stood there as I took the smaller pecans out of my pants pockets and started to climb the tree. I got far enough up to shake the bigger ones loose. She watched with interest as I maneuvered the tree, but I mistook her expression for amazement. I took a liking to her. In my effort to amaze some more, I swung my legs over a limb and hung upside down, making ape noises.

She laughed. I laughed. We picked pecans together. At times, our hands touched when we reached for the same ones. We laughed some more until her mother came outside and asked her to come inside. I said goodbye, then walked home, looking over my shoulder to catch a final glimpse of her smile. I had a girlfriend!

I walked with Chrissy to her house just about every day unless I was held back after school for not finishing some kind of work for Ms. So-and-So. As we walked, we'd revisit the events of the day. She was in a group with the smarter kids. Her English was excellent. So was her Spanish.

But the romance didn't last long. Chrissy moved away not long after because her father committed suicide. I didn't know what that was, but I thought it must have had something to do with her father being confined to a wheelchair. I later heard he'd been in the war and had suffered from some kind of disease affecting his brain. They called it depression. He didn't want to live in a wheelchair for the rest of his life. All sorts of rumors swirled among adult conversations. No one had heard of anybody committing suicide. This was a first for the community. All I knew was that he was dead. I didn't know what being dead meant, so it didn't matter even though I felt sad—a new emotion for me. What mattered was that his death took away Chrissy, my first girlfriend.

I got over it the next day.

Some Kind of Trouble

One evening, after the babies were asleep and Dad went AWOL for the umpteenth time, Mother, in an effort to entertain us, tore a sheet of paper from my Big Chief notebook. Nancy and I watched as she folded the paper from the corners, then kept folding until she produced a paper airplane. Not having seen this done before, we thought it magical. We were fascinated by her skills at keeping us busy with her little tricks, and our evenings became playing sessions that cost no money.

The special moments our mother gave us instilled a passion for learning. Not only was she talented, but she was also very smart. Keeping three or four young children entertained, she made the nights go by fast. We still didn't have a TV set, and the radio wasn't something we enjoyed, so keeping us entertained must have been exhausting for her. It was the little things she did that kept us busy for hours.

I tried to make my own paper airplane. Making folds here and there led me to different plane designs. I got so good at it, at the expense of Big Chief, that I took my knowledge to school. The last hour before we were let out of school one day, I started making one that would swoop through the air and fly for several feet. The bell rang, creating a mass exodus out the door. I ran

Robert Alfaro

out, flinging the plane through the air and desperately trying to catch it before it fell to the ground. I was showing off my newly acquired skill when José, one of the bigger boys in my classroom, ran alongside me, chasing the plane.

"Let me try," he kept repeating. I kept playing with it, not bothering to share my newest invention. "Let me try," he demanded, hoping to reach the plane before me.

The plane cut through the air like a floating missile, and the wind propelled it away from us. We both ran, hoping to catch it before it hit dirt. It was coming in for a landing when I reached out to grab it before it reached the ground. In an effort to beat me to the plane, José pushed me from behind, and I fell.

It happened so fast that I didn't have time to react. I landed on the back of my right wrist. I heard the snap! The bone broke right above the wrist. I lay on the ground, covered in dirt, as José ran away with the plane.

I yelled at him, cussing at the top of my lungs to give it back. "*¡Pinche puto! ¡Te voy a poner unos chingasos!*" ("You f—ing whore! I'm going to kick your ass!")

I managed to get up in spite of the pain and slowly walked toward my grandmother's house because it was closer than home. Crying and holding my arm to keep it from dangling, I noticed I could still move my hand. I didn't realize it was broken.

Grandmother (Ama) sent one of my aunts for my mother as she wrapped a towel around the arm. As soon as Mom arrived, I started crying all over again. Ama insisted Mom take me to Dr. Gibson. The hospital wasn't far, so we walked.

When we got there, it reeked of rubbing alcohol, which made me nauseous. We walked by the nurses' station, looking for Dr. Gibson. We were ushered into a room, and we waited. I didn't know what to expect and feared the worst.

"Don't let him cut off my hand," I cried.

"Nobody is going to cut off your hand, baby," Mom said. "The doctor has to see what's wrong with it."

She never asked me how it happened. We moved to another room. I only whimpered, trying not to show any signs of hysteria. Not knowing what was going to happen scared me to no end. I kept asking what I was to expect, but she didn't know. Now I was worried. *Is he going to do something to my hand that I won't approve of?* I wondered.

Dr. Gibson came into the room. Looking intently at the bulging wrist, he lifted my arm gently, moving it around and pulling on my fingers. By this time, the area around the wrist had swollen to twice its normal size. He never said it was broken.

He looked at Mom and said, "We have to take an X-ray."

I walked over to this machine, again not certain what they were going to do. "Please, Mom," I said. "*Ven con migo*" ("Please come with me.")

Then we were back in the examination room. Dr. Gibson told me it was fractured. He placed my arm on the table and cradled it between two metal splints. He stuck a lollypop in my mouth, and, just when I was about to savor the delicious morsel, he pushed the two metal splints together. The most excruciating pain I had ever felt made me fill the room with a horrifying shrill.

"*¡Pinche puto!*" I cried, yelling loudly. The lollypop flew out of my mouth, hitting the doctor smack on the middle of his forehead. He was holding on to the splints, Mother was holding me down, and I was yelling. I was going crazy. There was no anesthesia. No shot to numb the wrist. No warning.

After a few minutes, I settled down and allowed him to wrap it up with white cloth. He mixed powder with water to make a paste. He worked it over my arm from my fingers to my elbow. As it dried, it turned into a hard plaster that was hard as a rock.

Before we left, Dr. Gibson gave me another lollypop and told me I was a strong boy.

Bullshit! No amount of strength would have prevented me from cussing him out, even if it was in Spanish. He never knew I'd called him a man whore. Oh well.

In a week, I was back in school. No more airplanes for me. They were too hard on the old bones. Instead, I focused on learning to write with my left hand. In six weeks, I felt more comfortable writing with my left than with my right. Either way, if I didn't take my time, no one could read what I was writing anyway. To this day, I still write with my left hand on paper, but on a blackboard, I have to use my right. Funny.

Having very little money had an upside. It made us think of creative ways to entertain ourselves. I liked our little town. Well, I liked the part of town where we lived—south of the railroad tracks. The Mexican side. Fidel and Sam were always my accomplices. We ran around unsupervised, enjoying the openness and wilderness that lay beyond our houses. I used my imagination to create activities that would keep us busy for hours. Sometimes, my little brother Jesse would join us. But because he was still too little, we often left him behind.

Our favorite activity was hunting down desert lizards—those little creatures that scurry around looking for insects to eat. Lizards could camouflage into the terrain, which made them hard to spot. But to a trained eye, they were easy to find. When we found them, we'd use a hoe or a stick to slice off their tails. We'd get a kick out of seeing the tail still moving around as if it had a mind of its own. At times, we miscalculated the blow and wound up killing the lizard by splitting it in two. We'd spend hours killing them.

When bored of lizard killings, we'd pass the time catching horny toads. They were small and blended nicely under the brush. They weren't as fast as lizards, making them easy to catch. Horny toads were dumb. We'd turn them upside down in our hands and rub their bellies. They'd close their eyes and fall asleep. When they lay on the palm of our hands, just relaxing, it seemed strange. When the toad least expected it, we'd slam it on the ground. The startled toad would bounce up, wide awake, and make a run for it. Screaming, laughing, and jumping up and down like uncivilized humans, we'd run after it and do it again.

Tarantulas were different. They came out only after a good thunderstorm. Where they came from, we never knew, but they were there. We were scared of them, so we left them alone. We were told that if we made them mad, they'd hunch up on all legs and jump. When we least expected it, they'd fling black hair at us. If it caught us, it would sting, killing us instantly. Those were the rumors, so we stayed away from the tarantulas. If there was only one tarantula, flinging rocks at a distance was the game of choice. More than one scared us.

Tired of playing with lizards, toads, or tarantulas, we'd turn our attention to other forms of entertainment. Where we learned to make spears out of clothes hangers, I'll never know. We'd use a hammer to straighten out the hanger, then smash the end into a sharp point. With chicken feathers in our hair, we were wild Indians looking for something to scalp. We'd tie strips of old cloth around our heads to hold down the feathers, then dance around in circles, singing nonsense words.

One bright, sunny afternoon, with our shirts off and pretending to be Indians, we were whooping and hollering, our bodies glistening with sweat. The spears were used to hunt lizards. When we found one, we stabbed it and paraded it around like a bunch of lunatics. We danced barefooted, creating a swirl of dust as the lizard squirmed for freedom. With a small fire ready to cook the lizard, it was time for dinner. But the smell of burning lizard didn't sit right with us. It was a pungent smell none of us could stand. We passed on lizard dinner.

After some time, either the joy of killing lizards lost its relevance or we'd exterminated all of them that day. We eventually got bored and were thinking of what other things Indians would do if they were in our shoes. That's when I noticed Lucy.

Lucy, a young girl living next to our house, occasionally came over to babysit one of the younger kids—probably Imelda, who was the youngest at that time. Lucy was sitting outside in the shadows of a wooden door with the baby in her arms, rocking back and forth and singing some Mexican children's song. She sat on the steps with the door behind her, singing and enjoying the cool breeze coming in from the south. Lucy had thick, curly hair that stood out like an afro. Small in stature but very pretty, she never complained about anything.

Sam, Fidel, and I went behind the house and huddled up for a pow-wow.

"We make game interesting," I said in what I thought was Indian talk. "We make pilgrims scared. She run for life. We not kill. We scare. *¿Comprende?*"

We were to test our throwing skills by flinging the spear at the wooden door. The Indian who hit the door closest to Lucy's head would win the contest. We had to make the arrow stick to the door. If it didn't stick, then we would get two more chances. The losers would eat the burned lizard.

We snuck around the corner of the house. Lucy was still sitting there with the baby in her arms. I wasn't about to lose this game.

Fidel went first. He snuck around, holding the spear high above him. He threw and hit the door about four feet above Lucy's head.

"You need to stop doing that! What's the matter with you?" she yelled at Fidel.

Sammy was next. He threw the spear, and it landed on the concrete wall.

My turn. I came around the corner, dancing and whooping like Indians do in the movies. "I can hit the door closer to her head," I said. As I approached, the others followed. I raised my spear and swung, tossing the flimsy thing toward the door. The scream coming from Lucy's mouth struck fear in me.

I had stabbed Lucy right in her forehead!

"*¡Ay! ¡Dios mío!*" she yelled. The baby was dangling in one arm while the other reached for the spear still stuck to her forehead! I'd missed the door entirely.

"*¡A la chingada!*" I cried. I ran up and yanked the spear from her head, then ran to our teepee hideout—a pit my dad had dug at the back of the house where he used to toss things, like old tires, a refrigerator, and old washing machines. Shaken up, I flung the mangled spear into it.

Fidel and Sam ran home, leaving me to handle the explanations and consequences. I knew I was dead.

Mom was furious. She ran outside when she heard the crying. Lucy, holding her head, yelled even louder when she saw blood on her hands! She dropped Imelda and ran home. Mom grabbed me by the arm, yanking me while she spanked me on the butt with her hand.

She angrily said, "*Espera que venga tu papá, chamaco tonto.*" ("Wait till your dad gets home, dumb kid.")

I crawled under the bed and prayed to our Father and Mother Mary until I fell asleep. Halfway through my first nightmare, sure as dirt, when Dad got home, I got the beating of a lifetime. He grabbed me by the wrist, held me up, and started kicking me on my ass with his steel-toed boots. He then took a wide belt and whipped me like a crazed lunatic, yelling and shouting Spanish obscenities.

"*Chamaco pendejo. ¿Estás estupido? ¿La quieres matar?*" ("Dumb kid. Are you stupid? Do you want to kill her?") He yelled, swinging the belt over and over again.

Mother had to step in, yelling, "*¡Ya párale! ¡Lo vas a matar!*" ("Stop! You're going to kill him!") If she hadn't intervened, he probably would have killed me. He was that mad.

I was placed facing a corner, on my knees, and told to pray for forgiveness. When they weren't looking, I crawled back under the bed and prayed, falling asleep and moaning in pain.

I had some freaky nightmares after that whipping. They lasted for years after. I survived even though the beating left me black and blue.

A few days later, I had to go to Lucy's house and face her and her parents. With my parents there, I apologized. I was sent to a corner again and told to get on my knees and pray. With Lucy watching, kneeling in the corner seemed like an eternity. She sat there listening to make sure I was praying. The smirk didn't leave her face until we were ready to leave. The adults finished their coffee and chitchat. Again, I apologized to Lucy's parents. I looked back at her from the corner of my eyes.

I whispered under my breath, "*Puta.*" ("Bitch.")

Our family was growing, and we were still living in the midst of some poor, raunchy conditions. While I knew we were struggling financially, it didn't matter to us kids. As long as we were allowed to play outside, with the older ones taking care of the little ones, we were happy. We were becoming proficient at entertaining ourselves. Among siblings, we played stupid games, like chase or hide-and-seek. We had no bikes or bats. No store-bought toys. However, mud usually presented itself as a great pastime activity.

Using shovels my dad kept in the back of the house, we would dig holes, turn on the water hose, and make mud balls. Once they were dry, they became solidly pliable but not hard enough to hurt us when we flung them at each other. We had one rule: don't hit anybody in the face. Every other body part was a legal target. The reason for this had to do with evidence. We learned our lesson when I slung a mud ball at Jesse, hitting him on the cheek and leaving a red mark that eventually turned blue. This got me a beating. Not the serious type. But nevertheless, it was a good one.

Since I was the oldest, I would declare myself the referee. My job was making sure everyone had enough mud ball ammunition. Jesse always won because he could throw mud farther than anybody. Or, it could have been that other than me, he was the only boy. Our sisters were wimps and didn't know how to throw the right way. When they sided with each other, Jesse always won. On one occasion, Nancy decided to join Jesse against Wanda and Imelda. I had to declare a draw when Imelda started crying because she got hit in the face. It didn't leave a mark, so we were safe. No injuries, but what fun.

Oh boy, those were the days! Those were fun times!

1959

In the summer of 1959, I turned eight. It was the end of a decade. "Venus" by Frankie Avalon was being played on the radio. It resonated in the minds and on the lips of every kid in America. I loved to sing along when no one was listening.

Fidel Castro took over Cuba that same year. Alaska and Hawaii became states, and the deaths of rock-and-roll musicians Buddy Holly, Ritchie Valens, and the Big Bopper in a plane crash near Clear Lake, Iowa, shocked fans all over America. It had been five years since the Supreme Court brought down the ruling that segregation was unconstitutional. There were 4 million babies born every year in the 1950s, and we contributed to that total.

But what was happening in the country and the world didn't really affect us. We were too far removed from national events, much less world ones. We lived our lives in the streets, playing outside in our own little world called Mexican Town. We were happy kids with very few things to worry about. Even though our parents were still struggling and fighting, we kept to ourselves, did our chores, and pretended that everything was good.

By the time I got to third grade, which totally surprised the heck out of me, I was ready to get serious about school. The fact that I had somehow been promoted to third grade was a total miracle. Either that or I finally got through to Jesus Christ with my praying and everything.

School was getting harder, but I had time to enjoy it. I had acquired enough English to follow along with most of what the teacher was teaching us. Outside the classroom, we all still spoke Spanish, so practicing our English seemed almost impossible. We spoke Spanish at home, on the playground, in the halls, in the restroom, and just about anywhere we found ourselves. Even while standing in line and going to or coming from the restroom, music, library, cafeteria, or recess, we spoke Spanish. That didn't last long though. Our third-grade teacher would demand we not speak Spanish.

"You need to speak in English," she said. For the first time, I was constantly reminded of this. "You are in America, and we speak English. Do you understand?"

If we were caught using our native language near her or she heard us, we were in trouble. I made a commitment that year that I wouldn't do anything that would result in a spanking. It was 1959, and I was expected to be smarter, wiser, and in control. I tried really hard. Or at least I thought I did.

Third grade was tough. Demanding expectations were the norm. Mrs. Green, our teacher, was a drill sergeant. She was white, and she didn't know Spanish like Mrs. Falcon did.

Mrs. Green, who was often intimidating to me, was a big woman. She wore this strange dress, which was her favorite, that would make me dizzy. When she walked around the room, I had to be careful not to stare at her for too long. The lines on her dress were like pinwheels going squiggly up, down, and around. It played tricks on the eyes. When she walked by, my blinkers were drawn to her dress. In seconds, I felt hypnotized. In those instances, I wouldn't dare stand up for fear I'd stumble and fall.

Aside from her wonky dress, she did have kind eyes. But those eyes could switch in seconds if you talked, moved, or even

71

took a breath without her permission. She was a strict teacher. She didn't budge from the established rules of conduct. I learned big time with her.

By then, I'd finally mastered "Can I go to the bathroom" in English. I knew enough English to read some basic low-level stuff. I was still struggling with my pronunciation of words with more than one syllable, but I was getting the hang of it. Because I was so proud of myself, my confidence grew. I got the courage to attempt words whose meaning I didn't understand. Strange words appeared on the page without warning. I'd sound them out, doing my best to pronounce them correctly. But reading was not my forte. I was still embarrassed by my lack of reading skills. Third-grade reading books had fewer pictures. Therefore, it became difficult to decipher what was being said. Pictures gave me clues, making it easier to answer the teacher's questions.

"Okay, Robert," Mrs. Green said one day, standing close. "Now, in your own words, what is the author trying to say?"

"The hell if I know!" would have been my reply, but that terminology was unacceptable in this school. It got you sent to the principal's office. Instead, I said, "I think he is saying ..." Then I stopped, wondering what I had just read. "I think he is trying to say..."

"Read it again. This time, think about what the author is trying to say to you. Now, class, follow along with Robert."

Dang. I hated when she asked the kids to follow along. They were so much better.

"The baalue waaatters from the o ..." I'd say. "Okay. I got this. Osee ... a ... o ..."

"Ocean!" the kids blurted out.

Embarrassing.

Mrs. Green demanded that we learn a new list of spelling words each week. Every Monday, she gave us a list of ten words, and by Friday, we had to know how to say them and spell them. Each Friday, we had to turn in a paper with the words spelled ten times. Then we had to get in front of the class, say the words, and spell them with no mistakes before we could sit back down. If we didn't have our spelling words, couldn't pronounce them, or lacked the courage to spell them in front of the class by Friday, we were to bend over in front of the entire class, place our hands on the teacher's desk, and get ready for a spanking. She would come around and give us three swats with a pretty good-sized paddle she kept hanging behind her desk.

I won the paddle contest, which really wasn't a contest at all until Troy bet me and three other fools he could take the most swats in one month. The bet included no crying. I was competitive. Troy was the shortest kid in class, and he stuttered. His stuttering would get worse when he got anxious or excited. It took a lot of patience to stand there and let Troy say what he wanted to say. Sometimes we made fun of him and stuttered ourselves just to piss him off. This was not called bullying. It was called making fun of others. His friends would make guesses as to why he stuttered.

"He stutters because he was dropped on the head when he was a baby," one said.

"No, no. His head was crushed when he was born," another replied, laughing.

"His tongue is too small," another added.

"His brain is faster than his mouth!"

Eventually, someone came up with the notion that Troy stuttered for no reason other than he was slow in the head. At some point, we stopped making fun of him. Troy was a fast runner. And although he was short, he could outrun most of the boys in class. If we made fun of his stuttering, he would chase us, trip us, and kick us two or three times in quick succession before we could get up. The idea was to make fun of Troy, then run. All we had to do was outrun Jaime. Jaime was the fat one. We all thought that if Jaime stopped eating, his legs would grow faster than his stomach. Maybe then he could run faster.

One day, Troy convinced us that if we didn't partake in his scheme, we were *mariposas* ("butterflies"), which meant "gay." It was his way of calling us sissies. On the third week of not turning in my spelling words, I just got up to the front of the class and simply bent over the desk, awaiting the swats. This time, Mrs. Green reared back and placed three good ones on my skinny ass, and I started crying. I didn't jump, scream, and hold my butt like Troy did.

On week four, I not only turned in my ten words, spelled correctly, ten times over, but I'd memorized and pronounced them correctly. I'd learned a good lesson: don't get sucked into bets made by eight-year-olds.

I walked by myself to school, which wasn't more than two or three blocks down from my house. On the left side of the street was a spooky-looking house. I had to pass directly in front of this house, which was obscured by overgrown shrubs and trees, to get to school. The front lawn had a short brown fence with a gate that opened out into the street. Sometimes, I would hear a moaning sound coming from the house.

"Stay away from here!" came a shrilling voice from within one day. I wasn't anywhere near the house, but I could hear this voice.

"Ha, ha, ha! Stay away," the low shrill came again.

This would happen just about every morning. I would feel fear creeping down my spine. I finally spoke to Mom about it, and for a couple of days, she walked me to school.

"There," I said one of those mornings as I pointed at the house. "It comes from that one."

"I don't hear anything," Mom said. "It's just your imagination. There's no one living there. Otherwise, they would trim those shrubs."

I wasn't convinced.

A tall, dark boy with bushy eyebrows and dark circles under his dark eyes started to appear behind the bushes. He seemed to be about twelve years old. He would come out and sneer at me, telling me to stay away from his house. Then he would run out the gate, yelling obscenities while holding his pants up with one hand and threatening with the other. I'd bow my head, avoid eye contact, and keep walking. I decided that if he came out into the street, I'd run. I made up my mind that this guy was either crazy or missing some brain cells.

Why is he not in school? I wondered. *Why is he always there in the morning? Why is he always asking me to stay away from his house? Where are his parents?*

Weird guy.

I started leaving for school earlier, hoping to avoid him. For a while, it worked. I would walk very quietly when I went by his house, avoiding his wicked face. By the end of the week, I'd decided to remain calm and confront him. Maybe if I was pleasant to him and said, "Good morning," he would leave me alone.

That morning, he was waiting for me. I kept walking. He yelled so loud that I turned around. I saw his hand fling something through the air.

A smooth, round rock hit me right between the eyes! I yelped, turned, and as ran as fast as I could toward school and straight to the nurse's office, crying. I told her all that happened, and she wrote a note to my mother.

Mom must have spoken to the parents of the dumb kid because after that, he never came out of the house in the morning. I walked around with a two-inch bump on my head for a week.

Third grade taught me two things. One: Troy became a good friend. Sometimes I needed a good friend. He taught me patience. Two: Reading would be an ongoing struggle. Knowing I was a poor reader created a determination to learn.

Continued Struggles

School was out for the summer. It was 1960. We didn't get our last report card until two weeks after the end of the school year. This gave the teachers time to calculate grades and make any comments they felt needed to be recorded for future reference. The report cards were mailed home to parents. They not only had the comments and grades, but they also had the most important information for students. The last page included a statement that revealed whether you were promoted to the next grade or whether you needed to repeat the grade. The report card was the most sacred educational instrument feared by students. Especially me.

Each day, I waited patiently by the mailbox in anticipation. Was I going to be promoted or not? I had my doubts. Every time the postman came by, I'd make the sign of the cross, take a deep breath, then run to the mailbox before anyone noticed. Finally, the day arrived. I picked up my siblings' report cards, quickly tossed those aside, and tore mine open. I flipped over to the last page of the card and closed my eyes, saying, "Our Father, who art in Heaven ..."

Nervously, I opened it.

It read, "Robert has been promoted to the fourth grade."

I jumped up and down, forgetting Jesus Christ, and ran inside to tell everyone that I had made it to the fourth grade. I handed all the report cards to Mother. She opened them, asking me to read the contents one by one. Nancy was already reading by the second grade, so I handed them to her. She was quicker at it. She wanted to read mine, but I yanked it away.

"Let me see it," she demanded.

"No. I can read it to Mom myself. Keep your dirty hands off."

"You won't tell her the truth," she remarked.

"You're stupid. That's why you're in second grade."

"Stop it. Both of you," Mom said. "Now, *mijo*. Read it to me."

I made myself look better than what the teacher wrote. Like I said, I wasn't a stellar student. How I got promoted to the fourth grade, I'll never know. After I read the comments and grades to Mother, she gave me a hug. I'd fudged on the comments.

"I'm so proud of you. I knew you could do it," she said, smiling proudly.

It was time to enjoy the summer months!

By this time, I wasn't too interested in what my parents had going. They weren't getting along. And I was around friends whose parents didn't argue like mine did. I knew the difference. I was old enough to understand that Mother wasn't a happy camper. Money seemed to be at the root of all arguments. Dad worked odd jobs, never really having a skill that qualified as a profession. During the summer months and the vegetable season, he worked in the fields. He hated working like a *bracero*, or a worker from Mexico. When summer work was over, he'd take odd jobs. Nothing permanent.

Chuy had a serious problem. When he got paid at the end of the week, he'd go straight to Cowboys' Place, a local bar. He would start Friday afternoon and go into the night, drinking with friends instead of thinking about feeding his family. He'd come home drunk with little left for the week. He didn't care.

It would be many years later before I figured it out. He was homesick. It wasn't an excuse for his behavior, but it was a common occurrence among men from his hometown. Work, get paid, get drunk, buy your friends beer, play pool, repeat. I got to see this for myself later in life. It didn't matter whether he had children to care for. How this didn't bother him, I would never understand. Many times, we went to bed hungry because he'd selfishly spent the little money he'd earned on his emotional state.

There was a store on 2nd and South Nelson Streets, about two blocks west of Main Street. An old Southwestern Bell Telephone building sat next to it, and right across was the fire station. Sotero's Grocery Store was much bigger than Fidel's. It catered to the Hispanic community, but since it was farther away from home, we required a car to go there. Many of our neighbors didn't shop there. It was located in the upper reaches of the barrio, closer to the railroad tracks that separated Mexican Town from the more affluent white sections of the city.

Many years later, when I was discussing our upbringing with Mom, she shared a story that was very difficult for her. I could see the hurt in her eyes as she recounted the incident.

"You must have been about four," she told me. "Nancy was three and Wanda two. I was pregnant with Jesse. I wasn't showing yet, but nevertheless, I was carrying a new baby. I had very little food. It had been two days, and Chuy had not been home. I knew he was out spending his paycheck. The little ones were crying. I knew it was hunger. You complained as well. I'd make coffee for the three of you. Nancy and Wanda would drink it from a baby bottle. That was all I had. I made some *atole* for you as well. I took flour, mixed it with water, added cinnamon and sugar and made a sauce for you to eat. I'd tell you it was a special dessert. I could feel the hunger pains, so I knew you all were suffering. When all were asleep, I walked to Sotero's. Because it was late, the store was closed. Behind the store, in the trash bins, I searched for rotten potatoes or any other vegetables that had been thrown out that day. The store owners threw out vegetables they didn't sell by a certain date. Rummaging through the trash cans, I found some. It wasn't much, but it was enough to make soup. I walked five blocks home in the dark, hoping none of you had woken up. I cut out the bad parts of the vegetables and made soup for the morning. When you got up, you asked for coffee. Instead, I handed you a cup of soup. You ate it all, saying it was the best you'd ever had. You had three cups."

She went on to say the soup fed us for two days. She never told anyone else that story. Why she decided to share it with me at that time, I'll never know, and I never asked.

Chuy

My dad, Jesús Navarette Alfaro, was born in Sahuayo, Michoacán, Mexico. His early stories revealed he came from a family of *zapateros*, or shoemakers. His father was a shoemaker, his father's father was a shoemaker, and his great-grandfather was a shoemaker, so it was expected that Dad should do the right thing and be a shoemaker just like his family. But he hated wearing shoes. The entire business repulsed him.

To be more precise, he shared once that this family really didn't make shoes like one might think. They made the upper part of huaraches. Using cow or calf skins, they cut long strips of leather, then sewed them into leather soles of various sizes. These were then sold to American businessmen for fifty cents a pair. The buyers would then take the upper part of the shoe, or huarache, and have a plastic heel sewn or glued on. Once the shoes were complete, they sold them at department stores for fifteen to thirty dollars a pair. Ten pairs of huaraches at fifty cents each would bring in enough money to buy a great meal for the entire family.

Dad didn't understand the significance of these earnings. He didn't like the smell of leather, the banging of hammers to smooth out the leather, or the time it took to make a pair of shoes. He'd much rather run the streets with other boys and simply enjoy his freedom, which, at times, led to mischief. It was certain in a neighborhood crowded with people, cars, and animals, all moving about until all hours of the day and night.

By the time he turned eight, schooling was not for him either, making him a third-grade dropout. Disgusted with his attitude, my grandfather decided to teach him the intricacies of the business whether he liked it or not. He demanded a work ethic from my dad, eventually molding the boy into one who despised the making of shoes. The family had created a business that brought in enough money for them to enjoy what middle-class families wanted—to be respected by others. This ideology soon fell off Chuy's plate of principles to live by. He did learn the trade, but only to appease his father. The older he got, the more clear it became to everyone that in no way was he going to be a maker of huaraches. He was the youngest of five children. By the time he came along, his parents had little time to work on discipline. So, with all the adults busy creating a thriving business, he ran the streets with other kids until he was old enough to take matters into his own hands.

Dad lived in a modest two-story house in the middle of the barrio, surrounded by aunts, uncles, cousins, and friends. With very little supervision, he had the freedom and independence he so enjoyed. Once children were given free rein to wander about the neighborhood, it was not unusual for them to get into trouble. When it happened for Chuy and his father found out, discipline came in the form of physical abuse. My dad had learned it from his dad. Eventually, that abuse would be passed on to his children.

The home was modest at best. They had enough money to buy the necessities of life and then some. There was always plenty to eat and drink. My grandmother ran the household and looked like Granny in the sitcom *The Beverly Hillbillies*. She supervised the housecleaning crew while preparing the meals of the day.

Hyper, with a relentless supply of energy, she moved about, shouting orders to the crew. Where the energy came from, no one knew. She never stopped moving! I don't believe obsessive-compulsive disorder, attention deficit disorder, or attention-deficit/hyperactivity disorder was something people in Mexico understood, let alone thought someone like my grandmother had. They simply chalked it up to excessive energy. She ran the kitchen and managed the household needs, the children's needs, and my grandfather's needs. She was one of the first to get up in the morning and the last to call it a day. When I met my grandmother, I could not keep up with her. I tried. She was nearly eighty years old, and I was pushing twenty-five.

My grandfather, on the other hand, was the typical *mañana* type. He was not one to be in a hurry, yet he kept the business running day in and day out. I heard he was a tall, light-complected man with white hair that stood straight up in the air and made his large head look even larger. He was an easygoing guy who loved music, drinking, dancing, singing, and more drinking. He provided for all the family by making sure the shoe business was producing the quotas demanded by American businessmen who came down to inspect the merchandise every so often. There wasn't much my father said about my grandfather. I never got to meet him, although, to me, it seemed strange that Dad seldom mentioned his father.

He did recount the day my grandfather died. Chuy was about fifteen or sixteen years old when that happened. My grandfather, Francisco Navarrete Alfaro, apparently slipped and fell from the top of his home's spiral staircase, drunk. In his drunken state and completely oblivious to the number of steps on the stairwell, he missed one and fell to his death. That's how my dad described the incident.

With the head of the family gone, Dad became restless. He didn't want anything to do with the business. Besides, his two older brothers were handling it just fine. Days after my grandfather's passing, Dad left on a pilgrimage to Mexico City. What sort of pilgrimage? It was never described, but he said it was one. Since the majority of Mexicans were Catholic, I assumed it was a religious pilgrimage. In reality, he was just hungry for adventure, and the thrill of going off to the big city seemed the perfect solution. Without a father around telling him what to do, his sense of adventure took over. The obsession left him with a longing to travel as far away from Sahuayo as he possibly could. He wanted to see places he had only heard about, especially the enchanting Cuidad de Méjico, or Mexico City.

Mexico City, the land of the rich and famous, beckoned, and Chuy left as quickly as he could. Shoemaking days were over. He was an adventurer who could not stay home and carry on with the family business. Something different and savory kept calling him. Seeking romance, entertainment, glamorous clubs where he could dance the night away, and a place to work without being told to make shoes, he arrived in Mexico's capital. Unfortunately, not fully understanding the city's culture presented unique challenges. He lived in the streets and worked at odd jobs, barely making enough money to live the dream. Extended family lived there, but living with them would be like living at home with people telling him what to do and what he needed to do. That was what he was running away from.

My brother Jesse behaved the same way. The apple doesn't fall too far from the tree.

Years later, out of curiosity, I asked Dad why half of his ear was missing. I hadn't noticed the missing part of the ear until I was about ten. He began to recount the story of this unfortunate incident with a troubled smile.

He had been living in the streets alongside other homeless people in Mexico City and had been paid for doing temporary work of some kind. He and some young men he called friends decided to spend some of the money drinking and gambling in local bars.

"I had earned a few miserable pesos that week," he said. "One of my amigos invited me to a bar not far from where we had been camping out. We were being rowdy, singing and dancing around the tables and flirting with women at the bar. We were just kids. There was no law or rule determining the drinking age. Even if there was, no one enforced it. We'd been drinking most of the afternoon. We all sang the last songs played on the jukebox before we were thrown out of the bar."

He stopped to think.

"The street hustle was a way of life in Mexico City. If one was to survive in that overpopulated city, they needed to know whom they could trust. I must have been eighteen or nineteen by then. We ran out of booze late into the evening. Some street guys I didn't know ambled over to us. One said he could get more beer down the street if we had money. Of course, I told him I did, proud of the fact that I did have some. Staggering, we followed him. The drink made us laugh. The store was a house, the front room being the place where this family sold goods and beer." He stopped as if he needed time to put his story in the proper sequence.

"We were walking down the street, drinking beer and savoring tacos bought from a corner stand, when a group of older men approached us. They wanted some of our beer. '*Están pendejos? Esta cerveza es para nosotros! Vayan a la chingada!*' ['Are you all stupid? This beer is for us. Go to hell!'] An argument ensued. One of them pulled a knife, yelling, '*Los vamos a capar, cabrones.*' He promised he was going to cut off our balls."

I put my hands over my mouth and laughed. He stopped briefly, like he needed to think about the next part. Then he continued.

"We all ran in different directions. Then the man with the knife shouted, '*¡Les vamos a cortar los juevos, cabrones!*' ['I'm going to cut off your balls!'] Hoping to avoid castration, I ran away from the others. I had the sack of beer in one hand, which made it difficult to run as fast as I should have. One of them caught me, dragged me down, and held me until the others caught up. My friends were gone. I knew then they were going to castrate me for sure. I tried to fight them off, but I was so drunk, I couldn't land a punch, much less fight off three of them. They took my beer and what little money I had left. The guy with the knife said, 'Hold him!' He took the knife and sliced the tip off my ear!"

Chuy laughed, shaking his head back and forth as if to erase the memory. He paused for effect, looked at me with a slight smile, then turned around and went outside.

Not long after that incident, he decided Mexico City was too violent. He realized very quickly how difficult it was going to be for him. His only skill was making huaraches, which he hated. Living in the streets was not what he'd envisioned. So he set on a course leading him out of the city and away from the hustle and bustle.

Discouraged and out of money, he hitchhiked back toward his home. He stopped in San Luis Potosi, a less populated city, hoping a friendlier place without so many distractions might prove better. The last thing he wanted was to show up in Sahuayo and be looked upon as a failure. He didn't want to face the humiliation. Being out on his own was not pretty. It was difficult. He had to find a way to make a living other than hustling in the streets. But after a few more years of going from town to town, he finally arrived back in Sahuayo. While at home, he reluctantly rejoined his brothers in the family business.

Some cousins who had been to the United States told stories of the wonderful things they'd seen and done. They told of the jobs they'd had, the apartments they'd lived in, the food they'd eaten, and the women they'd dated. They talked about the cars they could afford to buy with the money they'd made. It sounded as if jobs in the United States paid so well, anyone could afford an apartment and a car. They kept talking about how much money they were making—enough that they could send some back home to their parents and still keep some to sustain themselves. Stories they shared sounded thrilling and adventurous as they sat in a circle around the patio after a hard day's work. As was customary, the workers discussed America as if it was the greatest place on Earth. Other friends, who had been to the United States before being caught as illegal aliens and deported, recounted stories of jobs, cheap cars, pretty girls, and who knows what else.

Chuy made up his mind. He was going to find a way to get there. Los Estados Unidos was going to be his new home. The cousins continued to sensationalize the wonderful time they'd had while in the United States, drawing even more appeal for him. Houston, Dallas, Chicago—these were places he wanted to see for himself. He was convinced it was not hard to pick up American girls who liked Mexican men.

Chuy decided to head to El Norte with his two friends, Jorge and Camilo. Their destination was Chicago—a city where many people from Sahuayo had settled. It was far enough from the border, and the US Border Patrol was less likely to be there. So it was safer for Chuy and his friends.

They mapped out a plan, convinced that leaving in the late winter would put them in the US by early spring. Folks from Sahuayo told them of a community of Mexicans from Michoacán who could help them out while they got settled. Some of those people were relatives or friends of folks from Chuy's hometown. The stories these townspeople shared with him were enough to convince the three young men that Chicago was a place made in Heaven and that it should be theirs as well. Jobs, girls, beer, cars, and more beer!

They heard stories regarding what path to take. It was not going to be easy by any means, but if they were careful, they could make it by hitchhiking, taking the bus, and/or jumping on the train headed north. Hitchhiking through the desert and some of the roughest parts of the country was dangerous, they were told, but not as dangerous as jumping on the train.

"Avoid the train at all costs if possible. You don't want to be caught by Mexican immigration or by the bandidos lurking at train stations looking to rob passengers," was a warning shared by most.

By the time they got to Matamoros, Mexico—the sister city to Brownsville, Texas—Chuy and his friends were exhausted, hungry, dirty, and smelling of rotten potatoes. They'd crossed half of Mexico with great difficulty, yet they were determined to keep going. They were so close.

In the meantime, they needed a place to stay for a few days until they could figure out a way to get across the border. If they languished too long in one place, they were fearful they'd succumb to the dangers that had befallen many a comrade who'd waited too long—eventually losing all their money to bandidos. Crossing into unknown territory with a coyote—a person who transported illegals into the US—was out of the question. It cost too much. The three friends barely made enough money to eat, much less get someone to cross them over.

The trio did spend some time in Matamoros, scouting the area for a perfect place to cross the mighty Rio Grande. They discussed their options, considering crossing late at night without the help of others and making a run for the city of Brownsville, at which time they would either walk or find a ride through Texas.

The major obstacle they had to overcome was getting across the Rio Grande without drowning. Numerous Mexicans were swept away by the current. This created a sense of caution for them. This was the last thing anyone wanted. They were so close to making a new life in the United States. Drowning was not an option.

Matamoros served as a getaway destination for many Mexican and American workers. It was the place to relax after a week of toiling in the hot sun. They could eat, drink tequila, enjoy mariachi music, or simply hang with others, sharing stories of adventure.

Mexico provided plenty of hired hands for the farmers' demands. The valley, a fertile section of land extending from Las Palmas de Zapata down the Rio Grande to Brownsville along Highway 83, was a farmer's dream. It provided a perfect spot for growing just about any kind of vegetable or fruit one could dream of. The abundance of crops provided seasonal work for many documented and undocumented workers.

As luck would have it, my dad and his friends noticed a group of men having dinner and drinks in a small Mexican café not too far from the border in Matamoros. These men were Texan farm contractors who hired Mexicans to work the fields of produce and cotton. They held work visas, which allowed them to move back and forth between the two countries. My dad and his friends quickly introduced themselves. The Texans shared their need for more workers and asked my dad if he was interested. If he, Jorge, and Camilo agreed, they could apply for work visas, which could be obtained in a few days. Or they could take their chances, cross illegally, and know there was a job waiting for them on the other side.

The three travelers didn't want to wait any longer. They would take their chances and cross the river. The Texans promised them a job picking watermelons and cantaloupes for the season. When those crops were done, they would move on to pick cotton. If they worked for three months, they could save enough money to get them to their final destination—Chicago.

The three made the decision to cross the Rio Grande by night with the aid of the moonlight as it reflected off the water. Holding on to an inner tube, the three kicked their feet hard enough to move the tube slowly down the river. The current, which was not at full strength, carried them away from the US side. So they held on to the tube for dear life and kicked until they felt the rocky bottom.

They were across.

"I thought we were never going to make it. The water was cold, with the current fighting us all the way across," Chuy recalled.

Regaining their footing, they walked onto the Texan bank, breathless and tired. Still in danger of being seen, they ran through tall grass, away from the riverbank and deeper into the unknown.

In wet clothes and shivering from the cold, they ambled through the alleys and back roads that led them away from town. Still not safe from the prying eyes of residents, who reported illegals, and La Migra, (the Border Patrol), they worked their way toward a small farming community a few miles from Brownsville.

They didn't find the Texans who'd promised them jobs, but they did manage to find a location where contractors picked up people willing to work. The three were added to the group of laborers and, within an hour, arrived on a farm close to Weslaco. There they met the majordomo, or contractor/boss—Francisco Gonzales Fabela, an older Hispanic man—who gave the three a job picking fruit.

After a few weeks, the little gang of three decided it was time to move on. Chicago called. With two weeks' wages—enough to get them as far away from La Migra as possible, they were ready.

But hesitation on my father's part did not sit well with the others. He was faced with a dilemma he would never have anticipated.

The people in this working community included several young women. One who had caught my dad's eye was a small, skinny girl who, at times, found herself working a row or two from him. His flirtatious nature amused and alarmed the girl. He made her smile and laugh with his corny jokes and silly stories. Her name was Virginia Velasquez Fabela, and she would someday become my mother. She was one of the daughters of the majordomo, who was my grandfather.

"I'm going to Chicago with my friends as soon as the work is done here," he told her.

"That must be far away. Do you live there?"

"No, not now. But it will be my home. I have friends there. My home is in Méjico."

She found him attractive and liked the attention he gave her. They kept talking, becoming comfortable with each other's company. In two weeks, he managed to gain her confidence enough that she began falling for him. He liked her manner, her looks, her work ethic, and the way she paid attention to his dramatic stories. She liked him too.

Was it love at first sight? If it was, they never said. My dad was not the kind to admit he had fallen in love with her. She was smitten by his handsome looks and his older, more mature nature. By the time the three men were ready to leave for Chicago, Chuy told his friends he was going to stay and travel with the group of farm laborers until he could accrue enough money to drive to Chicago in a car instead of hitchhiking all the way.

They left. He stayed.

As soon as the farm job ended in south Texas, the group of workers moved on to the Texas Panhandle, reaching a small, dusty rural town called Muleshoe. There they worked picking cotton for the season, which ended in late November.

Mom and Dad carried on with their little love scene until her family decided they would move back to their hometown when the job finished. After a few weeks, the Fabelas packed their meager belongings and headed back to Fort Stockton, Texas.

My dad followed. Once in Fort Stockton, he and my mother spoke of marriage. This sealed the future for the two. Dad's dream of going to Chicago disappeared. Against her family's protestations, she insisted on marrying him.

"He's too old for you. He's trying to take advantage of you," said one of her sisters.

"He doesn't belong here," said the other.

"Why are you wanting to marry someone who has nothing to his name? How are you going to survive?" asked one more.

Mom's younger sisters were the most vocal as they tried to convince her that she was making a huge mistake. The only exception was Mother's oldest sister, Aunt Minne. She'd say to the others, "Leave her alone, and mind your own business. If she wants to get married, she should get married. Now go back to work and stop harassing her!" She was more understanding. She supported my mother's wishes most of the time.

The sisters' continued insults, compounded by their negative actions toward my dad, eventually took their toll. They were cold to him, taking stabs at his lack of education, lack of a permanent job, lack of money, and lack of respect for them. He knew the younger sisters didn't like him. Yes, he was several years older than my mom, but they loved each other. Eventually, with all the negative comments coming from her family, his relationship with the Fabelas deteriorated.

The result was a separation from her family that lasted for many years. He prohibited my mother from having anything to do with them. He would never forgive them, nor would he forget how they made him feel. Mother let her family's remarks fall by the wayside, but my father never forgot how they treated him. This caused a lasting resentment just short of downright anger. On occasion, my parents did attend family gatherings, but he said very little to her relatives. In his heart and mind, he knew they were not the kind of people he trusted or even liked. This would create family problems for years.

Mom

Virginia Velazquez Fabela was born in Fort Stockton, Texas, on January 2, 1932. January in West Texas has always been cold, with northern winds sending temperatures plummeting to near freezing. It doesn't rain very often there, but when it does, especially in the winter, it turns to snow and ice, making it difficult to stay warm. The grayish skies rarely let the sun show its face, which can offer a respite from the gloom of the day.

A small town with a ridiculously small hospital belonging to the only doctor in town, Dr. Gibson, Fort Stockton was my mother's birthplace.

Her father, Francisco Gonzales Fabela, was originally from Matamoros, Mexico. He'd married a fourteen-year-old woman, Romana Velasquez, who was from a railroad town known as Marathon, Texas. He was eight years older than her. When they ran off together, he was twenty-two years old and already a seasoned businessman. Grandfather was a tall, lanky man who didn't have much education but did possess a great deal of common sense. A kindhearted man who rarely took the Lord's name in vain, he was religious yet seldom set foot in church. He loved to work, loved his family, and enjoyed the outdoors. He would venture into the US periodically, buying and selling goods. He mostly entered the US to sell what he grew in his fields, which wasn't much more than beans, wheat, corn, or hay.

Grandfather Francisco grew up working the land around Matamoros and eventually graduated to owning a small plot of land near what today is known as La Mula, Mexico. He took advantage of a law that gave land grants to those willing to work the land. It would remain his as long as he worked it, but he would never legally own it. The day he stopped working the land, it would revert to the Mexican government.

Up until just a few years ago, Sarah's Café in Fort Stockton was the central gathering place for the local Hispanic community—a place to join family and friends who enjoyed good, authentic Mexican food. The music, the food, and the continued flow of beer gave the place a "back home" feel, especially for those coming from Mexico. Everyone spoke Spanish there. The conversations filled the dining room, giving people who frequented the place a sense of community. Sarah made them feel at home no matter where they came from. "*Mi casa es su casa*" probably came from visiting Sarah's Café.

It became my grandfather's favorite place when he ventured into town to sell his crops. He did this several times a year, so many there knew him. At times, he conducted business with American customers at Sarah's. The food, beer, music, and business and social opportunities that presented themselves among friends drew many to this place. This was where my grandfather met my grandmother.

They were married in Fort Stockton and moved to La Mula, away from her family. It wasn't long before they started having children. Thirteen in all! The more the merrier, right?

No. The more kids one had in those days, the more free labor you got. The first four were born in Fort Stockton. (Mom was the second oldest.) The middle six were born in Mexico, and the last three were born in Fort Stockton.

What little schooling Mother received did not get her beyond the sixth grade. But it gave her enough English to understand well enough so she could help out her father with business dealings. She was never proficient but did manage to mix English with Spanish to get deals done. Gringo or Mexican, everyone spoke Spanish. Her shyness prevented her from speaking the language correctly, so she didn't speak much unless she had to.

She attended Butz Elementary School, the same Mexican school I would eventually attend. It was the oldest school in the city and was located between Front and Gallagher Streets in the middle of Mexican Town. She learned math rather rapidly, but reading took longer for her to grasp. She was proficient in Spanish, so reading Spanish books came easy to her. However, school was fun for her, and it was this experience that solidified in her mind the worth of knowledge and education. She would never forget this.

Grandfather took everyone back to La Mula in 1939. News around the world caused alarm for all Americans. Germany had started a war by taking over several countries along its borders. But the lack of a TV set limited what most people in remote Fort Stockton knew about the impending war. The Hispanic community, with a mixture of gossip and news from the local radio station, learned very little about the global discontent among nations. It would be two more years before America was drawn into World War II. On December 7, 1941, the Japanese bombed Pearl Harbor, forcing President Franklin Delano Roosevelt to declare war on Germany, Japan, and Italy.

Staying close to the radio late one evening as the local disc jockey announced the nation's declaration of war, the Fabela family discussed how it would impact them. The US government needed men to fight the aggressors and help bring a quick end to the war. Not long after, an announcer reported to the nation that implementing a military draft would shore up the ranks, forcing young men to enter the war. The announcement of the military draft kept my grandfather in Mexico. He feared that this war, which he knew little about or simply didn't understand, would take his young boys away from him if he returned to the US. The idea of placing his sons in foreign lands to fight a foreign war he knew nothing about was not worth the risk. However, staying in Mexico was not a good idea either.

Life in La Mula was riddled with poverty, which at times made it extremely difficult to feed so many mouths. Many Mexican families relied on a simple diet since there wasn't much to go on. People lived on beans, tortillas, fideo, and potatoes. Money was hard to come by with the war going on, and this prevented my grandfather from venturing into the US. Selling his produce became difficult. Mexico as a nation was struggling also, as were many countries around the world. Shortages in food, clothing, and manufacturing made things hard.

By the time the war was over, the situation in La Mula had become desperate. Grandfather was prepared to make some tough decisions. It was because the family was struggling that Grandfather, agonizing over his inability to provide for so many people, decided to separate the family. In such times, a father must make these decisions. It made sense for him to send the four oldest back to the US. He sat them down, explaining that the family could not survive unless the four went back to the US to find work. The opportunities there would be greater for them since there was very little to be had in Mexico. He explained that if he left as well, he would lose the lands he had worked so hard to keep. He needed to stay and tend to his farmland. Meanwhile, the four oldest children, unhappy with the decision, prepared to leave the rest of the family behind.

Mother cried.

The four left La Mula and headed toward Presidio, Texas, on their way to Fort Stockton. Mom was only fourteen years old in 1946—the year she waved goodbye to her mother. She and her three siblings were to live with my great-grandfather in a small all-adobe house on the westernmost outer reaches of the town, in Mexican Town.

A few adobe houses made up the southwestern boundary of the city. It was approximately a ten-by-ten-block area south of the railroad, east of Highway 385 and west of Nelson Street. This community was inhabited entirely by Hispanics. Fort Stockton— even though it didn't have the population to be a village, much less a town—would become the home for the oldest Fabela kids.

The four worked the seasonal crops, picking, cutting, plucking, and loading. Whatever other jobs they could find during the offseason provided some stability. The money they made kept them barely alive. After sending money back to help out those in Mexico and paying money to my great-grandfather for staying at his place, there was very little for them to do but work. Mom and the others settled into a routine, often working late into the night.

At the age of fourteen, Mom worked as a farm laborer. She was a shy, quiet girl. She was not very tall and was skinny, weighing in at almost ninety pounds. But she had guts. She didn't cry or complain, knowing full well that what she and her siblings were doing would keep them and the family back home from starving. Either she wasn't interested in boys or boys weren't interested in a shy, skinny, poor girl who wore tattered clothes made from flour sacks sewn together by her grandmother. It wasn't a good time for a young girl to enjoy the life of a teenager. Even after a long day at work, she fell back to work at her temporary home, helping with cleaning, cooking, and taking care of the younger cousins who all lived with my great-grandfather, Don Sabastian.

By 1947 and 1948, with the war over, the numbers of men who did return home were not enough to help the country rebuild its economy. In an effort to fill the labor shortage, the

US government passed a bill allowing immigrant workers to come into the country. These workers were called *braceros*, or laborers. The US government worked out a temporary work visa for workers from Mexico. Those who took up the call with the promise of jobs and money crossed into California, Arizona, New Mexico, and Texas. These braceros filled the gap that existed mostly in low-paying farm labor, but many also worked in the motel and hotel cleaning industry. Others drove transport trucks, cooked in restaurants, cleaned people's homes, and joined the construction industry.

Grandfather, who continued to struggle with his farming venture, eventually decided to bring everybody back to Fort Stockton. He rented an adobe house along Alamo Street, which was at the upper end of the armpit of the city. The house resembled a barracks, with three or four rooms lined up in a straight line connected by inside doorways. This would be their home for several years.

The seasonal migrant work attracted my grandfather, who had enough experience as a businessman to solicit contract work from the gringo farmers. He assembled a crew of laborers, which included his own children, and followed the seasonal crops. In 1948 and 1949, there was an abundance of much-needed work in Texas. Picking cotton was lucrative, and he had experienced hands to deliver the product on time. This kind of work ethic filtered down to Mother, who used these experiences to learn from him and his business practices.

By the middle of 1949, while working in cotton fields in the southern part of Texas, my mother found herself face-to-face with a stranger who had just joined the crew. His name was Jesús Navarrete Alfaro.

The Struggle Continues

1960 was a trying year. Mom was struggling with Dad's lack of responsibility. Right after Christmas, she moved out of our house and into my grandparents' place, taking with her six kids. Nora, the youngest, was born on August 30, 1958. So she was two. I was eight. My grandparents had moved to a bigger house near Oklahoma and Callaghan Streets, up from the adobe three-room house we'd lived in. It was a wood frame house with running water, electricity, and a gas stove. With many children still living at home, they needed more space to accommodate them all. The place offered a bigger lot, where Apa, my grandfather, could park his trucks and cotton trailers. I was glad they'd moved to a bigger house. They certainly deserved it.

Ama, my grandmother, was a good cook who prepared some delicious home-cooked meals. With an apron tied around her midsection, she was forever in the kitchen, cooking and carrying on a conversation with anyone who was present. She was old school, offering anyone who came by something to eat, regardless of the time of day. Papas, fideo, and beans with freshly made tortillas never faded from the menu. She was never stingy with food. And when meat was available, she spread the love with a good meal.

It was a cold winter day when we arrived at my grandparents' house. We'd been there about two weeks when the shit hit the fan, as the adults would put it. Every day, Mother worked around the house, helping out with the cooking, washing, or cleaning up after the men, who went to work every day. Mom's oldest sister was married and gone. That left her younger sisters and younger brothers still at home. With us there, a total of seventeen people lived in that house. When you live in such close quarters, there's bound to be some arguments. Two of my aunts were not very pleased with us being there.

"What are you doing here?" one would say to Mom.

"We don't want you here. You need to go back to your no-good husband and have him provide for you and your kids," said another.

"You are taking room here and eating what little food we have. There isn't enough room for you and those *huercos*," they would say.

Mom would not argue. She simply tried to avoid them. Their constant demeaning, insulting words were said when our grandparents couldn't hear. I'd hear the negative comments but would not say anything. I couldn't. It wasn't my house. This continued to be an everyday occurrence. Mom eventually got tired of being scolded and harassed by the two. She'd had enough. One morning, she woke everyone up. Angry and still distraught over the negative comments, she'd decided to leave. It was winter, and the cold wind blowing strong from the north sent a chill throughout my body.

"Get your coat and help Nancy with hers," she said to me. She wrapped each of us up in our meager winter clothing. As she walked out the door into the bitter cold, I could see tears in her eyes.

It started to snow. We walked through the snow-covered streets, trying to avoid the cold wind biting into our faces. Mom, holding baby Nora with one hand and pulling Imelda with the other, demanded we move faster. As we tried to avoid slipping, I held Nancy's hand while she held Wanda's. We walked. Jesse followed.

"Wait up, Mom," I cried after her. Motivated by the cold and her anger, her pace was fast and deliberate. When we were halfway to the house, which was still about five or six blocks away, one of her sisters pulled up in the truck and yelled at Mom to get in. She refused. She was insistent that we were going to walk to the adobe barracks we called home without assistance from anyone, much less her family.

It was cold inside when we arrived at our rental. She turned on the gas stove, slowly warming up the place. It would take some time before we could shed our clothes. She was still visibly angry. Dad was nowhere to be found. We drank coffee to keep warm.

By the afternoon, she said to me through clenched teeth, "Go to the bar and tell him we're home."

I knew where the bar was because I'd been there before. He'd stopped going to Cowboys' Place, giving it up for Joe's Place. It was more to his liking since it was frequented mostly by Hispanics. It was a long one-room adobe building with an overhang protecting the screen door from rain that seldom fell. The green paint didn't hide its age. Above the overhang, in large, fading cursive red letters, was the name of the place. The overhang didn't look too sturdy, but those entering the place didn't mind. I thought if a strong wind came blowing through, it would topple the whole dang thing. I suppose drunk men didn't care. The place had two pool tables and three or four tables along the back, where men played dominoes or cards. A twelve-foot bar on the left protected the beer coolers. Joe, the owner, a tall man, was permanently affixed behind the bar. He had dark hair and a face punctuated by dark circles under his eyes. He wore a green apron and moved back and forth the length of the bar, serving customers.

My dad became a regular. The first time I entered the place, I thought Joe looked familiar. At first, I couldn't place him. He was in a different environment when I had last seen him. But he looked familiar. *Where do I know this man from?* I asked myself. It would take a few more trips to the bar before it clicked. He was my godfather! He was responsible for my confirmation! Small world for a small kid.

That cold day, I opened the screen door and looked around the place, giving my eyes time to adjust to the darkness. Joe saw me and waved me inside.

"He's over there," he said. "You need to take him home."

I looked toward the end of the place, focusing on a table where four men sat. I found Dad sitting at one of the domino tables, drinking beer, laughing, and smoking. As I walked toward him, I looked up at other men standing around talking. Some acknowledged my presence by smiling at me, while others just went on about their business. I was definitely out of place and felt intimidated by these strange men. I bowed my head and avoided making eye contact. I knew I should not have been there.

I got close to Dad and said, "*Mama quiere que te vayas a la casa.*" ("Mom wants you to come home.") I pulled on his shirt and said it again.

He laughed and yelled to Joe over the loud music to get me a pop. He wanted to finish his game. I could tell he was nearing drunk status.

I looked toward the bar, and Joe waved me over. Slowly, I approached the bar and jumped up onto a stool. Grabbing the end of the bar, I could now see Joe up close. He was a smiling character who seemed to enjoy running the place. He had been there for some time and catered to clients who were never many.

He made a living selling beer, soft drinks, cigarettes, and chips. He also kept two big jars on the counter. One was filled with what looked like pigs' feet swirling in yellowish liquid. It was full. The other was filled with hard-boiled eggs. They, too, floated in yellow liquid that smelled like baked beans, just like Chuy's farts. Each time Joe opened the jar to swoop one out with a long spoon, the smell almost made me gag.

Joe grabbed a Coke and asked me if I was hungry. I nodded. He gave me a bag of potato chips.

"I'm glad you are here for your father. He's got money in his pocket. You need to get him home before he loses it all," he warned me.

I just nodded and asked him if I could have another Coke.

About thirty minutes later, Dad got up, stumbled a little, and grabbed me off the stool with a big smile on his face. He carried me out the screen door, put me down, and asked me to walk with him.

I walked toward the house, and he followed. How we managed to get home in his condition, I'll never know, but we did it.

By then, I knew that on certain Fridays, Dad would get paid and take what he'd earned to Joe's Place. As soon as I got home from school, I'd put my stuff away, then ask Mom if I could go. She knew exactly what I meant.

"*Sí, por favor. Dile que necesitamos comida.*" ("Yes, and tell him we need groceries.")

I would run out the door, hoping that when I got there, Joe would invite me for a Coke and chips. When I got to the bar, I'd open the screen door just enough to see if Dad was there. If he was, I'd walk in, jump on the stool, and talk to Joe with my feet dangling. Every time I came in, he'd pull a Coke and some chips, then hand them to me without even asking if I wanted them. We'd talk for a few minutes, and he'd ask me how school was going. I'd reply eagerly between sips of soda. He would then rush to clean off some table vacated by customers. He'd point to where I was sitting, telling Dad I was there for him. Eventually, I'd beg Dad to come with me, but not until I'd had my fill of soda and chips.

Mom was at her wit's end. Dad's trips to Joe's Place at the end of the week before coming home made her incensed. I could see the frustration on her face, yet she'd seldom complain to us.

In sheer desperation, she'd exclaim, "*Ese hombre no sabe que necesitamos muchas cosas en esta casa.*" ("This man doesn't understand we need things around the house.") It was a pattern that tended to repeat itself quite often. This did not add to her sense of compassion. In her mind, his behavior was getting close to a come-to-Jesus conversation. What was she going to do about it? She had too many children to take care of. She was stuck with no remedy in sight. When she did complain, not necessarily to us, she vocalized her desperation. But it made very little difference in his behavior.

If we were lucky, at times, he would get home before he ran out of money. On those few occasions, we would relish the few groceries we had for the week. It was never anything fancy. Just the usual—beans, tortillas, eggs, potatoes, and, during good times, ground beef. I'd always plead for bologna. It came in handy when ground beef was scarce. Apparently, there were some paydays that were better than others because even though he got home after being at Joe's Place, he still had enough left over to keep Mom from getting angry with him. As if in his drunken state, he cared.

On those occasions, Mom would stash any leftover change in a coffee can she kept hidden in a drawer. With time, those dimes, nickels, and quarters amounted to just about enough for a rainy day. She would use this money to put some clothes on layaway for the coming school year. Nancy, Wanda, and I were now going to school, and three sets of clothes didn't come cheap. It would take Mom several weeks to get the clothes paid for before school started.

I would turn nine in July and was growing rather quickly. So I would require a new set of clothes by January. This made Christmas a no-brainer. I knew what I was getting.

The new decade looked promising for the country. It saw, for the first time, a Catholic president. John F. Kennedy was young—younger than any other president. Embracing a can-do spirit, he gave hope to the American people. The Hispanic community felt hope for a better life for the first time. They believed in this president. Pictures of President Kennedy hung on the walls of almost every Hispanic house in the barrio. They all liked him so much that it was no accident his picture hung close to the picture of Jesus Christ. They had faith that Kennedy would provide security, jobs, and a better future. With this president, poor people would have the opportunity to achieve the ever-elusive American dream: to be independent from welfare status. Kennedy was hope.

In July of 1960, I turned nine. On July 15, a few days before my birthday, Chubby Checker released a record that had everyone dancing a new dance—at least in my house. "The Twist" hit the charts with a bang and made Chubby Checker a household name. Everyone could do the twist. Women loved it. They swore doing the twist would make their hips sexier. Even people with two left feet could dance to this song!

As the country twisted to the music, other events were occurring that were not as popular. 1960 brought about the beginnings of the civil rights movement, the Cold War, the space race between the US and the Soviet Union, and the escalation of the Vietnam War.

We knew very little of what was happening in America other than Kennedy being president. The Alfaro clan was remotely aware of such events, as were most working Hispanics in the barrio. We were trying to understand why things were so bad economically. Mom and Dad had their disagreements, and they started openly arguing more often. Mom was becoming more aggressive with her demands, taking a hard stance on his drinking and his lack of a full-time job. She finally realized things were not going to get better unless she took more responsibility instead of just being a housewife committed to taking care of the kids. She'd had enough. She was orchestrating a plan. It would take some time, but she was determined.

Things must have gotten pretty bad during the summer of 1960. We got evicted again and were forced to seek out a place we could afford. This time, it was toward the southernmost part of Mexican Town. This area was the *sobaco*, or the armpit, of the neighborhood. The house we moved into was within a block of the center of the armpit, making it the most deplorable area one could live in. This move pushed us back to the lowest rung of the poor ladder. We were not moving forward.

The hood was cluttered with the oldest houses in town. Ours was rated one of the worst. There was nothing modern there other than running water and electricity. There were no streetlights illuminating the night. The streets were dirt, mostly caliche—powdery white dirt that left dust everywhere, even when the wind wasn't blowing. When a car or truck came rushing by, it left dust swirls lingering in the air. The dust was so pervasive that it made breathing difficult. Sometimes, the wind picked up the dirt, causing small funnels that swirled upward toward the sky. Many a time, the dust just settled in the air like a brown cloud, making it hard to see.

The neighborhood, which was made up mostly of adobe houses that were all small and close to each other, had its own cultural aura. Music flowed throughout the homes, especially during the Tejano radio hour. Up the street, closer to downtown, houses made of siding—something unique and strange for our part of the neighborhood—marked the boundary between the armpit and the rest of the world. On the southernmost part of town, where the desert began, was our barrio. It was not much more than mesquite, cacti, lizards, horny toads, and rattlers.

The house was small. It consisted of a kitchen and a bedroom/ living room combination separated by a curtain hanging on the door. It had dirt floors, a small gas stove, and one light bulb that dangled from the kitchen ceiling, giving just enough light for us to see.

We had gone from being poor to being really poor. Dad wasn't making much money, thus making it difficult to afford anything better. Mom, who was seven months pregnant with Waldo, was becoming very concerned about our welfare. We found ourselves going backward, but somehow it didn't matter. At least it didn't matter to me. I didn't know any better. I thought everyone in Mexican Town lived the same way: poor. I was young and naïve. Besides, what could I do?

The Armpit

fter settling in as best we could, I wandered around, trying to get familiar with the new environment and hoping to see if there were any neighborhood kids. Most of the residents were older. I longed to find something to do with kids my age.

Strangely, the kids living there would come out to play only in the evenings. The heat kept them indoors. But it didn't take long to make their acquaintance. On warm summer evenings, they would come out, one at a time, until there were enough to play ball. Two doors down from us, on the same side of the street and in a better house, lived the Garza family. There were five boys and one girl, who was the youngest. They were always the first to come out. Juan, who was my age, was one of them. I'd never seen him at school. I don't know how I could have missed him, since he was tall for a Mexican kid. The friendliest of the bunch, he was easy to get along with. Soon he was inviting me to the Saturday baseball games.

These games weren't the kind one might think of. They were the kind poor kids play. One of the guys had a wooden bat but no ball. In the absence of a ball, we used rocks. The guys had it all figured out. To prevent someone from getting hurt with the rock, they used the small round ones. They put the rock inside a white tube sock and tied the end into a knot. When the rock was hit, it sailed across the field and hit the ground, with the understanding that no one should catch it in midair. It was thrown underhand in time to get the batter out. We played in the middle of the street right in front of our houses. Between us all, we had two gloves we shared, depending on what position we played. The catcher got a glove. The pitcher rotated the glove with the first baseman. We would play until dark or until we couldn't see the rocks coming our way.

It was an incredible activity that helped us gain excellent hand-eye coordination. If someone hit the sock rock straight at us, ducking was the way to not have to call an ambulance. If it was hit high in the air, getting out of the way showed agility and dexterity. We didn't want to be anywhere near the rock when it was coming down. I quickly learned to let the ball drop, then pick it up and throw it to first base. I caught on quickly.

The only part of the game I didn't particularly care for was when we were choosing teams. The two oldest boys would be the captains. Someone would toss the bat in the air. As it was coming down, one of the captains grabbed it. The other captain would place their hand on top of the one who caught it, and they'd take turns going up the bat handle until someone reached the top. That person would be the first to choose a player. I never wanted to be the last one chosen because everyone knew the last two or three chosen were the worst. No one said it, but they didn't have to.

When we got so engrossed in the game, we kept at it until nightfall. (There were no streetlights to keep the game going.) If one of us got hit with the rock ball, the captains immediately called time-out. If there was no blood, the game continued. If there was, we all ran home. But very few of us got hurt because our reflexes adjusted to the ball's speed. If the ball was coming in fast, we let it go by. If it wasn't, we caught it. That was rule number one. For those who didn't live by rule number one, having the sock on the rock lessened the pain.

Problem: Parents started complaining—complaining that too many socks were going missing. It wasn't unusual for some of us to show up with socks that didn't match. What fun!

The Garzas finally came up with a real baseball one day. But it didn't make catching the ball with our bare hands any less painful. That's when we started using socks again. We'd wear them on our hands. The thicker socks were the best. But it wasn't long before our parents took those away as well. As we lost players to accidents, we looked for other options to keep us entertained.

Hide-and-seek was one of my favorites. The neighborhood had old sheds behind some of the old, dilapidated adobe houses, as well as carports built from used lumber. These were used as storage places. They were also great places to hide in. The rules were set by the older kids.

"You can't hide in your house or in somebody else's house," one of the kids said, stating rule number one.

"What about the garage? Can I hide in the garage?" one of the youngest asked in a meek voice.

"No, you can't. You just told everybody where you're hiding, stupid."

"If you're found, you can't go somewhere else and hide again. You're out, and you get over here. Understand? The last one to be found wins the game, and they get to choose who will be it. Now get ready," the older boy explained.

Seven or eight of us played this game. The person chosen to be it was blindfolded and asked to spin around till the count of ten while the others ran and hid. The younger kids took a long time to find anyone, so they were seldom picked. Why one of the younger kids was told to be it one day was a mystery. As soon as the game started, I ran to one of the nearest sheds. I got in, shut the door, and hid behind some old boxes. It was dark, with very little light coming in from the cracks in the walls. It was hard to distinguish what was in there. I silently stood there. Suddenly, a small voice startled me.

"This is my place. You need to find another place."

It was the youngest Garza sibling. The girl. Her name was Sandra, and I thought she was the prettiest girl in the whole town. Even though she came from Hispanic parents who had dark hair, brown eyes, and brown skin, Sandra was blond and blue eyed. She was gorgeous.

So there I was, in the dark, in a shed, with the prettiest girl around. Well, she was the only girl I knew in the neighborhood other than my sisters. It was tight quarters. My heart was pounding, and I thought the sound would give us away. I could hear it in my ears. Being that close to her made me nervous.

"You have to go!" she demanded.

"It's too late. If I open the door, Danny could be there, and he'll find us both," I whispered back. I convinced her we could both hide. If I was seen first, I wouldn't tell Danny she was there.

"Well, be quiet then," she said, putting her finger to her lips.

There wasn't much free space in the shed. It was packed with junk. The little space we shared forced us to stand close to each other. I was close enough to smell her hair. Her blond hair was thick with dangling, uncombed curls at the ends. Although her hair was all over the place, covering most of her face, she still looked amazing.

"Who combs your hair? Your mother?" I asked in a hushed voice.

"Shut up. You're going to give us away."

That was the last thing I wanted. I just wanted to stay close to her in the dark. I leaned slightly closer as she peeked through the crack in the wall. I could smell her hair. I placed my nose right up to the back of her scalp, taking in the sweet fragrance of soap and sweat mixed together. Wanting to look at her face, I squeezed closer to her. *What if I kissed her?* I wondered.

We sat quietly for what seemed an eternity, then I started to feel nervous. *Why am I so nervous?* I thought. I'd never been this close to her. Was it proximity? Was I too close? And then it hit me. It took a second for me to realize that if one of her older brothers caught me in there with her and was thinking what I was thinking, I could get expelled from the group. If I was lucky, I might avoid a beating. I could just hear one of them saying, "What were you doing in there with her?" That made me nervous.

The door popped open. Little ol' Danny poked his head inside, squinted, and let his eyes adjust to the darkness. He took one look, and just when he got ready to close the door, she shoved me with no warning. I came crashing into little ol' Danny and smashed him in the face with my elbow.

He made me. I was the first one out.

What nervous fun!

Errand Boy

Whenever Mom needed something, I was the first to be sent to the neighborhood store. Although Doña Lucia's store was only a few blocks away, Mom could trust I wouldn't get lost.

One warm summer day, she handed me a dime and a small piece of folded paper with something written on it.

"Give this to Doña Lucia, and you can buy a candy with what's left," she said.

This wasn't the first time she'd sent me to the store with a piece of paper. She'd do this at least once a month. But I didn't know why she'd sometimes hand me a piece of paper when most of the time, she just told me what to get. I never questioned what was on the paper. Paper was a luxury and hard to come by, so she'd tear a piece off the end of a brown paper bag, write on it, fold it, then hand it to me.

I'd run and deliver the note. I'd hand Doña Lucia the dime, get a couple of pennies in change, and spend them buying hard candy. Then she'd give me something securely wrapped in a paper bag. Content with life, I'd walk home slowly, chewing on my treat. Curiosity never tempted me to look inside the bag.

This warm summer day was like any other day. I got a dime and a folded piece of paper with instructions, and off I went.

I couldn't say I was getting to be a proficient reader in third grade, but I knew how to pronounce letters even if I didn't know what they meant. My curiosity got the better of me on that day. *What's on that note?* I wondered. *Why is it always folded? Why am I asked to hand it to Doña Lucia? Why can't I just read it to her?* These were thoughts crammed into my head as I walked lazily to the store.

The desire to read the note was compelling. I had to know. The secrecy of what was written tempted me to no end. I was walking along the side of the dirt road, thinking that perhaps the note contained something special. I couldn't stop thinking about it. My mind wandered, and I finally succumbed. I had to know. I mustered enough courage to open the little piece of paper.

Nervously, I looked, and, to my astonishment, it only had one word! What was so secretive about this word? Why couldn't I just say it to Doña Lucia? I could read, couldn't I? I convinced myself that with all the English knowledge I possessed at my age, I should be able to read this word to her. I decided I would surprise Doña Lucia with my reading ability.

So, instead of handing the paper to her, I thought it would be great if I just told her what Mom wanted. On my way to Doña Lucia's, I practiced reading the word.

"Kkk ... ooo ... tt ... eee ... xxx." I'd say it again and again until I had the two syllables down.

"Kotex," I mumbled. I kept saying it in my head. "Kotex, Kotex, Kotex." Proud of myself for being able to read it, I walked in the store.

Doña Lucia came out from behind the curtain and looked at me. That stern, disapproving look on the old woman's face was enough to scare anyone.

I handed her the dime.

"Doña Lucia, Mom wants Kotex!" I blurted out, giving her my best smile.

I felt it before I saw it. Doña Lucia reached over the counter, smacked me on the side of the head, and proceeded to sneer at me with her old-woman look.

"Don't you ever open a note from your mother!" she yelled angrily. "Now, give me the paper!"

"Why did you do that?" I asked her. "I just told you what she wants. Why did you hit me?"

"*Chamaco pendejo. Esa nota es para mi. Es personal. Entiendes?*" ("Stupid kid, this note is for me. It's personal. Understand?") She lifted her hand as if to smack me again.

I reared back, not understanding why she'd hit me. I walked home stunned. I so desperately had tried to understand what was so secretive about the word *Kotex*. What was it? Why couldn't I say it? I didn't understand.

I didn't tell Mom what happened. When I got home, I just handed her the box carefully wrapped inside a brown paper bag. There wasn't any candy for me on that day. The mean old lady kept my two pennies.

On South Gillis Street, two houses down from where we lived, a woman in her late twenties would stand inside her screen door and smoke a cigarette. This was most mornings. I would see her but couldn't really make out her face. She lived alone. One morning, as I was walking past her house, she called me over.

"Are you going to the store?" she asked.

"*Sí. Voy a la tienda.*" ("Yes. I'm going to the store.")

"Will you do me a favor and pick up some cigarettes for me?" she asked, opening the screen door just enough for me to see her face for the first time. "I also need some other things," she said. "I'll write them down for you. Can you do that?"

"Sure."

"I'll pay you," she said, letting me in her front door.

I was excited about her paying me. My eyes lit up at the notion of having some money in my pocket. I stood just a step inside and noticed a tidy but small house. My eyes gravitated to what she was wearing—a thin white nightgown that flowed to just above her ankles. I tried to avert my eyes, slightly embarrassed at what I was seeing. I'd never seen this type of clothing before on a female. I could smell a sweetness about her. A perfume. I instantly liked her. She turned around and handed me a piece of paper, the cigarette wrapper, and some money.

"I'll be right back," I said. Then I turned and ran to the store.

Her name was Sandra, she told me. I found this older woman very attractive. There weren't many like her on that side of town. She was slim, of average height, and had big eyelashes that made her brown eyes smile without having to work at it. She gave me a look of polite kindness mixed with sadness—something I'd not experienced before from the opposite sex. She had curly brown hair that didn't need combing, as it fell smoothly down the sides of her face. She was the picture of beauty, and I felt lucky to be her errand boy.

When I came back with her groceries, she opened the door and asked me to come in. She had changed clothes. A pretty white cotton dress with light-colored flowers fell loosely over her shoulders. She looked younger without the cigarette dangling from her lips.

"Thank you. You can put those things on the table," she said.

I gave her the change. She picked out a dime and a nickel. It was more money than I'd seen in a long time. All mine!

I ran errands for her at least once a week. I never saw her outside her house. There was a car parked on the side, but it never moved. *How strange*, I'd tell myself. When I did run errands, I'd get no less than fifteen cents.

Coming home from school with the rest of the kids one day, I saw that her front door was open. She never had her door open. I went to her house and knocked.

No answer.

I knocked harder and waited. Something was not right. A peculiar feeling swept over me. *Is she hurt?* I wondered. *Is she home but not answering? Why is the door open?* I knocked again, harder.

She pulled the door all the way open, but not the screen door. I could tell she'd been crying. She wasn't acting her normal, pleasant self. A heavy sadness was clearly visible on her face. The little makeup she used was not in the right places. A housecoat, house shoes, and pajamas made her look old. I'd never seen her like this before.

She told me she didn't need anything, asked me to wait, then turned and went inside. She returned, gave me a dime, and said, "Thank you."

I never found out why she was so sad. Word in the street said she'd lost her husband, who was off to war. In 1960, the only war we had going on was the Cold War, where very little actual fighting happened. I didn't question it.

Other strange things happened that year. Sandra losing her husband was bad enough. Then, not long afterward, she disappeared. She moved away without letting me know. It didn't make sense. I'd lost my only source of income. I had to find out where she'd gone. People didn't move very far from the barrio. I asked around. I listened instead of talking, gathering information from old people who would sit around the kitchen table and swap stories about other people living in the neighborhood. It wasn't long before Sherlock Robert found out where she had moved.

St. Joseph's Cemetery, where they buried all the Hispanics, was near a cousin's house. A few weeks later, as I was walking down El Paso Street, which was across from the cemetery, I saw the place people said she had moved to. I walked up to the door and knocked, not knowing if she would be there or whether she even lived there. I waited for what seemed an eternity. No answer.

I knocked again, this time feeling like an intruder. I was just a kid interested in either the money she would give me for running errands or just seeing her again. What was going through my mind that day was uncertainty.

I could tell someone was there because of voices coming from inside. The door opened. Shocked to see a man open the door, I took a step back.

"What do you want?" came the booming voice.

"Does Sandra live here?"

"Yes, but she is not here right now."

I could tell he was lying. "Would you tell her Robert came by?" I asked.

"Yes, sure." He closed the door.

Then I forgot about Sandra. For weeks, I wondered instead who the man was. One day, I was standing next to my mother when a neighbor asked her, "Have you heard?"

"Heard what?" she replied.

"Sandra's boyfriend killed her, and then he committed suicide."

I froze. *Sandra? My Sandra? Killed? What is suicide? Her boyfriend committed suicide?*

Her boyfriend, a Vietnam vet, had lost it. I never saw her again. My only money source was gone. Forever.

Responsibilities?

By the end of the summer, I was tired of being home and taking care of the younger kids. There were too many of them, and they were always needing something. Wanting something. Asking for something.

"I want to play outside!" said Jesse.

"I'm hungry," demanded Imelda.

"Someone needs to pick up Waldo. I think he needs changing. Robert, Waldo needs changing!" hollered Nancy.

"Why am I always having to change that shitting kid? You do it," I protested.

How I got this responsibility, I still can't figure out. I was doing just fine, staying away from the house whenever I could. I wouldn't venture too far, just far enough so as not to be assigned any more jobs. We all had chores to do. According to Chuy, chores came with living in the house. Mom had found a job, and she left Nancy, who was eight, in charge.

Fine by me.

On some winter days, the wind blew the coldest through the desert plateaus, gaining strength as it swooped down on Mexican Town. When that happened, the temperature dropped below freezing. Our little house kept us warm during the day, but at night, we wrapped ourselves up in blankets. Nora and Waldo were still in diapers—the white cloth types. The two oldest were responsible for changing their diapers when Mother was gone. That would have been Nancy and me. Mostly me.

When Nancy was making tortillas, changing diapers fell on me. I would take their tiny legs and hold them up with one hand while I swiped their ass with a warm washcloth. I'd take Vaseline, grab it with three fingers, and plaster their ass with it. I'd bring the diaper around their belly and up from their crotch, then pin it together. Mom insisted we use Vaseline to prevent the babies from getting a rash. When they took a crap in the diaper, I would take the diaper and stick it in a bucket full of water that sat right outside the front door. After soaking them for some time, I would dip the diapers in and out of the bucket until the crap was off. Then I'd place them in another bucket of water with Clorox. After half an hour or so, I'd take them out, rinse them, wash them in detergent by hand, rinse them again, wring them out, and hang them on a string across the kitchen to dry. It was a long, exhausting process.

On a particularly cold day, one of the little kids pooped, and we had no diapers. I went outside, took a stick, broke the ice encasing the diapers, and stuck my hand in to pull one out. I went inside with baby shit frozen and stuck to the diaper. Every time I did this, I would gag. This stuff was nasty, and I didn't like it.

I stuck the diapers in warm water, hoping to get them warm enough so I could wash them in a tub of hot water. I'd take a large pot, warm up some water, pour it in a tub, scrub the soiled parts off, then proceed to rinse them with cold water. I hung them up to dry next to the stove while the baby sat naked and pissing all over the bed. I took one of the few towels we had and managed to pin it around the squiggly butt until the diapers were ready.

When Mother came home that evening, I told her about a radio announcement. A company called Pampers had invented disposable diapers, and I insisted she should try them. For the next year, my job was to shake the shit from the diapers, place them in a bucket, wash them, dry them, then fold them for the next time the babies crapped! No Alfaro child ever wore Pampers.

We weren't paid an allowance, a word I never heard until I turned twelve. One time, I made the mistake of asking for one.

"Mom, can I get paid for taking care of the kids?" I had lost my errand job when Sandra moved away and got herself killed. I wanted to have some money for candy.

"You are getting paid," my mom said. "You live here, don't you? You eat here. That is your reward."

I didn't buy it. In our house, performing these chores was an expectation. We were rewarded by not being swatted in the ass with whatever Mom or Dad had in their hands. There were no options. The oldest had chores, period.

Nancy was learning how to make tortillas, and, because she was so good at it, this became her job. She did it every day after she got home from school until she was old enough to move out of the house. She made the best tortillas ever!

Wanda's job was sweeping the floors clean enough to avoid an infestation of ants or mice.

Jesse was too young to have a job, but it was his responsibility to make sure the bed was made.

Imelda washed dishes. The few we had.

I made coffee, made sure everyone got ready for school, ran errands, threw out the trash, and did anything else as assigned. We became so adept at making sure the house was clean that, to this day, the oldest siblings, including me, dislike a dirty, disorganized home. It was beaten into us by our dad. If things weren't in order, Chuy would start yelling, cussing, and threatening to throw us out.

"Estamos pobres, pero no somos cochinos" ("We might be poor, but we are not dirty") was his favorite saying. The older he got, the more demanding he became. The older we got, the more work assignments were placed on us. It was part of living in his house.

First Party

We never invited kids to come to our house. It just wasn't something we did. It was either out of embarrassment or because we didn't know any better. Growing up, we went to other people's houses, like our grandmother's or our great-grandfather's. There were times when we were invited to some of our relatives' houses. But they were never invited to ours. Except for Sandra's place, I'd never entered a house unless it was a relative's. I don't know why. We just didn't do it.

Until I was invited to a birthday party.

Roy Urrutia and I were the same age and in the same third-grade class. We didn't hang out together, nor did we play together. We seldom spoke to each other. He had his friends, I had mine. He was better off than me economically. You could tell by the clothes he wore. He came from a family that owned a business in town. They didn't live in an adobe house with dirt floors. His house was a block down the street from Joe's Place. It was nicer than most of the houses around there.

For the most part, I hung out with my buddies from the armpit neighborhood while he hung out with those living closer to downtown. Everyone knew that anyone who lived closer to downtown was better off financially. Those who did have money were second- or third-generation Mexican. They'd assimilated to American ways. They had businesses or steady jobs. Some had special training, like those who owned hair salons or barbershops. They weren't filthy rich, but they weren't starving either.

I got an invitation to attend his birthday party, but I hadn't been expecting one. The Monday before his party, he came to school and asked the teacher if he could pass out invitations. At the end of the day, the kids around him got one. I was sitting at my desk, waiting for the bell to ring.

"Here, this is for you. You can come if you want," he said, as if I was an afterthought.

I tried to hold on to my self-worth by not appearing too happy. At that moment, I realized the invitation spoke volumes about who I was. I was somebody. I had been recognized by someone better off than me. I felt privileged.

I really wanted to go to this party, no matter what. I'd never been to a classmate's party. I didn't even know there was such a thing. I was surprised he had thought of me. I later found out his mother had told him to invite the whole class.

"I got an invitation to a birthday party!" I told Mom on Wednesday before the party. "I want to go to Roy's party. Everybody is going from my class," I pleaded with her.

"We'll see," was all she said.

I crossed my fingers behind my back for good luck.

The party started at noon on a Saturday. And it promised to be fun. I brought it up with Mom again on Saturday morning. With Dad gone, I had a chance. He would never let me go. He'd complain about us having no business being with folks from downtown. "*Esos sun a va vitches* think they run the town," he'd say, scorning them but never pinpointing who the sons of bitches were.

"You need a present, and we have no money for a present," Mom responded, not looking up from the pot she was stirring.

"I don't have to take a present," I objected.

"You just don't show up to a birthday party without a present."

"I'll make something for him!"

"No, you won't. You are not going!" was her last comment before she walked away.

I wanted to cry. I sat down and put on the saddest face I could muster.

Mom was a sentimental woman. A kind, good-hearted woman who cared very much about how her children felt emotionally. She knew how much this meant to me. She was the nurturer, and she cried when we cried. She laughed when we laughed. She was sad when we were sad.

I wasn't going to cry, but I knew that if I did, I might be able to change her mind. I moped around, making sure she saw the make-believe sadness on my face. I tried to portray a look of pity, hanging my head down and shuffling my feet whenever I came close to her. I even practiced in the mirror when she wasn't looking. I knew that if I just looked sad and dejected, Mom would come around. She always did.

It wasn't long before she caved.

"Here's a dime. Go to Ben Franklin's, and see what you can find," she said, smiling.

I ran to the department store—the same one that had thrown me out a few years back for trying to steal BBs. I prayed the man who kicked me out wasn't there. I could still hear him yelling at me to never come back to his store. I wanted him gone. Dead, gone, or fired.

I placed my face up against the window, looking for the man. When I was sure he wasn't there, I walked inside, looking for something that wouldn't cost too much. I only had a dime. I saw things I knew he would like, but they were too expensive. There were things that cost a quarter, fifty cents, or even a dollar!

Then I found a water gun. It was a nickel! I could afford this. I could afford two! Each gun was in a clear plastic wrapper. I picked a blue one and an orange one, took them to the counter, and paid. Then I ran home. I thought about keeping one and only giving him the orange one. He would never know.

"I don't think you can go," Mom said when I got back.

"Why?" I asked, wondering why she had changed her mind. *Dad got wind of this,* I thought.

"I don't have wrapping paper. I don't have ribbon."

"We don't have to wrap it!" I calmly said to her.

"You cannot show up to a party without a wrapped present. Don't you understand?

"Look! It's already wrapped," I cried as I held up the guns in their packaging.

She looked around and found a brown paper bag used for hiding the Kotex boxes. She pulled scissors out of a drawer, cut the paper, and wrapped the toys. No box. She just covered them.

"This is going to have to do," she said. "Get me Nancy's head ribbon. We are going to have to make this work." She wrapped the package nicely, tying the ribbon around the brown bag. "There," she said. "Good luck! Oh, and by the way, don't forget to bring back your sister's ribbon!"

I ran to Roy's house. When I knocked, I was invited in.

"You can put your present there, with the rest of them," some woman said as I entered the house.

"Bueno. Thanks," I replied. While no one was looking, I took the present out of my pocket and placed it between the other presents, hoping no one would find it. It was embarrassing. There were so many presents so beautifully wrapped in colorful paper, with pretty ribbons and bright bows.

I felt out of place. I knew I didn't belong there, but I stayed. I walked in and just marveled at the furniture, the roominess, the curtains, and the beautiful floors. Walking through the house to get to the backyard, I also noticed some of the moms placing food and drinks into coolers. *Where did all this come from?* I wondered. I'd never seen so much food. Well, except in the school cafeteria. Never in a house.

The place was packed with kids running or chasing each other in the backyard. Some I'd not seen before. They were all dressed in their Sunday best—nice pants, new shoes, button-down shirts with sleeveless sweaters, even though it was warm. The girls had shorts with tops matching their socks. They wore summer dresses with ribbons in their hair. Everyone looked great!

I had on a clean shirt, clean pants, and a pair of tennis shoes that weren't too worn out. Although I was conscious of my appearance, I didn't let it bother me. I stood back, hoping to recognize some of the guys I hung out with at school. I figured they probably couldn't make it. I did see Roy, who was the center of attention. I walked slowly over to him.

"Hey, Roy. I'm here," I said.

"Yeah, good," he replied as he ran off to chase one of the girls.

Everyone was excited because word had it that we were going on a ride in a big truck. Finally, a dump truck pulled up to the house and honked, sending all the kids into a wild frenzy. I scampered outside with the rest of them, looking up at the gigantic truck. It was huge! Bigger than a mountain, I thought. The wheels were bigger than anything I'd ever seen before.

Twenty-five kids all loaded into the back of the dump truck! I never questioned where we were going. I didn't care. I was having fun. Someone overheard the adults talking about going to the roadside park, a few miles east of town. How exciting! While the truck rambled down the highway, we cheered, sang, pushed, and shoved each other. Those who were bold enough stood up, letting the wind hit them in the face. On a dare, one of the girls stood up, looked over the rim without holding on to anything, and was blown halfway across the bed of the truck. We all started laughing. I stood up, grabbed the rim, then opened my mouth, letting the air puff out my cheeks. I loved the sensation. Funny how simple things give such joy. I was having the time of my life!

We arrived at the park several minutes later, along with some of the parents, who'd driven their cars, loaded down with gifts and food. We all gathered in an area I would never have called a park. Three beat-up picnic tables sitting under a tin roof made it hotter than being in the direct sun. The only area that had grass became our playground, which we used for a game of tag. The girls stayed with the ladies near the gifts and the food. There were no swings, no monkey bars, and no kind of playground equipment. I wanted to participate in the game of tag but wandered shyly around, hoping to be included. These were not my friends, so it made it difficult to engage with them.

I spotted a small kid sitting by a withering tree who looked like he probably felt the same way. I moseyed over and sat next to him. He wasn't having much fun. Neither was I. His name was Thomas, and he and I sat there while the others played. We didn't say a word to each other.

When the kids were done playing, Roy stood next to the cake, and we gathered around to sing "Happy Birthday." He blew out the candles, and we ate. Then it was time to open the presents.

With the biggest smile, Roy worked his way to the middle of the crowd of kids. His mother picked out present after present, announcing who it was from. Unwrapped gifts revealed button-down shirts, sweaters of every color, a pair of tennis shoes, caps, more sweaters. These presents looked expensive. I prayed he wouldn't open mine. How embarrassing to know it was all I could afford. As the pile of presents neared the end, mine sat there among the scattered wrapping paper.

Roy's mother picked up mine, the smallest present of all, and said, "This present is from ..." She looked for a tag that might identify who it was from. Then she handed it to Roy and asked, "Who brought this one?" She looked at the children, who also looked around for the giver.

Embarrassed, I hesitated to identify myself. That moment lingered longer than expected. I felt bad and did not want anyone to know that the smallest present came from the poorest kid there. But reluctantly, I raised my hand.

"Oh," Roy's mother proclaimed. "It's from ... What's your name?"

I just smiled and said nothing.

Roy tore into the brown paper wrapping and pulled out the water pistols. His eyes lit up! He stood up. Smiling, he yelled, "Water guns! I love 'em! Let's play!" Then he ran toward the only water faucet in the park. He handed one to Joe, his best friend, and they went around chasing and squirting kids with warm water.

My present contained the only toys he got! I couldn't believe that a pair of water guns costing ten cents outweighed all the fancy clothing he got that day. *What were these people thinking?* I wondered. *This is a kid. Why not buy toys instead of adult things?* I couldn't understand the reasoning. I would think toys would have made more sense. Oh well.

The rest of the afternoon passed by too slowly for my comfort. I wasn't having much fun at all. This would be the last birthday party I would ever attend with this group of kids. I just didn't belong. When it was time to leave, I was ready to go home.

"How was it?" Mom asked me when I got there.

"It was fun. We went to the roadside park. We played chase."

"Did you eat?

"Yes. We had sandwiches made of something called ham."

"Did you like it?"

"It was okay. I would have rather had bologna."

"By the way, did you remember to bring back Nancy's hair ribbon?"

I gracefully reached into my pocket and pulled out a yellow ribbon, a blue one, and, finally, a red one.

"Here, she can have all three," I said. "They were going to throw them away, so I took them."

Fourth Grade

The hot desert summer days were ending. I could feel it in the air. Leaves on what few trees adorned the barrio were turning brown, losing their luster and vibrancy. Back-to-school announcements on the radio advertised specials on paper, crayons, pencils, tablets, and such.

Meanwhile, I had to mentally get ready for another school year. It was time to face the truth about my education. If I didn't work harder at school, what were my chances of success? Would I be a dropout? Would I not be a successful student? This would be my last year at Butz Elementary, but only if I didn't fail. The idea of being a failure in school was beginning to weigh heavily on me. I could only imagine how it would affect Mom, who had high hopes for me.

Being in the oldest group of kids at Butz was exciting. By this time, I knew the routine: go to school, learn as much as I could, pay attention to the teachers, stay out of trouble, get along with others, and pray a good spanking was not in the cards. My English was better even though my reading still sucked. The lack of English books at home contributed to my dilemma. I'd never been to the public library. I didn't know we had one.

"I'll do better this year," I told myself. I believed it, too, even though it wasn't convincing. In July of 1961, I turned ten. On May 5 of that year, millions of Americans watched in amazement as Alan Shepard, a young navy pilot, flew the Freedom 7 space rocket from Cape Canaveral, Florida, making him the second person and the first American to fly into space. President Kennedy asked Congress for $531 million to put a man on the moon before the end of the decade. The space race against the Soviet Union was well on its way. Other events unfolded in Europe, making many Americans nervous. Many were building bomb shelters in case of a nuclear war with the Soviets. That same year, Germany was being split into East Germany and West Germany by the Berlin Wall. Tensions were reaching critical stages between the Soviets and the rest of the Western world.

But these events were far removed from our lives in the barrio. Our world revolved around survival. The price for surviving for many still living in the hood was getting harder to meet. The average cost of a brand-new house was an overwhelming $12,500, when the average income per year was only $5,315. The adobe house we were living in probably didn't cost over $300 to build. If my parents brought in $2,500 dollars a year for a family of nine, we were way below the poverty level. The average cost of a new car was $2,850! Where in the world were we going to get that kind of money? We couldn't even pay for a full tank of gas in the used truck when it cost twenty-seven cents a gallon. Highway robbery! It cost sixty-seven cents for a pound of bacon and thirty cents for a dozen eggs. Way out of our league. Bologna was cheaper.

When school started, I was ready to learn to read better. As I gained confidence in my English abilities and always tried hard to speak it when opportunities presented themselves, I was well on my way.

On the first day of school, Mom made me promise I would do the best I could. Personally, I was ready for whatever the new school year might bring. I was fortunate to be in the fourth grade. I was not going to repeat the mistakes I'd made the previous year. I was ready!

The days at school were the same. But what made this year special was my discovery of music. The music teacher, who was vibrant with too much energy, made music enjoyable. I came to like her style. She was a young Hispanic woman who could play the piano really well. Expanding our knowledge of culturally different music, she had us singing, dancing, and playing simple instruments with gusto. I don't remember her name, but I do remember she always wore a dress layered with a colorful sarong tied around her waist, complemented by western-style blouses. She wore beads around her neck that shimmered in the light. Her black shoes made a *clack, clack, clack* sound when she walked. She was always singing or humming some song and moving her fingers as if she were playing air piano. She was a performer who dreamed of directing a musical on Broadway.

She got her wish that year. If she couldn't direct a play in New York, subjecting her fourth graders to a school play would be good enough. Each year, the grade levels put together a play of some sort for parents. First graders put on book plays, marching around the gym with costumes from children's books, while the second graders kept their traditional Thanksgiving Day celebration. They dressed up as pilgrims, Indians, and cornstalks. I played a cornstalk once. Not the most fun. The third grade did a Christmas performance, and the fourth grade did a variety musical. This year, the music teacher decided we would do a western play depicting Texas history. On a Monday, she introduced the class to a play script she apparently wrote.

"I want you to take these pages and read them. This is a play where everyone can participate. We are going to have fun, and on Parent Night, we will show off your talents. I want volunteers for each of the characters."

Kids were all vying for the best parts. There was to be a girl lead and a boy lead. They would be the main attraction. The most popular kids who could speak English with very little accents raised their hands. The teacher went around the room, filling the character slots one by one.

I remained in the background, hoping to be picked for some static part, like a telephone pole or a tree. They didn't have to say anything. Being in the fourth grade called for a longer play with longer lines that had to be memorized. I was not very good at memorizing the times tables, much less the lines in a play.

When the teacher reached the last of her characters, she picked the rest of the leftovers to be dancers. I was a dancer. I did not have to memorize lines, but I did have to memorize dance steps. *That should be easy*, I thought.

Our teacher had written square dancing into the play. Four boys would be paired with four girls. Four dancing groups on stage would swing back and forth, switching partners as the music played on. She showed us how to move our feet and skip at times for effect. I didn't have any trouble with that. I could skip and chew gum at the same time. I loved square dancing.

Loella, the cutest girl in our class, was also a dancer. I wanted her to be my partner, so I stood next to her, hoping the teacher would place us together. If we were paired together, we got to hold hands. I thought that would be nice.

Standing next to her, I pulled all the courage I could muster and said, "We're going to be the best dancers on stage." I got no reaction, but she didn't run away. Good sign. I stood quietly.

Our teacher came up on stage, making changes to the pairing. "Robert, you come over here. Sandy, move over there. Joe, you go here. There, it's perfect."

Instead of Loella, she fixed me up with Manuela.

Oh no, not Manuela! I thought. I was taken by complete surprise, my ego shattered. Nobody wanted to dance with Manuela. Why did the teacher change me? Manuela was a pretty girl whose two separated front teeth gave her a goofy, stupid smile. She was tall for her age and towered over everybody. I think her height had something to do with her neck. She had the most god-awful long neck. We called her "Horse" behind her back. I didn't want to dance with Horse!

The music started, and we skipped along with it, back and forth, side to side, round and round.

We did this back and forth, holding hands with different partners and sashaying around the stage over and over again. After going back and forth a few times, we all started sweating. It was hot in that gymnasium. Each time I came back around to Manuela, we locked arms as I swung her around.

I first saw the sweat forming on her upper lip, then it started to build up on her forehead. Her long neck showed signs of a hurricane-force rain running down her blouse. She was sweating profusely. About halfway through the song, she came back to me, and we held each other as we danced. It was then that I smelled a recognizable odor on her. It didn't take me long to figure out what it was. She smelled like bologna! It was stifling! I wanted to gag. I was quickly reminded of the time my uncles and I ate half a roll of bologna we had stolen from the Gandy's truck! It was unbearable. I couldn't breathe!

When the music stopped, I walked over to our teacher and said, "Miss, I don't think I can dance. Can't I be a cornstalk or something?"

Sounding irritated, she replied, "No, Robert. You are dancing with Manuela. Now, get back in line."

I went home in frustration and confessed to Mother how I was feeling about dancing with a girl who smelled of bologna. Then I said, "There is a play next week, and I am going to need black pants and a white shirt, Mom."

"Where do you think we are going to get black pants and a white shirt? We are not made out of money, you know," she replied.

"I don't have a choice. My teacher told me I had to be in the dance part of the play."

"Well, you tell your teacher that we don't have the money to buy you those things."

"Mom, I can't tell her that. I don't want to dance, but she is making me. Besides, I'm dancing with Manuela, and she stinks of bologna!"

"Don't be mean and don't cry," she said. "We'll make it work."

By Friday of the following week, I had black pants and a white shirt. How Mom managed that, I'll never know. That money could have been used to buy us food. I was thankful but regretted taking away from the family. The pants and shirt were not brand new. Maybe she borrowed them from someone. Either way, I didn't have an excuse for not being in the play.

The teacher provided everyone with a straw hat and a red bandana. As the curtains opened on Parent Night, the music started, and we proudly stood, all nice and clean, in front of a full audience. Then we pulled apart, leaving the main characters up front talking about Texas and how we came to be.

The play wasn't long, and it kept the audience's attention. I'm sure there were parents like my own who didn't understand everything that was being said. But the play was a success. Everyone clapped after the show. We all came out on stage and bowed as the curtains slowly closed.

To this day, I hate square dancing. It took me a while to get over Manuela's smell. However, being on stage in front of an audience was enlightening for me.

Poorest to Poor

S ettling into the old adobe house took some getting used to. In September, Waldo, the last Alfaro kid, was born—a fat and happy baby. When Mother brought him home, I asked, "What are you going to name him?"

"His name is Waldo," she said.

I had never heard the name Waldo. Why he was given that name baffled me. I stared at the pink-faced baby, thinking no Mexican should be named Waldo. *Kids are going to make fun of him*, I thought. *Who names their kid Waldo?*

I didn't ask Mom where the name came from. I simply turned and walked away, scratching my head in total confusion. I thought maybe she was running out of English names.

There were seven Alfaro kids now. The good news was that Mom wasn't having any more. The bad news was we were still poor, and one more mouth to feed was painful.

Mom was determined to work full-time. She could not rely on Chuy. She didn't ask for permission. She just went looking for a job, and she found one at a restaurant—a diner—with an Old West-style décor. Railsback Restaurant, on Dickenson Boulevard, would employ her for at least three years. A counter with fixed stools set four or five feet apart added to the look.

Against the windows facing the boulevard were red vinyl booths. It wasn't a big place, but it was popular with the citizenry.

Dickenson Boulevard, the main road running east and west, accommodated traffic leading into and out of town. From San Antonio to El Paso along Interstate 10 is about 551 miles. Fort Stockton is located smack in the middle of this route, making it a natural stopping point for weary travelers. In the 1950s, there weren't any restaurants along the interstate, so people had to veer off into town to get gas or something to eat. There were plenty of hotels or motels if they chose to stay the night, but few places to eat. So, Railsback attracted hungry travelers. It catered to the locals, but many travelers stopped by for some great grub, including their famous corn biscuits.

It could have been that with seven children under the age of ten and a husband who regularly drank a good portion of his salary, Mom had no choice but to work. That left me, the oldest, to take on more responsibilities around the house. We all did our chores without too many complaints. In a way, we understood Mom had to work if we were going to get out of being the poorest family in town. We certainly needed the extra cash.

"We are not going to live in a poor house any longer. You deserve better," she would say each night before she went to work.

Respecting her decision was all we could do. We were getting older and demanding more things she knew we couldn't afford—like black pants and a white shirt for a play. I grew to admire her courage and determination.

For a few months, we continued to struggle. Chuy found a better job—still unskilled labor, but at least it was steady. Now both our parents were working. Mom worked the late shift at the restaurant, and since we didn't have a car, she walked almost three miles to get there. She could not count on Dad to get her there. So she walked. At night. By herself. She might have complained, but I didn't hear it. Dad sometimes walked Mom to work, then met her halfway when her shift ended around eleven at night.

There were times she'd bring home a bag of leftover biscuits and cornbread. After a day or two, the biscuits and cornbread would get hard as a rock. Instead of throwing them away, the restaurant would let her take them home. On some mornings, we'd get up to the smell of fresh coffee. Exhausted from the late-night work, she'd get up and make coffee for us all. We all drank coffee in the morning. We found that dipping both the biscuits and the cornbread in coffee lessened the hardness and allowed us to eat without chipping a tooth. It was a much better breakfast than atole, the pasty stuff she used to feed us. This would be our breakfast before leaving for school. I loved the cornbread. It was much better than the biscuits. Corn bread, biscuits and coffee became a staple, and we didn't complain.

Our parents weren't deeply religious. But they did practice some of the rituals of the Catholic Church. We respected the Bible and its teachings but didn't go to church on a regular basis until much later. However, giving us a good education in Christianity was important for both Mom and Dad. So, we four oldest were forced to make our first communion. Mom claimed this would keep us on the righteous path to God. Also, we were all baptized as babies, making us officially God's children. I was the only one who was confirmed through the church—something I would never wish on anyone. That experience traumatized me for years.

We were beginning to understand the importance of religion because we were dragged to church on Sundays. Our parents believed we needed to attend because we needed all the help we could get. For an hour, we sat, kneeled, stood, sat, sang, prayed, and gave thanks to God and Jesus Christ for all good things, which weren't that many. I was taught to ask the Lord for forgiveness if I did something wrong. Prayer was the key to getting closer to God, who protected us against evil.

What I didn't understand was why I had to pray right after I got disciplined. Evil to me was getting whipped with such ferocity that no prayer was going to stop the beating or the pain. Either way, if Jesus prayed, we had to pray. If it was good for him, it was good for us. But I didn't ask for forgiveness. I asked for food, a TV, a bike, new clothes, and a diamond ring. Perhaps I should have asked for a kinder dad.

Although the older kids learned to pray the Our Father and Hail Mary ever so diligently in both English and Spanish, the younger ones avoided such rituals. They weren't held to the same standards as the older children were. When we did go to church, not everybody went at the same time. There were too many kids to keep entertained for an hour of worship. By the time Nora and Waldo came along, my parents had given up on them making their first communion. Tiredness coupled with leniency prevailed. I suppose I could have prayed for the younger kids, but I was too busy taking care of my own skin. Mom and Chuy had other things to deal with, just like most parents from the barrio.

One evening in late fall, the air turned fresh and cool, bringing some relief from the hot summer days. I sat watching the last of the leaves fly off the few trees growing naturally in some yards. Mom asked me to run to the store. It was a pleasant evening. The night was exceptionally dark. It was difficult to see with no streetlights. The glow of a random porch light threw shadows into the darkness. At times, the moon's light illuminated the barrio's very existence. I didn't like going to the store by myself on scary, dark nights, and I told her so. But my whining didn't make a difference. Having no choice, I took the money from her hand and grabbed the door handle.

When I opened the solid wooden door that led onto the street, the kitchen bulb dangling from the ceiling cast a stream of light onto the street like a flashlight beam. A car whisked by at a fairly good clip, stirring up dust into a cloud that hovered over the middle of the street. It swirled around, hanging serenely for several seconds. The light from the house struck the dust, giving the illusion of an eerie apparition. The image of the Virgin Mary coming up from the dust appeared before me! She stood there like the pictures on religious candles, looking at me. Her hands were by her sides with palms facing up, as if she was saying, "I'm here."

I stood paralyzed. Instead of accepting her hand of guidance, I shook in terror. Stepping back inside, ever so slowly, I closed the door. Panting with my heart pounding in my chest, I turned around to face Mother.

"Mom, I just saw the Virgin Mary," I said, visibly shaken.

"You see, she wants you to go to the store. She will protect you," she told me nonchalantly.

"Mom, I don't think the dust is going to protect me!" I cried. "I can't go. I'm scared. You come with me."

She could see the fright in my eyes. After some thought, she said, "You don't have to go. I can get salt in the morning."

Sometime after, I was consumed by the image. It wouldn't go away. I could see her in my dreams and in the thoughts swirling in my head. *What if she was trying to tell me something? I* thought. *What if I offended her by not staying and listening to what she had to say? What was I scared of? Wasn't she supposed to protect me? Will she come again, wanting to say something to me?*

This image would not appear to me again, although I wanted it to. I'd open the door on dark nights and peer out, hoping to see her again. It never happened. Much later in life, I still recalled the image and would find myself wondering if my religious upbringing had anything to do with that night. I was convinced the Virgin Mary would look after me in life. I would come to rely on her often in times of crisis after crisis. *What if …* I'd ask myself.

Fall turned into winter. Desert winters can get extremely cold, especially when you don't have the appropriate clothing. Things were getting better now with both Mom and Dad working. Still struggling to make ends meet, we were always sure there would be plenty of tortillas, beans, and potatoes for everyone. Mom didn't have to water down the beans anymore. We stopped going to bed hungry. We were growing so fast that it was hard to keep up with clothes that fit. Like all other families in the hood, we passed clothes down to the younger kids. Since I was the oldest and there were two girls between me and Jesse, by the time he could fit into my hand-me-downs, they were out of style and quite worn.

Dad's favorite clothing store was Winkler's. It was as high end as you could find in that town, and the prices seemed exceedingly high. But Dad would insist that their clothes were high quality, which only the better-off could afford. I believed him.

Mr. Winkler was a Jew who, rumor had it, had been a prisoner of Nazi Germany during Hitler's reign. He had a series of numbers tattooed on his arm, proving it was so. After I heard about this, I always looked for evidence of the tattoo.

Edward Winkler was a tall man with large eyeglasses. He never wore a short-sleeve shirt. He was all business and never smiled. But he was eager to show off the latest fashion he proudly displayed. He was always impeccably dressed, with a suit and tie of the latest fashion, complemented by a pair of nice, shiny shoes. He ran a clean store, which attracted the ladies who were looking for fancy new fashions.

We went there only for special occasions, like when one of us was either making our first communion or being baptized.

Mom and Dad would buy from Winkler's if they were going to a quinceañera or a wedding. Edward Winkler knew most people from the hood couldn't afford to shop there. In order to attract these infrequent buyers, he would hold items for them on layaway, just like Gibson's did.

Dad bought me a coat at Winkler's once—a silver topcoat that was too big for me. I didn't like it, but he insisted on buying it, swearing that, "Only rich kids wear these coats. I think you should have it." It looked like an adult midget's coat hanging near the adult men's suit section, so I knew it was not a young kid's coat. I didn't like it, but he insisted. And because it was on sale, he was determined to convince me this was the best thing I would ever get. He told me to put it on and get in front of the mirror.

He said, "*Mira que bien te miras.*" ("Look how good you look.")

"*Es muy grande. Mira las mangas. No puedo ver mis manos.*" ("It's too big. Look at the sleeves. I can hardly see my hands!")

I looked at myself in the mirror, thinking, *I'm not wearing this to school. Why couldn't I just get a regular kid's coat?*

There was also Anthony's down the street, and it catered to regular poor people like us. Then there was Gibson's discount store. They had kids' coats with a layaway plan. I didn't pursue my disapproval. I was getting something new. What if it was an adult coat? Either wear a coat or freeze.

I wore the coat.

Spring came sooner than expected that year. Trees bloomed, flowers donned their petals, and the flies multiplied. There were always flies—flies everywhere. We went through fly swatters like we went through toilet paper. Complaining didn't help matters. Complaining only got us slapped upside the head. Flies were an indication that winter was over, and we would now be expected to be outside more often, meaning we could play outside with the neighborhood kids.

I loved spring! Anticipating our regular street baseball games, we gathered outside. Someone produced a real ball. There were more gloves to play with, but most of us still played without. Playing without shoes made the soles of our feet hard as rocks. No one wanted to ruin their only pair of school shoes.

One beautiful spring day, the kids were gathered in the street for one of our regular baseball games. I stood watching from a distance because I was supposed to take care of Waldo. But the game was too enticing, and I found it easy to ask Nancy to take care of the baby. I stuck him in a walker so he could jump around and entertain himself. This gadget allowed babies the freedom to roam around and helped them get used to walking. What I did not think about was the surface of the front yard. It was full of small rocks that could keep him from moving forward or backward. But I left him there with Nancy and walked over just in time to get selected for a team.

Not long into the first inning, Nancy came running out into the street, yelling that Waldo had fallen and was stuck to the tree, crying his little heart out.

I ran back to the house.

Yes, he was stuck! He had rocked the walker enough to where it fell forward into the tree. A small branch at perfect eye level protruded from the tree. It had caught him right on top of the left eyelid. There was blood everywhere! It was running down his face, into his diaper, and down his little legs. He had been stuck for at least a couple of minutes, and he just couldn't pull himself away. He was six months old. You'd think he'd know better!

I cried, "Oh shit! I'm getting it good this time." I yanked him off the tree branch, picked him up, and, while I was holding him, told Nancy, "Grab the hose and run some water over his face!"

But he wouldn't stop moving. He was crying as blood spilled onto my clothes. I couldn't see the injury because of the blood.

I placed an old diaper over his eye, praying it wasn't the eye. Once the blood stopped, I noticed the cut was not deep.

"Maybe if we put Scotch tape over it, no one will notice," I said to no one in particular.

Mom got home. Waldo was asleep, and I went about pretending nothing had happened.

"Waldo cut his eye," mumbled Imelda.

Stupid tattletale!

"Mom, Waldo cut his eye, and he had blood," she repeated in her little childlike voice. Mom jumped up, almost knocking the kitchen table over. She found Waldo asleep, with the pacifier in his mouth and the eye swollen shut.

"*¿Que pasó aquí?*" ("What happened here?") She had a stern look on her face as she examined the injury.

"He tipped the walker into the tree! I didn't see him," I pleaded.

"He was playing baseball and left him alone!" cried Nancy.

Another stupid kid who can't keep her mouth shut, I thought.

"You'd better get ready," Mom said. "When Chuy gets here, *te va poner una porrieada.*" ("He's going to give it to you."). She was yelling and pointing her finger at me. "You'd better pray he didn't bust his eyeball!"

I knew what that meant. I was getting my ass beat.

Barred from playing baseball for the rest of my young life, I braced myself. *It was all Waldo's fault*, I thought that night, when I was recuperating from the ass-whipping. Yet, I prayed that the swelling, once it went down, would reveal he wouldn't be a one-eyed Waldo.

He was never taken to the doctor. The accident didn't leave him blind in one eye like I thought it would. But it did leave a scar above his eyelid as a reminder to me: don't ever leave young kids alone.

A lesson never to be forgotten.

Benefits

Moving up the poor scale, my parents were able to afford some luxuries. Not much, but something new at least once a year.

To my surprise, Chuy walked in the house one day with a box containing a small electronic object. I stared as he opened it. I had heard about these things but had never seen one. It was a small black-and-white TV!

He plugged it in, turned it on, and it came alive! He moved the antenna, and, with a static sound coming out from behind the object, I saw moving pictures for the first time. Once he pulled the antenna out to its full length, the images became clearer. All nine of us stood back and stared at the thing. Dad moved the antennae back and forth, and voilà! A man appeared, calling himself Walter Cronkite and talking about the news! Mouths agape, brains confused, we sat quietly as the screen showed images of world events. It was a miracle! We were captivated by the technology.

That night, a dinner of watery beans, potatoes, and fresh tortillas was served to each kid. We took our plates and sat down in front of the TV. The first movie I remember watching was a western called *Rawhide*. It was amazing. We were so caught up with the movie, plus the commercials, that some of us didn't eat for fear of missing something on the tube.

This contraption would become our tie to the rest of the world. It was our entertainment when we were good, our punishment when we weren't. Losing the right to watch our favorite movies was worse than getting a beating or being stuck in a corner, on our knees and praying for forgiveness.

Chuy liked westerns and war movies with Gene Autry starring as the soldier war hero. He believed Gene Autry was a real soldier and considered him the best soldier America ever had. He said that if it weren't for him, we would not have won World War II.

I didn't put up much of an argument, believing what he said to be the gospel truth. Since action movies were about the only thing we watched, my little brain started thinking like the heroes. I could win at anything. Well, maybe not in schooling, but I could win if I was a soldier or a cowboy.

The Rifleman was a great movie, with *Gunsmoke* coming in a close second. *Gunsmoke*, starring William Conrad as Marshal Matt Dillon, was awesome. *Rawhide*, with Clint Eastwood as Rowdy, was even better. *Have Gun–Will Travel*, starring Richard Boone as Paladin, was another cowboy series. Paladin was a tough cowboy who was fast with the trigger. He sported a mustache that flipped on the ends and wore a black hat that never fell off his head. John Wayne was a great soldier and a cowboy who never lost. He always killed the bad guys. There were other movies on TV about shooting and killing bad guys.

Some TV shows portrayed an America where no poverty existed. There were also no quarreling parents, no anger, no language issues, and no major problems. *The Andy Griffith Show*, *The Danny Thomas Show*, *My Three Sons*, and *Lassie*, which was my favorite, depicted what the rest of America was supposed to be like. I believed this was how it was in real America—not the one in our hometown.

The Ed Sullivan Show was popular, and *Perry Mason* was excellent. I loved it. The problem I had with the shows at that time was the lack of Mexicans, Blacks, Asians, or any people of color as actors. *Is this what the rest of America looks like?* I wondered. Every member of the cast in each show was white. They spoke good English. They wore nice clothes. They drove nice cars. They had good, clean homes with all sorts of appliances. *Is this the real America?* I wondered.

On a Wednesday night, October 27, 1954, *The Wonderful World of Disney* debuted in color. I would not experience a color TV—something unheard of and unimaginable—until 1966, when *Batman* came out. We knew it would be televised in color. But not everyone had a color TV. They were rare in the barrio.

Armando, a kid I met in school, came by to play baseball with us one day in 1966. The topic of Batman and Robin came up. Armando had a color TV. With my arm around his shoulders, I said, "If you let me watch the show with you, we'll let you play ball with us any day."

He lived a few blocks north—closer to the railroad tracks but still in the barrio. He and his grandmother lived alone in an old adobe house with a porch facing the busy street. She welcomed us, happy that Armando had friends over. On the Sunday of the *Batman* premier, we sat in his living room, glued to the TV. It was a miracle! The show was amazing. We talked about it for days. We were mesmerized by the vibrant colors of the superhero costumes. Amazing.

Only three channels competed for viewers: NBC, CBS, and ABC. All three went off the air at midnight and did not start up again until seven in the morning. We were beginning to see America and the world through the eyes of reporters like Mr. Cronkite. We now had something to talk about other than what was happening in our own little isolated world. TV opened a whole new perspective of America for us. I was hooked forever.

Back at school, there wasn't much going on. I was getting better with my English but wasn't doing much better with spelling. As a matter of fact, I don't think I was doing better in math either. I did like history, but only if the teacher read to us. I stayed awake when I got to hear real stories about real people doing real things. I found it fascinating. Our teacher read to us so eloquently. That was something I hoped I'd master before I went to Heaven.

I don't know why reading was extremely difficult for me. And because it was, I didn't like to read. Our fourth-grade teacher would sit us all around in a circle. She called it round-robin reading. I'd keep my head down, hoping she wouldn't call on me. I'd tremble with embarrassment when she did. An overwhelming feeling of despair would consume me. It felt like I was having this horrible nightmare in which huge words were coming closer and closer, then swallowing me up before I could run away. It was a repeat of the third grade all over again.

The only consolation was when I followed Troy the stutterer. The other kids would get impatient with him and blurt out the words when he got stuck. If I read after him, even though I read slow, kids didn't mimic me as much. The teacher would usually ask for volunteers, and, of course, the girls were the first to raise their hands since they could read really well. I never raised my hand unless it was to go to the bathroom, and I did that often during reading time.

My fourth-grade teacher was overly patient with me. I don't remember her name, but I do know she was kind. I could tell she liked being a teacher. But with her patience and caring treatment of me, at times, I felt like her genuine efforts were wasted on me. Here I was, ten years old, and I was already a failure. That bothered me.

The Butz teachers decided that since the fourth graders would be leaving to attend another school as fifth graders, they wanted us to have a graduation ceremony. The announcement was made one evening during a PTA meeting, which my parents did not attend. But I did because someone from the family was expected to be there. Most parents didn't attend because they couldn't speak the language. Besides, since students were expected to attend, we could always go back and tell our parents what was said. The parents who were there were all excited about the idea of a graduation. I was, too, even though I wasn't too confident I would make it to graduation that year. Either way, it sounded exciting.

Growing up, we never called our parents "Mom" or "Dad." We always referred to them by their first names. It was much later that I began calling them "Mom" and "Dad." I'd heard other kids call their parents "Mom" or "Dad." One day, I tried it. I wanted to see what kind of reaction I'd get. At first, it felt weird. However, the more we used these terms, the better it got. I think Mom liked it much better than being referred to by her first name.

When I got home after the PTA meeting, I said, "Pino, the teachers said we are going to graduate to fifth grade, and you have to attend the graduation." I handed her the paper we were given.

She gave it back to me and said, "Read it to me. Can't you see I'm busy?" She would always say, "Read it to me." I didn't realize at the time that this was her way of having me practice my reading. She could read a little. She could speak Spanglish—Spanish and English mixed together.

"It says we will graduate in May, the last day of school. It says we have to wear black pants and a white shirt. It says you have to pay a dollar for the cap. It says it starts at seven p.m."

She hugged me and told me she was proud of me. I don't know if this graduation thing inspired her to bring up graduation every year after that. She would never let us forget what the end result was—graduation from high school for every kid. She never failed to remind us of the goal.

"From now on, that is the goal," she said. "You will all graduate! Understand?" She saw graduation from Butz as an opportunity to practice for the real thing when we reached high school. She was determined to see all seven kids graduate, and at every opportunity, she pounded this into us. Her trust in teachers was never questioned. In her mind, they were doing their job and were always right, even if they could be wrong. If we got good grades, she showered us with adulation. Bad grades brought forth a sadness that teared her up. Many a time, I didn't want her to see my report card. My heart saddened when she cried.

"Robert can do better if he tries harder," was a comment on one report card.

"Robert is well-behaved, but he needs to study harder."

"Robert is a good student but still needs work in reading."

My grades were never great. The only good grades I got were in attendance, PE, and music. Reading, math, social studies, and writing were not stellar. They were marginal at best. The core subjects reflected grades closer to Cs, Ds, and Fs, depending on how hard I'd worked at it, or on whether I had turned my work in on time, could read better, or had done my spelling. I barely squeezed by with these subjects. I felt hopeless. Such depressing thoughts made me hate school.

Graduation day was filled with excitement. I didn't know how it happened, but I'd made the list of those who would walk across the stage! I was overwhelmed with emotion. My name was on the list to pass on to fifth. I had new black pants, a new white shirt, and new shoes! New shoes! I never got those at the end of the year. I liked this graduation stuff!

We all lined up in a classroom as we watched our parents beaming with pride. Being excited to see their children advance in such a celebration made their day.

I liked all the fuss. The teachers came around and placed dark-blue graduation caps on our heads. Girls were giggling and trying not to get their hair messed up. Hundreds of bobby pins hung from the teachers' mouths, waiting to be used in an effort to hold down those caps. We were told to get ready: "Stand still. Keep your hands down by your side. Stand still."

The music started. We perked up.

"Stand up straight!" one of the two teachers demanded.

"Robert, stop talking," my teacher said, giving me the look only teachers can give.

I was so excited! "Pomp and Circumstance" was played. We marched into the gymnasium, which was crowded with families all dressed up as if they were going to church. As I marched on stage, facing parents and friends, I caught sight of Chuy and Pino.

Both my parents are here? I thought. *Unbelievable! Where are the kids? Chuy never comes to these things. Why is he here?* These questions raced through my mind faster than my beating heart. I could almost hear the pounding. *Is it my imagination?* I wondered. I got this weird sensation in my belly—a feeling of joy mixed with pride. I was glad both were there. I wanted them to be proud of me.

The ceremony didn't take long. The principal said a few words in English. He was a white guy we rarely saw except when someone got in trouble. My name was called. I got up and walked toward the principal. I grabbed the piece of rolled paper tied with a blue ribbon with one hand and shook the principal's hand with the other.

Smiling, happy, and proud, parents clapped for each child as they marched across the stage. I could see it in their eyes. I was searching for Chuy and Pino. Looking beyond the few parents gathered there, I desperately wanted to catch a glimpse of them. I wanted to make sure they saw me. We made eye contact. Their smiles assured me they were proud of what I'd accomplished.

Every student was scanning the audience in hopes of receiving the same from their parents. We wanted to impress those we cared most about and those who cared about us. There weren't many of us, and, apparently, we all graduated. Even Roy! By golly, and me!

We marched out just like we'd come in, with the same music being played. We went back to the gym to enjoy Kool-Aid and cookies. Parents were mingling, talking to each other like they'd not seen each other in ages.

The excitement of that night and the ceremony's purpose had reaffirmed the importance of education. I wanted to graduate from high school. I thought I could. *If I can make it this far*, I thought, *imagine what I could do in the next few years*. I felt hope.

I spotted Mother and rushed to her side. Smiling, Pino put her arm around me. I noticed a tear in her eye, and I hugged her again. I was happy. My parents were happy. What a day! What a feeling!

My euphoria wore off the following day as doubt set in. *What if I didn't pass and the event was just a ploy?* I asked myself. *They can't take that diploma away, can they? They can't leave me behind. Everyone saw me cross the stage. I must have passed.* I was nervous, thinking the worst.

The report cards arrived a few days later, and, as always, I ran to the mailbox to retrieve the mail before anyone else did. The report card was the Holy Grail for me. It was the only official document that stated whether I had really passed to the fifth grade. It came in a small manila envelope. I made the sign of the cross, shaking with anticipation yet reluctant to even open the darn thing. I said one Hail Mary, then asked for a miracle.

I opened the envelope, reached inside, and read the contents. Slowly, I flipped the card over to the back page—the page that contained the verdict.

"Robert is promoted to the fifth grade."

The initial shock made my eyes tear up. I'd made it. I was going to a new school. A bigger school. A newer school. I ran inside to show everyone.

"I passed, I passed!" I shouted in unbelievable joy. I raced into the kitchen, holding the prize open for everyone to see. The last column of the report card showed the progress made over the entire year. I showed Pino, pointing out the beginning of the year and the end of the year. While there was little difference in my grades, on the row outlining attendance, I had a perfect rating. I hadn't missed a day of school! In the row indicating how I had done on the other subjects, it showed a mix of Cs, C-minuses, C-pluses, and at least one B. Not a single A.

In the comment section, it read, "Robert will have to learn his multiplication tables and read at least three books during the summer months. Robert is a good student, but he must work harder in the fifth grade."

Work harder? I asked myself. *I can't work any harder! I'm giving it all I got.*

Good Sadness

In July 1962, I turned eleven. The first Beatles single, "Love Me Do," was released, the first oral polio vaccine was used to combat the disease, Marilyn Monroe was found dead, the Cuban missile crisis took the world to the brink of war, John H. Glenn Jr. became the first American to orbit the Earth, and the first Walmart discount store was opened.

Back at the barrio, we were dealing with what seemed to be better times. We found ourselves moving again, but this time, we were only moving a block down, farther west, to the last house at the end of town. You couldn't go any farther. This was where the town ended.

The green frame house with a kitchen, three bedrooms, a living room, and one bathroom made us feel special, even though it was old and in need of a lot of work. The entrance to the kitchen, the only place we used to get into the house, had a screened-in patio. In the back of the house stood a detached wooden garage that the previous occupants had transformed into a storage shed. We had running water, gas, and electricity. The floors were made of wood! Imagine, us having wood flooring covered with slightly worn linoleum! It was soft yet sturdy, old but better than we'd ever had before. Excitement was in the air. We had plenty of elbow room and were moving on up! We still lived in the barrio, but for the first time, we had a real house with a real floor!

We carried what few possessions we had and walked to our new house. Chuy borrowed a truck to haul the rest. The rent was reasonable, according to Pino. This would be home for the next ten years.

Dad bought a car later that summer, and we all rode around the neighborhood, feeling like the rich and famous. We were hanging out the window with no seatbelts, wanting kids to see us. We'd pass by our friends' houses, showing off our new car, which wasn't new at all. But it was a car, nevertheless.

Chuy and Pino seemed happier now that both were working. Within a year, we were moving into the poor-plus category. That's when you're still poor but don't know it.

Chuy managed to land a good job working in the oil field business as a construction worker. He was building a reputation for working hard and being on time. He'd also built some friendships along the way, which was surprising, since he didn't like many people.

The Colonia family seemed nice enough, and he got along well with the father. I knew my dad liked to hang out with Manny Colonia. They rode around in Manny's station wagon. What I didn't know was that Manny had a questionable reputation—a reputation that went along with the shadiness of his character. Manny was one you couldn't trust or depend on. However, he and Chuy seemed to get along well. Chuy still hung out at Joe's Place after payday, but he wouldn't stay as long as he used to. He still got drunk. He still lost money playing dominoes. He still was mean. But all that was overlooked as long as he was making money.

One Saturday afternoon, Manny came by to pick up Dad. How I managed to talk them into taking me along for a ride, I'll never know. That ride led to several hours of barhopping with me either going in the bar or sitting in the car while they went inside, depending on whether the owner allowed me in or not. At Joe's, I was considered a regular. I'd been going there since I was six, so that wasn't much of a problem.

After several hours, they decided to leave the bar scene and head toward Rooney Park. They sat in the car, talking and drinking while I sat in the back, minding my own business. The minutes passed slowly.

"I'm getting hungry," slurred Manny. My dad agreed. I did too. So we drove to a small convenience store appropriately named The Trading Post at the corner of Dickenson and Rooney Streets.

It was a run-down store owned and operated by a big, fat white guy who wore a felt cowboy hat cocked to one side. To keep his pants up, he wore suspenders with a belt over his big belly. A loose shirt with a couple of buttons missing gave him that raunchy "I don't give a damn" look. He stood behind the counter, elevated by a raised floor so he could have a clear view of the store. He had been robbed so many times that he kept a pistol strapped to his waist, hoping it would deter potential robbers. The store sat by itself on the north side of Dickenson. It was always crowded, so it made it an easy target for those wanting to take things without paying.

It was a cold day. Manny and Dad had on bulky jackets. Chuy wore a green military-style jacket with big pockets, and so did Manny.

"You go to the counter and ask the man for a phone book," Dad told me as we headed into the store. "And don't ask for anything else. Look for Juan's name in the book, and ask the man to help you find it."

"I don't know any Juan except for my friend. He doesn't have a telephone," I replied.

"Just pretend you are looking for him."

"But he doesn't have a phone at home. Why would I want to look for his name when he doesn't have a phone?" I pleaded.

He gave me a stern look, so I followed instructions. It didn't sound or feel right, but I did it. I walked in the store and asked for the phone book. I forgot what else I was supposed to do.

Dad was in the store, and I went looking for him. But there was no one else there. I didn't think it would take me long to find him. The store wasn't very big, but it was packed with so many items stacked on shelves that the shelves were too tall for me to see over. I went around the corner and stopped by the refrigerators where the meat was kept. That was when I saw Dad sticking luncheon meat under his coat. He didn't see me. I pretended I didn't see him either. In the meantime, Manny took a loaf of bread and did the same thing. Putting it in his coat, he zipped it up and grabbed a bag of chips. He stuck the bag on the other side of the jacket.

My dad is stealing! I thought. *How could anyone steal from a man who carries a gun?*

This was not good. I remembered what happened to me when I was caught stealing BBs. I was an accomplice to a crime! The thought of spending time in the cold, dark, dank place called the county jail frightened me. I wanted no part of this, so I went out to the car, got in, and prayed no one would get shot.

Within a few minutes, out came the two men, smiling, laughing, and hurrying to get in the car. Once in, they drove back to the park. Then, out of their coats came candy, bologna, bread, potato chips, and a six-pack of beer!

I was mortified!

The shock didn't last long though. Sitting in the back seat, splurging on stolen goods, I was content. My belly was full. I reminisced about when I had stolen BBs from the five-and-dime store years earlier. I was indeed my father's son.

Too young to care what happened to adults, my mind was now occupied with more important things. Chuy and Pino were working. We had a better home, where I could have some room to be alone. I even had my own room. It was the official living room, which no one ever used. We'd never had a living room before. It sat alone much of the time. The room must have been added after the original house was built because it had no gas for heating or electricity for cooling. It was always hot in the summer and cold in the winter. An extension cord was brought in through an opening at the bottom of the door that separated the living room from the rest of the house. I used it to plug in a lamp. With clean, folded blankets kept on the side, the couch served as my bed. There was an old record player at one end of the room, a couple of chairs, a lamp, and a small end table. We had very few official visitors, so having the place for myself was a luxury. No one argued with me for taking over the room because there were other bedrooms for the kids.

I felt special and grown up. I liked my room, and I added posters and pictures of my idols, Batman and Robin. It was a place I could use when I needed to get away from the others. It was where I'd ponder my lack of social activities.

Eventually, it also became Chuy's drunk den. Coming home from wherever he'd gotten drunk that day, he'd avoid Mom's terrorizing glare by going there and playing mariachi music. If I was caught sleeping there, he'd wake me and make me play music on the record player.

Javier Solís, his favorite singer, reminded him of his beloved Méjico. He couldn't play the record by himself because he couldn't stand still long enough to put the needle on it. He didn't have many albums, but the ones he did have were played repeatedly during these periods of drunken mourning. I'd put on Javier Solís and sit down with him as we listened to the voice of sadness and despair—a melodic voice that resonated through the speakers like sails in the ocean, smooth and clean. The entire album was one of the best he ever recorded. The melodies he sang came from the heart, reminding Dad of the family he'd left behind. I could feel the loneliness he must have felt when I heard Javier sing. Every song spoke of leaving and missing someone or someplace. It was beautiful music. Even today, when I ask Alexa to play Javier Solís, it brings back those memories. It still gives me a good sadness.

Javier Solís sang with a full mariachi. One of Chuy's favorite songs, "La Media Vuelta," spoke to him in a way no other song did. He would have me play this song over and over while he sat there on the doorstep, head hanging, body swaying. During these moments, when he was still awake, he'd confide in me and tell me about his home in Mexico. He'd share his stories of growing up and wanting desperately to come to America.

"*Me fui a los Estados Unidos porque mi papá se murió.*" ("I left for the United States because my father died.") He spoke of his sisters and brothers, who he had not seen in years.

"*No saben si estoy vivo o muerto,*" he'd calmly say. ("They don't know if I'm alive or dead.") He'd recall his father's efforts to teach him the family business and how demanding he would be. He'd carry on this way until he fell asleep.

When I thought he was asleep, I'd head for the door, hoping to relieve myself of the redundancy of his thoughts. Just when I thought I'd escape, he would lift his head and tell me to play it again. This could go on for an hour or so until he finally dozed off or Mom came in the room.

"That's enough," she'd say. "You can't be keeping everybody up just because you're drunk."

I'd help her get him to bed, take off his boots, then retreat to my room, hoping for some peace and quiet. To this day, I love mariachi music and will always remember Javier Solís singing "La Media Vuelta."

Why was Chuy so sad whenever this song was playing? Whether he missed someone he'd left behind or played it to upset Mother, I never could figure out. I often wondered but would never ask him. The words didn't mean much to me at a young age, but in retrospect, I could see the marriage was in trouble again. Pino was frustrated to the point where she was challenging Chuy, telling him he needed to get his priorities in order.

"*¡Ya basta!*" she'd tell him the next day while he was dealing with a hangover. She'd complain, "*Ya me canse mirar te borracho.*" ("I am tired of seeing you drunk.") Meanwhile, he'd hold his head in his hands and look for a beer to ease the suffering. "You need to think about how we are going to pay for the things we need," she'd say.

She was getting to the point where she thought she could handle a household without the man around. When he came home drunk, she'd tell him to get out of the house and not come back until he sobered up. This would repeat itself many times over the next few years.

Obviously, as I listen to the song now, I can feel his hurt. I can feel his loneliness. I can see the sadness in his eyes. To Chuy, this song was a threat to Mom. It was saying just the opposite of what she was thinking. The machismo the song represented said she couldn't make it without him. Even if she did find another man, Chuy still owned her.

I sensed at the time that things were beginning to change. I reasoned that once Mom found the balls to confront Dad, things would get better, and he'd understand how much she detested his ways. I was proud of her determination in the face of such an emotional and traumatic life with him.

While she stood her ground against many of his machismo antics, she tried really hard to keep her frustration from us. She loved us and didn't want us to believe this was the way parents behaved. But sometimes it was unavoidable. When they argued openly, I would round up the kids and take them outside. I often wondered how she remained so strong and determined. Mom could be so inspirational and full of hope. She often saw the silver lining in things while I only saw despair.

"Don't think this is the way all families live or behave. We love each other, but one of us has to have the sense to make things happen. For the good of us all," she would lecture. "We will survive, and all of you will achieve in life what the good Lord put you here for. You are good *hijos*. Now go and play. Supper will be ready in an hour."

What she didn't foresee was that her kindness, words of inspiration, and trust gave us permission to be creative with our free time.

Chaos in the Hood

O ur friends were still close by, and we continued with baseball games. We still played in the street if there were enough kids to create two teams. But the original group members were slowly disappearing. Some were pulled away to work the fields, while others went to Mexico for the summer. And perhaps we were just getting older and our interests were taking us elsewhere—talking to girls, swimming, hanging out, or simply just lying around watching TV. By the middle of the summer, we seldom played. Yet, the older we got, the more daring we became. Venturing into the unknown became my favorite pastime. This summer was going to be one to remember!

My great-grandfather on my mother's side, Don Sabastian, lived on the corner of South Texas and West Sherer Streets, a couple of blocks just north of us. Like many of the houses in the barrio, his was made up of two adobe structures separated by a portico made of wood with a tin roof. You had to go outside to get from one building to the next. The smaller of these two was the kitchen. The bigger building was long and narrow.

The living room, which also served as a bedroom, was Don Sabastian's favorite hangout. Two small bedrooms separated by cloth curtains accommodated his family. The property, made up of two lots, was big enough for a chicken coop, an outhouse, and a storage shed where he kept his tools. My great-grandfather was quite a handyman. He walked two miles every morning to an old white woman's house to take care of her yard. Mrs. Williams kept him on a meager salary so he would keep the property up. Her husband had passed on a few years back, and she needed a handyman. He'd walk to this part of town every day except Sunday. If Mrs. Williams had some emergency that required his attention on Sunday, he would comply.

Don Sabastian, whom we referred to as Abuelito, lived a long time with extraordinarily little stress in his life. The coop kept his most loved possessions—chickens. He loved his chickens and took great care in making sure they had enough to eat and drink. The chickens roamed around freely early in the morning. Sometimes, he would let them run wild until he came home for lunch. The chickens ran around all over the place, at times crossing the street into the *monte*, or llano. It was an empty area just before you got to the Marathon Highway. We loved this area. It was our playground.

One day, Fidel, Sammy, and I walked over to his house. Along the way, we decided to stop by the chicken coop. On this day, the chickens were all gathered there and not loose.

"How many chickens can you hit with a rock?" I asked Sammy.

Sammy was so vulnerable, he would try anything. He picked up tiny pebbles and threw them into the cage. Fifteen chickens, all walking around and pecking at everything on the ground, were not hard to hit. For no apparent reason, we disliked those chickens. We thought Don Sabastian loved them better than he loved us. Or at least that was our rationale.

We opened the gate, and Fidel walked in and scooted them out. As they walked out, we threw rocks, not pebbles, and chased them across the road. Running after them, we flung rocks, hoping to knock one out. We didn't realize it was lunchtime. The chickens were making such a commotion that Abuelito came out, shouting and yelling for us to stop.

"*¡Chamacos cabrones! Dejen las gallinas en paz!*" he yelled. ("Damn kids, leave those chickens in peace!")

We ran into the bushes, hunkered down, and kept quiet until he left. When the coast was clear, we walked over to my grandmother's house, which was across the street from Abuelito's, and entered the kitchen. We were sweaty and thirsty. My grandmother, Romana, gave us goat milk with a piece of bread she had just cooked. She didn't ask what we were up to, and we didn't volunteer any information. She was a wonderful, kind woman who took the time to talk to us. She'd always try to feed us no matter what time it was. She'd ask questions about how I was doing in school, what my hobbies were, or how my parents were doing. These rare conversations led to a relationship I had with no other. I loved my grandmother.

As soon as we settled down to eat our bread, Don Sabastian walked in the house and said, "*¡Estos chamacos me andaban matando mis gallinas! ¡Necesitas aplacarlos!*" ("These boys were trying to kill my chickens. You need to settle them down!") Then he walked out.

Grandmother gave us a stern look, but as soon as her father left, she smiled at us.

"Leave his chickens alone. Those are what keep him alive. He loves those chickens. Find something else to do. Now eat your bread and go play."

I couldn't believe my great-grandfather had called us *cabrones*. That meant war! Outside, we plotted our next move. The chicken chase was one thing, but our next move was daring. We'd make his life miserable by attacking his house. Pretending to be Jack from the book *Jack the Giant Killer*, we went looking for ammunition. It came in the form of rocks collected and placed into mounds of a dozen or so for each one of us.

Shielding ourselves with a piece of tin roofing found in the yard, we prepared to attack from across the street. The idea was to create havoc by tossing the rocks onto his roof. Because it was made of tin, it would have a loud hailstone effect.

"On the count of three, we fire our rockets and explode the house," Sammy said.

"I don't know if we should be doing this," was Fidel's response.

"I think we should fire the bombs and see what happens. That old man will never catch us," I explained.

"One, two, three!"

Rocks went flying through the air, making loud clanking noises as they landed on the tin roof. The reverberation of rock hitting metal sent a chilling sound throughout the neighborhood. We kept throwing until Don Sabastian ran out, yelling obscenities and pronouncing us *hijos de la chingada* (sons of the damned).

We ran north, away from his house, and kept running until we were sure there was no more chase. We laughed and bragged about how many bombs had hit the roof. We were all Jacks.

But sooner or later, we had to return to the scene of the crime. We looked around to make sure the coast was clear. Fidel and Sammy returned home. I calmly walked to my house, but I had to pass right by his house. I walked fast and cautiously.

We didn't hear too much about the incident from either my grandmother or my mother until a few hours later. We had gotten away from Don Sebastian's wrath. I was feeling safe, thinking the old man had learned his lesson. I let out a slow, continuous breath, wiped sweat off my forehead, then walked inside. I went straight to the refrigerator, looking for Kool-Aid to quench my thirst. With a glass full, I sat down.

"Mom, Robert's home!" Wanda yelled across the bedroom. She was on the floor playing with Imelda. "You're gonna get it," she said to me. Then she laughed.

"*¡Roberto, ven aca!*" ("Roberto, come here!")

Uh-oh! I thought. *Trouble.* Mom never called me Roberto unless there was trouble.

I walked to the front room, calmly drinking my Kool-Aid, and my eyes popped wide enough for everyone to notice my fright.

Don Sabastian was sitting, having a cup of coffee with Mom. He had tattled on me and the others.

He got up to leave. And as he walked toward the door, he gave me a sly, wicked look that said, "I got you, you little piece of shit!" As soon as he left, Pino tore into me.

"You can't upset the old man. It isn't proper, and I didn't raise you to be cruel. This old man is your great-grandfather. You and your uncles need to go over and pick up all those rocks you threw at his house. You could have hurt somebody. Now get back there and pick them all up."

She was not a happy camper. I went to Grandmother's, picked up the two boys, and headed out to Don Sabastian's. We collected the rocks, put them in a bucket, and hauled them off to the monte.

"What about those still on the roof?" Sammy asked.

Fidel and I looked up. The roof was cluttered with rocks.

"Those must have already been there. We didn't throw that many rocks," I exclaimed, looking nervously at the number of rocks on the roof.

"We can't climb on the roof. That would be suicide," Fidel, the smart one, said.

"I agree. It is sulbeeside. Whatever Fidel said," I mimicked.

"It's *suicide*, not *sulbeeside*," Fidel replied. "That's doing something stupid that gets you killed."

"Well, whatever," I said. "Leave them. You can't see them anyway if you're looking down."

So we left them there and walked away with smiles.

Chuy got home, and I was certain as a rattler's tail shaking a warning that it was coming—the beating of a lifetime. To my surprise, when he came in the room, he told me it was not right to disturb an old man.

"Stay away from his house," he told me. Then, through God's miracle of miracles (though by this time, I was questioning God's good motives), Chuy turned around and left. I thought I caught a smile on his face as he walked away. I believed in God once again!

I ran to my grandmother's house and found Fidel and Sam working in the backyard, cleaning up trash from the weekend before. With very little supervision and a lot of time on our hands, the three of us decided to explore beyond the barrio.

It was hot, and the sun was bearing down on us. But we walked three or four miles, following surface roads leading away from the barrio. Fidel led the way, since he'd been in this area a couple of times with Don Sabastian. If we traveled far enough northwest beyond the railroad tracks, the town changed dramatically. In this part of town, there were large, picturesque houses with paved driveways and manicured lawns with real grass. Nice cars were parked outside or in the enclosed garages, making this neighborhood appealing. This was gringo territory. The affluent white people lived in this neighborhood, and we had no business being there.

We were to stay away from this part of town, according to our parents. I had heard of this neighborhood from friends and family members who had ventured there for some reason or another. Some of our relatives worked there, cleaning houses, mowing lawns, or running errands for families that lived within these castles. In the back of these houses were alleys with huge trash bins called dumpsters. Word had it that one man driving a truck with special equipment could pick up each dumpster, empty it into the truck, and put it back in its place with one fell swoop. I didn't believe it. In our neighborhood, it took three men. One drove, and two stood in the back of the truck, picked up the trash can, lifted it, and poured its contents into the truck. Three men!

On this day, we were on a hunt for treasure.

"I read on the back of a milk carton that if you cut off the top of the carton and collect ten of them, you could get a free game of bowling," I said to the two as we walked at a leisurely pace.

"A free game of bowling? What's a bowl?" Sammy asked, surprised at the thought.

"Not a bowl. Bowling is a game rich people play with balls that roll. You hit some thingy things. The idea is to make those thingies fall," I explained.

"It's a game you play by rolling a ball down a path at some white bottles," Fidel, being the smart one, chimed in.

"Yes. All we need is thirty, and we can go bowling," I said. It seemed like a good idea even though I'd never been bowling. I kind of knew what it was supposed to be like and wondered if it was worth ten, tops. Curiosity egged me on as I walked and thought about how long it would take me to get ten carton tops. After some serious calculations, I figured it was going to take over two months. We had milk around our house only for coffee. Since milk had gotten expensive, coming in at an astonishing fifty-two cents for a half gallon, the kids were barred from drinking it. By my calculations, adults drinking two cups of coffee per day equaled a carton a week. So, that added up to ten weeks.

"Why would you do that?" Sammy asked with confusion on his face.

"Because the more you crush them with the ball and make them fall, the more points you get," I told him. By this time, I knew I was getting nowhere with my explanations.

"What do you get for the points?" asked Fidel.

"I don't know. But do you guys want to play or not?" I asked.

"I don't have milk cartons," Sammy exclaimed. "Why milk cartons? Can we take cigarette tops? We can find those everywhere."

"No, it said milk cartons. Now, do you guys want in on this, or am I going by myself?"

"We don't have milk cartons!" cried Fidel. "Where are we getting milk cartons? This is stupid," he said, then turned to walk back down the alley.

Then it hit me.

"Where? Right here in the gringo alleys, where they throw their trash!" I said. "We can go and search through the big trash cans. I bet they have milk cartons. Gringos don't have use for milk cartons!" I shouted with excitement.

We managed to open the plastic lid of the first dumpster. Sammy, being the smallest, was chosen to go into the bin. We picked him up by his legs, then swung him over the top and into the dumpster. He crawled around in the trash until he found what we were looking for. It was taking him a long time.

"It smells in here." His voice echoed from inside.

"Don't breathe," I told him. "Just look for the milk cartons, okay?"

After several minutes, he threw out two milk cartons.

"I told you we'd find some here!" I said, jumping up and down and smiling. "Okay, let's go to the others. I bet we can find enough for all of us!"

Fidel and I walked away from the first dumpster, excited to look into the next.

"How am I gonna to get out of here?" Sammy's little voice cried out. "I need someone to help me get out! Hey, guys, I can't get out."

In our excitement, we had forgotten that Sammy was too small to get out by himself. His size didn't allow him to reach the rim of the dumpster. I lifted Fidel over the top. He tried pulling him out, but he couldn't.

"I can't get him out! He's too heavy!" Fidel called out. By this time, Sammy was crying hysterically, calling for Romana, his mother.

"Shut up! You're going to get us caught, and we're all going to disappear!" I shushed him. "Be quiet. We'll get you out."

I don't know why I felt like we were stealing. It was trash. But what if we got caught? The police would surely take us away.

By one of the other bins, we found two old plastic boxes used to carry soda pop empties and brought them back to the dumpster.

"Stand back, Sammy. We're going to throw these boxes inside. Use this to reach the rim and pull yourself up," I told him.

We could see his hands coming up over the top, and we finally pulled him out.

"I'm not getting into that nasty thing again!" Sammy demanded.

I looked at Fidel, the genius. "If you want to, you can do it," I said.

"I'm not gonna do it. I'm not!" He was determined not to.

By the end of the first three alleys, we had accumulated a total of eight milk cartons, thanks to Fidel's eventual willingness to go in the dumpsters after all.

"See, I told you we would find these here," I said.

"I'm going home," said Sammy. He started walking back in the direction we had come from.

"Okay, let's go home. Tomorrow we can come back and find some more," I said.

Then we headed back. My clothes, shoes, and hands smelled worse than a sewage treatment plant. I had to get home before my parents found out I hadn't been home.

It took us almost a month before we had enough for all three of us to go bowling. Problem was, we didn't know where the bowling alley was. The only person we could ask was Uncle Juan. He was a cool and smart teenager. He was determined to be the first to graduate from high school and old enough to have a girlfriend. He knew how to drive, so we asked him if he would take us to the bowling alley.

Yes, Fort Stockton had a bowling alley. It was in an old building just north of Rooney Park along the Sanderson Highway. It was a good distance from where we lived and not a place we would walk to. After some cajoling and pleading, he finally agreed. He dropped us off, and, as he drove off, he let us know we had to get home by ourselves. Somehow, we didn't hear him say that—probably because we all rushed to the front door, pushing and shoving each other to be the first to go inside.

We had a paper bag with forty Gandy's milk carton tops. I went up to the counter and placed the bag in front of a gruff-looking man.

"We want to go bowling," I said.

He counted the box tops, then asked, "Do you want shoes? If you want shoes, that will be a dime each."

"No, we don't want shoes," I said.

"Well, you can't bowl in those shoes. You are going to have to bowl in your socks. Do you have socks on?" he asked, leaning over the counter to look at our feet.

We had socks on.

"Take lane number three," he said.

We walked over to lane three. *What now?* I wondered. *How do we play this game?* We looked at the other people playing and, after a few minutes, decided we had it down.

"I go first," I said. Then I told Fidel he'd go second. Sammy would go last.

"I found most of the boxes. Why am I last? asked Sammy. We answered him by paying him no mind.

Somehow, we figured out the game. We threw the ball, hoping it would reach the end without going into the gutter. We took turns. Keeping score was out of the question. We were having a blast knocking down bowling pins, amazed at the robot that came noisily down from the top of the pins to pick those standing up from the neck and swipe the rest down into the abyss.

We just kept pushing the button that said, "Next." At the end of the first game, we kept pushing the button, and the robot would stand the pins back up. I think we bowled for two hours. Sammy finally had enough, so we decided to quit.

As we were walking toward the door, the man at the counter said, "You guys owe me three dollars."

"Why?" I asked.

"You played three games."

"I don't have three dollars, sir," I said.

"Well, when your parents come to pick you up, you need to let them know you owe me three dollars."

"Okay," I said.

We kind of ambled around the door, and when he turned to help another customer, we snuck outside and ran as fast as we could until Fidel said, "Stop! Which way do we go?"

We didn't know the way home.

"If we can get to Main Street, I know the way to Butz," I told the guys. "We can find our way home from there."

"How far is it to Main Street?" asked Sammy.

"Don't know, but if we go that way," I said, pointing west, "we can find it."

It took us an hour to get home. No one missed me. No surprise.

That summer, Chuy and Pino were working, and Nancy was taking care of the younger kids with Wanda's help. That left me with loads of time. I had the freedom to continue enjoying the days, exploring, and letting my curiosity take me into parts of town I'd never seen before. Fidel, Sammy, and I were like brothers roaming the Wild, Wild West, seeking out new adventures. The property west of our homes was mostly empty range with nothing but sagebrush, mesquite, and tumbleweeds, with an occasional patch of tall Johnson grass. The dirt road running north and south was Texas Street. We had nothing to do after the bowling fiasco but fight boredom.

"Why don't we make a bow and arrows," I said. "We can go into the monte and cut branches out of some mesquite tree and make a bow. I've seen it on TV. Chuy has string he uses to measure things. We can use that to make our bows!"

"Where are we going to get arrows?" Fidel interjected.

"We'll make them too!" I said, pointing at a wooden box used to deliver fruit to Doña Lucia's Store. "I bet we can find some of these boxes over at the store."

We grabbed a wood saw from the shed, and off we went, heading into the monte, looking for the perfect tree with the perfect branches to make the perfect bow. I was insistent that the branch had to be exactly right, so it took us a while to find the perfect mesquite with bendable branches. I climbed the tree, found the perfect branch, and sawed it off.

"Tell me which one you want!" I yelled at the two. "I'm not climbing back up here, so pick one."

Fidel pointed to his, and I cut it down. Sammy asked for a smaller one, and I cut that one down too. We headed back to the house, looking for knives to scrape the bark off. Once we had the branch completely peeled, we sanded it down, then cut grooves in the ends to tie the string. The string had red powder on it for marking cement floors. We had red powder on our hands, face, and clothes. A dead giveaway if Chuy were to see us.

By the time we were through with the bows, I complimented our work. They looked pretty good. Now it was time to test their flexibility.

"What about arrows?" Sammy asked. "Where do we get arrows?"

"Let's go to Doña Lucia's. She has some wooden boxes in the back. We can use those," I suggested.

We walked away from the back of the store with a box each. Once we got back to the shed at my house, we took them apart, saving the long side boards for arrows. Splitting the boards with a hammer and a large kitchen knife, we made sure each sliver of wood was cut straight. We whittled the long pieces with our knives until they were as straight and round as we could get them. We sanded them from top to bottom until we were sure there were no splinters that would dig into our hands when we fired them off. This was a long, tedious process that took at least two days. But an abundance of time was what we had.

Sammy's job was to find nails, so he roamed all over nearby family houses, looking for straight ones. He found a big box of them in Chuy's shed, and we used wire to tie the nails onto the tips of the arrows.

We snuck into the chicken coop. Abuelito wasn't home. Scooping up as many feathers as we could, we headed back to base camp. The next step was to find glue to attach the feathers. Elmer's glue was a much-needed supply, and at the end of the school year, we got to keep what hadn't been used. So it wasn't hard to find.

Now, the hardest part was cutting the feathers in half and gluing them to the other end of the arrows. That done, we were now ready for the hunt.

I would turn eleven in July; Fidel was ten and Sammy nine. Here we were, playing with knives, hammers, and nails carefully affixed to the end of sticks and getting ready to pretend we were Tonto from the movie *The Lone Ranger*. Tonto was the Lone Ranger's sidekick, and he rode a neat-looking pony. All Indians respected Tonto.

I went home to get a bandana, placed it on my head, and stuck a feather between my hair and the bandana. With Mom's lipstick, I drew two lines on each side of my cheeks, running from ear to ear. Taking off my shoes and my T-shirt, I asked the two uncles if I looked like Tonto. It would be a few years before I was told that *tonto* is the Spanish word for "crazy." Oh well, who's not crazy at eleven years old?

"Well?" I asked Sammy and Fidel.

"You don't look like Tonto, but you look like an Indian," Fidel said.

I did Sammy's face, then Fidel's. We were ready to roam the range and kill bad men. We gathered in the monte, just the three of us, to test our skills. I strung the bow, pulling on the string to check for tightness. I got an arrow, placed the feathered end on the string, pulled back, and shot in the air. It went a few yards, passed some cacti, and landed on its side.

"Why didn't it stick?" asked Fidel, the smart one.

"I don't know. Maybe we should aim higher," I said. Then I pulled on the next arrow, letting it go straight up. "Run!" I shouted.

We all scattered, stopped, and looked up in the sky as the arrow was making its way down. *Swoosh*, it came down and stuck in the ground without breaking.

We clapped. We smiled. We had conquered a new task. Jumping up and down, excited that we'd actually made this work, we gave each other high fives.

Fidel went next, and for the next few hours, we played a game of chicken. We shot the arrows up above us, then waited until the last second to scatter as the arrow came crashing down and stuck in the ground.

"Chicken!" we yelled at the first one to dive away from the incoming arrow. Even Sammy was having fun. How none of us got injured playing this stupid game, I'll chalk up to nothing less than a miracle from Jesus.

But the adrenaline from the thrill of danger wasn't over yet. We had bad cowboys to shoot. Smiling and laughing, we picked up the arrows and walked home, chatting about our adventure. We gathered at my grandmother's house and set up targets in the backyard, getting better with our bows and arrows, and naming each target. But that got boring after a while. The game was no longer exciting.

"We need a moving target," I said, sitting on the ground Indian style. Sammy looked at us, and instantly I knew what he was thinking.

"I'm not going to run and have you and Fidel shoot at me! I'll tell Mom," he said. That idea didn't appeal to any one of us, so we sat there trying to figure out our next move.

"The feathers are falling off. We need more feathers. Let's go to Don Sebastian's house and get more feathers," Fidel suggested in his infinite wisdom.

We walked over to Don Sabastian's backyard and climbed up onto the shed overlooking the chicken cage. Then, like a light beaming from the sky, it hit me! A brilliant idea.

Looking at the others, I said, "Let's shoot the chickens." The coop was large enough for the chickens to move and fly around, so they would be perfect moving targets. "I go first," I said. I strung the bow, reached for an arrow, and shot it inside the coop, not hitting a thing.

"Look, I almost got one!" I yelled out.

"Shoot that one," Sammy demanded. "Shoot the red one!"

"That one's too fast. I'm going for the fat white one!" I yelled.

The chickens went crazy, squawking and making all sorts of noise. They were flying as fast as their little wings would carry them. They were all over the coop.

We were shooting our arrows, trying to nail one or two, when we heard a voice screaming, "*¿Qué cabrones están haciendo, chamacos pendejos?*" ("What the hell are you doing, you stupid kids?")

It was Don Sebastian, running toward us as fast as his little old legs could carry him.

We were faster. We jumped off the shed and ran into the coop, letting some of the frightened chickens out as we picked up the evidence and ran into the monte.

We lingered around in the empty desert for what seemed like hours. When the evening sun began to cast long and slender shadows on the ground, we went our separate ways, walking home. I hid my bow and arrows in the shed, then climbed the two steps into the kitchen. Just in time for supper.

The next day, Don Sabastian came to the house to see both Mom and Dad. He brought an arrow with him—one of the arrows we must have missed when we rushed out of the coop. I not only got a scolding, I got a good whooping. It wasn't a "call 911" kind of beating, but still a good one. It could have been worse. Chuy didn't appear mad when he was swinging the belt.

"Stay away from the old man! You hear me?" he said. Then he smiled and walked away after a few swings. I was placed in the corner to pray for forgiveness. I recovered in minutes and promised to throw away *las flechas*—the arrows. I kept the bow for several years. I thought it was a great piece of work for an eleven-year-old.

The summer of 1961 was a long one. Bored and hanging around the house with nothing to do was depressing. There was only so much TV a kid could watch. However, one Saturday morning, a commercial advertising a skateboard caught my interest. Young boys and girls were standing on it with one foot and pushing with the other, making the board fly down the pavement. They'd balance themselves on it when it gained momentum, which allowed them to stand and ride like the wind.

I was intrigued. I asked Pino if I could have one. Of course, the reply was always, "*¿Dónde crees que vamos obtener el dinero?*" ("Where do you think we're gonna get the money?") That was the end of that story. No use in pushing it.

One day, I was scrambling in the shed, looking for something to do, and I saw a box. After moving some old furniture, I found, toward the back, a box full of toys. Down at the bottom were two rusty metal skates, each with four wheels. The previous owners must have left all the stuff. I assumed they didn't want it, so I pronounced it my own.

The roller skates were stuck together, but after some expert finagling, I managed to unhook them. I oiled the wheels. After soaking in oil for a day, they became loose and functional. They were too small to fit my shoes, so I took them apart and screwed the two sides to a piece of two-by-four wooden board.

I stood back and marveled at my new toy. I had invented the poor man's skateboard!

We didn't have any sidewalks, and the skateboard didn't travel well in dirt. So I walked a mile west to the place that was going to be my fifth-grade school. It had plenty of sidewalks. The main building, which housed the principal's office, library, and a teacher's conference room, sat on top of a slight hill. The school had five wings, which housed the five grades and were connected by sidewalks. This was the perfect place to try my invention.

I started by trying to balance myself on the two-by-four, adjusting my balance so as to stay upright. I had some difficulty. The board was too thin. This wasn't working out. I tried putting one foot on the board and pushing with the other, but I kept falling off. My efforts at staying upright didn't look like the commercial.

I went to the top of the hill, sat on the board, and let gravity pull me down to the end of the walkway. That seemed to work pretty well. The poor man's skateboard rolled. As it gained speed, I hung on for dear life! I grabbed the board tightly with both hands while my feet hung slightly in front of me.

But problem! I didn't have a way to stop the damn thing unless I let my feet down, and that didn't seem like a good idea at the moment. So I let it roll.

The sidewalk curved at the bottom of the hill. There was no way I was going to make that turn. With my eyes shut, I waited for impact. After crashing down the end of the pavement and rolling several times, I came to a complete stop. Surprisingly, there wasn't any blood. Good sign.

I slowly got up and checked to see if there were any broken bones. Nothing. My butt hurt a little, and I noticed grass burns on my knees. But I was safe to see another day.

After several tries, I learned how to use my feet to slow myself down until I could make the turn at the end. Now it was time to share my invention with my uncles.

I went back to the house, repaired my skateboard, and made another one for them. We spent countless hours skateboarding on our butts but never mastering the upright position! We laughed. We fell countless times. We had fun.

My Friend Troy

U p the street from our house was Troy's house. I'd met him long before he and I were in third grade. Troy was shorter than I. How he and I became friends was sort of strange. He lived caddy-corner from the old Coleman House, a rundown building with one resident living on the bottom floor. I was walking toward Lucia's corner store when I ran into him. He'd just left Lucia's. Eating an empanada and holding an RC Cola as he walked toward me.

An empanada looks like a tortilla folded in half with pumpkin, apple, or cherries inside. Some moms like to sprinkle cinnamon on the outside, giving it a sweeter taste. As it cooks, the outside turns brown and soft, just like a tortilla. They're delicious.

I asked Troy where he got his. He stuttered out, "A-a-a-ke-ke-ke Lu-lu-lu-Lucia's!"

"How much."

"Two—two—two—two for a-a-a-a nic-nic-nic-nickle."

"Can I taste it? If I like it, I'll buy one," I said, knowing full well I didn't have the money to buy anything.

"He-he-he-he-here. You can ca-can—can, ha-ha-ha-have this one."

We sat on the side of the street and ate the empanadas. We got to talking. Or at least, he got to talking. He pointed, "I–I–I–I live there."

"I've never seen you there. Where do you go during the summer?" I asked.

"Work, wi-wi-wi with my fa-fa-fa-father."

"Why do you talk like that?"

"Ah-ah-ah-ah-ah don't know.

After a few more minutes of this, he asked me to come by his house. I forewent Lucia's and walked over to his house. It was big—bigger than ours. In the back of the lot, his father had an open shed where he kept all sorts of tools hanging off wooden pegs. He had scissors—big scissors, little scissors. Some had cords attached to the ends.

"What are those for?"

"The–the–they–they–they're for sheep."

"What?"

"To she-she-she-she-sheer sheep."

"What's that?"

"To cu-cu-cu-cut off their hair."

"Oh. Cool. Who lives at the Coleman house?"

"A bl-bl-bl-bl-black guy. He th-th-th-th-thr-throws p-p-p-p-p-parties and bu-bu-bu-buys b-b-b-b-b-b-beer for b-b-b-boys."

"*¿Es un joto?*" ("Is he queer?")

"*N-n-n-n-n-n-no s-s-s-s-se.*" ("I don't know.")

"How do you know about the parties?"

"C-c-Chris te-te-te-te-te-tells me."

Chris was his older brother. Much later, through rumor and gossip, I found out that the resident at the Coleman house was a black man who lived by himself. His name was C.D. On certain nights, he would invite some of the older boys to his house, buy them beer, and try to seduce them. It was a dark place made of solid gray rock with a receding porch lit by one dim light that hung hopelessly from an extended wire coming off the ceiling. The yard was a mess, with dead grass and weeds sprinkled about.

When we walked by at night, if the light was on, supposedly a party was going on. We couldn't tell if there were any boys there unless we saw them going in or coming out of the house. No one drove a car, so without cars there, it was hard to tell whether teenagers were inside.

The older boys would drink his beer and who knows what else. You had to be a teenager to get invited to the Coleman house. We had several years to go before we could get an invitation. By the time we did come of age, C.D. had died. Not that we would ever have gone, but who knows. The parties ended, and the building became another one of those desolate old places destined for demolition. Eventually, the city tore it down, leaving the lot vacant for many years until it was bought by unknowing purchasers. We had to go with the rumors and the gossip. I leaned toward wanting to believe them. It was creepier.

Three weeks after he shared his empanada with me, Troy and I were hanging out. His father had picked us up, saying he needed help loading his truck with hay for some sheep he was taking care of. We piled onto the bed of the truck, and off we went to the *molino* at the end of town. The molino was a gin where bales of alfalfa were brought from Belding Farms and processed into small round pellets used for animal feed.

While Troy's father was inside the store, Troy and I decided to go exploring. We found some stalls where they kept the alfalfa unbundled and just spread all over the floor.

"I've got to take a piss," I told Troy.

"M-m-me t-t-too," he said.

We stood over the alfalfa, spraying a long stream over it.

"Let's see how many letters of your name you can write. You have to write your last name, too, because *Troy* is too short," I told him as we continued to urinate. I was on the last *r* of my name when I heard his father say, "*¿Que cabrones estén haciendo? Súbanse en la troka.*" ("What the hell are you doing? Get in the truck.")

He walked away, visibly irritated with our childish antics. I was taken off guard by his unexpected loud remarks, which forced me to cut off my peeing and fail to finish my name. I had one letter left, but at his bark, I rushed to put my thing away. When I pulled on the zipper a little too fast, I caught my pee-pee's skin. (Since no one told us what the correct term was for it, we all called it a pee-pee.)

"*¡Chingada madre!*" I yelled, turning around so no one would see my skin stuck to the zipper. I tried pulling the zipper down, but it exacerbated the pain. It really hurt. Crying would only bring embarrassment to an already bad situation. So I kept jumping up and down, hoping that would release the zipper and eliminate the pain. The last thing I wanted was to damage the goods for good!

With one last pull, I managed to zip down, and out came the skin. I went out and sat on the back of the truck, waiting for Troy's dad to tell us where to get the hay and pretending nothing had happened. I kept my hand on the jewels.

As we were loading the truck, Troy couldn't stand it any longer. He bellowed out a laugh that sent spit flying in the air. Funny how laughter didn't make him stutter. He laid down the pitchfork, grabbed his stomach, and fell to the ground, laughing and pointing at me.

I gave him a *cometa*, an equivalent of the finger but without holding it up for everyone to see.

I got paid twenty-five cents for helping out that day. It wasn't enough money to pay for the pain my pee-pee suffered at the hands—or should I say the teeth—of the zipper. I often wondered if Levi's came out with button-down jeans because of boys like me getting their thing caught in zippers. Who knows.

It would be an entire year before Troy's father took us on another job. One day, Troy mentioned that his dad had a sheering job at a sheep ranch. He asked me if I wanted to go. His father needed helpers to gather wool and stuff it into large sacks.

I wanted to go.

Early the next morning, with the truck loaded, we set off to a ranch several miles east of Fort Stockton. We arrived at a gate and drove onto a dirt road, and it looked like we were headed into a mountain range. Then we came upon a ranch house surrounded by animal pens. We stopped next to another set of animal pens that held what I thought was a sea of sheep.

After they unloaded the equipment, the men were ready to start. They'd grab a sheep and turn it on its back. With electric shears whirring away, the wool began to fall off the animal. They'd place the sheep's head between their legs, hold it steady, and chop off the back and the sides. The wool fell to the ground, piling up around the men's feet.

Troy and I picked up the wool and stuffed it into burlap sacks. Once a bag was filled, we tied the top with a string, lifted it onto a big trailer, then moved on to the next load.

This went on for two days. By the end of those two days, our clothes, bodies, and hair were covered with nasty grease from the wool. Our clothes looked like someone had spread brown lard on them. Our hair was lardy. Our hands. Lardy. Our skin. Lardy.

When I got home and Pino saw me, she cried out in disgust. "*¿Qué cabrones hiciste con tus pantalones y camisa?*" ("What the hell did you do to your pants and shirt?")

I pulled out four dollars and gave them to her with a smile.

"I made four dollars working," I said. "I got this way because the sheep had lard on their wool. When I picked up the wool, it rubbed against my clothes, and I just got dirty."

"*Quítate esa ropa y ve báñate.*" ("Take off those clothes and go take a bath.")

I was never allowed to go back to the ranch with Troy. It was fun, but it was a dirty job. I don't know what happened to the four dollars I gave Pino. I never saw a dime. I could have used it to get new clothes for the following school year.

Pets

The summer dragged on ever so slowly. Like all kids, I tried to keep busy but lacked the motivation. I'd amble around, thinking of things to do. Being occupied with my thoughts did pass some time, but after so many days, even pondering things I wanted to do wasn't possible because they required money I didn't have.

Being bored had a tendency to make me think of things a sane person would not attempt. I could only think so much, then it was time to get up and act on thoughts requiring no money. So one day, I headed outside, hoping to find something in the shed worth tinkering with.

Stepping into the warm summer morning, I saw the dogs. We didn't own a dog per se. They hung around the house, so in a sense, they adopted us. They were neighborhood dogs unless someone decided to make one their own. To do that, all one had to do was feed it and give it water. For the most part, we just left these dogs alone. When a female had puppies, the presumed owner, if they could not give them all away, suckered us young 'uns into falling for one or two of them.

Baby dogs are cute and cuddly. Dogs make good pets. They bark when strangers come around or when someone knocks on the door, and they warn you of unwanted visitors. Dogs are okay because you can train them to do things. Like, sit, roll over, sic 'em, and fetch. They go places with you, run with you, play with you. They ask for very little, making them very low maintenance. Given time, they can become your best friend.

I didn't have a pet dog until I was much older. Pino didn't want us bringing stray dogs to the house. She and Chuy would complain, saying," We barely have enough to feed you kids! Bringing another mouth to feed takes away from you."

It wasn't worth the effort, so we simply considered stray dogs as neighborhood dogs. We fed them if there was anything left after feeding nine people or when Pino brought bones from the restaurant to make broth soup. Then we gave the bones to the dogs. Most of the dogs that hung around were just mutts anyway. They wandered from house to house unless we fed them. If they stayed long, they just became ours. We never named the dogs because they weren't bought at a fancy store, and we didn't get them from the pound with a name already attached to them. If the dog was brown, we called it Brownie. If it was black, it was Blackie. If white, yes, you got it—it was Whitey.

Cats, on the other hand, I considered unfriendly and useless. At least the ones hanging around our place. They would amble around looking for food, and once they'd eaten, they'd sleep. Mother had major allergies, one being to cats. This was one gene we all must have inherited from her. We all had allergies—mostly to cats. So cats were never allowed in the house.

I didn't like cats. They never did anything wrong. I simply didn't like them. For one, I thought they had entitlement issues. *You owe me food. You owe me a hug. You owe me warm milk. You owe me, owe me, owe me.* Second, I'm allergic to them. Finally, they were always mysterious creatures. Sometimes people portrayed them as evil. Black cats were the worst, so I was told. They were bad luck, and they hung around witches, warlocks, and wizards. If one crossed in front of you, it brought bad luck. I heard plenty of crazy, scary stories about cats, especially black ones.

Most adults didn't believe these stories, so they tolerated cats. They were a necessary evil, I thought. I was told cats could keep mice and other rodents away from the house. They could also allegedly fight snakes, and we had plenty of them, since we lived so close to the monte. But these stories were hard for me to believe. I had never seen any cat catch anything. Pino thought they were good to have, so she made us feed them. I didn't know what role they played in the neighborhood, much less around the house.

Of the three cats that lived outside our house, the black one was the oldest and meanest. It would not let you pet it or get close enough to grab it. It would just run away. But I caught it once when it was drinking expired milk. I gently picked up the cat, called out to the young 'uns, and climbed the ladder to the roof with it under my arm. I'd heard that if you dropped a cat upside down from any height, it would land on its feet. At the time, it seemed like a great idea. But I needed witnesses on the ground. So I yelled again for them to come out.

"I'm going to drop this cat and see if it lands on its feet. I need you to watch and see if it does!" I called down once the kids were all outside.

They all stood there, one horrified, the others looking up, chanting, "Drop it, drop it, drop it." The only objector was Nancy. She, being the second oldest and probably much smarter than any of us put together, did not like the idea and threatened to tell Pino.

"You'd better not drop that cat!" she yelled, looking up at me. "That's Mother's favorite, and if you hurt him, she'll kill you."

"Drop him. I won't tell," snickered Jesse. The cat was screeching and meowing, probably anticipating the obvious, but I hung on to him. I thought about what Nancy had said. I didn't want Mom to be mad at me, so I walked down the ladder halfway and dropped the cat. It landed on its feet and quickly ran away!

"See, I told you it would land on its feet," I said.

"I'm telling," Nancy said. "You just wait until Mom gets home. I'm telling."

I brought more milk for the cat. This time, three cats showed up. The black one was the first. As it was lapping milk, I picked him up again. I really didn't like this cat. I had heard that cats had nine lives. Who I'd heard it from, I can't say. *If this is true*, I told myself, *then I want to see it.*

I went into the shed and brought out a long extension cord Chuy used to run lights when he was working on the car at night. I tied the wire around the cat's neck. I tied the other end of the wire to a cinder block. If I could throw the block over the branch, the momentum of the block would hurl the cat into the air. But I couldn't pick up the block and throw it while hanging on to the cat. So I called Jesse over.

"Here. Hold the cat," I said. Then I climbed the tree. Using the wire tied to the block, I pulled it up. I rolled the wire around the block to shorten the distance between block and cat.

"On the count of three, let the cat go!" I yelled at Jesse. "One, two, threeeeeeeeee!" I counted. I dropped the block, and the wire tensed, pulling the cat up in the air by its neck. I watched as the cat dangled halfway up the tree, clawing at the wire. Half the kids were crying. Nancy was screaming, and Jesse was laughing.

Then, out of nowhere, Mom appeared.

Oh shit, I thought. *There's no explaining this one.*

She yelled at me. "*Abaja ese gato! Estás tonto. ¿Qué no sabes que un gato negro es bad luck! Y si lo matas, te va venir a buscar y te va colgar! Vas a ver cuando Chuy venga.*" ("Get that cat down." Are you crazy? Don't you know that black cats are bad luck? If you kill them, they will come for you and hang you! You wait until Chuy gets home.")

The cat didn't hang for long. Maybe three seconds. I got it down, turned it loose, and watched it run away. It never did come back. Later, in the corner and on my knees, I prayed. I wasn't praying for forgiveness for trying to hang the cat. I was praying the cat would not come back to haunt me, take me away, boil me, or turn me over to some wicked witch. I couldn't explain to Mom the story about a cat having nine lives. She wasn't talking to me.

Cats are not like dogs. A dog wouldn't come to get you and try to hang you, like Mom said the cat would. That remark resonated with me well into my teen years. I don't like cats, and I don't think I ever will. I will avoid a black cat any day. If it crosses in front of me, I will go around. I don't walk under ladders, and I certainly don't pick up a cat, no matter what color it is.

The Big City

Our parents had been working steady for almost a year. They were bringing a bit more money. Not a lot, but enough to have nice things, like real toilet paper. Not the expensive kind, but toilet paper, nevertheless. Gone were the days of the Sears & Roebuck catalog.

Chuy and Pino seemed to be getting along for a change. Fights between them were infrequent. Chuy still enjoyed the cantina but limited his drunkenness to maybe once a month. One Saturday, he and Mom decided to go to Odessa to sell some aluminum he had collected. He would hoard aluminum cans and copper to sell for some extra money. This also gave them time away by themselves.

Odessa was the largest city within a three-hundred-mile radius. It was located about an hour and a half northeast of Fort Stockton and rested in the heart of a vast oil-rich area known as the Permian Basin. As the demand for oil grew during World War II, the population exceeded ten thousand, making Odessa the world's largest inland petrochemical complex. By the 1950s and 1960s, the population had grown to well over eighty thousand. There were more businesses there than anywhere else, so it made it a haven for those looking to buy things they couldn't get in Fort Stockton.

Mom and Dad had been to Odessa before with other family members, but this time, they were going by themselves. They came home late that night, talking about the big city with the big lights. So impressive was their first solo trip that their description of the place made it seem magical. Mom showed off a tiny new ring to the girls, talking about all the beautiful jewelry she and Dad had seen. She swirled her hand around, looking at the ring with pride. Chuy talked about the visit to the downtown stores.

Mom said, "*Tenian todo lo que una mujer o un hombre desea. Y no cuesta mucho.*" ("They carry everything a woman or man desires, and the prices are reasonable.") She was talking about the pawnshops—stores where people took jewelry, tools, bikes, TVs, radios, and an abundance of other personal items and got money for them. If someone didn't pay the pawnshop broker back by a certain date, he would take those items and put them up for sale to the general public. It was from one of these pawnshops that Chuy had bought her the ring.

They talked about Odessa for days, hoping to go back soon.

In late July, another trip to Odessa was in order. Chuy and Pino were discussing the trip when my name came up. I heard them talking in the kitchen about the traffic in the city. Chuy seemed legitimately concerned.

"Come here," he said, motioning to me. "I need someone who can read and tell me about the lights in Odessa."

"What lights?" I asked, totally confused. I didn't understand what he was asking.

"The city has put traffic lights on poles that sit to the side of the street, and I don't know which one I'm supposed to follow," he stated. "I almost got in trouble last time. I can't get caught driving there. I haven't gotten my license back yet."

"I know nothing about traffic lights," I answered.

"But you know how to read, don't you? Just read the signs."

And with that, I was going to the big city.

The confusion lay in our limited knowledge of how traffic was controlled. The only traffic lights our little town had were those that sat in the middle of the intersection. There was one light that controlled traffic on all four sides of the street. They were easy to follow: Red, you stop. Yellow, you watch out. Green, you go. Easy. But as Odessa grew, the city found it difficult to control the emerging flow of traffic, so they'd switched from the single traffic light in the middle of the street to pole lights on the side of the intersection. Chuy didn't know which one to follow. He needed me to read the signs, tell him which of the traffic lights he needed to follow, and when to go or stop.

The confusion on his part presented me with the opportunity of a lifetime. I would get to experience the big city. This would be my first time going on such a trip. I was excited!

The day for this adventure finally arrived. I woke up early, had my coffee, and, with a buttered tortilla in hand, ran to the car before they changed their minds. To my surprise, I was not the only kid going. Nora and Waldo, the two youngest, were accompanying us.

"Why are they going?" I asked. "Who is going to take care of the kids when you go shopping?"

"You two get in the back with me," Mom said to Nora and Waldo.

I didn't get a response. She ignored my questions, probably thinking I didn't deserve an answer. I didn't want my brother and sister to go. They would only take up space. I was being selfish. I wanted to be the first child to see the big city.

The five of us packed into the two-door Ford Fairlane hardtop. Nora and Waldo sat in the back with Mom, and I sat in the front with Dad. I felt so grown up, riding shotgun and all. Nancy was given the responsibility of taking care of the other three. My eight-year-old sister was in charge!

"We'll be back soon. Take care of the kids, and make sure they eat something," were the instructions left for her.

We left early and got to Odessa around nine in the morning. The pawnshops would be open at the time we arrived. As we entered the city limits, the desert took on a different appearance. There were four lanes of traffic—two on each side. Stores catering to the oil field business lined both sides of the street. The city was big compared to little ol' Fort Stockton, and I was mesmerized by the sheer number of people. There were so many people in so many cars and trucks. Chuy was driving slow, allowing other drivers to pass us. He reasoned they knew where they were going, and we did not. Our objective was to get to Main Street, where these pawnshops were. Businesses lined the main road coming into the city, each attracting customers by the dozens. After we traveled for what seemed miles, I could see the tall buildings a few blocks ahead.

"I need you to watch the signs and lights and tell me which one I'm supposed to look at," Chuy told me.

I still didn't know what he was talking about. My brain rotated questions I couldn't answer just yet. *What signs? What do they look like? Where are they?*

As we got closer to downtown traffic, the signs appeared. They were everywhere. Railroad Crossing Ahead! Flashing Light Ahead! 4 Way Stop Ahead! Right on Red! Bus Stop! The traffic slowed down. About a mile into it, I noticed a flashing light indicating there was a traffic light ahead. I stuck my head out the window and saw for the first time what he was talking about. The traffic lights were not in the middle of the intersection like in Fort Stockton. There were lights everywhere! Each street had its own lights telling the drivers facing the lights when and where to go. Or stop. Or yield. The confusion lay in the fact that there were too many lights.

"You have to follow that one," I said, pointing to the next light facing us. "You can go when it turns green."

We came to a place where the road swerved left, but some lanes went straight. It was confusing. There were now two lights giving us instructions.

"Stick to the right! Follow those cars!" I said, pointing and trying to keep my voice calm.

"But I want to go left to that street," he said.

Too late. We were caught trying to squeeze into the left lane, but I kept telling him to go right. Cars were honking, humans were giving us angry looks. We were trying to avoid a collision, which would most certainly be our fault. I nervously pointed to a certain light instead of telling Chuy what to do. He was busy driving, trying to avoid getting us killed.

I yelled, "Watch out!"

He barely missed going over the curb and into oncoming traffic. Confusion and frustration dominated some fearful moments. Navigating the maze of highways, which went in all different directions, almost brought me to tears. How could adults put this kind of pressure on a kid?

After several attempts, we made it onto Main Street. Now, to find the stores they wanted. It took us a while to master the modern traffic lights, but once we did, the terror subsided. Chuy pulled into a parking lot and stopped the car. Everyone took a deep breath, made the sign of the cross, and smiled. We had survived the chaotic streets of Odessa. But my job as a navigator had brought me no joy. This was way beyond my level of intelligence. And the problem still existed. How were we going to get back safely?

Once we got out and milled around the pawnshop, we forgot about the traffic. We walked into stores, lingered around windows, and looked without buying much. I couldn't imagine the items people would pawn and lose because they couldn't pay back what they borrowed. Although many items were used, they were still in pretty good condition. Chuy gravitated toward the tools. Pino wandered over to the jewelry. I got stuck watching the babies. I was thirsty and hungry. A buttered tortilla gets you only a couple of hours of fuel. The young ones had their bottles, so they were okay.

After a day of visiting pawnshop after pawnshop, we started on our way back home. I wanted to eat at a diner whose billboard displayed pictures of hamburgers, hot dogs, and French fries. I started to salivate. Out the window, Furs' Cafeteria, with all kinds of delicacies, went by. There were Mexican restaurants, as well as Chinese restaurants, lining the streets. I'd never eaten at a Chinese place before. All this was so enticing. I was hungry.

"Stop there! Look, there's a place to eat!" I yelled. "Look, there's another!" All the pointing fell on deaf ears. Chuy just kept driving and telling me to watch out for traffic lights. Before we got to the outskirts of town, he stopped at a little convenience store.

"You wait in the car. I'll be right back," he said, then went inside.

"Mom, I'm hungry. When are we going to eat?" I asked while she was changing diapers in the back seat. Within minutes, Chuy walked out of the store with a brown paper bag.

Between Odessa and the cutoff heading south toward Fort Stockton, we stopped at a desolate roadside park that harbored one picnic table under a decaying pergola. We all got out and shuffled over to the table. The bag was unpacked, revealing the contents. It contained half a pound of bologna, cheese, Fritos, bread, jalapeños, and mayonnaise. Instead of a restaurant meal, we were having bologna.

Who could complain? Bologna it was.

Mom made us sandwiches, which we ate as fast as she could make them—one slice of bologna with a slice of cheese between two pieces of bread covered with mayo. It was as delightful as it could get. The bologna was better than the kind we bought at home. When I asked why it was so good, Chuy explained the workings of a meat market.

"We should buy our bologna from a meat market then," I said between bites.

"Yes, we should," was all he said as he bit into his sandwich, followed by a big bite of the raw jalapeño.

We sat in the afternoon sun as it slowly moved farther west. After washing everything down with an RC Cola, we loaded up the car and headed home, satisfied and not thinking about those fancy restaurants we'd seen in the big city. That picnic meal would have rivaled any ol' restaurant any ol' day. I thought about how pleasant the day had turned out! I might not have gotten anything from the pawnshops, but I got to eat fresh bologna straight from a meat market!

It would be months before I got to go to Odessa again. I begged Mom and Dad to include me when a trip came up. I didn't think about it much, but I supposed I'd done a fairly good job of helping Chuy understand the workings of traffic lights. Now he didn't need me as a guide anymore. So, a couple of brownie points for me.

I didn't realize I'd be needing them soon.

A New World

O n May 17, 1954, a landmark decision was handed down by the justices of the Supreme Court. It would present a problem for children of color. We now had to attend schools with white kids.

In Brown vs. Board of Education, which was litigated by the NAACP Legal Defense and Educational Fund, a unanimous United States Supreme Court declared segregated education systems unconstitutional. School districts had to find ways to integrate brown and Black children with white children in all public schools. No longer was "separate but equal" a crutch used by white segregationists to keep children of color apart from white students.

It would take several years before brown children in Fort Stockton would be fully integrated with the white children. Eight years had gone by since the ruling, and I was now entering an integrated school. Alamo Elementary was closer to where I lived than Butz School. The younger children from the barrio had been separated and not allowed to be educated in the same school as white kids because of the color of our skin. But for the first time in my twelve years of existence, I would get to sit next to a white student.

Hispanic and Black kids had their own school in Butz, but only up to the fourth grade. Alamo Elementary had grades one through five. So, in the fall of 1962, I entered a whole new world of public education.

The school looked and felt new compared to Butz Elementary. Everything about this school was new or seemed new. The library was fully stocked with shelves and shelves of colorful, interesting-looking books. It was even carpeted! The music room had an array of instruments, from drums to flutes to xylophones—instruments I'd not seen before. Classrooms were spacious, painted in bright colors, with student desks that were neither carved into nor nearly falling apart. The bathrooms were free of urine smells, with working toilets and actual toilet seats. Campus grounds were clean and well-maintained.

The grass glistening in the early morning sun gave off a freshly cut fragrance. The greenest lawns surrounded playground equipment, which beckoned, "Come play with me." It was full of equipment I'd never seen before—slides, swings, tetherball poles with real balls, merry-go-rounds, and monkey bars—all standing just high enough for children of all ages. The monkey bars were in the middle of this enticing playground. I imagined myself climbing and swinging from one bar to the next. A plethora of delight. It was amazing! It took some time to soak in the differences between where I'd come from and where I'd arrived.

There were more kids there than at Butz. The student body consisted mainly of white students—more than I'd ever seen in one place at one time. Most entered their classrooms wearing new school clothes. I noticed a difference between what the white kids were wearing and what the Hispanic kids were wearing. Ours were cheap, simple clothing. Some of us didn't have clothing that matched. On the other hand, the white kids did, especially the girls. Boys wore jeans and shirts, while the girls wore dresses or skirts. Shorts were not allowed.

Even though the differences between us were abundant, a sense of excitement filled the classroom. To my awareness, these differences on this first day of school didn't seem to matter to the white students. But to me, it was quite obvious: We didn't belong there. I didn't belong.

When the bell rang, teachers stood outside next to their classroom doors, welcoming those prancing in from the playground. Our fifth-grade class was in the last wing closest to the main building. It had large windows across the entire side of one wall. When the curtains were opened, it allowed us to occasionally look out into the world beyond. I couldn't believe I had made it this far.

I was assigned to Mrs. Smith's classroom. Upon entering the room, we were asked to stand in a circle around the desks. Mrs. Smith called out our names in alphabetical order, pointing to the seat where she wanted us to sit. Naturally, having the Alfaro name put me up front and center—not a very comfortable position for me, since everyone could see me. I would have much preferred the back of the room. A place to hide.

Aside from the student differences, what was most noticeable about the school were the teachers. Most were white. There were no Black or Hispanic teachers teaching fifth graders. None in the fourth and none in the third. I didn't pay much attention to the primary grade teachers, but I assumed there were none there either.

I immediately took a liking to Mrs. Smith. She was a big woman who wore nice, colorful dresses. Female teachers were not allowed to wear pants or shorts. Mrs. Smith was kind. She was older than most of the others. I could tell by her demeanor that she liked teaching kids regardless of who they were, where they came from, or what they looked like. With a wonderful sense of humor, punctuated by a perpetual smile, she spoke kindly and respectfully to the children. Her blond hair—perfectly coiffured, as if she'd been to the beauty shop every morning—complemented her appearance. A slight touch of makeup on her round face and ever-so-light lipstick on her lips gave her confidence and purpose. When she walked by, she left a fragrance of baby powder in her wake. She was definitely the kindest, most appreciative teacher I'd ever had. She was the best. She made me feel like I belonged there because she showed no indifference toward the Hispanic kids.

This was going to be the best year of my life.

Or so I thought.

It didn't take long to realize that making friends at this school was going to be difficult. The differences in culture, language, and expectations resonated within the walls. In Mrs. Smith's class, three boys, including me, had come from Butz, which made it easier to adjust to this strange environment. At least I knew them. I could play with them. There also were girls from the Mexican school who'd made it into Mrs. Smith's class. I was glad they did. I could ask these familiar kids to help me when I didn't understand Mrs. Smith's instructions.

Everything was in English. Not wanting to draw attention to my lack of English skills, I mostly stuck to myself. My survival depended on knowing who I could ask for help and who to avoid. I would have to figure out the lay of the land before I made any attempts at befriending strangers. The white kids were friendly enough, but they stuck together, just like the Hispanic kids stuck to their own. We played separately, we sat in the lunchroom apart, and we befriended kids of our own color. I supposed it was the whole notion of safety in numbers. This behavior would become the norm for us, or at least for me, for the rest of my school years.

In the first two weeks, while playing outside during recess, I met Bobby. He was a white kid dressed in typical cowboy rancher-style clothing. He wore boots, jeans, a cowboy shirt with snap-on buttons, and a belt with his name engraved in the back. The buckle, sparkling in the sunlight, showed a cowboy roping a calf. His name was engraved on the back of it because, as he explained, "I won it in a rodeo contest." I didn't know what kind of contest gave away belt buckles. But it didn't matter. He seemed friendly enough. Bobby was about my height, and we both weighed in at ninety pounds. We weren't big kids, but we weren't puny either. His hat made him look taller. Not many kids dressed like Bobby.

"Do you want to play on the bars?" he asked as he came up beside me.

"How do you play?" I replied.

"Well, you jump, grab the bars, and try to push your partner off the bars by using your legs."

"Then what happens?"

"If you fall first, I win. But if I fall first, you win."

Sounded simple enough.

"Okay! Let's do it!" I said.

We played that game for what seemed like hours, laughing so hard we sometimes slipped off the monkey bars without grabbing each other. In a matter of days, we became best friends. We would look for each other anytime we were in PE or at recess. We would even eat together. Some of my barrio friends started calling me gringo.

"Why you hanging out with that gringo, gringo?"

"Think you're too good to hang out with us?"

"You are nothing but a smelly gringo."

"You can't play with us anymore, gringo!"

"Shut up. *Son una bola de cabrones* calling me a gringo. I don't want to play with you, *cabrones*," I said when such comments were made. I walked away, thinking this was not the way it was supposed to be. *Am I being a traitor?* I wondered. *Am I wrong in befriending a white kid?* I tried to justify my friendship by having a conversation with Bobby.

"Bobby, do you like being my friend?" I asked.

"Sure."

"But do you like being my friend? I mean, do other kids make fun of you for being my friend?"

"I don't have many friends. I have my family, who are my friends. Sometimes I get called names, but I don't let it bother me. I guess it's because of the way I dress. My family owns a ranch, and we're cowboys. I dress like this because I like it."

"So, you want to play?"

He was offering too much information that I wasn't interested in. I just wanted to know if he liked being my friend.

I loved my new school. For once, I was actually having fun learning. In this school, in this class, with my best friend, I was enjoying school. It was a dichotomy, to say the least.

Mrs. Smith made it so stress-free when she called on me to read. She was patient, helping me with words I couldn't sound out or pronounce. She gave me the encouragement I needed. She also made me feel safe from potential ridicule. I'd pronounce words teachers taught me at Butz with an accent, which made it sound wrong. Mrs. Smith would correct me without judgment. It was slow going at first, but because I got encouragement and didn't feel scared or stupid, I found that my confidence grew.

Students were friendly, especially Clara. Clara was a tall, blond, blue-eyed white girl who always matched her clothes with her shoes. She was nice to me. She'd seek me out to tell me about her friends, who she liked, who she didn't, and who liked who. I'd just listen, wondering if it was appropriate for a brown kid to be talking to a white girl. I don't know why I felt this way, but I did.

Should I be walking or sitting with this girl? I'd wonder. *Why am I so uncomfortable? What's so special about me that she has to talk to me?*

What if I don't act right? What if I say something stupid? What if, what if, what if?

As long as I didn't have to say anything, I didn't mind. I wasn't looking for a girlfriend. She wasn't looking for a boyfriend. She was just being friendly. She liked Bobby, and since I hung around with him, maybe she found it easier to connect with him if she talked to me. She never said either way. I just assumed. The three of us would play tetherball or on the swings. In time, I forgot what color their skin was. More importantly, I forgot what color I was. They were my friends, and that was enough for me.

The first month of school was the most enjoyable month for me. I was in a class with smart kids and a wonderful teacher in a nice, clean school.

I remembered people saying, "If it's too good to be true, don't be surprised when it isn't." That saying came to mind when the principal announced to the teachers that he needed to balance classes. That meant some teachers had more kids than others, and he needed to make sure all classes were about the same in number. Or at least, that was what he told us. On Friday of the fourth week of school, I was told I would be moving to a different class because Mrs. Smith's class was overloaded.

I was devastated. I wanted to cry.

I was yanked out of Mrs. Smith's class and thrown into Mrs. Bull's class. That wasn't her real name, although she looked like one. She was big, fat, ugly, and mean looking. She sported large black-framed glasses that made her look like a raccoon. Her hair was always in a bun piled high, and she always wore a dress that ballooned out when she waddled around the classroom, along with the biggest shoes I'd ever seen on a woman. Size 12.

She would eye us with piercing brown eyes. I was afraid of her. I'd never been afraid of a teacher before. Well, except maybe the psycho gym teacher who talked funny when he got excited.

Mrs. Bull was no Mrs. Smith.

I had difficulty adjusting to the new class environment. It wasn't long before I noticed something odd. The kids in this room were mostly Hispanic kids. There were more kids I knew from Butz in this class. What I didn't know at the time was this school operated on a practice of homogeneously grouping students according to ability. The practice, inherently flawed, called for three groupings of children. Those who were super smart were placed in what was known as advanced classes. Those with average ability were placed in regular classes. And those with below-average ability were placed in basic classes. Apparently, I was not supposed to be in Mrs. Smith's class, since she had a regular class. Those students were of average intelligence. According to the tests, I wasn't of average intelligence.

The educational administrators in Fort Stockton and across the entire nation believed that students should be grouped according to intellectual ability as measured by some standardized test. This supposedly made it easier for teachers to teach. Educational experts also said it was easier for students to learn. Unfortunately, I must not have done well on those tests, since they were all in English. So I was placed in a basic class with Mrs. Bull. She had the *tontos*—the slow students, who were separated from those who'd scored better on these tests.

Twenty-five years later, the same educational experts pronounced that this practice invariably hurt students.

The Supreme Court had determined that segregating students of color from the white students—who were more affluent, had more resources, and had been born into English-speaking families—was unconstitutional. However, once kids were in an "integrated" school, discrimination continued out of sight of parents and those who advocated for equity in schools. Hiding inside classroom walls, this school system continued to practice educational discrimination. This experience would create a lasting disadvantage for me and others like me.

Later in my career, I began to understand the societal and cultural issues facing the American education system. Behind the movement to desegregate the schools was the determination of those advocating for equal opportunities via civil rights. The sacrifice made by thousands of African Americans during this time paved the way for other minorities to demand equity in all aspects of life. It marked the beginning of a long struggle to dismantle long-standing practices that hurt students educationally. The war on inequality would continue to be fought well into the twenty-first century.

I was hurt and angry with this change. I just wanted to quit school or run away from it. I didn't want to hurt my mother's feelings with such awkward thinking, but this change affected me tremendously. When kids are unhappy in school, they tend to seek ways to cover up their disappointment or lack of educational ability. For many students, lashing out, causing problems in class, or finding any excuse not to participate in the learning adds to a teacher's stress level. Being unhappy leads to stupid actions on the part of the student.

I was there.

I was now back to being with the old barrio gang. Talacho ("Pickax"), a distant cousin of mine who was born with an odd-looking head, and Troy the stutterer were in this class. Manuela, the one we called "Horse," was there too. She still smelled of bologna when she'd sweat. Roy, or "La Marana" ("The Pig"), made it into the basic class. There were no more than five white kids in this class of twenty-five. The caliber of students who made up Mrs. Bull's class had little to be desired, and Mrs. Bull knew it. She wasn't happy with the number of dummies in her class. That was her problem. I had other things to worry about.

When you hang out with troublemakers, you invariably adhere to making bad choices. Some of those choices lead to trouble.

Mrs. Bull liked her bulletin boards. She kept a small box of thumbtacks on her desk to use when posting things—not necessarily students' work, but pre-made posters of places she had visited. She had pictures of national parks, cities, museums, and such. There were pictures of family and friends she traveled with. Under each picture, she would pin the name of the place. I didn't know any of them except for Disneyland. I had seen commercials on TV. Each morning, she would start by showing us words describing the adventures she'd had visiting these places. During our lifetime, most of us would never see these exotic places except through her pictures.

The trouble started out as a joke.

"Look what I got," Troy said, opening his hand just enough for me to see. He was holding some thumbtacks.

"Where did you get those?" I asked.

"I took them from her desk when she wasn't looking. I'm going to spin them like tiny tops when we get outside."

"I want some too! Hey, what if I put them on someone's chair and see if they sit on them?" I said.

We giggled.

Troy and I walked out to the sidewalk and started playing. By taking the tack's point between our fingers and twisting, we could make the tack spin. We were at the end of the walkway while all the kids were on the playground. I didn't think anyone had seen us playing with our newfound toys.

"Let's put them on Mrs. Bull's chair," Troy blurted out, smiling as if he had come up with the greatest idea ever.

"She'll sit on them and poke a hole in her big butt!" I said, laughing. "I think that is the best idea you've had since you were born!"

But we needed more tacks. Noticing Mrs. Bull walking away from her class and toward the teacher's lounge, we saw our opportunity to steal the tacks. Once she disappeared from sight, I snuck back in and took a handful of tacks. Halfway out the door, I turned around, placed three on Mrs. Bull's chair, pushed the chair back under the desk, and ran outside.

Troy and I went around the corner of the building, peered out the side, and waited for the Bull to come back. She went into the room, and a few seconds later, she was storming out like a raging bull, heading directly to the principal's office. Boy, was she mad! She must have sat on the thumbtacks.

I held my hand over my mouth to keep from laughing too loudly. We waited. Finally, she headed back with a face the color of canned turnips. Yelling for all the students to come back in from the playground, she looked mad. I thought it was the end of that story, but to my dismay, she started in on everyone.

"I want to know who came back to the classroom after I released you for recess."

No one said a word.

"Someone came back to the classroom, took something, and left the door open. Who did it?"

Silence.

"I'm having you go to the principal's office by twos, and you are going to tell him who came into the room without permission."

She was plainly upset. I looked over at Troy, put my finger to my lips, and motioned for him to keep his mouth shut.

I don't know how it happened, but someone must have seen us playing with the tacks. That someone immediately spilled the beans. It wasn't long before I was called to the principal's office. I thought that if I kept my cool, I could get away with this.

"Take a seat," the secretary said in a monotone as I arrived. "Mr. Henslee will be right with you."

Moments later, the principal called me into his office. He didn't waste any time getting started.

"Mr. Alfaro, I understand you took some thumbtacks. Is that right?" he mumbled under his breath. "Did you place them on your teacher's chair for her to sit on?" He looked at me suspiciously.

I stood in front of his desk, pretending to be shocked by such accusations. I stared at him with that "I don't know what you're talking about" look. I shook my head in silence.

How could anyone have known? I wondered. *We were careful not to be seen. Who told? Who saw us?* All these questions lined my young, feeble mind. But I said nothing.

"Well, I happen to know that you did it," he proclaimed, looking me straight in the eyes.

"I didn't—

"Don't lie to me! You will get double punishment," he threatened.

"I didn't do any—"

"Okay, Mrs. Jones! Bring Troy in."

There it was. Troy the stutterer. *That blabber-mouthing little piece of dog dung!* I thought. *He squealed!*

We were caught. There was no point in delaying the inevitable. Troy admitted he and I had taken the thumbtacks and placed them on our teacher's chair. At least he didn't put the entire blame on me alone. By this point, I was shaking, fearful of the actions to be taken by this man called the principal. I couldn't run. I couldn't hide. My shoulders slumped as if the air had been sucked out of me.

"You boys could have really hurt her. Thank goodness she only sat on one. I won't ask you why you did it, but after I speak to your parents, you will be placed on probation for six weeks."

"What is that?" asked Troy.

"Each of you will get three swats with the paddle. If you get into any trouble within six weeks, I'll double the paddling. Understand? Now, who goes first?"

I'd never admitted to the crime. But I went first. I grabbed the front of the desk and stuck my ass out like I was instructed. The first hit almost buckled my knees. I didn't cry. I grabbed the desk tighter, waiting for the second and third, which came in rapid succession. Tears flowed out of my eye sockets on their own.

I kept it clean for six weeks.

But that episode didn't go well for me for the rest of the year. Mrs. Bull did me no favors. She'd call on me and hit me over the head when I couldn't pronounce a word during oral reading. Embarrassing. She was determined to fail me. I knew it. I could feel it. Many times, she just ignored Troy and me when we asked for help.

"If you boys can think of ugly games to play, then you can figure this out by yourselves. Now, go back to your seats, and don't come back up here," she'd say.

I didn't blame her. That stunt was meant to be funny. I didn't think about her feelings because I was so consumed by mine. We were never asked to be first in line or clean the erasers. And we were never first when it was time to go to PE or recess. There wasn't much I could do but keep my head down for six weeks. I felt her form of punishment was worse than taking a spanking from Mr. Henslee. If I didn't regress educationally, I did regress in my thinking that all white people were good. I suppose I deserved it.

Oh well.

The year went by ever so slowly. Mrs. Bull forgot about our prank, eventually assisting me when I asked. But she was still leery and continued to look at me with suspicion. However, within time, that sneer disappeared as well.

Low Expectation

T rying to understand the civil rights movement or how it affected us wasn't a concern for people my age. I was in a new environment, and that was perplexing enough. I really liked Alamo Elementary even though I was moved to a class I didn't like. I liked being around white kids. They were interesting. I didn't feel the bigotry from them, and they were different. Some knew some Spanish and tried very hard to accept us by speaking to us in our own language.

Even though I knew we were different from them, I was beginning to question other things—mostly adult behaviors. I'd ask myself, *What do the adults see in us that is so different from the white students other than language? Are these differences perceived, or are they real? What are the differences between brown and white students? Why are some not very friendly toward the Mexican kids? Why do they call us Mexicans?* All my siblings and I, like many kids at that time, had been born in Fort Stockton. Not in Mexico. *Why did it take so long for us to be admitted to a nice school? Why were we placed in basic classes? When something goes wrong, why are we looked upon with suspicion?*

It took a long time to adjust to a culture considered to be better than ours.

At home, the days were going by faster than usual. Eventually, I acclimated to the new environment. Attempting to assimilate into a culture I didn't fully understand made me realize just how much English I was speaking. Now I was careful to enunciate words correctly and not butcher the language. However, the educational system made it difficult for me to fully adjust. Even though I was only ten, I was aware of discriminatory practices, whether intentional or not, coming from adults. I could see the difference in the treatment of students. White students were rarely sent to the office for discipline. And the poverty difference stood out more. I struggled to fully understand why that was.

I still spoke Spanish with my friends in all places except the classroom. We were never allowed to speak in our native tongue there. If we were caught, it could mean a spanking, a snarky remark, an abusive slap on the side of the head, or a sneering look. Being brown and poor added to the subtle, unfair treatment we received from teachers. Some, but not all, made us feel inferior.

This resonated with me because of one unusual experience.

The librarian asked the advanced and regular students to write a one-page book report on their favorite author. They were taught how to do research. In contrast, the same librarian asked our class to draw a picture of our favorite book and color it. A stark difference in expectations.

When teachers went on a break to get away from the kids for a few minutes, we went to the library. Library time was meant for reading, but I knew better. Library didn't demand reading. The librarian—who was a typical-looking librarian, with glasses down her nose, hair in a bun, and a sweater—wasn't much of a teacher. She taught us how to find books by using something she called the Dewey Decimal System. It was easy if you knew your alphabet. I'd find books with pictures—lots of pictures. I wasn't advancing in my reading like I wanted to. I still detested it, so I'd spend my time with magazines or picture books. If we looked busy pretending to read, it was an easy S. Knowing we were from the basic class, the librarian didn't demand much. One day, she came up with a creative idea.

"Pick the book you like the best, and draw a picture of it. I want you to paint or draw a picture of what the book is about. The best pictures are going to be displayed here, and I will give ribbons to those who win. Now, get started. You have two weeks to complete this task."

I picked a book with a baby reindeer galloping through the forest. I did like to draw. Some would call it doodling. Drawing took me places I could only imagine. Scenery of mountains covered with snow, trees lining the background, and little animals leaving footprints filled my head with adventure. It didn't take long for me to draw the cover of the book. I handed in the final copy, proud of my work.

A few weeks after this assignment, as the class walked in the library, I saw my picture sitting high on top of one of the bookshelves. I was announced the winner and given a blue ribbon and a pat on the back. That picture didn't come down all year. It was one of my proudest moments as an amateur artist. I made an S on my report card for library. A proud moment for me.

Bobby and I continued to enjoy our playtime during recess, although we didn't have enough of it for those joyous struggles on the monkey bar. Since we didn't have the same recess period, it was getting more and more difficult to visit with him. If, by chance, we found ourselves in the cafeteria, we'd sit together and talk. Our conversations weren't overly complex. He enjoyed talking about what he did with his family on weekends. He'd talk about the rodeo, riding horses, and roping calves. The hunting, fishing, and exploring around the ranch sounded so enticing. I just listened. I envied him.

With the passing days, the grass turned brown, and the warmth of the summer disappeared into vestiges of cooler days.

Trees were turning into fall colors, shedding their leaves with the surge of northern winds. Thanksgiving was right around the corner, finally giving us all a break from Mrs. Bull. That year, Christmas arrived with a very cold snap that kept us indoors for most of winter break. Besides, there wasn't much to do during cold winters. Going outside was not an option because not everybody had a coat. We never ventured out to any place of interest. Having kids get sick was terrifying for Pino and another reason to keep us indoors. Her terror rested on the fact that if we got sick, taking us to the doctor was not in the cards. A visit to the doctor required blood. We had to be bleeding profusely to see a doctor because doctors were expensive. There was no such thing as insurance for the poor. A cold or the flu was fixed with Vicks or Mentholatum. For everything else, there was kerosene.

The semester ended before we left for the Christmas holidays, which meant it was report card time. We brought them home so parents could review, sign, and send them back. After seeing mine, Mom was concerned I wasn't doing well, so she had Nancy do some tutoring. It didn't help. This was the least of my interests. Holidays were for doing the things I wanted to do, not for doing homework. I neglected the time Nancy set aside for tutoring.

"I don't need your tutoring," I exclaimed after a few minutes.

"Mom said you needed help, so just do the words."

"I told you. I'm not doing it. I don't need to."

"That's fine. You're too stupid to learn anyway."

And with that, we parted ways.

The Christmas of 1962 brought few presents. Everyone got at least one thing, even if we didn't ask for it. Toys were reserved for the younger kids. I either got underwear or socks. If I was lucky, I might get at least one thing I did ask for. Every year, I'd write to Santa, as required by teachers, asking for coats for my sisters, nothing for my brothers, and a set of colored pencils with a drawing notebook for me. Ever since I'd won first place for the library drawing, I wanted to become an artist. I also asked Santa for a diamond ring. Don't ask why I wanted a diamond ring. It was probably a status thing. Those who had diamonds weren't poor.

Santa lost his hearing that year. Or so I thought. Somehow, the man with the red suit heard I wanted colored pencils and a drawing notebook, and he delivered. Colored pencils, Can you believe that? I'd seen students with them, so I knew they existed. To pass the time, I got into drawing during the break. But that hobby didn't last long.

Mischief

B efore leaving for the holidays, I'd overheard some of the boys talking about asking Santa for a go-cart. I didn't know what it was, but it sounded interesting. Sitting in front of the TV one day, I saw go-carts being advertised. They were the in thing for Christmas that year. Sleek, fast, and expensive, this motorized car could go a hundred times faster than a car. You could win races if you owned one of these. They were cool to drive. The TV said so.

I wanted one. But I couldn't understand how anyone could afford such a wonderful piece of machinery. While Pino and Chuy were at work, my face was glued to the TV set as I watched go-cart commercials. I knew I wasn't going to get one, so I decided maybe I could build one.

The shed not only provided some respite from the cold wind, but it also contained numerous items of interest—tools, small motors, old tricycles, tires, lumber, and an assortment of odds and ends. In the middle of the shed sat an antique barber's chair. I dusted off the chair, sat on it, and pretended I was *The Thinker* from our history book. It was quiet in the shed, and I could think. No one was asking me to take care of the young 'uns. No one could pester the thinker.

But instead of using this time to reflect on schoolwork, I used it to think of building what I couldn't afford. After a few minutes of pondering, I fell on an idea. I'd seen Dad work on these small electrical motors in this very garage. He would use them to grind garden tools, knives, and an assortment of metal objects. I knew how they worked. Don't ask me how I knew, but I did.

The picture of a go-cart emerged in my mind. I cut a board in the shape of a rectangle, built the sides up with two-by-fours, took apart the tires from the tricycle, and hammered and screwed all the pieces together. I took an old lawnmower, removed all the wheels, and attached them to the bottom of the rectangular board.

After a few hours of work, I stepped back to admire my creation. It looked like Frankenstein, but cuter. By the next day, I was almost finished with it. The thing didn't have a steering mechanism. Figuring out how to tie the tricycle handlebars to the front wheels proved daunting. I took the electric motor off the table and assembled a wooden box at the rear of the cart to hold it. After some creative maneuvering, I had the motor strapped to the cart with a fan belt attached to the back wheels.

Where am I going to get power to run this thing? I wondered. Three extension cords hung by the door. I connected them together, which gave me enough length for the go-cart to travel in a circle with a circumference of about forty feet.

"I think this will work," I told myself with a sliver of confidence. The steering problem still puzzled me. I needed a welding machine. I'd never used one, but I had an idea of how it worked. Asking Fidel and Sammy presented no results. It was probably a good thing they didn't know. No telling what damage I could have caused.

Finally, I asked them to come back and look at my go-cart. So we all ran to my house.

"This thing's not going anywhere," Fidel commented, looking dumbfounded. "This doesn't even look like a go-cart! It has no steering wheel. How you gonna to steer it?"

"Get in and hold on to the sides," I told Sammy as I pulled the electric cord toward the electrical panel on the side of the house. "I'm going to plug it into the wall. You can't go forward or backward because the cord is not long enough, so you are going to have to go in circles! Fidel, turn the wheels so they go left in a circle."

Then I plugged the cord into the socket and yelled, "Sammy, HOLD ON!"

The motor fired up, and the go-cart jumped three feet and stopped. Electricity shot a spark flying across the panel, burning out all the fuses to the house. The sockets were black with soot from sparks flying all over the place.

What could have been a hell of a fire, with God's good graces, didn't happen. The house was an all-wood structure! I tried to unplug the cord, but the heat from the shock melted the ends into the socket. Oh shit!

The boys, laughing and pointing at my creation, were not impressed.

"You almost burned the house down!" cried Fidel. "I'm going home. Come on, Sammy. Let's get out of here before Chuy shows up."

The house not burning down promised I was safe from a beating that would have easily turned into murder. Chuy would have beaten me to within an inch of my life. But I had to find a way to fix the fuses in the electrical panel. After taking my prized creation apart, board by board, I put everything back the way it had been and went looking for pennies. I had seen Chuy put a penny in the socket where the fuse went in. This would complete an electrical circuit and bring back the lights.

I didn't find any pennies, which was a good thing. I probably would have electrocuted myself. That would not have been good. But how was I going to get rid of the burned area around the fuse box? It was all black. That puzzled me.

Mom got home first, and I immediately beat everybody to the punch.

"Mom, I connected a cord to the socket outside. It sparked, and the fuses burned out. I don't know what happened."

I didn't tell her about the go-cart. My brothers and sisters were not aware of anything other than that the lights had gone out, which was a usual occurrence.

Mom saved my life. She gave me two new fuses with instructions on how to replace them. Once I did, I turned on the electric handle, and the lights came back on. It would be days before Chuy noticed the burned section around the fuse box.

My days as a wannabe race car driver were over.

There was plenty of time during the holidays to play with whatever toys we got—that is, if we were lucky to get anything. One Saturday proved to be a cold day. Even with the sun shining, it was still cold. Several of us decided to investigate a place the older kids called *la calechera*—a pond not much bigger than half a football field and surrounded by brush that grew only in the desert. It was about three miles from our house. This remote place was outside the city limits. From there, we could see the Marathon Highway and an occasional truck or car coming into town. The radio station, KFST, was out there somewhere, not too far from our destination.

We headed there on a pretend vacation. Thinking of camping out away from home, we decided it was to be our Christmas vacation.

Carrying jugs of water, potatoes, knives, spoons, forks, and butter, the seven boys and girls marched through cacti and mesquite trees. Someone even brought a skillet, hoping to cook some potatoes for us to eat once we explored the area. While the older kids explored, my sister Nancy was giving instructions to Fidel, Sammy, and me.

"You need to find some firewood so we can start a fire," she said.

Finding dry wood was not a problem. Shrugs, grass, and trees out there were drier than usual.

"Bring more firewood!" she hollered as she cut up the potatoes, skin and all. She was determined to make lunch.

We piled rocks in a circle, then brought twigs, branches, and anything else we could find. While the potatoes were cooking, someone came up with a game to play. This game, Stomp It, required dexterity, speed, and accuracy. Who came up with the game, I'll never know. To play, Nancy lit some matches and threw them on the dry grass. Once it got going, Sammy, Fidel, and I stomped out the fire with our feet. We did this several times until she decided that stomping out the fire too soon was not appealing to her sense of daring.

"Let it get bigger, then you can stomp it out," she declared. She threw the match into the grass, and when it got going, she shouted, "NOW!"

The fire got too big, engulfing shrubs that were close to the surrounding tall trees. We stomped as fast as our little feet could stomp, but to no avail. The fire grew, sending billowing dark grayish smoke higher into the sky. The bigger kids, seeing the smoke, ran back and yanked some of us away from the burning shrubs. The intensity of the fire created a whirlwind of heat.

The fire was out of control and headed toward the radio station.

"Run!" someone yelled.

We picked up what little we'd brought and started running back home, dodging mesquite branches and jumping over cacti. On the run back toward the neighborhood, we were dropping potatoes, pans, and water bottles. Anything that was holding us down landed on the desert floor. The older kids didn't wait for anybody. It was every man for himself. I didn't look back. I just kept running.

Somewhere between la calechera and the house, curiosity got the better of me. I stopped, looked back, and watched the smoke rising high above the ground. It wasn't coming toward us.

We ran the three miles back to the neighborhood in record time. As soon as we got to the edge of it, we dispersed in all directions. Nancy, Fidel, Sammy, and I lived closer than the others, so we went inside the house and grabbed glasses of water. Washing down the dirt and smoke lingering in our throats felt good. Through the back door, we could see smoke curling farther and farther into the sky.

Apparently, the radio station had seen the smoke and called the fire department. We were standing outside looking at the smoke when the police drove by. The car stopped and backed up to where we were standing. The officer called to us. I walked over. Jesse followed, wearing nothing but his underwear.

"Don't say nothing," I told him.

"Did you see anyone coming from the direction of the fire?" the officer asked.

"No, sir." We all shook our heads.

"Have ya'll been down there?"

"No, sir."

"Someone said there were a bunch of kids running this way."

"It wasn't us, sir," I said, trying to keep my voice calm. I could feel my legs shaking. What if he suspected us? We would all go to that jailhouse my father frequented.

"You need to stay away from the area. The fire is still burning."

"Yes, sir!"

He drove away. We looked at each other, flabbergasted and surprised. The police officer probably needed glasses or something. If he'd seen the soot on our shoes or noticed the smell of smoke on our clothes, he didn't say a word. We were lucky he didn't take us in for starting a fire where we had no business being.

I didn't hear the word *pyromaniac* until many years later when some kid tried to burn down the high school when I was a student there. The word brought back memories of the fire we'd started and how easily we could have burned down the only radio station for miles around.

Once we realized we were free and clear from the danger of going to jail, I was hoping school would start soon. We were too dangerous to be left running loose.

El Cucuy

C huy bought an old Chevy pickup truck, and on weekends when he didn't work, he'd take Mom to her day shift at Railsback Restaurant. I would ask if I could go, but my requests always fell on deaf ears.

One ordinary Saturday morning, right before we were to go back to school after Christmas break, Chuy asked out of the blue if I wanted to go. He'd been listening! I was excited and feeling special. Not the special ed kind—just special.

On this trip, I learned Mom was a dishwasher working in the kitchen. I'd always imagined her as the pretty young lady taking orders, balancing plates of food, and delivering them to customers. Where in the world did I get this image of her as a waitress?

TV.

Railsback Restaurant, like many other small-town restaurants, had the look and feel of an old-fashioned diner, just like the ones you'd see in a Norman Rockwell painting. It had tall picture windows in the front, brick around the sides and back, and strange animal heads hanging all over the inside walls. After we dropped Mother off in the back, Dad and I went inside and sat at the counter. A white woman came out and asked us what we wanted. Dad ordered a cup of coffee with some toast. I got an orange Coke.

"What kind of Coke do you want?" she asked me. Every soda was a Coke in our world. So, if we wanted an orange drink, we asked for an orange Coke. Funny.

This was a big event for me, to be sitting at a restaurant and drinking an orange Coke. I reached over, took a slice of Chuy's toast, spread butter on it, and took a bite. It was good. I felt important and all grown up to be mimicking the adults in the room—how they sat, talked, and looked at one another. Sipping on my orange Coke, I marveled at the plates full of food coming out from the kitchen. I wasn't hungry. I'd had my cups of coffee and stale cornbread from this very restaurant at home.

I looked around the place, taking it all in. Then, my eyes rested on the kitchen door. The metal door would swing back and forth as the waitress picked up customer plates from the kitchen and brought them out. The door had a small round window pretty much at eye level with adults. Those coming and going from opposite directions had a clear view of each other, thus avoiding a collision. Because these outings were few and far between, my wandering eyes took everything in, prompting questions in my mind. On this occasion, I wasn't coming up with good answers. So, instead of inventing some, I asked Chuy.

"Where does all this food come from?"

Chuy didn't answer.

"Who cooks it?"

No answer.

"Where do these people come from?"

Ignoring me, Chuy kept talking to a man he obviously knew.

"How can they eat so much? Who is that man staring at us?"

On the other side of the metal door, a man kept looking out and quickly disappearing from view. His head slightly leaning to one side, with one eye closed and the other barely open, he kept staring at us. I quietly looked away, hoping the man had not seen me staring back at him. He reminded me of an ogre. Igor the Ogre. I had read something in school about an ogre—a legendary monster usually depicted as a large, hideous manlike being that eats ordinary human beings, especially infants and children.

When I was little and not wanting to behave, Mom would threaten me with El Cucuy, the boogeyman of legend. I was told he lived in a cave at the top of the mountains south of Fort Stockton. When children refused to go to bed or were being disobedient, he would come down to murder or kidnap and eat them. I couldn't tell whether this man on the other side of the door was El Cucuy or the one-eyed ogre. Either way, he was scary enough for me to want to know more. Only then would I decide how many Hail Marys and Our Fathers I'd have to say at night. I pulled on Chuy's shirt cuff to get his attention.

"That man is looking at us, Chuy," I whispered, looking in the direction of the door through the corner of my eye.

Dad turned around, looked toward the kitchen door window, and laughed. "*Horale! Ese vato es Miguel.* He works here," he said, waving at the man.

"Why does he look like that?"

"He was born that way."

"What do you mean? He was born with one eye?"

"No, he was born with two eyes, but only one works. He also can't talk very well, so he doesn't say much," Chuy said, looking at the door as another one of his acquaintances came into the restaurant.

"What's he doing there?"

"He works here. You will see him come out when customers leave. He will pick up the dishes, clean the table, and arrange the chairs back the way they were."

"Does he get paid for doing this?"

"Of course. *No seas pendejo*." ("Don't be stupid.")

I didn't like the fact that Igor the Ogre, or El Cucuy, worked in the restaurant with Mom. I didn't say much after being called pendejo, so I kept my mouth shut and longed to get out before "it" came out to clean tables and pick up dishes. I didn't want to see what the rest of his body looked like. I was scared for everyone. I tried very hard to suppress my anxiety.

When Dad got out his pocket change to pay, I bounced off the stool and ran to the truck, happy to be outside and out of reach of the monster. I was going to have nightmares. I knew I was going to have nightmares. I made the sign of the cross and got in the truck.

My fear of ogres, goblins, old pigs, monsters, *la llorona*, and all scary legends was Chuy's fault. At night, to keep us calmed down, he would tell us stories of wicked people haunting the streets of Sahuayo. The story of the woman dressed in red was his favorite.

"She would only come out at night," he would tell us. "When the moon cast its shadow on the deserted streets. She wore a red dress, tattered and worn down. She always wore this dress. Blood red. She had no face, but she could see you. Especially young children out at night playing after hours. The streets were dark. When the full moon casts a faint light from above, the windows are boarded to keep out the mysteries of the night."

We would listen in terror as he continued. "She would walk the street, and all you could hear was the tapping of one shoe on the cobblestones. *Clack, clack, clack*. Her moans cried out for her lost child, who was taken by someone living close by. Who could it be? Was it us? Was she looking for one of us? *Clack, clack, clack*. She wandered the streets moaning. Ooooh. Ohhhh. Oooohh. There she was, looking through the window!"

We kids would all get closer together, hovering under a blanket for support. But Chuy would just keep going.

"She had no face. No eyes. No nose. But she could see by touching each child with her long fingers, scratching their eyes, if it was not her child. *Clack, clack, clack.* She opened the window ever so slowly until she was RIGHT BEHIND YOU! LOOK! THERE SHE IS!"

Chuy would pull the blanket away from us. Screaming, huddled close to each other, and hoping not to be taken by the woman made me pee. Not much, but enough for someone to see through my jeans.

I had nightmares for days after these stories. To this day, I'll bypass a horror movie any day of the week. Nope. That's not for me. I blame Chuy.

Life Goes On

The holiday season was over, and I'd prepared myself for the second half of the school year. The country celebrated the dawn of a new year—1963. A Tuesday. I watched the countdown on the small black-and-white TV set. I saw the New Year's ball coming down the tower in New York City's Times Square while my siblings slept. Not wanting to wake anybody up, I kept the volume down to almost zero. This was the most excitement the Alfaro household was going to have. Because we were living from paycheck to paycheck, celebrating New Year's Day didn't happen. To us, it was just another regular day.

In January of that year, "Go Away Little Girl," by Steve Lawrence, became my favorite sing-along, and "Limbo Rock," by Chubby Checker, became my favorite dance song. I didn't have to know how to dance to do the limbo rock. Some of the kids in the neighborhood liked to limbo because it only required a stick—usually some mom's broom—held up by two people while the others formed a line and tried to go under the broom by leaning back without falling. The stick would be lowered each time someone went under. It was so much fun that we would do this until someone fell flat on their back, creating a hilarious moment for the rest of us.

"Big Girls Don't Cry," by the Four Seasons, "Return to Sender," by Elvis Presley, and "Bobby's Girl," by Marcie Blane, became the girls' most loved songs. The tunes were catchy, giving anyone with half a voice an opportunity to sing along.

Much of the news in the United States was dominated by the actions of civil rights activists as well as news of those who opposed them. The US role in Vietnam was growing at an alarming rate, along with the costs of that involvement. It was also the year four long-haired British musicians started a phenomenon known as Beatlemania, and President John F. Kennedy visited West Berlin, delivering one of his most famous anti-communist speeches. The telephone company introduced the first push-button telephones, thus moving away from the bulky rotary ones. A first-class postage stamp cost five cents, and the average cost of a new home was about $19,000, still too expensive for most Americans. A gallon of milk was forty-nine cents, and a gallon of gasoline averaged thirty cents nationally. The federal minimum wage was only $1.25, making it extremely difficult for poor people to enjoy luxury items, like toilet paper, food, or a new car, even though a new car or truck cost a little over $3,000. Above all, while I didn't know there was a University of Texas at Austin, the tuition to attend one year of classes as a resident was only $100. The population of the world was 3.2 billion, less than half of what it is today. I was getting older but not wiser. I didn't fully realize the country was going through some critical cultural and economic changes that would eventually dictate part of my life.

The two weeks of winter break went by faster than expected, and the Alfaro kids were back in school. How Chuy and Pino were able to keep us fed and clothed at a dollar twenty-five an hour was a shocker to me. We did get some new clothes for Christmas, making the return to school bearable. It was January of 1963, and I was more excited about the new clothes I'd be wearing than going back to Mrs. Bull's class. I was ready to see my friends who lived in other parts of town that were far enough from my house to prevent me from seeing them unless we were at school. I was excited to see Bobby, my cowboy friend.

January was typically cold and dreary, but there were days when cloudless blue skies allowed the sun to shed warmth while we were on the playground. On this type of day, the teacher allowed us to go outside to soak up some sun and expend some energy. I ran to the monkey bars, looking for Bobby. I waited for what seemed an eternity, but he didn't appear. So I finally gave up and diverted my attention to a tetherball game going on at the other end of the playground. I played with the other kids but took breaks to scan the playground for Bobby. He never showed up.

A week went by. No Bobby.

Horrible news finally came. A few miles up the Marathon Highway, closest to the mountains that lay on the southern horizon, ranchers leased their property to mule deer hunters who came from all over the state. Deer hunting season always came right after Thanksgiving and typically ended on December 13. Since many hunters and their friends were off work during the Christmas holidays, this was one of the biggest sporting events for them. Bobby's family were among them. The details of the accident were not revealed until much later. I didn't read it in the newspaper. It wasn't there. I heard it.

Bobby was running after the hunting truck and holding his rifle by the barrel. When he jumped on the back of the truck, the rifle hit the bumper, firing off a round and killing him instantly.

The news of his death terrified and shocked me. *How could an eleven-year-old kid be out hunting in the first place?* I asked myself. *What was he doing with a deer rifle? Why was he allowed to use one at his age?*

I was devastated. I could not believe that someone so close to me was gone. Forever. I had not experienced death before, which made it difficult to comprehend. It didn't seem possible.

Thoughts of death and dying saddened my heart and soul for many days after. I couldn't believe my best friend was dead.

I didn't attend his funeral because I didn't know about his passing until much later. I walked around the playground, thinking about how young he was. *What a shame. Where was God? Why didn't He protect him? What am I going to do now?*

East Hill Cemetery was regarded as the "whites only" cemetery in Fort Stockton. It was located due east of town. It was here where Bobby's body was laid to rest. I knew where the cemetery was since we used to pass it on our way to 7-Mile Mesa, but I had never entered its stone walls. The wall surrounding the cemetery was built to keep the living out after hours. The arched gates were always locked, which I thought unusual. It was totally opposite from the Mexican cemetery, which was open to all visitors all day and night.

Sixty-three years later, as a grown man, I finally entered East Hill Cemetery and looked for his grave. A lot can disappear, even tombstones. I didn't find it, but standing inside the walls, I took a moment to finally say goodbye to Bobby.

Life, as unpredictable as it is, must go on. Even though such a loss can be emotionally difficult, one has to adjust to it. As a youngster, I was confused. I wondered why God took away someone so small and kindhearted. The more I thought about it, the more confusing it became. At times, while playing on the monkey bars, I'd look for him. I'd forget his absence was real. Sadness would bring a shudder of disbelief. But somehow, I managed to move on, letting Bobby's image fade away with the years. It took time to forget, but I did.

School activities became my distraction. PE was one. Our coach, a big white guy with too much energy, made PE fun. I didn't have to try hard to earn an S for *satisfactory*. If we could breathe, we'd pass the class with flying colors. I liked PE and the coach. He was young and eager to teach us different sports.

Always challenging us to run faster, jump higher, and hit balls farther, he was blessed with more energy than any adult I knew. He taught us the rules for soccer, baseball, basketball, and boxing. I liked to play team sports, but when it came to boxing, I drew the line. I was a little too timid, preferring to hug rather than fight. I'd seen boxers get the hell beaten out of them, and I wanted no part of that sport.

But one day, the PE teacher announced we were going to learn to box. He called it a sport. I failed to see anything sporty in boxing, and I wanted to tell him so. But courage was not my strongest asset either.

"You need to find a partner. When I call your name, you and your partner will come to the ring, put on your gloves, and start boxing like I showed you," he proclaimed.

Felix was in my class. With a hunched stature much like an old man's, he seemed a likely candidate to partner with. So, when the coach asked us to grab a partner, I moved over to him, saying, "Let's be partners, okay?" Felix lived farther north of town. And while I'd talked to him on occasion, we really didn't hang. Much later, after telling my account of the boxing match to my father, I learned Felix was a second cousin on my mother's side.

He was shorter than I. His puny physique made him stand out. I figured if I was going to box someone, it might as well be him. How could anyone that small hurt me with a punch?

Something about Felix should have told me to stay away from him. He looked sinister, like a mobster. Where he lacked in looks, he made up for by showing gangster tendencies. Baggy khaki pants made him look puny. But he wore a red bandana in his back pocket and a sleeveless tank top under his oversized button-down. He wanted people to think he was badass.

I knew better. Some kids called him by his nickname, "Talacho" ("Pickax"), because of his awfully big, protruding forehead. He walked leaning to the right as if his head weighed more on that side. His lopsided appearance was enough to scare anyone.

I waited our turn, nervously biting my fingernails and hoping our time would not come. The kids coming out of the makeshift ring were sweaty with red splotches on their faces from hits. There were no boxing helmets. I kept looking at the clock behind the coach's desk. If it moved faster, the bell would ring, and we'd be safe.

"Felix and Robert. It's your turn," announced the coach.

We got up, got our gloves on, and circled around the ring, sizing each other up. Apparently, we weren't getting into it fast enough to satisfy Coach.

"You guys need to start punching!" he yelled.

I had sixty seconds before the coach rang the bell for us to stop. I thought, *I can do this!* I moved closer toward Felix, covering my face like Coach showed us, and threw a punch at his head. I connected, but his head didn't move! I hit his gloves and tried to move them out of the way so I could hit his head again. Pow! I swung hard, and still his head didn't move. He punched me several times around my belly, but it didn't hurt.

The gloves were getting heavy, and the seconds ticked away slowly. I kept aiming at the side of his head. He swung and got me good on my right kidney, and I almost fell. I was getting mad. I got close, holding up my gloves, which, by this time, weighed a ton. I looked for the right opening to hit him again. I set my footing and punched hard. I got him right in the forehead. He fell. I fell. I was clutching my hand. I'd hit him so hard that my hand throbbed. Hitting his head was like hitting a rock. I just knew Talacho's head had broken my hand. It hurt right through the padding.

Exhausted, we both stood up, shaking. The bell went off. The coach came over to check, making sure we were alright. Now I knew why they called him "Talacho."

This was the first and last boxing match Sugar Ray Robert ever participated in. I knew then that I didn't like being punched anywhere on my body. Not even with padded gloves. Call me a crybaby. I don't care.

Simply Life

E very evening, the war in Vietnam dominated the news with Walter Cronkite. Since the war started, the first thing he reported was the number of young American soldiers killed or missing. This was quickly followed by updates on the fight for civil rights. African Americans continued to demand their right to sit at the front of commuter buses and drink from water fountains that said, "Whites only." They were going into restaurants and diners serving whites only and sitting at the counters or tables, asking to be treated equally. Many were threatened by the KKK or by their own white neighbors. The problems between the two skin colors were escalating in many Southern states, including Texas. The country was at war with itself.

Meanwhile, back in our hood, we carried on with a life of isolationism. These events were so far removed from our daily lives that I didn't make the connection between what was happening in our schools and what was happening around the country. At times, I would question the disparities between us and the white folk, yet I wasn't smart enough or worldly enough to understand the seriousness of the inequities. I thought this was a fight between African Americans and gringos. This was not our fight. The images on TV did not include Hispanics or

Latinos, so I figured, why should we interfere in what is clearly not our business? It would be later in life when I would become a recipient of racist behavior. It would be then that I started rooting for the African Americans and their rights. They were fighting for people of color. I was color.

Whose fault was it? Who was to blame? Was it because there were so few Blacks in our town that racism remained so distant? It was hard to interpret. Looking back, I can see that it did exist, but it was not so noticeable. It was subtle. My parents didn't question the disparities between us and the white kids because they didn't know any better. They didn't see the lack of educational standards being applied to us in comparison to more affluent children. They didn't see the opportunities not available to us.

In the barrio, there were no team sports to participate in after school. We played baseball amongst ourselves in the streets. Our parents didn't sign us up for after-school activities. There were no official Little League baseball games played on a real baseball field. At the elementary level, there were no opportunities for us brownies to join a sports team like tennis, soccer, football, basketball, volleyball, or swimming. There were no leagues of any kind to participate in. We didn't go to summer camp. There were no after-school art classes. When school was out for the day, we all went home to deal with our own issues. We were left out of those activities. Somehow, I found imaginative ways to entertain myself.

Chuy brought home some old beat-up bikes someone had placed by a dumpster on the north side of the tracks. He claimed they were trash. "See what you can do with these," he said as he took them out of the back of his truck.

I took remnants and looked for ways to make two bikes out of three. I pulled a chain off one, a seat off the other, handlebars off all three. I took all of them apart and assembled Frankenstein bikes. They were good enough for us to ride around the neighborhood. At times, parts would fall off if we went too fast. The biggest problem was keeping the chain from falling off and wrapping itself around our feet. That hurt!

Fidel and Sam had a bike between them—a banana bike, which could seat two people if needed. We had two Frankensteins. Waldo was just old enough to ride one of the smaller bikes. Because we lived across the street from nothing but brush, dirt, mesquite, cacti, and more dirt, we rode there, dodging mesquite branches and praying no one would fall on a cactus. There were races, which sometimes ended in collisions with each other as we tried to avoid brush and holes.

Attempting to build a bike ramp, we dragged shovels, hoes, and picks out into the desert. Overlooking the dirt road across from our house, we managed to carve out a thirty-foot trail. Once done, we'd race our bikes from about two or three hundred feet out and ramp off the hill, high into the air, and land on the street. Mastering the task of landing on both wheels when hitting the ground in the middle of the street took some time. Fidel and Sam were better than me. They had the better bike. Fidel, Sammy, and I could pedal harder. Doing so gave us the momentum needed to ramp off the hill. Jesse and, of course, Waldo couldn't clear the hill, which caused fear and frustration.

"Like most things," I explained to the others, "if you do it long enough, you not only get better, the macho takes over. When you reach macho stage, you can do anything." I was trying to instill courage in the hope they would try the jump.

"Look at me! I'm almost landing in the middle of the street," I hollered, slamming on the brakes when I landed and avoiding a crash. I rode back around and went at it again.

"See how easy that is?" I smiled and tried another heroic jump.

"My turn, my turn!" cried Waldo. "I want to do this. When can I do this?"

"You are too small to ramp that hill," I said.

"No, I'm not."

"Yes, you are. If you get hurt, Chuy will kill you and me!" I protested.

"I want to ramp! I want to ramp!" He kept on whining.

Jesse, not wanting to hear Waldo's continued bellyaching, said, "Let him try once."

"Okay," I replied. "But if he gets hurt, it's your fault. You stand by the ramp and watch for cars. If you see any, you whistle so we can stop him."

Waldo got on the bike and tried to gather enough speed to ramp the hill. Twice he stopped short, not having the courage to see it through. Jesse ran to the end of the ramp, watching for cars coming down the street.

"You can do this," I whispered in Waldo's ear. Then I pushed, giving him the extra speed he needed to clear the ramp. I stood back and watched as his little feet pedaled the little bike straight at the ramp. Two hundred feet and gaining speed. One hundred feet, getting faster. We were all staring at this little kid's daring. *Is he going to do it this time?* I wondered. *Will he hit the ramp and fly into the air?*

Jesse kept looking at him as he rode right up the ramp. Waldo lifted higher than expected and landed on the other side. From where I was standing, I couldn't see if he'd landed on the street. Jesse, in his excitement, had forgotten to look for cars. By the time he saw the car, Waldo was in the air, flying right into the rear fender of a car that was moving slowly down the road. The bike hit the car, and Waldo flew over the handlebars, hitting the fender with a body slam.

We ran toward the hill, with Jesse yelling, "He's hit!"

The driver must have been drunk, because he never stopped or looked back to see what hit his car. I don't think he even heard Waldo crashing into him.

We reached Waldo and found him lying on the ground, crying and obviously in pain.

"He's alive!" I stammered, half shocked at his luck. He'd scraped the right side of his face, arms, and legs. Dusting off the dirt, I stood him up, checking for broken bones.

Fidel and Sam got on their bike and peddled home as fast as they could. They didn't want any part of the accident. Jesse and I managed to calm Waldo down by promising to buy his favorite candy if he stopped crying. After a few minutes, he settled down. We picked him up and carried him inside the house. No one was there. Chuy and Pino would be arriving from work soon enough.

"What do we do?" Jesse asked me.

"We put him in our room and shut the door."

"What if he starts crying? We're gonna get it this time," he cried. "Chuy is going to beat us until we die or bleed to death!"

"Look, give him these. He'll fall asleep." I handed him two Bayer aspirin from a tin can. This was what was given to us when we had any kind of ailment, so I figured it would work on him.

"Someone is gonna find him," Jesse protested. "We have to tell Mom."

"No, we don't. Give him the aspirin and put him under the bed. No one will find him there. When he gets better, we'll let him out."

We put Waldo under the bed. He fell asleep.

Chuy and Pino got home from work. They must have been exhausted from work because they didn't ask us how our day went. Not even, "What did you do all day today?" They never asked much about our day anyway.

Our evening went on as if it had been a perfect day. Chuy looked around to make sure the house was clean. He expected a clean house when he came home. Nancy knew exactly when to start the tortillas. She had them on the table, ready for when Mom was ready to start dinner. The tortillas made the house smell wonderful. We were like little puppies drooling over them. Chuy sat on the bed, calling for one of the girls to pull off his boots. He never pulled off his own boots.

Mom came in, smiled at us, and washed her hands to peel potatoes. The radio spilled out the Spanish hour, playing good ol' Tejano music. It was a typical day. No one missed Waldo. No one asked for him. Jesse and I went outside to solidify our plan for how we were going to deal with the Waldo fiasco.

"I'm scared," murmured Jesse, shuffling his feet like he normally did when he needed to pee.

"Just stick to the plan. If we get caught, we'll say he did it on his own."

"Waldo will blame us when he wakes up."

"No, he won't. We'll give him more Bayers."

Striking up conversations with anyone, we acted as normal as two kids guilty of murder. We were pretty much ignored, like usual. The radio played on. Fred the Man played Tejano music with some true Mexican music thrown in every once in a while. We enjoyed *The Fred Show*. I turned up the volume just in case the accident victim woke up and started crying. I sang to the music, drowning out any noise coming out from the other room.

The kitchen table was not big enough for all of us to sit at once, so we took turns sitting with Mom or Dad. Most of the time, we sat in front of the TV in the so-called living room with our plates across our legs. Beans, potatoes, and an occasional helping of ground beef mixed in with some tomatoes and onion was the meal most days. Jesse and I sat at the table with Chuy. I kept looking at Jesse to make sure he wouldn't turn on me.

After dinner, Chuy and Pino went off to listen to the rest of *The Fred Show* while the girls cleaned up the kitchen. I grabbed a tortilla, made a taco, and snuck it out without anyone noticing.

Waldo was waking up. I handed him the taco and told him to take it with two more Bayer aspirin. He was still under the bed. He came out, ate, then got into bed.

In the morning—it must have been a Sunday—I got up, looking for any signs of bruising on Waldo's face. He had a gigantic black-and-blue spot on his right arm and scratches on his face that were visible to the entire world. He kept complaining that he hurt. I gave him two more Bayer aspirin and told him to get under the bed again.

Between Jesse and me, we managed to feed him for another day, secluded from our parents and the girls. Day two passed without incident. However, as we all sat around waiting for dinner to start that evening, Pino asked, "Where's Waldo?"

"Shit, here it comes," I mumbled to myself. No one had missed Waldo for two days. I reckon with so many kids all going and coming during the day, no one had asked for him. Jesse, the idiot, turned state's witness, volunteering, "Waldo is under the bed because he crashed on his bike, and Robert let him do it."

That little shit, I thought. *I'm gonna kill that little snitch.* I stood up quickly, stammering like a girl. I needed to find a way out of this.

"He's alright. He just fell off the bike."

"Well, go get him," Mom said, giving me the stern look she always managed to give when she was approaching a state of hysteria. Her determined face clearly told me it was going to become another incident in which a beating was in store.

Chuy continued to eat, then looked at Jesse and me, shaking his head as if to say, "I'm going to hurt you."

I went to the bedroom, woke up Waldo, and told him not to say a thing. "I'll explain what happened," I told him. Waldo walked up to Mom, looking bewildered. She put her arms around him, looking for evidence of mistreatment.

"What happened, *mijo?*" she asked. At that very moment, I knew whatever Waldo said was going to incriminate me and only me! And Waldo spilled the beans. Between sobs, he managed to say, "Robert and Jesse told me to jump the ramp. When I did, I hit this car, and it broke the bike!" Catching his breath between sobs, snot coming out his nose, he showed Mom his head. "It hurts," he said, pointing to his noggin. In our state of hysteria, we hadn't noticed or bothered to look at his head. He had a good-size lump the size of a Ping-Pong ball. Since he had a full head of hair covering his entire head, we'd missed it.

Two miracles happened that weekend. Waldo survived a car crash, and we didn't get beaten to death. We just got beaten, me more than Jesse. I was the oldest and should have known better.

"You are supposed to take care of them. Not get them to do stupid stuff," remarked Mom, giving me the evil eye.

"It wasn't my fault. He was crying that he wanted to ride the bike. Why is it my fault?" I asked, knowing full well it wasn't going to get me any sympathy. Being the oldest, I got the brunt of Chuy's fury, so by the time he got to Jesse, he was done hitting hard.

Of course, there was no such thing as "child abuse" in those days. There wasn't even a hotline or a 911 number we could call to report parents who beat on their children. Even if we did, the police would absolutely side with them. As long as there was no noticeable bruising, bleeding, or broken bones, parents were safe. Sometimes I wonder if this type of discipline, beating on children, helped them behave better. I know it didn't work for me.

We were barred from biking for a long time.

I should have known better.

The Work

The desert was blooming with signs of life, including desert flowers from the natural landscape—or weeds, as I call them. This phenomenon created sinus problems for us all. Spring was here. Desert flowers on top of cacti bloomed yellow. Red yucca plants bursting with purple and red dominated the area. The mesquite trees, which give very little shade during hot days, sprouted leaves from twigs that still looked dormant. The Santa Rita prickly pear showed off its long stems adorned by red flowers. This was a beautiful sight early in the morning.

The smell of the desert after a light rain sent a clean, fresh fragrance throughout our end of town. Early in the morning, before heading off to school, I would sit on the concrete steps outside the screened-in porch, marveling at the sight of the sunrise. Bursting in yellow, orange, and red, it made me smile. I breathed deeply, taking in the sweet smell only the desert can give. It was amazing! This scene never ceased to amaze me. My favorite part of the day was when the sun's face slowly crept over the horizon and said hello.

I'd lived to see another day!

School would end in a few weeks. All I needed to do was keep my nose clean, do my work, be nice, and not burn down the house, and I might live to see sixth grade. If I was lucky and passed, I would only spend one year at Alamo Elementary. Spring was turning into summer, and before we knew it, we'd be done with Mrs. Bull.

Before the last day of school, every student had to be tested again to see whether there was any improvement according to a standardized instrument. The testing determined how a student would be placed when entering the next grade. Now it would determine what kind of classes I would take in junior high school. It was important to the school that we take this test very seriously. I didn't pay much attention to these intelligence tests, but the teachers made a fuss over them: Get a good night's sleep. Go to bed early. Bring a No. 2 pencil. Be focused.

We would take a whole day to test, taking intermittent breaks and chomping on bananas or apples to help our minds stay fresh and alert. We drank milk or orange juice from little cartons, all in an attempt to help us do better on the test. It didn't matter to me whether I was an average kid or not. In my heart, I knew I was better than the average bear. I never saw the test results. Whether it impacted my placement or not was insignificant. Besides, these tests had no bearing on whether we would pass to the next grade or not. I didn't take them seriously.

The school year ended without fanfare. As we walked out of the building for the last time, a group of boys and I threw away an amalgamation of a year's work. Beyond the teachers' eyesight, we flung every piece of paper up in the air, letting the wind dispense with negligible waste. Alamo was over, and I wanted nothing else to do with it. I prayed I would pass.

It came as no surprise when Chuy announced, "Get ready. We have to work." According to him, this would be a new adventure for us. What he meant was, "Get ready to work like a slave after school lets out." His plan was to get us to appreciate an education by having us perform child labor.

He mapped out a plan, which he would introduce immediately after school. "You don't know what it's like not to be educated. I could have gone to high school in Mexico and owned a business by now. Without an education, you will work like braceros," he lectured us a couple of weeks before school let out. "You don't study and work hard in school," he said, looking straight at me. "You are always getting in trouble. Let's see if you like to be dumb." He was obviously echoing Pino's sentiments because she just stood there and nodded.

No doubt, the lecture was intended for me. Nancy and Wanda would become collateral damage. In their minds, I needed to learn to appreciate a good education.

School was out on a Friday, and on Monday morning, he woke Nancy, Wanda, and me at five thirty. Mom had been up for some time, preparing tacos for breakfast and lunch. The smell of coffee, eggs, bologna, papas, and tortillas filled the kitchen. I was rubbing my eyes as I walked into the kitchen.

Mom said, "Go wash your face and put on old jeans. I have a shirt here for you to wear. Here, you'll need this too." She handed me a straw hat. The girls were already dressed and sitting at the table, drinking coffee.

"Why are we getting up so early?" I complained, rubbing my eyes.

"Just get dressed. And while you're at it, get those scissors and put them in the truck," Chuy said to me.

"Pino, why are we up so early?" I asked, looking directly at her.

"You and the girls are going with Chuy to the onion fields to work."

"Why?"

"Because he said."

"We don't know how to do that. Why are we even going?" I asked one more time as I put on my shirt.

"Just do as he says. It's not hard. Have fun."

Fun? We were in for the surprise of our lives. Apparently, Chuy had joined a group of barrio families who were going to Belding Farms to pick onions. It was a few miles just east of the city. I'd heard of it but never been there. I was curious.

Chuy started barking orders. "Pick that up! Get your shoes! We are leaving in ten minutes! Bring that jug of water! Get in the truck! The girls get in front, and you get in the back!"

Off we went to the first day of work like ordinary child laborers. On our drive to Belding, I lay in the bed of the truck, wondering, *Why are we even doing this? Is it so financially bad at home that we have to work like adults?*

I didn't know the first thing about picking onions, but we learned fast. Once we got there, the field supervisor gave the adults instructions on how many rows of onions each family was to get. Onions, as far as the eye could see and spread over rows of dirt plowed under by tractor blades, came in all different sizes. Tractor blades uprooted the onions so we could easily grab them by the stem. Chuy showed us how to cut the roots. I took the odd-looking scissors, bent over a row, and picked up several onions by the stem, like he'd shown us.

"See, you grab two or three, shake the dirt off, like this, and cut these hairs sticking out the bottom. Get it?" he asked.

I shook the dirt off the roots, then cut them off, leaving the onion bald. Next, I'd cut the stem off, making sure the onion, and not my fingers, fell into a bushel basket. Once I got the hang of it, the process went faster. We filled basket after basket of onions. Chuy and I would then take the basket and pour its contents into a burlap sack.

I looked around to see how the other families were doing, hoping they weren't outperforming us. The more experienced were grabbing four or five onions at a time, moving fast through each row, and filling baskets very quickly. By the time other families had finished one row and were starting another, I was almost a fourth of the way through the first one. Once I filled a basket with about fifty to sixty onions, I'd grab a sack, dump the contents into it, and start the whole process again.

We took a quick break for lunch, then continued picking until three o'clock. Everyone quit at three because the sun was a beast at that time of the day, and most people couldn't work in over hundred-degree temperatures.

We were back home by four, completely exhausted. I headed straight to the coolest place in the house, lay on the floor, and let the coolness flow through my aching back. I stretched and wiggled in pain. I imagined my body looking like the Hunchback of Notre Dame. After bending over all day, it felt good to straighten out.

The smell of tortillas cooking on the comal woke me up an hour later. I was famished with all this work stuff. Huffing and puffing, I rolled off the floor. My body ached. But the power of tortillas cooking gave me the strength to amble toward the kitchen. I picked one up, smeared butter, and rolled it up. After my first big bite, I felt better. Dessert before dinner. Mm, mm. Nancy had performed another miracle. Those tortillas were amazing. She didn't like us eating them before dinner, but I could steal one if she wasn't looking. She'd smack us with the tortilla roller if she caught us. She didn't care if she inflicted pain. The last thing she needed was to make another batch.

Dinner was usually a quiet activity. I don't know if we were too tired to talk or just had nothing to say. We ate. Then, one by one, as we finished dinner, we floated off to our own spaces.

I slept through the entire night until a pat on the head woke me up. Chuy had been up since five in the morning, getting things ready for the day. We loaded up again, grabbing brown paper bags that contained tacos of beans, potatoes, and egg. By five thirty, we were riding off in Chuy's old '51 Chevy pickup truck. I rode in the back, thankful I would have at least thirty to forty more minutes of sleep before we got to the fields.

We did this for three weeks until all the onions were picked, loaded on trucks, and sent off to be processed at a nearby factory. With all of us donning Band-Aids on most of our fingers and smelling like onion, we were glad it was over. I was okay with the Band-Aids, but the smell was difficult to remove from our bodies.

At the end of the three weeks, I made the mistake of asking how much we'd made. I was told to mind my own business. Later, I found out that we were paid a dime for each basket! Ten cents! It took ten of those baskets to earn a dollar! This business was not going to make anybody rich.

After a few days, Chuy found another spot for us. The picking continued.

Coyanosa is a farming and ranching community a few miles northwest of Fort Stockton. Back then, it boasted a population of about a hundred and thirty residents, including domesticated animals. We marched out into the field like old hands, looking like the rest of the pickers already there.

We settled down into our already internalized routine: picking, bagging, and loading onions until it was time for lunch, which was always the simplest of tacos—potato, eggs, and beans. If we were lucky, we got a Spam or bologna taco. My favorite. We all drank water from a large orange water jug. Much later, these became better known as the Gatorade water jugs seen at football games. Ours kept the water very cold when Chuy dumped in large blocks of ice from the local icehouse. It was so good that it necessitated frequent trips for water, much to Chuy's dismay.

"If we are to make any money, you need to work faster. Stop taking time for water. We're going to run out before noon!" were his words of warning. He just wanted us to keep working and not goof off.

By midafternoon, some of the families started loading up and quitting for the day. They were fast, finishing their given rows early. We kept going until Chuy told us we could pack up. That was usually an hour or so after everyone else was gone. We were slow. Looking back over the rows of onions picked, I tried to estimate how much money we had made that day. On a good day, we could make as much as twenty-five dollars. Chuy was never satisfied, thinking that if we got to the fields earlier and left later, we could double our money. That never panned out. It was exhausting work.

Imelda and Jesse kept pestering Chuy to let them go with us. They were eight and seven years old. So, one morning, he got them up, saying, "If you want to go with us, be ready in thirty minutes." They jumped out of bed, excited to finally be included in what they thought would be an adventure. They only lasted one day.

Picking onions in the hot sun over a period of several weeks made our skin smell of onion. Somehow, the odor penetrates skin. People could smell us a mile away. Lying about what we did during the summer didn't fool anyone. People could identify an onion picker as soon as they came within fifteen feet. After being around onions for some time, I couldn't smell it on my body, but others could.

We toiled in the sun for three more weeks until the entire field was picked clean. There were families that did this kind of work for most of the year, traveling from town to town, state to state, picking and gathering vegetables and fruit wherever they were needed. Some left town to pick strawberries in California, lettuce in Oregon, and peaches in Florida. We went home. Thank God Chuy had the sense not to follow the migrants.

The summer was creeping along at a slow pace. I missed my own twelfth birthday. Perhaps I was just too tired. I don't remember doing anything worth remembering for it. I wanted desperately to get school started back up so I'd get away from work. Afraid Chuy would find other summer jobs in the fields, I started complaining to Pino.

"Why do we have to work so much? We don't get a chance to play or anything," I whined. "Other kids are going swimming, and we work. That's not fair. Can't we just take a break and do something else? How much money do we really need anyway?"

Mom seemed sympathetic, but all the crying wasn't going to change her mind. She believed work was a way to instill responsibility, endurance, and pride—pride in knowing hard work made us better people. "You're going to work for the rest of your life," she commented. "You might as well get used to it."

That was it. That was her logic.

I received my report card three weeks after school let out for the summer. When the postman delivered it, I ran to the mailbox. Hands shaking, I walked back to the house. I knew I was on the fence with grades.

"*El nombre del padre, del hijo, del espíritu santo. Amen,*" I said as I made the sign of the cross, then opened the envelope. It was a five-by-seven report card with the last-semester grades on the inside page. I had made three Cs, one B, two Ds, and an S in PE. On the last page, I read, "Robert Alfaro has been promoted to the sixth grade!" The comments section stated, "Robert is a good student but needs to work harder. He will have to read at least five books from the recommended list for next year. Have a good summer!"

"Thank you, Jesus!" I shouted to everyone, happy as a lark. "I passed to the sixth grade!"

Pino looked at the report card. By this time, she knew how to read and knew the differences in letter grades. I couldn't pull off my scheming any longer.

"Remember when I told you about working for the rest of your life?" she said. "Well, with these grades, you'll be picking onions every summer."

Terroristic threats were not going to make me a better reader. Summer was here!

Comanche Pool

Instead of worrying about school, I thought it seemed like a good idea to gather up the guys from the hood and sell them on the idea of going swimming at Comanche Pool. With my powers of persuasion, it didn't take long for all to agree.

Saturday was the perfect day. No work. No problem. It must have been eight in the morning when I tried sneaking out of the house without asking for permission. In my attempt to not wake Pino or Chuy, I walked out with my shoes in hand. Arousing suspicion would only deter my objective.

"Where are you going?" Pino asked between sips of coffee. I hadn't realized she was in the kitchen.

"I asked you yesterday if I could go swimming today, and you said yes," I said.

"I don't remember you asking me."

"Please, Mom," I cried. "The guys are going, and we haven't been in a long time!"

"Do you have money?"

"No. But Fidel said he would pay for me and Jesse," I lied.

"Take Waldo."

"Mom! I can't take Waldo. He is too young, and he can't swim! What's he gonna to do there if he can't swim?"

"Teach him."

"Mom! He's too young, and he'll want to come home early. We're walking. He's gonna get tired."

"Carry him."

So, Waldo, Jesse, and I walked over to my grandmother's house to pick up Fidel and Sammy.

"What's that pea brain doing coming with us?" asked Sammy, looking at Waldo.

"Pino wouldn't let me go if he didn't come too."

"He's always getting us in trouble. *"Está medio tonto*," exclaimed Fidel.

For hundreds of years, Comanche Springs had been known as the sixth-largest freshwater spring in Texas. Considered a truly spectacular water oasis in the middle of the desert, the spring was fed by the Edwards-Trinity Aquifer, which provided water to Native Americans, settlers going west, and those who settled in the area. The free-flowing waters made irrigation possible for farming. In the early 1960s, the springs eventually stopped flowing because of farming west of town. A two-story pavilion was built around what was known as Comanche Chief, the largest of the springs. This became a haven for local families during hot summer months. Comanche Springs Pool, as it was known, also served as a place kids could go if their parents worked during the day. On weekends, it was packed with children all vying to enjoy the cool, fresh water. All for a dime! The pool entrance was on North Spring Drive, the westernmost section of James Rooney Memorial Park.

This was a perfect day for swimming. The weatherman at KFST radio announced the temperature would reach a cool one hundred degrees. Anticipating the cool waters, the great music, and me jumping in and out of the pool left me eager to get there. Splashing water at the girls walking by added to the fun. I envisioned dancing to my favorite songs while splashing around in the water. Which girl would I try to impress with my swimming talents? There would be many. I was so looking forward to this day!

We picked up two more kids who lived down the street from Grandma. Our cousins Pedro and Jaime were our age. They seldom hung out with us, but on this day, Fidel had invited them. We walked from South Texas Street and down Ryan Street. The pool was at least ten blocks east of us. A pack of brown-skinned, black-haired kids marching across town, daring each other to jump off the high board, must have looked like a modern-day gang. We wove in and out of traffic, making sure Waldo wasn't left too far behind. Like all kids our age, we kept trying to one-up each other.

"I'm going to splash water on the high school girls," one of the kids remarked with a sinister look.

"I want to see those girls run and watch their boobies bounce up and down!" yelled Jesse to no one in particular.

"Shut up! You can't be saying that!" I scolded him with images of boobies bouncing in my own head.

The gang of seven headed east toward Butz School, navigating across the playground, toward St. Joseph Church, then circling between the Annie Riggs Memorial Museum and The Grey Mule Saloon. Comanche Pool was just a few more blocks north. Chattering while walking the several blocks, we were all excited about how cool it would be to have swimming races even though not everyone could swim.

"Does everyone have their dime?" someone asked. As if on cue, everyone stuck their hands in their pockets, reaching for loose change. We were at Rooney Park by now and quickly realized we didn't have enough money.

"Stop. Let's see what we have," I said. We huddled around as I put my hand out. "Put your money in my hand."

Pennies, nickels, and one dime. Most had nothing. Between the lot, we couldn't even come up with seventy cents. There wasn't enough money for everyone. Somehow, there was an expectation that the older kids would pay for the younger kids. A discussion regarding what we were going to do started, with looks of despair on all our faces. Waldo and Jesse didn't have a nickel between them, and I certainly didn't have enough for all three of us. Everyone was talking at the same time, with no one paying attention.

"Wait a minute. Stop talking, everyone!" I practically yelled. A final determination revealed some startling news to the younger kids. "You are not going swimming. Stay in the pavilion until we come get you. Understand?"

Then came the whining words of displeasure. "I want to swim! I want to swim!"

"We've come this far. We can't go back!" someone stated.

The younger kids started whining again, threatening to walk home and tell. Someone mentioned us sneaking in without paying.

"How we going to do that?" asked Sammy.

"Look, if we can find a way to sneak in, we can use the twenty-five cents to buy candy or a soda," Pedro said.

But how? The pool wasn't open. We got there too early. The gates were locked. Nobody was around, so we sat by the curb and toyed with several ideas.

"We sneak in one at a time. The first one pays. Once he's in, he can act as a scout. Once the workers aren't looking, one by one, we sneak in," I said.

"That's a bad idea," Fidel replied. "If we send Jaime in first, he doesn't know his head from his ass! He'll get us all thrown out."

"Leave him alone," demanded Pedro. Jaime was his younger brother, and he was a little slow in the head.

"The tunnel!" Fidel and Sammy hollered at the same time.

There was a drainage tunnel that had been built in the early years to deflect rainwater from the pool. Situated in an obscure location about two hundred feet from the pool, this tunnel was approximately six feet tall and five feet wide. It had been screened off with a wire fence to prevent people and varmints from entering. It was dark and clammy. The stench of rotting leaves and who knows what else added to some people's hesitancy to go in it.

The tunnel stretched several feet under North Spring Drive and went up the hill toward downtown. When it rained, it came in torrents, causing drainage problems for the businesses. These tunnels had been built to divert rainwater toward Comanche Chief and away from the pool.

One couldn't see the tunnel entrance from the road, and most certainly not from the pool concession stand, where the lifeguards took a dime from every person entering. The tunnel was hidden from view because this part of the park was covered with tall trees, shrubs, and grass high enough to conceal small kids. But first, to get to it, we had to climb a six-foot chain-link fence.

"Let's get to the tunnel," Fidel said. "We can change our clothes there. When the lifeguards are not looking, we can sneak in from behind the bleachers."

"Why not?" I asked. "We can all sneak in without paying."

We snuck around behind the fenced-in portion of the pool area. Sammy would scout the traffic and warn us if anyone was coming. The pool would open at ten in the morning. We knew parents would bring their kids and drop them off while they went about their business, which happened on most weekends during the summer. By eleven, the pool would be full of people, mostly elementary and junior high kids, with a smattering of adults. Since there were a lot of kids, the lifeguards couldn't tell who'd paid and who hadn't. If we wanted to swim without paying, this was our best option. It was our only option.

Once over the fence, we got into the tunnel and changed into our swim gear, always on the lookout for any official from the pool.

"We can't all go at the same time," I mentioned to the group. We have to go in pairs until everyone's in."

It was a foolproof plan. But while the older kids, including myself, were strategizing our next move, the three younger kids, with Waldo in the mix, weren't paying much attention to the planning session we had going.

"Okay, now. Sammy, you and Pedro go first," I said. "Make sure the lifeguard is looking away before you go. Once you get to the pool, Fidel and Jaime will follow. Fidel, you give it about five minutes before you go."

With our heads huddled together like a football squad planning the next play, we were ready. The lifeguard whistle blew so loud that it broke our concentration. We looked up from our huddle. The whistle sounded like it was coming closer. I stopped talking.

"Where are the kids?" I whispered, looking around. The younger kids were missing. "*¡Chingada madre!*" I muttered under my breath.

We ran toward the bleachers, and what did we see? Waldo, Jaime, and Pedro being pulled out of the pool by one of the lifeguards.

"Get out!" yelled the lifeguard.

The three kids had jumped into the shallow portion of the pool. In their foolhardy anticipation, they'd jumped in without anyone else there. The pool wasn't even open yet!

"*¡Que pendejos!* How stupid can they be?" I exclaimed in whispered shock.

They were hauled off to the concession stand, interrogated, and told to leave and never come back.

"What do we do now?" Fidel asked, being all cautious and everything.

"Let's get out of here before they come looking for us too!" Sammy yelled.

"Wait. Let's see what happens," I said.

"*¡Chingada madre!* Some of the lifeguards are looking for us!" I said.

The younger kids had told them where they had entered the pool. Running back to the tunnel, Fidel, Sammy, and I, with our clothes in our hands, jumped over the fence. We headed toward the front entrance of the pavilion as the younger kids were walking up the stairs. Once we realized no one was following, we grabbed them and slowly, so as not to attract too much attention, ran toward the picnic tables farther down the park.

Swiping sweat off our brows and thanking God we weren't caught, we finally relaxed. We waited, pondering our next move. We couldn't go back to the pool, but we did have to get our stories straight just in case somebody blabbered and told on us. In all the commotion, with everyone talking at the same time, the young ones started pointing and blaming each other. Then we noticed that Waldo was missing. Where was he? Did the guards keep him?

"Where's Waldo?" I asked.

"He was right behind us!" Sammy cried.

"Well, he's not here! Someone has to go back and find him!" I yelled.

As I hurried back to the pool pavilion, praying he wasn't being held captive by the cops, I panicked. Going down the stairs toward the concession stand, I felt anxious, wondering what would happen if the lifeguards found out. I had to find him fast.

Sneaking into the dressing room, I looked under the stalls and in the showers. No luck. When the guards weren't looking, I walked past the concession stand toward the pool. By this time, there were several people around. No Waldo. Panic set in. *Where's this damn kid? Did he walk home? Did the cops get him?* I couldn't think clearly. I just knew I was in huge trouble.

I had turned back toward the concession stand and was just past one of the concrete columns when I heard him laughing— that distinct childish laugh that Waldo was famous for. As I moved around the column, I saw him. Two teenage girls were sitting on their towels, basking in the sun, and Waldo was right there between them, talking to them as if he knew who they were.

I grabbed him by the shirt collar and walked back up the stairs, almost strangling him as I walked.

"Stop! You're choking me! Stop!" he yelled. By this time, he was crying and asking why I was so mad at him. "I was just talking to the girls. They were going to buy me a Coke! I told them you were in the dressing room, and they were just talking to me!"

Once we got to the picnic tables, I sat him down and told him, "If you say anything about what happened today, I'll never bring you back! You understand? You'll never go swimming with me again!"

Then I started walking back home. Everyone else followed. Waldo never mentioned what happened that day to Chuy or Pino. He never said anything. Maybe he understood the trouble we could have gotten into if they'd known. Or maybe not. He probably just forgot, because once we got home, he went to sleep.

The weekend came and went, and I was still mad. Not because the young 'uns got caught, but because they ruined a perfectly great Saturday. So much for a fun summer day!

We did get to swim several times that summer though. Sometimes we paid, sometimes we snuck in via the tunnel. The next time, I made sure there were no more than two or three of the older boys. We were never too early, and we were always sure the pool was crowded before we snuck in.

The pool was simply the most beautiful place to me. We lived in the desert, for Christ's sake, and this oasis was so inviting. It was also the biggest one around for miles. The fun started when we'd spot some girls, mostly our age. We'd irritate them by jumping close and splashing water on them. Toying with them was the fun part. Some would retaliate by dunking our heads in the water, then swim away. We'd swim after them, returning the favor of a cool dunk.

"Stop it!" they'd yell.

"You stop it."

"I'm telling!"

"No, I'm telling!"

Very childish.

The cool blue water was beyond welcoming for us all. The teenage lifeguards were always playing music, which added to the joy. The melodies blaring from speakers, located around the outermost part of the pavilion, sounded out the latest hits. My favorite was "The Loco-Motion," sung by American pop singer Little Eva. Surrounded by screaming kids, I'd be dancing in the water alone, shaking and moving in circles, my arms extended. I'd tune it all out. It was just the music, the cool waters, and me, singing and swaying to the rhythm.

I loved Comanche Pool. Couldn't get enough of it. When I had money, which was seldom, I paid the ten cents to get in legally. Getting Pino to give me a dime was not difficult after I'd worked the onion fields. I figured this was the least she could do for me. She could afford a dime. When I was invited to go with some of the neighborhood kids, I'd either pay or sneak into the tunnel, change quickly, then join the others. Even though I feared getting caught, the idea of not being part of the group was out of the question. The embarrassment of getting caught by the lifeguards in front of my friends worried me. But it didn't keep me away.

Comanche Pool became my favorite place, where I'd disengage from the seriousness of home life. Forgetting I came from a poor family, I'd swim. It came naturally to me. As time would have it, it became a place to gather on weekends, even after the summer months were gone. As I got older, it also became a place to meet girls, including some who came from the surrounding towns.

Within a few years, there seemed to be a subtle yet simple change occurring in our town. It wasn't noticeable at first because I wasn't expecting it. Comanche Pool was going through a transition just like the town itself. As a youngster, I didn't notice the change because I was naïve and oblivious to those changes.

The city built a community pool between James and Everts Streets. Talk around town was that the pool was private and only for those living north of the railroad tracks, who so happened to be mostly white. We were still too young to grasp the significance of those changes. Comanche Pool was a favorite spot for many white folks, but it seemed to be the only place for Hispanics. Either way, Comanche Pool was the place to be during those hot summer months, regardless of how many white families were leaving to go to the other pool. It was the early 1960s, so who cared whether segregation came in such a subtle form. I certainly didn't. Not at my age anyway—until the first and last time we entered City Pool.

Comanche Pool and City Pool were the same distance from our house. Troy, Fidel, and I decided to go see what was happening at the City Pool. We didn't know the rules. All we knew was that there was a pool north of us. We grabbed our trunks and headed north. Once we crossed the railroad tracks, the scenery changed. Nicer, more modern cars and trucks were parked in paved driveways next to nice brick homes. Just beyond Railroad Avenue, we could see City Park. A large grassy area with playground equipment surrounded by a chain-link fence took up at least ten acres. On the eastern side of the park was the pool, which was new but smaller than Comanche Pool. There were several cars parked there. Mostly white kids and parents were walking inside the chain-link fence. At first, we stood looking through the fence like a group of homeless kids.

"It looks like fun," I said.

"L-l-l-l-look over there!" Troy managed, eyes wide and protruding past his eye sockets. He was pointing toward the deep end of the pool. I thought he was pointing at the high diving board. But as we followed his finger, our eyes landed on a group of older girls. They appeared to be of high school age. Their long blond hair, flowing in the warm breeze, made them look like goddess statuettes. They sported tiny polka-dot bikinis in different bright colors that showed more skin than we'd ever seen on a girl before. It was like they didn't care if they showed that much skin. We stood staring through the fence, mesmerized by the beauty of these girls, not caring whether anyone noticed. If this was a window, we would definitely have been called Peeping Toms! We didn't notice any teenage white boys standing around or swimming. Only the girls.

"Should we go in?" Troy was the first to move toward the entryway. Fidel and I followed.

"What does it cost to swim?" I asked the boy standing guard at the entryway.

"Twenty-five cents," he said, staring at us with a perplexed look on his face.

I was ready for him to tell us we couldn't swim there. Instead, I just mumbled, "Wow."

"I got money. I'm going in," Troy said without stuttering for the first time. He held out his quarter for the guard and quickly moved past us toward the dressing rooms.

"Well, I don't have money. I thought we were just going to check it out," I complained.

"I've got money," Fidel said. "Let's go in."

We followed Troy into the dressing rooms. As soon as we came out, one of the white guards said, "You have to shower before you go in the pool."

"Take a shower? Why? We're going to get wet," I explained to the kid.

"Rules," he said.

We headed back into the dressing room and stood under the showerheads long enough to get wet. Then we headed back outside. No sooner had we walked out than a guard blew a whistle. All eyes were on us. I felt embarrassed and somewhat humiliated. People stared.

"You can't go in the pool with those," he said, pointing at Troy's cutoffs.

"Wha-wha-why? I–I–I–I–I p-p-p-p-p-paid already!" he said, ready to throw a fit. Fidel and I were standing next to him, and I couldn't find a way to take the scene into a more private setting.

"Those are not legal here. They have to be sewn like theirs," the guard said, pointing at Fidel and me. "Or, you have to have regular swim trunks."

"I'm going home and getting other shorts. I'll be back!" Troy exclaimed. Then he took off, running out the entryway and back across the tracks.

They could have told us about the shorts before we paid. I wanted to leave, but I didn't think the guards would give us our money back. So Fidel and I walked toward the pool. Some of the parents were calling their kids to get out, but most of them stayed, still staring at us. We jumped in the pool as if nothing was wrong.

Troy didn't come back. After an hour or so, we decided this pool was simply not as much fun as Comanche. We didn't even change back into our regular clothes. We just left. We never returned to City Pool. Ever.

Reflection

On August 28, 1963, a march of protest was taking place in Washington, D.C. Many people were protesting the inequalities facing the American citizenry. It was organized and attended by civil rights leaders, including Martin Luther King Jr. More than two hundred thousand people of all races congregated for a peaceful march for the purpose of forcing Congress to enact legislation that would establish job equality for everyone. On this day, Martin Luther King Jr. stood on the steps of the Lincoln Memorial and shared with the attendees his "I Have a Dream" speech. The speech led the way for many Americans to rethink the treatment of minorities and poor people. The speech solidified the national civil rights movement, becoming a slogan for equality and freedom.

Out in West Texas, far removed from the actions taken by people of color, it didn't affect us. Sitting in front of the black-and-white TV, I watched with mixed feelings as Martin Luther King Jr. delivered his speech. *Will we have access to the same rights as white citizens?* I wondered. *How long will it take?* It was confusing.

Happening at the same time was probably the most bizarre event, but it wouldn't affect me until much later. The country was showing concern over the escalation of war looming in Vietnam. It was a time when Americans were questioning the country's priorities, especially when it came to supporting a country many of us knew very little about. According to the politicians, communism was evil, and we needed to contain it. It was spreading into a democratic country, and we needed to stop it. President Kennedy was hoping to stop this expansion by sending "advisors" to teach the Vietnamese how to protect themselves. This conflict was slowly creeping up on us, and we, as a country, didn't realize it until it was too late. America was not ready to jump into a full-scale war. Neither were those eighteen-year-old boys recruited to protect democracy. I was too young to fully understand the significance of this travesty. But I would come face-to-face with it at eighteen.

For now, the summer was upon us. In our world, August on any day is always the hottest month of the year. Temperatures in the dry desert soared upward of a hundred and ten degrees! In the shade! The evenings were the worst, making everyone uncomfortable and short-tempered. I couldn't even sit for too long watching TV, as it was so hot. Chuy had bought a used evaporative swamp cooler. It was a water-cooled contraption used mostly in dry, arid desert environments. It wasn't big, but it was good enough to cool down a room. Water trickling through straw pads located on its sides cooled the air going into the house. Once it was placed in a window, it could keep things cool, but only if the water was running down the pads. The house was old and built by some dumb person. The rooms zigzagged throughout the house, preventing cool air from reaching the other rooms. Chuy placed the swamp cooler in the living-room window because the only water source was found there. Problem was, it would only cool the living room and one bedroom. If the kids wanted to stay cool at night, we had to sleep either on the floor in the living room or outside on a cot in the screened-in porch. We all tried sleeping on the floor. Chuy and Pino shared a bed with Waldo, Nora, and sometimes Imelda. They were younger and didn't require much space. As for the rest of us, if we wanted fresh, cool air, we slept on the floor. The room was small, making it difficult to reach the bathroom without stepping on a body. If we could make it to the bathroom, we'd better hope no one was in it. One bathroom for nine people, five being female, left the boys with very few options. It was easier to walk out the front door and pee outside. At least for the boys.

One hot, dry summer evening, I decided to climb onto the roof of the house. The roof's asphalt shingles would cool off when the sun went down, making it a nice, quiet place to relax and get away from the young 'uns. I'd lie there, looking up as the sun slowly disappeared into the western desert and created vibrant colors against a darkening sky. The sun's retreating rays gave off an array of colors that bounced off the clouds. The evening turned into night, and the brilliance of tiny stars would appear, revealing the majesty of the universe. For me, it was a great place for personal reflection—a place where I could collect my thoughts regarding my place on Earth. Not deep thinking. Just superficial enough to stimulate my brain. I'd think of how tiny the Earth must be in the largeness of space. It generated amazement in my young mind, especially when I saw falling stars dashing through the night sky. I'd quickly make a wish even though I didn't believe wishing upon a star would bring me riches. I'd do it anyway, just in case people were right. I didn't want to pass up the opportunity to buy that diamond ring I'd always wanted.

I wondered where God resided in the immensity of it all. Was He up there looking down on us? The peacefulness, coupled with the serenity of it all, made me realize how lucky I was to be in the presence of God, who never complained about anything. I felt secure. I thought about staying on the roof and making it my permanent residence. But after some time, I climbed down, grabbed a blanket, fixed up a bologna sandwich, and filled Chuy's thermos with Kool-Aid. I was set for a nice evening under the stars. With God.

I hauled my stuff back onto the roof. Quietly eating bologna wrapped around a tortilla smothered in butter, I couldn't ask for more. I wasn't a very religious kid, but I thanked God for letting me share this night with Him and hoped Jesus and the Virgin Mary would not get jealous. This was amazing.

It started getting a bit cooler as the night progressed. Wrapping the blanket over me, I lay back. Sleep overcame me within minutes. Chuy and Pino either didn't know I'd gone missing or were too tired to care. I was the oldest. Therefore, I was expected to know better than to fall asleep on the roof. I didn't fall off the roof that night. That was a good thing. If I had fallen off the roof, maybe I would not have done it repeatedly. I so loved the desert night in the summer with God.

Summer came and went without further incidents or crazy thoughts. I had survived the summer of 1963. That was another miracle. It was late August, and I had to think about school again. It was going to be a great year because I was going to the big school.

Parents were now buying school clothes for their kids. When Gibson's Department Store began setting up school supply displays, we knew it was time. I wondered if we would be getting our clothes from the Van Man.

Money was always at the center of everything for us. I knew we didn't make much, but apparently, we made enough to afford new school clothes. A few weeks before the beginning of school, Mom heard from the neighborhood women that the Van Man would be coming around soon. The man sold clothes out of the back of his old white van. One morning, the van came past our house, moving slowly down the street.

Mom yelled, "Go stop him!"

A couple of us quickly ran outside, chasing the van, yelling for him to stop, and waving our hands, hoping he would see us through his rearview mirror. He stopped in the middle of the road.

Between breaths, I pointed at Mom and said, "*La señora quiere mirar la ropa.*" ("That lady wants to see the clothes.") He turned around and headed toward our house. When he opened the back doors, we were amazed at the amount of clothing he had for sale. New and used clothing was everywhere. Clothing for adults. Clothing for children. Lots of clothes piled high.

We surrounded the van, seven kids gawking at new clothes with mouths open and eyes wide. Pino kept us away while she looked, sizing up the clothing and checking tags for prices. We stood there like zombies, immobile and calm, hoping to get something.

"He needs pants, she needs a dress, he needs a shirt ..." she said. We lined up like kids in a candy store. Pushing the others aside, I said, "Me first."

Measuring me up with one look, the Van Man pulled out a pair of tan trousers. How he knew my size by just looking at me was surprising. He handed them to me to try on. Excited, I rushed inside the house. You'd think the man didn't know what he was doing, but to my surprise, they fit! I rushed back outside, pushing the door wide open and shouting, "They fit! They fit!"

Toward the back of the van was a red-and-black checkered shirt with hints of tan that would complement the pants. By golly, next to the shirt was a matching pair of socks. They were perfect. It would complete the outfit. The socks were more maroon than red, but it didn't matter—the outfit was going to turn girls' heads once I got to junior high.

I held on to the outfit, marveling at my luck, and stood back to give the others a chance to pick their stuff. Nancy and Wanda got to pick their outfits with Mom's help. Excited about the new clothes, I couldn't wait to put them on. I wanted to show them to my grandmother.

When Mom was finished picking out our outfits, she handed the Van Man some money. He took out a large clear plastic bag, and as he held it open, we hesitantly placed our new clothes inside. Much to our dismay, the man tied a knot in the bag, marked it "Alfaro," and stuck it back inside the van.

What the? I thought. "What happened?" I asked Mom as the van moved on to the next sucker. "Why did this guy take our clothes?"

"He'll be back in two weeks. I'll pay some more on the clothes. Don't worry. By the time school starts, I'll have paid for them," she explained.

That was how we got our new school clothes for that year. But school was still far off in the future. As much as I hated to see my new clothes drive off, I couldn't help but wonder if I'd ever see them again.

We had two weeks to clean up, get a haircut, and convince Pino it was never too late to get us some school supplies. The priority, though, was to get the onion smell off my body because the smell lingered on. At first, that pungent odor was overwhelming. Now, I couldn't smell it on me even though I knew it was there. *Can other people smell it on me?* I wondered. I supposed it was like cow shit—once you've been around it for so long, you can't smell it anymore. Nevertheless, I felt self-conscious, so I kept washing my hands. For days after the last onion field had been picked, I felt it on my skin. When it got too terribly hot, I swear I could still smell it on my sweat. I didn't want anybody at school to know I was an onion picker. I believe the other kids whose families also picked onions, like the Garzas, felt the same way. I was too embarrassed for anyone to know because field workers were considered poor. I didn't want to be thrown in with that group. I don't know if pride had anything to do with it or not, but I just wanted the other kids to think of me as normal, like them.

I took great pains to remove the smell by bathing regularly. Regularly was at least twice a week. In my house, bathing was a pain in the ass. We had a pink bathtub in the bathroom, but it was off-limits for bathing because the faucets in there did not work. To flush the toilet, we had to bring water in from the kitchen or from outside. Chuy thought it would be easier if he ran a water hose from the outside, pushed it through the window, and filled the tub. Then we'd use a bucket to scoop water and flush the toilet. It worked rather well unless someone forgot to follow the process. That became a big problem during the hot summer months. Urine mixed with poop was a perfect combination for making us gag when we entered the bathroom. It was bad. "Someone forgot to flush the toilet!" was a common cry, mostly from the girls.

We had no running water in the bathroom, and, therefore, no hot water. Apparently, the hot water heater had blown up some years back and had never been replaced by the landlord. So we took Pino's kitchen pots filled with water and set them on the stove. Chuy had bought a used aluminized steel tub some years back for bathing and washing clothes. We hauled it from house to house. That was our bathtub. I would take the water hose from outside, run it through the screened-in porch and the kitchen, then fill up the tub. When the water was hot, it went off the stove and into the tub. The tub did not fit in the tiny bathroom, so the next best place was the kitchen. Problem was, we had to wait until everyone was asleep before we could bathe in private. Ivory soap was cheap enough for us to afford. There was no shampoo, but there was plenty of Ivory. It didn't work as well on the hair, leaving it stiff and hard to comb.

The weekend before school started, I went to my grandmother's house. I wanted her to smell me. She was the only honest person who would not make fun of me for asking. She told the truth.

"*Ama! Ama!*" I said. "*Quiero que me huelas.*" ("I want you to smell me.")

"*Hay, mijo. ¿Por qué?*" ("Oh, son. Why?")

"*Porque no quiero oler a cebolla.*" (Because I don't want to smell like onion.")

After a couple of stiff sniffs, she told me I smelled like soap. Mission accomplished. I was ready for school.

We got our clothes from the layaway Van Man that week. We all looked pretty good for a bunch of dark-complected Mexican kids. Either from working in the onion fields, swimming, or playing outside, the gang and I would shimmer in the sunlight from our tanned bodies. We were dark-skinned kids, and we loved it.

Junior High

Going to the sixth grade meant no more baby stuff. No longer would there be one teacher who taught us all subjects. Now we had several. There were horror stories trickling down to the sixth graders by those who'd been there. That only scared us, and it didn't help matters.

"No more childish behavior, or you'll get beaten by the eighth graders."

"Fear the girls. They're bigger than the boys and can knock you out with one punch."

"Stay away from the seventh- and eighth-grade girls if you want to survive this school."

It was advice to be taken seriously.

Even the sixth-grade girls were growing bigger than the boys. Manuela, the one we called "Horse" in elementary school, was taller than most adults. No one called her "Horse" anymore.

The teachers weren't any better. According to lore, they were mean, uncaring, short-tempered, obnoxious, demeaning, and, above all, ugly.

The junior high school was located straight up Texas Street, across Railroad Avenue, and one block west. There were four buildings within a six-block area. For a twelve-year-old, it was quite intimidating. This entire area rested between Oklahoma

Street and South Colpitts Boulevard, bordering north and south. West 2nd Street was the front of the school. The football field, stadium, and a large practice field rounded out the north side of the complex. The school was only eight blocks away, but for me, it might as well have been on the other side of the moon. It was farther from home than any of the other schools I'd attended. The oldest building was three stories high and ran along Oklahoma Street. This was the sixth-grade campus. The other buildings housed various departments, the cafeteria, band hall, choir hall, gym, and administration offices. This was where you would find the dangerously intimidating seventh and eighth graders—the bullies, rascals, hippies, smokers, drinkers, and cursers.

I was familiar with the different campuses because the fifth-grade teachers had taken us to the junior high on a field trip. On this trip, I saw them—boys sporting unshaven mustaches and girls wearing makeup. It was horrifying. They looked so adult-like. As we passed by them going from one building to another, they stared and whispered among themselves, loud enough to hear.

"Wait till they get here. I'm killing that one."

"No, leave that one to me. I call dibs."

"I'm breaking that kid's arms!" yelled an eighth-grade girl, pointing at me.

We bowed our heads as we passed by, hoping they wouldn't recognize us the next year. My hope was that the one girl would pass on to high school and I could avoid broken bones.

This trip revealed the truth to sixth graders. We were dead meat, and the older students were going to have a field day with us. Rumor had it that the best way to avoid them was to hang out in groups. I didn't believe the rumors, but I needed to make new friends. The entire trip frightened us! I had nightmares.

My first day in school went without incident. I felt secure knowing that some of the kids from fifth grade were in many of my classes. Some things didn't change. The cafeteria, for example, still served the same meals I was used to. No surprises there. I never ate breakfast in the cafeteria. They didn't serve biscuits and coffee to students. For lunch, there was the usual— meat of some sort, a veggie, a biscuit, a roll or a slice of bread, milk or juice, and potatoes. Since Pino and Chuy didn't make enough money, we all ate free. We were still in the governmental poverty range. Pino would sign the free or reduced-lunch papers so the government could pay the district to feed us. We never were part of the reduced-lunch program. Always free.

Everyone had to take six subjects in junior high: English, math, history, reading, PE, and an elective. I had signed up for PE instead of athletics. I was too skinny and puny to play football and too lazy to play basketball. I hated to admit it, but PE was for losers, me being one of them. It's not that I didn't want to be in athletics. All the popular kids were in athletics. But Pino didn't want us playing contact sports.

She'd say, "*Ay. No, mijo. ¿Si te lastimas, quién va pagar por el hospital?*" ("If you get hurt, who is paying for the hospital stay?")

PE wasn't going to be that bad. The only consolation was that I knew for sure this was going to be an easy A on my report card. All I had to do was show up, do a few calisthenics, learn to play fair, and listen to the coach. The PE instructor gave us an orientation on what was to be expected and told us we all had to take showers at the end of the period.

"Showers?" I turned to the boy next to me and asked, "Did he say we needed to take a shower?"

"Yes."

"Coach, where are the showers?" someone asked.

When the instructor showed us the showers, I panicked. From an entryway, we could see a large room with at least ten showerheads next to each other. There were no curtains, doors, or walls separating those taking showers.

"You mean we all have to take a shower at the same time? Naked?"

Yes and yes were the answers.

I'd never taken a shower or bathed in front of other boys. At my age, I'd never bathed in front of anybody! How embarrassing! The last thing I wanted was another human being looking at my skinny body and all those body parts that come with it! I was a lot like my mother when it came to nakedness—modest. Some of the kids didn't mind getting naked in front of the others, but I wasn't going to. I'd wait until the coach left, then I'd put on my regular clothes, dash to the sink, and wet my hair. We had to pass right by the coach inspector as we left PE. My wet hair would tell him I'd showered.

The last period of the day was band. I'd signed up for band, determined to learn to play the trumpet. My uncle Domingo was a trumpet player, and I really enjoyed watching him play with his little band. I wanted to play trumpet and only trumpet. Most of the kids had their own instruments. Especially the white kids. They had been taking private lessons since they were babies. Those like me and the other barrio kids did not. When asked what I wanted to play, I smiled and boldly said, "The trumpet."

"I'm going to need at least seven to ten trumpet players, five drummers, three French horns, and twelve clarinets," said the band director. I raised my hand when he asked for trumpet players. Man, I was excited. I was in the band! I loved it.

But the problem was that I didn't have a trumpet. The band director gave those who did not have an instrument a chance to choose another instrument. Some picked from those the school provided: a tuba, drums, baritone, or French horn. I didn't want to play any of those. Three days later, the band director gave me a French horn. I didn't like it. French horns were for girls.

My aunt Patricia decided on the drums. She wanted to play the flute, but that cost money too. "Why don't you play the drums?" she asked. "It doesn't cost much. All you got to buy are the sticks. How much could that be? Cheaper than a trumpet."

I sulked for the rest of the week. On Friday of the first week of school, the band director announced that a music company from Odessa would be in town displaying instruments for those who wanted to buy or upgrade.

"The music company will be here next Friday from four to six p.m.! Bring your parents!" the band director shouted over the noise. I took the flyer he handed out, put it in my pocket, and ran out the door.

The week went by with very little fanfare. I got to know my way around the campus. Plus, I learned to avoid the upperclassmen. Finally, it was Friday again. In my excitement about the approaching weekend, I forgot about the music company. I was too busy playing baseball with the neighborhood kids. Up at bat, I hit the ball and slid into first base. Safe! I pounded the dirt off my jeans. That's when I felt it. The flyer in my pocket.

I ran home and yelled, "Pino, we have to go to the band hall right now!"

"*Por qué?*"

"The band director told us we have to be at the band hall before six. We have to go! Please!" I begged.

"*No. Es muy tarde.*" ("No, it's too late.")

"*¡Por favor!*" I grabbed her hand and pleaded with her, on the verge of tears.

She relented. "*Bueno. Trae mi cartera.*" ("Bring me my purse.")

She got up from the kitchen table, put on her shawl, and headed out the door. We practically ran the eight blocks.

"*Mira, mira. Esta es una trompeta.*" ("Look, look, this is a trumpet.") I picked up the trumpet, feeling it in my hands. It was a thing of real beauty. I could see myself playing music in front of large crowds. I put it up to my lips and blew. Nothing came out. I wanted this trumpet more than anything in the world.

279

More than a diamond ring. The salesman was talking to Pino. I ambled over, holding the trumpet in my hands and thinking I would have to interpret what the man was saying.

Nope. She understood.

"*No tenemos dinero para comprar esta cosa,*" she told me. ("We don't have money to buy this thing.")

"*¿Por qué? ¡Por favor!*" I cried. "*Si no me la compras, voy a tener que salirme de esta clase!*" ("Why? Please. If you don't buy it for me, I'm going to have to leave this class.") I was nearly in tears. "*Por favor, Mami!*" I'd never called Pino "Mami," "Mom," or "Mother." We all knew her as Pino.

The band director and the salesman kept talking in whispered tones a few feet from us. I was holding on to Pino's hand, pleading. A few minutes later, the salesman came over to Pino.

"Look, ma'am. I have a cornet for sale. It is not a trumpet, but it sounds like one. It is cheaper than the trumpet, ma'am. If you want, you can buy it, and we can put you on a payment plan."

She understood enough English to make out what the man was saying.

"How much money do you have now?" he asked.

Pino pulled out a five-dollar bill from her purse and handed it to the man. The man stared at the five-dollar bill, then looked at Pino as if to say, "Is this all you got?" He didn't say it, but the look in his eyes said it all.

I looked at Pino. My eyes said it all.

"Okay, now I'll take this," the man finally said. "And you still owe ninety-five dollars. You must pay until you pay this off, now. You can give Mr. Hanna (the band director) what you can afford until you pay this off, but you must pay it before the end of the year. I'll send you a receipt and tell you when it's paid off. You understand?"

"Sí. Yes, I pay for it," she told him.

And that was how I became a trumpet player. Well, a cornet player. I became a musician, just like my uncle.

"*Dios gracias*," I said. ("Thank God.") I don't know how long it took her to pay off the cornet.

We walked back to the house. I was skipping and jumping and talking incessantly about the songs I was going to learn to play. She didn't say much. She was probably wondering how in the world she had been sucked into buying a one-hundred-dollar instrument with no assurances that I would learn to play.

It was getting dark. Three blocks from the house, she said, "*¿Si no aprendes como tocar esa cosa, la voy a vender y te quedas sin nada. Entiendes?*" ("If you don't learn to play that thing, I'll sell it, and you'll be left with nothing.")

I learned to read music. I learned to play. Band became my favorite pastime. When I finally got the cornet, I read all the instructions on how to care for it. This was the most expensive item I would possess for the next ten years. But it was a little embarrassing. I was the only one in the trumpet section who had a cornet. It wasn't the prettiest thing, but it had a great sound. And it was affordable. This cornet would keep me out of trouble for years to come.

Oh, hallelujah. God works in mysterious ways.

Sixth grade went by without too much drama. I met a new kid by the name of Raul. He had recently moved from McCamey, a smaller town about an hour's drive from Fort Stockton. He lived with his mother in a small two-bedroom frame house not too far from school. He was a skinny guy with a full head of hair that went every which way. His small body almost looked sickly. He wasn't much taller than me, but he was skinnier than most kids our age. In the middle of the week, he told me that he'd gotten a new 1957 Ford Thunderbird model car. I liked cars, and I'd seen a picture of the Thunderbird in a magazine.

"I build model cars for fun," he said as we walked one day. "Something my mother encouraged me to do since I like them." He probably couldn't do much more, being all skinny and stuff.

I was intrigued. "Where do you get your model cars?" I asked.

"My mother buys them for me. They come in boxes with everything you need to put them together."

"How much you pay for this one?" I asked, holding one he'd pulled from his bag.

"I don't know. There is a Camaro that I want. She told me I could get it for my birthday. Hey, you want to see my other cars?"

To see a model of a real Thunderbird piqued my interest. "Sure. How far do you live?"

"I'm just up the street. Come on. I'll show you."

We started running toward his house. The house was modest. Small, yet in better condition than ours. There was no yard fence. Anyone could see his house from the alley. We went in the back door. He just walked in, and I followed. There was no screen on the door—just a wooden door that led right into the kitchen. The kitchen led right into the bathroom. As we stepped in, the bathroom door was open. His mother was in the tub, taking a bath. She was naked and didn't have time enough to cover her breasts before she yelled, "Shut the door!"

Too late. I couldn't unsee what I saw. My first female breasts. Tits! They were big! Her skin was white—almost almond colored—with a small nipple protruding from a darker round circle at the tip. She drew her arms up to cover her breasts, but it was too late. I saw.

Raul just went in toward his room, saying, "Oh, Mom. This is Robert. My friend from school. I'm going to show him my model collection." He never shut the bathroom door.

I don't know if I was in shock or just curious, but I stared at her for what seemed like a lifetime until Raul called out to me.

"Robert, come here. Look at my cars."

Snapping out of it, I walked toward his room as if nothing had happened. If he wasn't worried, I wasn't worried. Later, I learned to call them tits, knockers, twin peaks, or chee chees. Not breasts. Boys my age would laugh if they heard me call them breasts.

Raul tried to show me his model cars, but all I could think about were his mother's tits. I even dreamed of them. Normal, huh?

There were more things to do after school in junior high. There were football games, band rehearsals, girls' volleyball, tennis, cheerleading, and general hanging out with friends. While I did not have a lot of friends, I knew a lot of kids, and they knew me, but not as real friends. Apart from Raul, Troy, Juan, and José, all the others were merely acquaintances. We lingered about more than we hung out.

Lingering around after school usually led to boys getting in trouble. I'd stay as far away as I could, especially from the rowdy bunch, like Roy Urrutia and Joe Herrera. They were trouble. Raul and I were walking behind the athletic building one day after school when we ran into the rowdies. They were tossing and kicking around what looked like a white rag. They were kicking it at each other, yelling, "Blood rag is yours!"

"It's yours! When did you start?"

"No, it's your mother's!"

"It's your mother's. No, no. It's your sister's!"

They kicked it back and forth until someone yelled, "It belongs to your bleeding girlfriend!"

At about the same time, a female teacher walked out of the building.

Someone yelled, "Run!"

We all ran in different directions like a bunch of illegals in a Border Patrol raid.

Raul and I ran home.

"What was that all about?" I asked.

"I don't know. You know those guys. They'll make fun of anything."

"What did he mean, it belongs to Joe's bleeding sister? I didn't know he had a sister."

"I think they were making fun of a Kotex."

"A what?"

"You know. A Kotex. That's what girls use when it's their time."

"Oh," I replied, pretending to know what he meant. I didn't say much after the last comment. Raul talked about cars, and I was glad. We continued to walk, jabbering about whatever. But I was trying to make sense of the incident.

Do girls really bleed? I wondered. *How? From where? Do they do this all the time? How can they do that and still be alive?* I had so many questions. Who could I ask?

It was not until I was in high school that I finally learned about girls having periods. I learned it not from books or teachers or parents but from conversations boys had with each other. I finally understood why Doña Lucia slapped me upside the head when I told her Pino wanted Kotex. Now I understood. Or at least I thought I did.

National Tragedy

Toward the end of 1963, the world outside little Fort Stockton was changing at an alarming rate. The constant movement of change prevailed over the country, but for those of us living in our town, oblivion was the norm. New advances in the space race were dominating the news. Our country's desire to become technologically advanced beyond countries the likes of the USSR, had become a challenge. Advances in almost every aspect of the economy, business, technology, food production, and TV were becoming standard operating procedure to many Americans. Progress was moving America forward. However, only those who could afford such luxuries were reaping the rewards.

I was learning about these things because I watched TV.

Having a TV set in the house was a luxury most in our barrio still could not afford. How we came to own our small black-and-white TV is still a mystery. Chuy could have stolen it. I'd like to think he bought it from someone desperate for food stamps or something. It was small and reliable if the antenna was facing due north. Somehow, we came upon an outside antenna. How we got an antenna to go with it is also a mystery. If the wind blew hard coming in from the north, which it usually did, the antenna would stay put. If the wind blew in from the south, the darn thing would swirl over to the west, giving us a terrible picture. The only way to correct it was to climb on the roof and twist the pole until the reception was acceptable. Climbing on top of the roof and adjusting the antenna was my job.

"How does it look now?" I'd shout down from the roof as I turned the antenna one way or the other—something remotely akin to "Can you hear me now?" with cell phones today. I would adjust until the picture was clearer. It was never the best quality, but it worked for us. March, when the wind constantly blew at an alarming rate, was the worst time to try and adjust it. Once, when the wind was blowing in from the south, I wanted to watch *Gunsmoke*, a great western movie. I climbed up on the roof barefoot. When I got to the long aluminum pole that held the antenna, I noticed the wire was loose at the top. Instead of taking the whole thing down to fix it, I decided to climb the pole and try to reattach the wire. When I was almost to the top, about six feet above the roof, my feet started slipping. As I held on for dear life, with the wind blowing me back and forth, the pole started bending over the side of the house. Then it started to come loose. I knew the end was near! I slid down far enough to jump onto the roof, and the entire antenna and pole came crashing down on Chuy's truck.

If that didn't kill me, Chuy will, I thought.

I went looking for Chuy's ladder, hoping to fix it before he came home. I grabbed some nails, wire, and extra rope, then went to work. The pole was bent, but not enough to arouse suspicion. I attached the wire back on the antenna and lifted the pole to tie it down against the house, but I couldn't hold it and nail it at the same time. I needed help. *Who can help without squealing to Dad?* I wondered. *Waldo.*

Yes, Waldo wouldn't say anything. He'd think it was a game. So I went in and looked for him.

"Waldo," I said. "Do you want to play a game?"

"What kind of game?"

"Come outside, and I'll show you."

We got outside, and I pointed. "You see that ladder? Well, I'm going to climb it first, then you climb after me. I will nail the pole so it won't fall, and you hold it while I'm doing that. Can you do that?"

"Yeah. You gonna let me climb the ladder?"

"Yes. It'll be fun. Then you can climb it to the top once we finish, if you want."

"Yeah. I want to."

When we were done—with him still not knowing why he was up there—I asked him to come down the ladder. But he wouldn't do it.

"Waldo, you need to come down now," I said.

"I want to stay here. Look, I can hold on to the pole! Whee! Look!"

He was swinging off the roof, holding on to the pole. Explaining a broken neck would be near impossible.

"Get off that before you kill yourself!" I yelled. I finally had to climb up and pull him off. Once we reached the ground, Chuy pulled up. He never noticed the damage. Close call. Dumb kid.

About the same time, twenty-six-year-old Valentina Tereshkova became the first woman to travel in space in a Russian-built rocket, much to the astonishment of Americans watching.

Push-button telephones were introduced and would replace the old-fashioned rotary phones. We couldn't afford a rotary at the time, much less a push-button. Years later, we did get a rotary. It would be our telephone for the next twenty years.

The cost of postage was a staggering five cents. The US Post Office introduced a five-digit zip code to better manage postal deliveries. Studebaker, an American automaker, went out of business and ended production. Chevrolet came out with the

Corvette Stingray in 1963, which became the most collectible of all Corvettes. It rivaled any Jaguar or Ferrari in both styling and rear-end suspension. The manufacturer's retail price was an astonishing $4,525! It was an incredible car at a price very few could even afford. I didn't see a real Corvette until 1970! The Corvette inspired in me an increased interest in and love of cars.

The Andy Griffith Show, I Love Lucy, Perry Mason, Leave It to Beaver, and *The Rifleman*, popular TV shows, captivated audiences from differing cultures. "The Twist," by Chubby Checker, was still a sensation with young kids, who found twisting to the music enchanting. The women loved it because it had a tendency to slim the waist if done long enough. "Surfing USA" by the Beach Boys hit the number-one spot in Billboard's Top 10, giving young Americans the impression that California was the place to be. But it was Elvis Presley who dominated the rock and roll era of music. Girls went wild when his songs came on the radio. The nickname Elvis the Pelvis became an attack on the singer because he made moves on stage that alarmed the Baptists. Come to think of it, they alarmed many parents who felt his moves were despicable and undesirable. They believed that by gyrating his lower body, he sent sexual connotations they adamantly didn't approve of. When Elvis was brought on *The Ed Sullivan Show*, an extremely popular evening series, he was told the camera would not cover his entire body. It would cover him only from the head down to his chest.

The boys, including me, noticed how the girls went wild, so we wanted to be just like Elvis, styling our hair like his, wearing scarves around our necks, and gyrating to his music. I tried all these things, never getting the attention of one single girl. Eventually, I decided to give up on the style. I couldn't gyrate my hips like Elvis did, even though I tried it in front of the mirror.

"You need to stop doing that. You look stupid. You'll never get a girl to look at you if you keep doing that stupid dance," Nancy remarked once as she walked by.

"I'll get it. Just wait and see," I said.

It never happened.

Johnny Cash also had followers. He appealed to many who liked rough country music. His appeal was idolized by prisoners and former prisoners. Cash went to prison for some unknown reason, so he could relate to the inmates. John Lennon, Paul McCartney, George Harrison, and Ringo Starr—The Beatles—released "Please Please Me" in 1963. Beatlemania swept the world as music lovers from Europe to the United States embraced a new form of rock and roll. Young people, including me, began to change not only in demeanor but also in dress. We became rebellious toward the commonly understood standards portrayed on TV. We liked having long hair, dressing down, walking around in sandals, and such. The style of dress wasn't flashy. It wasn't impressively stylish either. Jeans and a T-shirt were the norm. I liked it because dressing down was inexpensive and accepted. A climate of change was in the air. But not in Fort Stockton. It would take a few years for the whole notion of being a free spirit to reach our little town.

President Kennedy was dealing with civil rights, the economy, the space program, Vietnam, the increasing growth of communism, and the national minimum wage—big-ticket items generating major controversial conversations from Washington, D.C., to the foothills of Alabama. The country was divided along racial lines. America was thinking differently. Conservatism vs. liberalism, old vs. young, racism vs. inclusion, segregation vs. integration, war vs. peace. It was all dangerously boiling over. At times, the tension led to killings as America turned on itself. But not in Fort Stockton. At least not yet.

It was a dollar and twenty-five cents an hour for an honest day's work. The country seemed to be rolling along. President Kennedy was still beloved by many. However, the civil rights movement did occupy much of America's thoughts. Virginia, North Carolina, South Carolina, Georgia, Mississippi, and Alabama were still very racist in their policies and Southern views. They still believed in flying the rebel flag of the Civil War. In Birmingham, Alabama, members of the Ku Klux Klan dynamited a Baptist church, killing four young Black girls. It created major US public outrage.

On June 12, 1963, in Tuscaloosa, Alabama, Governor George Wallace faced off with General Henry Graham from the US military. Wallace blocked the enrollment of two African American students, Vivian Malone and James Hood. Despite an order from the federal court, Governor George Wallace appointed himself the temporary university registrar and stood in the doorway of the administration building to prevent the students from registering. In response, President Kennedy federalized the Alabama National Guard. One hundred guardsmen escorted the students to campus, and their commander, General Henry Graham, ordered George Wallace to step aside. Tensions ran high among white and Black people on that day as each called out the other. Racial slurs were exchanged, tempers flared, and shouting increased the tension to a boiling point. If it hadn't been for Kennedy stepping in, using the federal mandate, the students would have never been allowed to register. The bravery of these two students, in light of the danger, opened the door for more Black people to attend colleges and universities in the South.

Kennedy addressed the public on June 11 of that same year in a speech that clearly demonstrated his position on civil rights. The bill he submitted to Congress was finally passed a year later. The Civil Rights Act of 1964 became the law of the land. It was simple to understand. It outlawed discrimination based on race, color, religion, sex, and national origin. It went further by prohibiting unequal application of voter registration requirements, racial segregation in schools and public accommodations, and employment discrimination. But it didn't change the thinking and behavior of many whites, particularly in the South. The power of the federal government to enforce this law was weak, and it would take years before it would challenge those who did not conform. It would take decades before Americans embraced it. Not all did. But some. Almost daily, there were reports of discrimination.

In our neck of the woods, many of us were oblivious to the events changing our nation. In our town, those who kept up with the events didn't say much in public. We just went about our business as if the rest of the nation's problems were not ours. Surprisingly, I would get a first-hand look at how racism affected me when I got to the seventh grade.

Meanwhile, back in school, it was just a regular school day. I left the lunchroom with a belly full of mashed potatoes, Salisbury steak, and green beans. I walked toward the stand-alone building housing the sixth-grade students. I was taking my time because attending English class bummed me out. I liked the teacher. Although she was young and trying her best to make our experience exciting, she wasn't reaching me. I hated English class. But I tolerated it. What choice did I have? The class was boring as all get-out. I lumbered into her classroom, where the desks were all in neat little rows facing the chalkboard.

The bell rang. We took out our books and, with pencils in hand, wrote the assignment from the board. About ten minutes into class, the principal appeared in the doorway and summoned the teacher into the hall.

November 22, 1963, had turned out to be a bright, sunny day. I immediately assumed the principal was looking for some kid who had done something wrong. I mentally reviewed the morning period by period, then hour by hour. Nope. I couldn't think of anything I'd done wrong. The conversation between the principal and the teacher didn't take long. It was maybe a matter of seconds. The teacher gasped and, holding her face in her hands, burst into tears. *She's the one who did something wrong*, I thought.

Then she and the principal stepped into the room, and the principal made a solemn announcement.

"Students, at around one this afternoon, President Kennedy was shot in Dallas, Texas, and has been pronounced dead."

The girl next to me cried out, "No! No! No!" setting a chain reaction that sent ripples of horror and disbelief across the face of every student. She started to cry softly into her hands, shaking visibly as the other girls quickly surrounded her and offered some comfort by placing their arms on her shoulders. They all cried alongside her. Hysteria overtook many of the students, especially the girls.

I was shocked. President Kennedy was dead? He was beloved by so many Latino voters, including my own family. I asked myself, *Who would do something like this? Why? What is wrong with this country? Who shot him? Where is Dallas, Texas?*

Things were quiet and solemn for the rest of the day as we progressed through our classes. Each teacher had something to say on the matter, which led some of the students to ask the same questions I'd been thinking about earlier. All after-school activities were canceled, and we all walked home to find our parents glued to the TV, waiting for Walter Cronkite's news report.

For the next few days, President Kennedy's assignation dominated the news worldwide. At about 2:38 that afternoon on Air Force One, heading back to Washington, D.C., Lyndon B. Johnson was sworn in as the thirty-sixth president of the United States. Kennedy would not live to see the Civil Rights Act become law, nor would he see a man land on the moon—something he'd promised Americans would do by the end of the decade.

The Games

In a few days, the country settled in for the Thanksgiving holiday with some solemnity. Kennedy's death weighed heavily on people. My grandmother spoke of his compassion for Latinos. She'd spoken of him as the president who would bring all Latinos out of poverty. The picture of John Kennedy and his brother Robert would remain on her living room wall for years. That's how much she adored them.

Being off for Thanksgiving offered some reprieve from the sad veil that enveloped our school, yet I looked forward to Thanksgiving, since it was a special time of year for people living in the barrio. Interestingly enough, it was also when we had plenty of food to eat. I don't know how we came upon it. The church would bring food to the poor folk living south of the tracks. That might have made us recipients. Chuy would bring a turkey or ham a day or two before the holiday. I don't know if he bought it or if someone gave it to him. We had turkey, dressing, potatoes, beans, tortillas, and an occasional pecan pie. These were good times. To this day, I still enjoy Thanksgiving probably more than any other holiday—except for Christmas, New Year, my birthday, Halloween, and Marti Gras.

I was looking forward to the Thanksgiving break, hoping for some cheerfulness at home. Spending time with the neighborhood kids was on the top of my list. We did not get together as often as we did before junior high. We all had so much going on in our lives as we grew older. Though we lived close to each other, we saw very little of each other. Not even in school did we hang out. Life was getting in the way of our time with childhood friends.

November in the Texas desert is still warm. Not as hot as the summer months of course, but still warm enough for us to spend time outside. We now played street baseball with real baseballs, real gloves, and real bats. We had to move our games to the baseball field at Alamo Elementary. There were more families who now owned cars, and the streets were not safe for children. Matter of fact, they weren't safe for animals either. Friday afternoons and Saturday mornings were the worst. That was when the drunk drivers headed home.

We were all getting taller, louder, stronger, and extremely competitive, to the point where arguments broke out among the baseball players. One Sunday morning at the Alamo Elementary ballpark, we started up a game. A group of boys from across the railroad tracks showed up with equipment in hand and challenged us. The game started. I played right field mainly because I didn't have a glove and most balls were hit either to center or left field. Right field was for the weakest player. That was me! I didn't care. At least I got to play. However, when I was up to bat, I would frustrate the pitcher by shifting the bat from left to right. I could bat left- or right-handed, a talent that gave him fits. Still, batting was not my forte.

"Make up your mind! Are you batting left or right?" he'd yell. I could sense his anxiety. In his frustration, if he pitched foul balls, I could walk to first base. He didn't like this at all. The ball came in slow. I hit the ball to right field, where the weakest player was, and it went past him. I ran to first base, rounded the corner, and was heading to second when the ball hit the second baseman's glove.

He shouted, "OUT!"

Clearly, I was not. An argument broke out.

"You are blind! I'm safe!" I yelled in his face, spit and sweat flying everywhere. He pushed me. Hard. I fell flat on my ass. The players on my side of the park ran toward the second baseman.

"You can't push him like that! He was safe!" one of my teammates yelled.

The other team ran out onto the field. That's when the fighting broke out. Punches were flying every which way, just like in the movies. There were boys wrestling in the dirt while others were just trying to stop the fracas.

I got punched in the back of the head, which left a small bump the size of a silver dollar. I didn't know where it came from. Crying, I walked away, holding my head.

The fighting ended as fast as it started. The older boys stepped in between the warriors and kept them apart. I didn't get a punch in; however, I learned a valuable lesson that day. I was definitely not a fighter and never would be.

I walked home holding my head. John, his arm around my shoulders, swore we would get even with the punks. It would be some time before I ventured out to the baseball field again.

The holidays came and went without much fanfare. Other than me getting smacked in the head, one day led to another. Fidel and Sammy were not to be found even though they only lived two blocks away. They were into other interests and seldom invited me to join in the trouble they were creating. The gloomy sadness that prevailed with Kennedy's assassination began to subside somewhat.

As things calmed down in our little world, classes resumed with some normalcy. Thanksgiving fell into Christmas. We were off again, not to return until 1964. With the new year, I tried to concentrate on my classes with little regard for how rapidly the year was passing us by. English and reading were still hard subjects and continued to haunt me. Without my command of the English language, I spoke Spanish when I was out of class or out of sight of teachers. I spoke Spanish after school. I spoke Spanish at home. I spoke Spanish everywhere other than in classes.

My English progressed slowly, but my music playing was moving along faster than I thought could be possible. Cornet playing became a passion, so I got better. I could now read music. It was thrilling to be able to read complicated notes on a sheet of paper. Why could I read music and not be very proficient when it came to reading Shakespeare? I couldn't untangle that one. Even though I wasn't as good as some of the other kids, I could hold my own. At least I wasn't last chair. Nobody wanted to be the last chair in any group. Last chair meant weakness.

The band director had a system for ensuring our playing got better. He'd put the best player in what he called first chair. Second chair was the second-best player, and so on, making the last chair player the worst. To move up a chair, a student had to challenge the player sitting up from them. Beating that person to a contest of playing and reading music meant moving up. The whole idea was to be the first chair. There were ten trumpet players in all. I had practiced enough to consider challenging the eighth chair.

I can move up a chair or two, I thought. But before I could propose a challenge, the last chair challenged me! I wasn't about to be last chair. No, no, not me. The challenge came on a Tuesday afternoon. We were both prepared to defeat the other, like warriors prepared to demolish the other. Each player would play a music scale suggested by the director, then he would listen to each of us play the piece we had prepared. I was nervous as hell. I played the scale. He played the scale. I played my piece. He played his piece. We waited for the verdict.

"Each of you has improved a lot since the beginning of school. Both of you should be commended. But ..."

I knew there was going to be a *but*.

"You are going to stay in your position for now. You were both good, but not enough to make a change. You can try again next time."

I was relieved. Playing next to the last chair is not very prestigious or rewarding. Anyone in this position played accompaniment and not the melody.

I waited for next time.

January and February were very cold. They soon gave into spring, offering us opportunities to play outside. But instead of indulging in silly games, I kept playing the cornet. You know you're getting better when your parents or siblings no longer ask that you "Shut the hell up." When they got aggravated at my playing, I'd go outside. The dogs howled when I played a B flat. I knew then I needed more practice. There were times when I'd just get in the back seat of the car and practice for thirty minutes, stopping only when I was told to come inside or when my lips started feeling numb. I could play a song from beginning to end.

The pieces weren't hard—they just didn't have the melodies the first trumpets had. The first three players carried the tune. The next three played accompaniment, but those at the bottom only played farting noises. At least, that's what it sounded like. I thought that if I could move up to at least second trumpet, I'd be content. To do that, I had to move up three chairs. Nearly impossible. But I practiced every day, hoping to beat out some of the guys. I practiced so much that my lips turned blue from lack of blood circulating through. After thirty minutes or so of not playing, they would stop vibrating.

By the end of the year, I was ready. I challenged the guy next to me, which moved me up! I was overjoyed. A month went by, and I tried again, failing miserably. There would be no further challenges that year. I settled into first chair, third trumpet. Not bad. Embracing my position as the Lord's decision, I ended the year satisfied.

The school year was coming to an end, and the PE coaches were gearing up for the end-of-year track-and-field day—the biggest event of the year. Everyone had a chance to participate without putting forth too much effort. The PE students had to participate as well. Not long before the event day, one of the coaches asked the PE boys to get in a line and run around the track. There were at least thirty of us. I had no idea what he was thinking. But I ran and almost passed out from lack of oxygen.

After the first lap around the track, he gave us each a number from 1 to 4. I was a number 1. Finally, I got to be number 1! I was excited, thinking I was one of the fastest runners even though I'd come in the middle of the pack. He gave each group a twelve-inch piece of pipe taped with a color on the ends. He showed us how to pass the pipe, or what he called a baton, to each other while we were running.

"You boys are going to be in the four-forty relay. Robert, you will start, then Henry will be second. You pass the baton on to Henry, making sure you don't drop it. Henry, you pass it on to Mikie. Then, Mikie, you pass it on to Joe. Joe will be anchor."

"What's an anchor, Coach?" one boy asked.

"The anchor is the fastest runner on each team."

"Coach," I said, turning to him. "If I'm number 1, shouldn't I be the fastest?"

"No. You are the slowest runner, and the slowest runner always starts first."

What the hell? I'm first, but I'm the slowest, I thought. *It don't make no sense.*

We practiced all week, passing the baton to each other without dropping it. It wasn't that simple. After several mishaps, we had it down. Then the day of the event was upon us. School let out right after lunch. The afternoon classes were canceled, so everyone could attend.

This is a great event, I thought. *No classes*! Some of the parents came early to help out and cheer for the athletes. We were being called "athletes." I'd never been called that. But there we were, a bunch of athletes, getting ready to participate in this major event. Imagine that!

"Ready. On your mark! BANG!" a coach yelled. Then a gunshot went off, and I started running, holding the baton in my right hand. I ran a quarter of the way around the track, about a hundred and ten yards, then I passed the baton to Henry, who dropped it and quickly picked it up.

I walked over to the middle of the track and started gagging. Vomit shot out, and I couldn't control it. I was embarrassed and hoping no one was watching me spill my guts. Then I saw two other boys spitting their guts out too! Whose damn idea was it to hold running events right after lunch?

Spitting out what was left of lunch, I walked over to the finish line just in time to see Joe, the anchor, running past all the other runners. He was fast!

"Run, Joe, run! Run, Joe, run!" we chanted. Joe, who was in front of all the others, came in first! Henry, Mikie, and I ran after him. With arms around each other, we jumped up and down, yelling, "We got first, we got first, we got first!"

The whistle blew for the next race to begin, and the coach came over to us, smiling.

"You guys did it! Now, get off the track and go support your friends."

We walked back, smiling and laughing over an unanticipated, magnificent win. That's when I saw her. In the stands, a few rows back, sat Mom! She was always supportive, but to come out in the hot sun to watch her oldest compete in a running race? Now, that was a big surprise.

She was proud. I waved, and she waved back. With my chest puffed out like Superman's on that day—in the hot sun, after running my first relay—I was an athlete!

At the end, we were given ribbons for our efforts. A blue ribbon for coming in first. That ribbon would adorn the fake mantel right above the fake fireplace in our house for years to come. It was the place where excellence was displayed. The blue ribbon sat there, right along with some honorary pictures, mostly of me looking rather prideful and arrogant. This would be a reminder of what we could accomplish if we tried. As the years went by, more awards from the other children crowded my ribbon. This would be the only blue ribbon I'd ever get in twelve years of school. As a matter of fact, this would be the only ribbon I'd ever get, regardless of color, for the rest of my school years. My days as an athlete began and ended on that day. My sixth-grade year was over.

The summer of '64 brought about some serious anxiety. Report cards were coming out soon. Even though I was getting better at many of the subjects, I was still very concerned about my standing when it came to promotion. Teachers would not tell us on the last day of school if we had made it or not. The year ending did nothing for my nerves. *Will I be moving on to the next grade?* I wondered. Teachers had to average all sorts of things to determine student outcomes, so I was left with this pressing anxiety for several days.

About two weeks after the year ended, those dreadful envelopes arrived in the mail. I was the only one in my family in junior high, and I knew which was mine even though it was addressed to my parents. I sat there holding the envelope in my hands, waiting for the inevitable. Was I going to pass to the seventh grade? I had my doubts.

I said, "*El nombre del padre, del hijo, y el espíritu santo.*" ("In the name of the Father, the Son, and the Holy Spirit.") Then, after making the sign of the cross, I carefully tore open the envelope and immediately went to the back page.

I knew it! Another miracle! Making the sign of the cross before I got any news became a ritual I practiced for the rest of my life. Despite my grades being low, I had barely made it. In the sixth grade, there were no more letter grades. We got number grades, which were more revealing of our performance. There were some 60s mixed in with some low 70s. I did manage a B in PE, and that was because I couldn't get myself to shower in a group. It just wasn't my cup of tea. I got an S for conduct in three of the classes. Imagine that. I also had a perfect attendance note on my report card. Imagine that. I hadn't skipped school since the first grade. I was beginning to like this junior high stuff.

Rite of Passage

hen we were off to the onion fields again.

On Monday, right after the last day of school, Chuy came in to tell us we had a job picking onions. The Sunday before, we'd sat outdoors, sharpening scissors and getting ready for another miserable summer.

Five o'clock in the morning came awfully early. We packed our lunch bags with egg/bean, egg/chorizo, egg/potato, or my favorite, egg/bologna tacos. Running out the door, we grabbed our hats as the clock approached five thirty. I'd sleep in the back of the truck until we got there, then I'd drag my butt out with a serious lack of enthusiasm. Nancy, age twelve; Wanda, ten; Jesse, nine; and Imelda, eight, didn't fare much better. There were now six Alfaros working the fields alongside the Garza, Rodriguez, Jimenez, and Fabela families—all of us from the hood. We were told money was needed to buy clothes for the next school year and put meat on the table.

We all hated it. Why couldn't parents just buy the clothes without having to put children into labor camps? Where were the authorities who monitored the child labor laws? Were there any child labor laws in the hood? I wasn't a child anymore. I figured I wouldn't be able to get out of this kind of work. What a bummer.

We toiled in the hot summer from sunup to sundown. I hated the smell of onion and hated the heat even more. The sun was not as excruciating between the time we arrived and lunchtime. By the afternoon, it was murder. At times, the air got so hot, I felt like I was breathing onions.

When the Garzas quit sometime around three in the afternoon, that was the signal for the rest of us to pack up and leave. Apparently, their father knew better than to have his children be smothered in the hot heat.

The job lasted for a month. There were no more onion fields to pick. I don't know how much money we made. Information like this was never shared. It wasn't our business to ask or our business to assume.

"You've been good. This is for you. Don't tell the others. You can buy whatever you want. But remember, this is all you're getting. Now, don't spend it all at once," Mom said to me one Saturday morning. Then she handed me five dollars!

I sat there staring at the most money I had ever had for myself. The most money I'd had since Jesus Christ was found on a manger somewhere in Africa. I couldn't believe her generosity. I looked up at her and smiled.

"Gracias, Mom," I said, giving her a hug–something we didn't do much of in that household.

In math class, we'd learned to calculate hourly wages. The teacher wanted us to learn how much someone would have to make in order to survive living alone. So I decided to apply my mathematical skills to calculating how the five dollars translated into an hourly wage. *Let's see,* I thought. *Four weeks, five days a week, eight hours a day equals one hundred and sixty hours, divided by five dollars equals thirty-two cents an hour. That's pretty good!*

I had enough to go swimming every day and pay my way in. Or I could go to the movies with a quarter. Or I could simply save the money for some important thing, like hanging out with friends and uncles. Five dollars was indeed a lot of money for any kid living in the barrio. I was a lucky guy.

But all those ideas were quickly nipped in the bud. On that same Saturday, Pino, whom I'd started calling "Mom" because some of my friends called their mothers "Mom," asked me to join her. I thought she was inviting me to go shopping. Instead, we walked north across the railroad tracks.

"Where are we going?" I asked.

"We are going to a woman's house to help her."

"Help her do what? I want to go swimming."

"You can do that later. Keep walking."

We stopped at a house with a large garage in the back. Mom had gotten a part-time job at a washeteria. Some old white lady had converted her detached garage into a place where people could come and wash their clothes. She charged folks two dollars an hour to use her machines. Those with money could afford to pay someone else to wash their clothes.

When they dropped off the clothes, Mom washed them. The machines were old washtubs with rollers on top that we used to squeeze the water out. She was paid one dollar for each load. In an old lady's garage, washing other people's clothing was how I got stuck being someone else's laundryman. I did this for a month until Chuy—I still called him by his first name—came home one afternoon and announced that we were going to the fields again. This time, it was to pick cantaloupe.

Coyanosa is a small farming community about thirty miles northwest of Fort Stockton. In the early 1960s, it boasted a population of six hundred residents, many of whom were farmers. It is considered one of the best areas for growing cantaloupe because of the potassium-rich soil. Over the years, it has been considered the place that grows the sweetest cantaloupes. Its farms brought people from as far away as New

Mexico, Oklahoma, Arizona, and, of course, all over Texas. As its harvest's popularity grew, the community turned it into a yearly Cantaloupe Festival. Before Coyanosa was famous for its cantaloupes, we were one of the families hired to pick them. The work of picking cantaloupes was hard on the back. Bending, picking up, and placing them in wooden crates was hard labor. The crates were hauled off to a large conveyor belt, where workers separated them according to ripeness.

After we were done picking cantaloupes, the day was not over. It was back to the washeteria for me. What a summer.

In July of 1964, I became a fully ordained teenager. I had survived thirteen years! Becoming a teenager in 1964 meant very little. It meant growing pubic hair, having your voice change and your bones hurt, and seeing plain ol' ugliness setting in. I was weighing in at almost ninety pounds soaking wet, which gave my grandmother something to worry about.

She would tell me, "*Necesitas comer, mijo. Te estás poniendo muy flaco.*" ("You need to eat, son. You're getting too skinny.") I could go there any time of the day, and she'd insist I eat something. Always in the kitchen wearing her flowery apron, which never came off, she insisted people eat. There was always a pot of something cooking in her kitchen. Frijoles, tortillas, eggs, and bologna were regular staples at her house, which meant if you wanted to eat, you knew what you were having. No second guessing.

On special occasions, she'd have a pot of chicken cooking on the stove for her *caldo*, or soup. A kind and considerate woman, she managed to hold down a household full of mostly adults, without a husband. My grandfather had died of a heart attack a few years earlier. How she managed this was beyond me.

I loved her. She was always kind to me. I loved being with her when no one was around. Some mornings, we'd share a cup of coffee, sit around the kitchen table, and talk about anything that came to mind. Our conversations were always in Spanish. She would throw in a *sun-a-va-vee-shee* every once in a while if she got upset. We would discuss the weather, my parents, her children, her health, and, most of all, my schooling.

Learning New Things

Istarted the seventh grade with a new pair of boots, new pants, and a very nice pullover shirt. They weren't called polo shirts. They were just shirts, and I liked mine. The boots were a size bigger than I would normally wear, but Chuy was insistent that I get a size bigger so I could grow into them. I went around the first few days of school making sloshing noises.

At thirteen, my brain must have grown too. I was now smart enough to find ways to compensate for such things. I borrowed an extra pair of socks from Chuy. If I wore two pairs, the boots would not rub against my toes or heels, preventing blisters. The extra pair also prevented the boots from coming off when I tried to run. This was the first time I'd owned a pair of boots, so it took some time to get used to walking in them. They weren't cowboy boots. They were work boots. They lasted me all year and into the next. No one made fun of them like they did everything else. I grew to love those boots.

Getting back to school meant getting back with some of my old friends and having the opportunity to make friends with kids from the north side of the tracks—not many, but certainly enough to get a feel for how the other side lived. Being invited to their houses after school showed me the differences. They had their own rooms. *How can a teenager have his own room?* I wondered. There were doors to keep people out! Their houses were bigger and better built. They had carports and yards with grass. They had real dishes, and they all matched. Large kitchen tables, where everyone could sit down and eat all at the same time, were a revelation. Their refrigerators were big and heavily stocked. How glorious. This was heaven.

I didn't get jealous of all the things my friends had. I just wanted the same things. Certainly, my own room, which I knew would never happen. Seeing all this got me to thinking about how my life would be when I could afford such luxuries. Daydreaming and wishing and planning were part of my being. I made up my mind. When I got old enough to get a real job, I was going to buy these things for my family. I wanted to be just like my northern friends. But that day, at that time, at least I had a pair of brand-new boots.

School slowly dragged on. I had different teachers every year, except for the band director, the PE coaches, and the librarian. Nothing seemed to excite me. I was still having a hard time fitting in, and I longed for friends outside of band. The problem was, the kids from up north were branching off to do their own thing, and I couldn't join them.

Why?

Money, or lack of it.

I felt lost, so I concentrated more on playing the cornet. In band, I could belong. Band became my safe place. I'd linger around after class was dismissed, hoping to learn and get ideas from the other kids. After we'd lingered around too long after class, the director would shove us off. I borrowed a baritone just to see if I could play it. No problem. Then I borrowed a trombone. It was more difficult to play, and I couldn't get the sound right. Next, I tried the French horn. I liked that it came easy to me, but one of my buddies told me this instrument was for girls, so I gave it up.

In the seventh grade, I was part of the seventh- and eighth-grade combined band. Graduating to that band was exhilarating. The seventh and eighth graders could play more than just one song from beginning to end. We were going places. And we were playing better songs. The band director praised players who were doing a great job and withheld encouragement from those who were not. Of course, the eighth graders were so much better than the others, but at least we were now playing more difficult songs.

"We are going to learn a song by John Philip Souza," the director said one day as he was handing out "The Stars and Stripes Forever." When I saw my part—I was still playing third trumpet—it had notes all over the place! How in the world could anyone play this song, let alone the first trumpet part?

But that wasn't all. He also handed us the school's fight song and "The Star-Spangled Banner." We had to learn them all.

"At the high school homecoming game, we will march with the high school band during the halftime show," the director told us rather abruptly. We had a few days to learn the songs AND be able to march while playing! This was way too much for a mere seventh grader.

Playing third trumpet just wasn't any fun. It was not motivating enough. I couldn't make out what I was playing. I wanted to play the melody associated with the first trumpet. So I borrowed the music from the band hall and took it home. Playing this part was enlightening. I learned to play the melody. (Unofficially.) I practiced the parts repeatedly until I could hit some of the high notes. The pace was difficult, but I had a good ear for what it should sound like. My confidence was building. The day before homecoming, we played "The Stars and Stripes Forever." How the band director knew I was playing first trumpet, I'll never know.

"Robert!" he yelled. "If you want to play first trumpet, you must challenge the player in front of you until you get to first trumpet. There are six people ahead of you. You'll have to challenge each one. Now, get your part and play that part. Understand?"

I understood. His remarks, said in front of all the band members, caused me to shrink into my chair. I would never play the first trumpet part. I could do it, but not while I was next to the last chair. Not in the seventh grade, anyway. I had to redeem myself and show everyone I could do this. So, I continued to practice. And I made it to second trumpet.

I tried to reason with logic. Could I continue challenging myself and make it to first-chair trumpet? I needed some reassurance. Some hope. A miracle. I looked at the guy next to me. I had to beat him plus three others before I could make it to first chair. In my heart, I knew I could, but in reality, it was not to happen.

January 1965 had me going back to school with a renewed interest. I was determined to beat anyone who got in my way of being first-chair trumpet. Practicing during the holidays reenergized my persistence. I could reach high notes that others could not. The band director was seeing the progress, so he encouraged me to challenge other players, which I did. I was much better.

Joey, this white kid, had a silver trumpet, and he was good. He'd been first chair since the sixth grade. That's how good he was. He was just a natural player. I needed just two more challenges to make it to first trumpet. Not first chair, but first-trumpet music playing. The year moved along. I never got to move any farther. I talked myself into believing I could do this! I thought, *If I can make it this far, imagine what I can do next year!* I had a goal.

I don't know if the seventh-grade teachers were the cause of my lack of enthusiasm or if it was that the curriculum sucked. We all had to take history, and history and I connected really quickly. Here was a subject I enjoyed. For some reason, it resonated with me. Too bad my history teacher, Mr. Hinkle, was not a very inspiring or creative teacher. In fact, he was the most boring instructor of all time. He had no class. No talent. No skills at making the subject come alive for the students. Mr. Hinkle was a military veteran who'd turned to teaching after his service was up. He still wore the military-style crew haircut—short all around with the front of his head sporting a few strands of hair that stuck straight up. He was a quiet man who was there, biding his time, until something better came along.

His classroom was in a portable behind the PE building. He taught Texas history and was not very good at it. As soon as the bell rang, he would stand up from behind his desk and ask everyone to keep standing. Then he would start off the period with, "I pledge allegiance to the flag of the United States of America and to the ..." And he expected everyone to recite it in unison with their right hand over their heart.

Our desks were in rows, all in a straight line, military style. We were expected to come in the room, sit down, grab our books, sit up straight, and wait for instructions. No talking, shallow breathing, no questions, no silliness. He was the drill sergeant.

Right after the Pledge of Allegiance, like good little children, we took our books from under the desks, all in unison.

"Page sixty-five," he said one day through clenched teeth, not looking up from his book. He gave us time to get to the right page. Then he looked at us with that military eye, the one where one eye is looking straight at you and the other is squinting, as if to say, "You'd better get there quick before I crack open your skull!"

"Jaime, start reading," he'd say. He always repeated himself when giving instructions, as if we needed to hear it twice because we were dense.

Jaime would read a few lines, then Mr. Hinkle would ask a girl. Boy read, girl read. Twenty minutes of reading out loud, then twenty minutes of reading silently. During this time, no one would say a word. The place would be quieter than the East Side Cemetery on any given night. There were no questions about what was being read. We'd finish a chapter, then we'd spend a day or two answering all the questions at the end of the book. Quietly. By ourselves. When finished, we'd exchange our work with the person in front of us.

Mr. Hinkle would give us the correct answer, one by one, while we marked in red those that were wrong. He'd have us calculate the grade based on how many we got right, then we'd turn in our answers for a grade. And on to the next chapter.

He did very little. He ran a tight ship. I learned very little. At the end, I got a good grade. We all did.

"I can do a better job of teaching this class than him," I mumbled to myself one day. "I know I can do a better job!" I loved history, and this man was making it so no one would ever appreciate the subject. I hated this class more than anything else. But because the class was easy, no one complained. If we did what we were told, which wasn't much, we could easily make an A. The tests were open-book tests. Any moron could ace this class. Even Troy.

"When will we get books, sir?" was a question a smart-looking blond girl asked on the first day of school.

"You don't need them. The books will be here under your desk when you get here."

"So how are we supposed to do our homework if we don't have books?"

"Like I said, you don't need books outside this classroom," he said.

This gave anyone else who dared ask any questions he considered to be ridiculously stupid little desire to speak. Later, I found out that he didn't like to check out books because, according to him, students were irresponsible. He could not afford to have them lose books he was accountable for. That assumption came from a classmate who was taking his class for the second time. I believed him.

I got up one Saturday morning to watch my favorite cartoons. We all got up early, grabbed a cup of coffee, and gathered around the set. It wasn't a big set, so if we wanted a front-row seat, we got up early. And we sat on the floor. Otherwise, we'd have to grab a chair or stand behind those who'd gotten there earlier.

Beginning the day with an hour or two of silly cartoons started our weekend. By ten o'clock, they were over. The TV went off, and we started our morning chores—making up our beds, getting clothes off the floor, cleaning, throwing out the trash, sweeping, and mopping. Getting the house clean before Chuy came back from wherever he went on Saturday mornings was an expectation. Threats of death and dismemberment were made if things weren't done.

Sometimes he and Mom would leave together and always come back right before lunch. By then, Nancy had made her tortillas while Wanda got the kitchen ready for either Mom or Chuy, depending on who was doing the cooking. If Chuy was cooking, he expected his favorite pans to be clean and ready to go.

Chuy was a pretty good cook when he set his mind to it or when he wasn't hungover from the previous night's drinking. He exposed us to meals from his motherland. My favorite were the strips of beef sliced thinly, salted and peppered, and cooked on a skillet to perfection with the aid of real lime juice. That was it!

When the meat was brown and sizzling, the strips landed on a hot flour tortilla and were topped with pico de gallo.

Then we'd chomp away, not waiting for it to cool down. This always brought on a delightful morning. Good stuff.

There were other meals I wouldn't feed to a dog. Liver and onions was a far cry from being tasty. In Chuy's mind, this was a delicacy to be enjoyed with freshly made pinto beans and slices of raw jalapeño. I'd try, at least once, anything he'd cook. But it was hit or miss most of the time. *Tripas*, or intestines—that terrible-tasting stuff that didn't go with beans, or potatoes, or anything, for that matter—were difficult to swallow. I learned my lesson when it came to that. Chuy brought it from the meat market one day. It looked like a small stomach wrapped and held together by these long strips of rope. It looked like a fat sausage. After adding the right number of spices, he'd cook it in the oven for an hour or two. When it was fully cooked, he'd sprinkle lime juice, pepper, and salt, then cut it into slices. Big fat ones.

"That looks good," I commented, eyeing the thing as saliva trickled down the corners of my mouth.

"Here, try a piece," he said, handing me a slice on a tortilla.

After blowing on it to cool it down, I bit a big piece off. With the first bite, the texture of the meat felt strange. I chewed. The longer I chewed, the nastier it got. I swear, the taste hit me, and I almost gagged.

Chuy looked at me with that stern look that screamed, "If you spit it out, you're not eating for a week!"

I tried really hard not to disappoint him, but I was chewing on a rubber tire tube. It just would not break up! I swallowed and almost choked on the slimy, awful-tasting stuff.

"*Está muy bueno*," I told him. ("It's very good.") He smiled, and as soon as he turned around, I ran out of the room with the intestine taco and gave it to Waldo, who was mesmerized by whatever was showing on the TV.

"Here. Eat this. Chuy told me to give it to you. And if you don't eat it, he will spank you good. Now eat it!"

He didn't take his eyes off the TV set. He grabbed it and started chewing. I stood there waiting for him to gag. He ate it! He ate the whole thing!

As I was leaving the room, I slapped him on the back of the head and told him he was a dummy.

After that episode, I vowed not to eat anything else Chuy cooked. If it looked suspicious, I gave it to Waldo first. If he didn't die, then I'd try it. Most of the time, Chuy's cooking was delicious. Food was to be enjoyed and not taken for granted. I ate what was given to me. We all did. Food was not to be thrown away. Therefore, there were no leftovers. Now, if Mom cooked, it was eggs, beans, potatoes, and fideo mixed with ground beef. Beef if we were lucky. Her cooking was simple and tasty. When we ate, there was no arguing or yelling. We ate what was given to us, or we didn't eat. Period.

Chuy was happiest when he was working full-time and making decent money. He still went out drinking, but he was slowing down. These were pleasant times in our house. They were the happiest as well. But as we got older, we fell into our own dedicated tasks. Wanda, at ten or eleven years of age, took over the lunch menu and learned how to cook Mom's recipes. I didn't mind her cooking because it was simple. It was to my liking. Sometimes too much salt killed the taste, but more often than not, even for a girl that young, she did pretty good. Nancy continued to make the tortillas until high school took over most of her time. By then, Mom had discovered Juana's tortillas. Juana made these gigantic tortillas that looked like flying saucers and sold them for a dollar fifty a dozen! They were perfect for a family of nine because it only took one tortilla to fill the belly.

Around eleven o'clock one Saturday morning, the girls turned on the TV and began watching a show with young people dancing. A guy by the name of Dick Clark, the host of the show, talked about the newest songs hitting the Billboard charts. He had bands playing the hottest and most popular music hits while the young danced away. Recognizing one of the songs, I worked my way toward the TV.

American Bandstand started as a regional show in Philadelphia in 1957 and gained popularity in the early sixties. I had never noticed it before. Maybe because we were expected to turn off the TV right after the cartoons. *American Bandstand* came right after cartoons, and we didn't even know it.

Anyway, on this Saturday, Dick Clark was introducing Elvis the Pelvis. He sang a song while the dancers swayed back and forth to the rhythm of the music. Later, Dick introduced a group of young men who called themselves The Dovells. They had a hit single called "You Can't Sit Down." As the music played, young men and women danced their hearts out. They were all white on a black-and-white TV. The girls wore fancy sweaters with nice skirts. No girl wore pants. The men were well-dressed. They sported a suit or sports coat. All the guys wore skinny ties held down by some shiny object called a tie clip. Feet were moving, butts were shaking. All to the rhythm of the music. While the music played on, cameras caught the dance moves up close. I stood there amazed and perplexed.

"How'd they do that," I said to no one in particular. These kids could move!

Dick used the show to feature artists who were fairly unknown, as well as those who were already famous, like The Beatles. I was fascinated by the show. This became my Saturday pastime for the next several years. I wanted to move like the dancers, so I'd practice right along with them. Every Saturday, I'd wake up, not caring about the cartoons anymore but more focused on the music young people were listening to and practicing the moves the dancers came up with. I was hooked. I loved that show!

Amy, my aunt, who was maybe five years older than I, invited me to a dance at the Community Center. I don't think it was her intention to string me along. It so happened that one Friday night, we were all listening to music at my grandmother's when Amy blurted out, "I'm going out! I'll be back later." Since I was a teenager, I felt like it would be a good idea to hang out with the older crowd. I didn't know where she and her friends were going, but I didn't want to be left behind.

"Can I go with you?" I asked.

"Don't you need to ask your dad or mom?"

"It's Friday, and they won't miss me."

"Come on then," she said, winking as she grabbed my arm.

We all got into someone's car, not worrying about who was driving or whether it was safe. We were off to the Community Center, a recreational teenager hangout located a few blocks toward downtown. Smiling from ear to ear and feeling all grown up, I couldn't believe my luck. I knew I was going to have fun with these people.

The place was dimly lit, the music playing loudly. We walked closer to the dance floor, watching several couples dancing. I stood close to Amy just in case something unusual happened. I'd heard some of these dances turned into fistfights when boys asked girls to dance. Infringing on someone's girlfriend was frowned upon. Not wanting to be picked on, I wasn't about to ask anyone to dance. The DJ played another song—one with a rhythm that compelled my foot to tap along with the music. Couples moved toward the middle of the dance floor and started dancing.

Amy looked at me and said, "You want to dance?"

"I don't know how," I said, shaking in terror at the thought. The last thing I wanted was to make a fool of myself.

"No problem. Just move your feet and hands, like this." She demonstrated with confidence. Before I knew it, she'd pulled me onto the dance floor, and I started moving like she showed me. I was stiff as a board. I couldn't make my feet do what I saw on *American Bandstand*, even though I'd practiced for weeks! My hands weren't moving either. My brain was not communicating with my body. I just couldn't synchronize my feet with my hands. My head was straight, like I was holding a basket on it. I was feeling self-conscious, wishing this song would end. Sweat poured down my armpits.

Is anyone looking at my stupid moves? I wondered. *Do I look like an idiot?* I closed my eyes and tried to pretend I was on *American Bandstand*.

It wasn't working.

The song finally ended, and the clapping started, with me clapping right along. No one noticed the spastic thirteen-year-old! Amy just laughed and pulled another kid onto the dance floor.

My first experience dancing in public was not what I thought it would be. I'd failed miserably. I was going to need a lot more practice if I was ever going to be a dancer like the kids on the show. Reluctantly, I danced one more song with Amy as she again pulled me onto the dance floor. By this time, I'd studied the other dancers, watching their moves and wondering how in God's name they could move like that. Confidence moves you in mysterious ways.

In my head, after seeing others dancing, I was ready to show the world I could dance. I had been eyeing this girl who'd been standing by herself most of the night. She didn't seem to have a boyfriend, and the chances of getting the bejesus knocked out of me were slight. I wanted to walk over and ask her to dance, but I had to find the right song—one I knew I could dance to while looking at least look halfway decent on the dance floor.

I'm going to ask her to dance on the next song. I'm going to. Yes, I am. I kept telling myself I could do this. I moved toward her. I held out my hand and asked her to dance.

She looked at me, and for a split second, I felt rejected. I was thinking I shouldn't have done this. Shyly, she put her hand in mine, and we moved toward the dance floor. I was shaking, nervous as all get-out, when the DJ played a song with a faster beat, much faster than my body could handle. I let go of her hand. I moved my arms and legs, and my entire body followed. Flailing away as if I were shooing flies. I turned, swung to the music, ignored her face, and closed my eyes. I pretended to be a dancer in a dance contest. I knew I just wasn't coordinated enough to pull it off, but I didn't care. It was too late to do anything but dance.

So, I danced.

The song ended, she went back to her corner, and I went back to mine like a boxer who had just gotten whipped in the first round. I wasn't going to be Elvis the Pelvis, but at least I didn't chicken out. I had asked a girl to dance for the first time in my life. It felt marvelous. I felt all grown up. I was proud of myself, wishing I could do this more often.

Maybe I will get invited again, I thought. *Maybe next time, I can ask more than just one girl to dance. Maybe I can dance more than one song.* I knew I could dance like those on the Bandstand.

But that day never came. My aunt didn't invite me to go with her again. Oh well. It was a blast. At least I had my one night of dancing.

Perhaps, I thought, *there will be more when I get to high school.* Awesome!

Changing Times

Even though I was concentrating on my schoolwork, hoping to do better with my performance in the various classes proved to be difficult. I was still a weak student, but my English was getting better. I knew every cussword in both languages. Teachers would write on the report card every six weeks that I had the ability to do better if I tried harder.

So I tried harder. But the teachers were not encouraging. They had this attitude that said, "If you want to learn, you have to apply yourself. No one is going to do this for you." Being a teenager, with all the changes my body was having to deal with, only made things worse. My brain was still growing, and with those spurts of growth, I was beginning to question authority. I don't know what happened. Maybe I grew a pair of balls. Who knows. What I did know was that I wasn't a good student who did everything the teachers asked. I turned in just enough homework to keep them from contacting Mother.

At home, I was being lazy and not helping out, always coming up with excuses as to why I could not take care of the younger siblings, take the trash out, or clean my room. I was questioning why I didn't have the things other boys my age had. Why we were always struggling to make ends meet. Why I had to ask permission for everything I wanted to do. I wasn't being a good son to my parents. I didn't care what Chuy thought, but I didn't want to disappoint my mother. She was so calming and supportive that I had to make sure I didn't disappoint. Schoolwork wasn't all that hard, but my heart was just not in it. I wanted to do other things. I wanted to play outside. Play baseball. Play soccer. Play football. No dancing. I was never any good at any of it, but I would rather get involved in things that interested me. Schoolwork was not one of them.

When I got tired of sitting around doing nothing or trying to avoid having to do something, I'd go over to my grandmother's house. She was my escape. She could tell when something was worrying me. She was always in the kitchen, the most comfortable place in her house. I'd come in, knowing she could put my mind at ease.

"*Siéntate*," she'd say with a smile. ("Sit down.")

"*Ama, ¿cuándo puedo manejar un carro?*" ("Ama, when can I learn to drive a car?")

"*Cuando aprendas como respetarlo.*" ("When you learn to respect it.")

"*Ama, ¿cuándo puedo tener una novia?*" ("When can I have a girlfriend?")

"*Cuando tu corazón pienza que es tiempo.*" ("When your heart thinks it's time.")

I could ask her anything about life, and she would answer with riddles. Half the time, I couldn't understand what she meant. When I'd ask her to explain, she'd say, "*Tu tiempo vendrá. No estés apurado.*" ("Your time will come. Don't be in such a hurry.")

Our conversation could go on like this for an hour or so while I ate or tasted her cooking. By the time I'd leave her house, my attitude would be much better. I don't know how she did this, but when I needed some reassurance, she was there to guide me with her platitudes, which I didn't quite understand.

During this time, the war in Vietnam was intensifying. My uncle Juan was graduating from high school with the expectation of joining the army. The draft had not started. He just wanted to volunteer before they came after him. On the day he left, my grandmother was extremely worried. She knew there was nothing she could do to stop him. She prayed for him and for the country. I just didn't get it.

He went off to basic training and returned six weeks later on military leave. During his two weeks at home, I was consumed by his stories, his uniform, and his determination to be part of a group of young men defending our country.

"Will you get to shoot your rifle?" I asked him.

"If I have to, I will shoot to kill."

"Aren't you scared?"

"Nah. We are soldiers. Soldiers are not scared."

"Would you really kill someone if they tried to kill you?"

"Of course," he said. "That's what the army teaches you."

"How long will you be gone?"

"Six months. Maybe more."

"Don't worry, I'll take care of Ama."

I don't know when he left, but he did leave. Several months later, a package arrived from overseas. Ama called me over, and I rushed to her house. She showed me an item Juan had sent her from Vietnam. It was a cassette player with instructions on how to use it.

"*¿Sabes que es esto? ¿Sabes como trabaja?*" She asked, wanting to know if I knew what it was and if I could get it to work. My grandmother apparently had more confidence in me when it came to things like this. I read the instructions ever so slowly, placed a cassette in the player, and, after several attempts, my uncle's voice came out of the speaker. Ama raised her hands to her face and started crying.

"*¡Ese es Juan! ¡Ese es Juan!*" she kept saying. ("This is Juan! This is Juan!")

In a clear voice, he let everyone know he was fine. He'd run into some good luck when the captain of the platoon asked if anyone knew how to type. Juan had taken some typing classes in high school, so he'd raised his hand and gave up his rifle for a typewriter. His new job kept him with some officer who expected him to type all correspondence going out of his office.

He told us the place was primitive and the people were poor. Vietnam was very green with lots of trees. He spoke of the daily routine, never mentioning killing or shooting people. I think he didn't want Ama to worry. He mentioned the peacefulness of the country when the bombs were not being dropped by US planes. He talked about the Vietnamese people and how friendly and hard-working they were. He could not understand why America was sending young men to such a place. Toward the end of the recording, he told us how to record Ama's voice and anyone else who wanted to talk to him, then send the recorded cassette back. He told us to keep the player. He would send more tapes for Ama to hear. He said goodbye to everyone. Then the recording came to an end.

We just sat there staring at this magnificent contraption. Letter writing had come to an end in this household. Anyway, Ama couldn't write. The tapes kept coming every two or three weeks, and when Juan took longer to send one, Ama would start praying, hoping nothing bad had happened to him.

Juan eventually returned from Vietnam with very little to say about his time there. The war in Vietnam would continue to escalate under President Johnson. The country was split between those who wanted to curb the spread of communism and those who thought we had no business being there. Protests around the country, especially among university and college students, continued to occupy the evening news. In the meantime, life in Fort Stockton moved on.

Sometime in early May, Mom was washing and combing Wanda's and Imelda's hair. It wasn't even a weekend! But there they were, getting their hair combed. I noticed that Nancy's hair was wet, shiny, and short.

"Why did you cut Nancy's hair?" I asked.

"*¡Estas chamacas tienen piojos!*" ("These girls have lice!")

The girls had been sent home from school because the nurse found lice in their hair. A note was also sent home, telling all parents to check their kids for lice. They didn't want an infestation at school. The note had directions on how to check for lice and get rid of them. There was a little box sitting on the kitchen table with instructions on how to use the product.

"What? How could they have lice? Yuck! How disgusting!" I said, moving away from them.

"They probably picked them up at school. So now we must make sure every one of you is checked. The school will not let you go back unless you are clean," Mom stated ever so calmly.

"It's because they don't wash their hair or comb it. No wonder they've been scratching their heads for a week now." I moved farther as Mom ran the fine-tooth comb through Imelda's hair.

"Look! See that. That's a *piojo*. These you have to pull out and kill between your thumbnails. These little black things are making these white little things. These are lice, and they will grow to become these black suckers," Mom said, holding the piojo between her thumbnails and smashing it.

I took a big step backward, hoping to prevent the ugly creatures from jumping and getting on me.

"You might have them too!" she said, pointing to my head.

"No, I don't. I wash and comb my hair every day."

"Don't matter. If you put your head down anywhere near where the girls slept, you might have them too. I have to check as soon as I finish with Imelda."

"I ain't got no lice, Mom. I don't need to have you check. I'm not scratching my head," I protested.

At that very moment, my hand went up to the top of my head, and I started scratching. *No, no, no, no*, I thought. *I can't have those things crawling all over my head. Why am I scratching?* In that instant, I wondered whether these nasty little creatures were found only on head hair. *What if they crawl all the way down to my privates?* I wondered. I was getting pubic hair down there, and the thought frightened me. Just thinking about it made my hand react. I reached down, and I started to scratch vigorously right above my nut sack. I turned away, walking toward the screened-in porch. Now I was scratching my head with one hand and my privates with the other.

I ran back inside the house, yelling, "Mom! I'm next!"

By the time she finished with the girls—washing, combing out the lice, killing the mama lice, and cutting their hair—she was too tired to work on me. But I knew that if she didn't inspect me, I'd be scratching all night.

"Mom, you have to at least check. I can't have these things crawling on me."

"Sit down," she finally said. Then she took the comb to my head, looking for critters. I sat very still, praying I didn't have them. After a few minutes, she stopped.

"I don't see any on you, but that doesn't mean they're not there."

At about that time, Jesse and Waldo walked in the house.

"What's going on?" remarked Jesse. "Why is everybody home so early?"

"¡Piojos!" We all blurted out at the same time!

"Mom's checking for piojos on everybody, so you boys are next, after me," I said.

The two boys ran out the back door toward Grandma's house. They were not about to sit still for an hour while Mom checked them. I didn't care. I was clean.

Regardless, by the time the weekend arrived, Chuy took us boys to Falcon's Barbershop on Main Street. Reluctantly, we all jumped in his truck, yet we were totally excited about getting a real haircut from a real barber. We'd never had a barber cut our hair before. One of the earliest investments Chuy ever made was a hair clipper. It was used and came from a pawnshop. It was missing some of the clips, so we never knew what our hair would look like after he or Mom ran it over our heads. It was hit or miss for us. But on this day, we were going in for real haircuts.

"Chuy, how are you doing, my friend?" asked Mr. Falcon.

"*Bien. Triago estos niños para que les des un corte.*" ("Fine, I brought these kids so you can give them a cut.")

"*¿Que clase de corte quieres?*" ("What kind of cut do you want?")

"*Dales un number uno.*" ("Give them a number one.")

I was listening to this conversation, wondering what a number one was. *Could it be something special, where I could comb my hair with a part?* I wondered. I wanted a part on the side, like those kids on *American Bandstand*. As soon as Mr. Falcon finished his last customer, I scrambled to be the first on his chair.

All three of us came out of the barbershop with no hair! No hair! Number one was the shortest clip he could find. We got in the truck, running our hands over our smooth heads. We would not get another haircut until the next school year. I was glad it was May and that school would be out in two more weeks. All I had to do was get by those two weeks without someone calling me "Baldy."

Troubled Times

For some reason, unknown to us kids, Chuy and Mom were not getting along. Perhaps it was because Chuy had lost his permanent job as a construction worker, which forced him to bounce from one part-time job to another.

It became difficult at home. I couldn't understand why he was having such a hard time finding a job and keeping it. *Why isn't he like other dads, who have steady jobs?* I wondered. *He likes to work. I'd give him that much. Could it be his lack of English? Or his lack of writing or reading? Why can't he get a job and keep it?*

Mom was maintaining two jobs while Chuy was out with some of his friends, supposedly looking for work. He'd come home disillusioned. That led to drinking. He often showed up at home drunk.

One evening, he showed up drunker than usual. He started cussing up a storm and talking nonsense. It was early evening when the argument started. I was in another room, listening but not paying much attention. Leaving them to discuss whatever was on their minds was my policy. Then I heard yelling.

"Get out of my house! You don't need to be here when you show up like this! Get out!" Mom screamed.

I went to see what was happening. Chuy was sitting on the bed, his head hanging down as if he was falling asleep.

"Get out!" she yelled again.

Chuy got up and staggered toward her just as I was walking in the room.

"You cannot tell me what to do!" he said.

"I said get out, you drunk!"

"Just go away. Shut up and let me sleep. Go away!" Chuy demanded.

"I don't want you coming home drunk. I've told you that. Go stay with your friends. Get out!"

Chuy got up from the bed and pushed her. Whether he came toward her, using her as a way to balance himself, or actually intended to push, I don't know, but Mom did fall back against the wall. She never fell down on the floor but fell backward. She hit the wall with her back, and I saw the fury building up inside her. She headed for the bathroom, returning instantly with a hammer in her hand, ready to crush Chuy's skull. She walked toward him, holding the hammer high over her head.

"Mom! You can't do that," I said, grabbing her arm. "He's drunk! You'll kill him!" I got in between them. As I faced Mom, I felt fear. "You need to stop this. Put down the hammer. The police will come if you continue to fight."

I managed to gently remove the hammer from her hand as I talked to her. She was crying and madder than a ton of hornets.

"I don't care," she said. "Call the police. They'll take him away!"

She left the room, and I grabbed Chuy, who was still standing, swaying back and forth with slobber running down the side of his mouth.

"*Siéntate. Necesitas calmarte*," I said. ("Sit down. You need to calm down.")

He sat on the bed, and I took off his boots. Bringing his feet over the bed, I helped him lie down. Then I covered him with a blanket. He fell asleep instantly, jabbering something incoherent.

I'd never come between my parents when they were arguing. When they argued, we all scattered in different directions like roaches when you turn on the light. We didn't want any part of it. Why I decided to intervene on this particular occasion is beyond me. But I'm glad I did. This was the last time Mom would try to beat the shit out of Chuy. Not that she didn't want to. I think she saw the fear in my eyes and decided it wasn't worth scaring the kids.

I'm thirteen. I should be able to intervene, I told myself. After that one time, I never did again. Ever. I didn't lecture them or tell them not to fight. I left them alone.

Chuy didn't stop drinking. He still came home drunk. But he never raised a hand toward Mom again. I believe Chuy, no matter how drunk he was that night, saw a half-crazed woman coming at him with a hammer, ready to smash his head in. I believe this image had something to do with him not getting close to hitting her again when he did come home drunk. I wouldn't have.

Mom got a job cleaning rooms at the Sands Motel. She was up every morning, including weekends, and walked several blocks from our house to the motel. On her way home, she would stop by the old lady's laundromat and wash clothes for other people. She would get home a couple of hours after we got home from school. This went on for several weeks until one Saturday afternoon, she showed up in a 1961 two-door hardtop Ford Fairlane. It was a beauty. The car was blue and had a radio and an aftermarket air conditioner. She wasn't driving. The car salesman had driven her home in it. It had a manual transmission, which she didn't know how to work, but she bought it anyway. I had never seen Mother drive. She learned quickly though. Her walking days were over. She had a car she could call her very own. "I'll never walk to work. Ever!" she said.

I wanted her to take us for a drive.

"We have to wait until Chuy comes home so he can take us all," she said with gleaming pride.

Mother owned a car! Imagine that. I didn't question how she got it or where she got the money, but apparently, she had been saving for a down payment for a long time.

Chuy came home and asked her about it—where she got it, from whom, and how she paid for it. We just wanted a ride. Everyone jumped in the car, and off we went around the block. Nine people in a two-door sedan. No seat belts. Kids hanging out the windows. Nobody cared. We were smiling and happy over such luxury. I was proud of Mom.

A few days later, I stopped by my grandmother's house. I wanted to tell her about the car. She was excited. We sat outside her house, letting the morning sun warm our backs. Sitting on a plastic lawn chair and drinking a cup of coffee, she began to tell me about pains in her stomach.

"I'm ready to meet your grandfather in Heaven," came out as a mere whisper.

We had not had this kind of conversation before. Ever. Now she was sharing her innermost feelings. Why me? Did she trust me that much, or did she want me to know before the others? We were close. I felt she wanted me to know.

"You're too young to be feeling sick and talking like that, Ama. You have to go see Dr. Gibson. He will give you some pills."

"*No, no, no. El doctor no sabe,*" she told me. ("No way, the doctor doesn't know how I feel.")

"*Pues, le dices que estás mala. Él sabe que hacer,*" I responded. ("You can tell him you're sick. He'll know what to do.") I was sure the doctor could do something for her. I felt helpless. Not wanting to increase her anxiety, I stopped talking. I just sat and listened.

"*No, mijo. Estoy lista para estar con Dios,*" were her last words to me on the subject. ("No, son. I'm ready to be with God.")

I wanted to tell someone so they could get her to the hospital, but I felt they already knew something was wrong. Most of her oldest kids were married and gone. Patricia, who was my age, hadn't said anything about her condition. I don't think Fidel and Sammy knew either.

Moving away from such morbid talk, I quickly changed the subject. "Wanna know how I dance a polka? I showed her how I danced, swinging my butt around.

She laughed so hard, and with teary eyes, she told me to stop. She'd take a breath and laugh again. I enjoyed those times with her.

As I walked home, my mind still doubted the seriousness of her illness. I was sure she was going to be alright.

A few weeks later, she was checked into the hospital. When I went to visit, I quietly walked in the door and saw my uncles and aunts around the bed. She lay there, pale and in obvious pain. My great-grandfather, Don Sabastian, was holding her hand and speaking softly to her. His attempts to reassure her fell on deaf ears. Moving her head back and forth, in obvious pain, she moaned, showing signs of labored breathing.

"*Ay, Papá. Como me duele,*" she said to her father. ("Oh, how it hurts.") She was crying like a little girl to her daddy.

I'd never seen my grandmother in such pain. I'd never seen her in any kind of pain whatsoever. I didn't know what I could do for her, so I just stood there watching, not saying anything. On the verge of tears myself and trying hard to remain calm, I didn't want to add to the stress and sadness present in the room. But I couldn't stand there any longer, seeing her suffer. Walking quietly out of the room, I left unnoticed.

Looking for some consolation, I spotted my mother quietly standing in the hall. I walked up to her and just hugged her.

Grandmother Ama passed away not long after in the middle of the night. Later, I found out that she had died from a tumor in her stomach. No wonder she was always complaining about her stomach.

The death of someone I admired and respected deepened the hurt in my heart. I knew death was traumatic because it had taken me a long time to get past my good friend Bobby's death two years before. Not even when my grandfather died a few years earlier did I feel like this. My grandmother's death left a lasting impression on my thirteen-year-old brain. Death was part of life. I knew that. The question in my mind was, Why does it happen to young people, like Bobby or my grandmother? I could understand old people dying, but this kind of passing troubled me.

"Why did Grandmother have to die?" I asked Mom after the funeral.

"Because when God needs you, He gets to take you. This is a good thing. Not a bad thing. God needed your grandmother. She is happier now and in no pain."

I wanted to believe her, yet I continued to question mortality and God's real purpose. *Is this how it's going to be when those I love and care for move on to God's presence?* I wondered. *If this is a good thing, why is everybody, including me, so sad? Why does death bring on such sadness of the heart? At what point do I accept that "from dust you came, and from dust you shall return." How could you be with God if you are dust? When someone dies, is this the rite of passage into Heaven? Is it earned, or does it happen automatically?*

Too many questions.

Ending Seventh Grade

School ended with kids flying out the doors, flinging papers all over the schoolyard. I joined in the revelry, throwing out all the bad memories, which included papers with lousy grades, tests with barely passing grades, and anything else revealing my lack of educational excellence. It was over.

As soon as I was out the door, I started to plan a summer of fun and freedom from schoolwork! I was determined to have all summer to play with friends, go swimming, play baseball, and sleep as late as I wanted.

Then it hit me. *What if Chuy is expecting us to work the onion fields again?* I wondered. *Is there any way I could get out of it?* If I couldn't think of something legitimate, I would only have Friday afternoon, then all day Saturday and Sunday to celebrate the end of the school year.

Chuy had indeed been out looking for onion-picking work two weeks before school let out. I prepared myself for the inevitable, but when Monday morning arrived, no mention of work was made. Nobody brought it up. Neither the kids nor me. Perhaps this would be the summer of no onion work.

That evening, Chuy started in on us. "*Mañana, todos van a limpiar la casa hasta que brilla como el sol! Quiero ver una casa muy limpia.*" ("Tomorrow you are going to clean this house until it shines like the sun. I want to see a perfectly clean house.")

The older kids were told that our job was to make sure every piece of furniture was moved and cleaned around, under, and above. That meant we were to clean every nook and cranny, no exceptions. Spring cleaning was replaced with summer cleaning. Not that we kept a dirty house. No, sir. Chuy made sure of that. He expected things to be clean and smelling of Pine-Sol, the cleaning liquid cheap enough for the poor folks. There were bottles of Pine-Sol, buckets of water, mops, brooms, and dust rags—one for every kid. The girls got to change sheets and make up beds while the boys moved furniture so they could sweep and mop. There was dusting, wiping, crying, washing windows, cleaning the bathroom, and, since we had no hot water, boiling water to mop the floors.

It took all morning. We did such a good job that Chuy made it a weekly expectation. For the next few years, it became a ritual. This became a regular thing every Saturday up until I left home my senior year of high school.

Having the summer off to enjoy ourselves didn't last long. The idea of a wonderful and fun-filled summer ended the very next Friday when Chuy announced we were joining a group of families going to New Mexico to work the onion fields. Only the older siblings were to go. We would follow the other families to Artesia, New Mexico. Nancy, Wanda, Jesse, and I would accompany Chuy in his '51 Chevy pickup truck. Mom, who still had the motel cleaning job, would stay behind with Imelda, Nora, and Waldo.

I was disappointed, to say the least. Another summer down the drain. When was this going to stop? When were we going to be allowed to enjoy summer?

On Sunday morning, the families began the journey from my friend Juan's house. One adult, a teenager, and three kids, packed into the front seat of the truck, some of us still half asleep, left heading north on Highway 285, or what most people knew as the Pecos Highway. We were headed into unknown territory. We kids had never been this far away from home. I looked out the window, excited about the trip but not looking forward to the work. We were going into a different state. Not that it meant anything to the younger kids, but to me, it was a big deal—something I would share next year on my first day of class when the teachers asked, "What did you do this summer?" This would set me apart from all the others. Not all kids in my school ever traveled this far.

The day was long. Each time we stopped for gas, we went looking for a restroom. We'd get off the truck, stretch our skinny legs, and massage our butts to get the circulation going after sitting for so long. We stopped in Pecos, Texas, before crossing into New Mexico, a barren and desolate place—worse than our part of Texas, with nothing but desert as far as the eye could see. We stopped again in Loving, New Mexico. There wasn't anything loving about it. It was a small western town with very little to offer other than gas, a restroom, and maybe a couple of restaurants, which we would never see the inside of. Mom had packed some tacos for our trip. The usual—bologna with egg, egg with potato, egg with beans, and just egg or just bologna. We ate when we got hungry, not stopping to enjoy the food. By late afternoon, we were in Carlsbad. Another godforsaken town.

In the early evening, with the sun still shining, we arrived on the outskirts of Artesia, following the other families onto a farm some distance from the main highway. The dirt road led us to a series of buildings made of blocks that sat right in the middle of what looked like a field. All around, all I could see were plowed fields. Nothing else.

We stopped at the first building. It wasn't very big, but it had bunk beds, a table, four chairs, a stove, a refrigerator, a gas heater, no air conditioner, and no toilet. The toilet was outside in a room all by itself. This was our home away from home.

After unloading our meager belongings, which weren't much, Chuy took us into town to buy some groceries. He bought eggs, corn tortillas, chili, ground beef, bologna, potatoes, Kool-Aid, and several cans of Chef Boyardee ravioli because they were on sale. After talking briefly with the other men, we headed back to our bunkhouse.

Monday morning came early. We packed our lunch, got in the truck, and headed out to the onion field. It wasn't very far from where the bunkhouses were, yet it was far enough that we had to drive. There were fields and fields of plowed ground as far as we could see. Every which way I looked, the flat land ended in blue skies.

We worked all day and into the week. By Friday, exhaustion set in. There was no TV or radio to help pass the time. But it was fine. After working all day, we were just too tired to do anything.

Chuy left Friday after work, saying he was going into town to pick up some things. He hitched a ride with some of the men, leaving his truck parked near the bunkhouse. Nancy cooked up some food. We ate and retired to our own little worlds. Jesse and I went outside to find something to do. We played around, throwing clumps of dirt at each other. After a few minutes, we went back inside. We all just sat around staring at each other, engaged in our own thoughts. After a hard week's work, I pictured Chuy coming back for us and taking us somewhere fun.

He never came back.

Saturday, we were up and ready, just in case Chuy came home. Nancy and I put together what little was left of the food he had bought earlier in the week. By lunchtime, the only thing left were the cans of Chef Boyardee ravioli. Noon came, and no Chuy. We ate ravioli right out of the can.

"I'm not staying here any longer!" cried Nancy.

"Where do you think you are going? There isn't anything for miles," I told her.

"I don't care. I'm going to the other bunkhouses to ask them for food."

"The next bunkhouse is at least a mile away!"

"Then I'm going into town."

"How do you think you're going to get there? Walking? You think you can walk that far? What if somebody takes you? We have no money to get you back! Go! Go ahead and go!" I said, pointing out the door.

"No. I'm taking the truck."

"You can't drive. I can't drive. No one can drive!" I said, equally frustrated.

"I don't care. I'm leaving. I can drive. I'm not staying here!" She stomped toward the door. By this time, she was yelling and crying at the same time. I didn't know if she was serious or not. I'd never seen her behave that way. Nancy was a quiet girl—shy and quiet unless she was mad. She got that from Mom.

She walked out the door with the truck keys. Imelda and Jesse jumped in the truck with her, and I stood in the doorway, looking on stupidly as she walked away.

"She can't drive," I mumbled to myself, not moving. I stood there, perplexed at her demeanor. I stared and waited to see what she would do. She got in the truck and started it up.

"Oh, shit!" I said, then I ran toward the truck. She put it in gear, and off she went, barely visible behind the wheel.

"Stop! You're going to kill somebody!" I yelled. "Stop!" Running after the truck, I was yelling like a madman. She was so short that she couldn't see over the steering wheel without sitting up close to the front. The truck lurched forward over rows and rows of plowed fields. It looked like a jackrabbit jumping up and down, leaving tire tracks and dust behind it.

It finally came to a complete stop about a hundred yards down the field. I caught up to it. Panting and choking on the dust the truck left in its wake, I stopped. I was scared. I prayed no one was hurt.

Imelda and Jesse were laughing. "Make it go again!" they yelled in unison. "Make it go again!"

I walked slowly to the driver's side, pulled open the door, and yanked the key out of the ignition.

"You've got to be the dumbest person in the world"! I shouted at her. You can't drive! You could have killed somebody!"

"Like who?" she asked. "There's nobody here!"

We all got down and walked back to the bunkhouse. Nancy walked behind, smiling. She'd had the guts to try. I didn't. Imelda and Jesse were disappointed in me because I didn't let Nancy drive them back to the bunkhouse.

Saturday afternoon found us eating more cans of ravioli. Chuy had not returned. Mr. Garza drove by and saw us outside. He stopped.

"What's your dad's truck doing over there?" he asked.

None of us said a thing.

"Where is Chuy?" he asked, looking directly at me.

"He went into town to buy something," I told him, trying not to show concern.

"Have you been here all day by yourselves? Have you eaten?"

We gave no answers. He drove away and told us he'd be back. Where he went, I don't know.

Sunday morning, Mom showed up in her car. About the same time, Chuy was dropped off by the same men he'd left with. He'd been in town drinking. Mom got the few belongings we'd brought with us and packed us in the car. Then she drove home, leaving Chuy behind. Onion picking for us was over for the rest of the summer.

When all the kids were asleep in the car, I asked her, "Mom, how did you know?"

"Mr. Garza called your aunt, and she told me."

"Was she mad?"

"No. I was mad for the both of us."

"Are you mad at Chuy?"

She didn't answer. But I could see her fuming. Her face told it all. The lines on her forehead wrinkled up, bringing both eyebrows closer together. These were clues that she was not a happy camper. She was thinking, stinking mad.

Nothing else was said about it. We would experience more incidents similar to this one before she realized that he would not change. In a few years, she would leave Chuy and file for divorce.

Lessons Learned

I turned fourteen in the summer of '65. On that day, the first four thousand 101st Airborne Division paratroopers arrived in Vietnam, landing at Cam Ranh Bay. The day before, President Lyndon B. Johnson announced his order to increase the number of US troops in South Vietnam from seventy-five thousand to one hundred and twenty-five thousand. The war raged on.

In the Southern states, mostly in Alabama, Mississippi, Georgia, and, to some extent, Tennessee and the Carolinas, tensions continued to fester over civil rights. In Selma, Alabama, on a day known as Bloody Sunday, a group of six hundred civil rights marchers were brutally attacked by state and local police. Pictures of these and other atrocities committed by white law enforcement officers, as well as white racist groups, flooded front-page news around the world. President Johnson, responding to the Selma, Alabama, crisis, told Congress, "We shall overcome." He believed that lifting the states' voting restrictions on poor and Black folks would help their cause. He advocated for the passage of the Voting Rights Act.

Dr. Martin Luther King Jr. led thirty-two hundred people at the start of the third and finally successful civil rights march from Selma to Montgomery, Alabama. Tensions mounted, but in August, President Johnson signed the Voting Rights Act of 1965 into law. Where there had been discrimination, the law increased the number of people registered to vote. Literacy tests, which were mandatory in some states, were outlawed. These tests had prevented illiterate adults from voting. The law also called for federal examiners who had the power to register qualified citizens in jurisdictions known for voting discrimination. The act shifted the power to register voters from state and local officials to the federal government.

These events were being televised worldwide. In turn, countries were casting doubt over whether America was still a wonderful place to live. Countries around the world took note of the atrocities committed against people of color. They begin to question, like so many Americans, whether we could survive the two wars: the war in Vietnam and the war at home over civil rights.

While the country mused over the issues of democracy around the world and equal rights here at home, I focused on living the life of a teenager—still a poor one but with hopes of one day improving our place in society.

The Alfaro household still had the small black-and-white TV set accompanied by a radio, which continued to blare music most of the day. I appreciated music so much more as a trumpet player. I didn't lose myself in books, much less hobbies I couldn't afford. But music did provide a pleasurable avenue. It provided relief from the ironies and hard lessons of life. My appreciation and understanding of music also became a distraction from the turbulent times the world was experiencing.

Any time I could get the radio to myself, I'd listen to the latest hits. The Rolling Stones, a group from England, had the number-one single in July of that year. "Satisfaction" not only had a rocking beat, but it also came with a clear message for young listeners like me. The lyrics cried out something about not getting any satisfaction. Elvis Presley had three songs in the Top 100 hits, according to Billboard. The Four Tops, an African American group, led with the number-two song, "I Can't Help Myself," made popular by the soulful lyrics. The Byrds sang "Mr. Tambourine Man." I'd sing along when no one was around. I loved The Beach Boys, a group out of California that made "Help Me Rhonda" popular. When no one was watching, I'd dance to the music of Sam the Sham and the Pharaohs with their song "Wooly Bully." The music scene was incredibly eclectic. It brought so much meaning to our lives. I loved it so.

In our little world, time moved slowly. The days slipped into one another. By the time I realized it, another school year was starting. I was now part of the upper class—the eighth graders. Teachers expected us to be role models for the incoming sixth grade. They couldn't have picked a worse group of eighth-grade teenagers—at least the group I hung around with. We weren't a gang like the kids from big cities we heard about in the news. We were just a group of kids trying to get by without bringing too much attention to ourselves. However, there were times when trouble seemed to come our way.

When you grow up with kids from the barrio, you get to know them pretty well. I knew where they lived, who they talked to, who their siblings were, which kids to stay away from, and who I could count on as a friend. Some had my back. Most did not.

By now you'd think I would have developed some rambunctiousness living so many years in the barrio.

Nope, not me. I was more interested in being an observer, not an instigator. I remained behind the scenes, timid and shy. Whenever troublesome incidents presented themselves, I could easily blend in with the nonparticipants. As eighth graders, we thought we were on top of the world. Our time had come, and we boasted of our superiority over the underclassmen. As we threw our weight around, I thought we were big shots—not necessarily me, but some of the boys I hung around with. Roy and Joe were two who were not afraid to challenge the status quo. They were bullies and the rabble-rousers in our grade. There were days when we'd stand outside the main entrance to the school, waiting on our friends so we could walk home together.

On one particularly hot day, four or five boys, including Joe and Roy, were standing under a big oak tree by the school's entrance. The last bell rang, and I joined the group, laughing at the jokes Joe was sharing. Most girls avoided the group and walked around them for fear of being verbally attacked. A new girl who didn't know the landscape walked past us. We didn't get many new students from out of state. She was not a true Texan. Her talk gave her away. With a Midwestern accent, she sounded funny. She had a milky-white complexion; long, stringy blond hair that fell well below her shoulders; and a skirt long enough to cover her ankles. A round face with a smile that could brighten any day complemented her look. Not a bad-looking girl, but quite tall. Much taller than any of the other girls in our class. Her name was Thelma. As she walked by, two boys stopped her by blocking the sidewalk. She stood there, wanting to get past them, but they would not let her.

"Are you from Mean-a-so-ta?" mimicked Joe.

"Why you so tall?" joked Roy.

"You Paul Bunyan?" added Joe.

"Ya?" one asked as they continued with their brutal degrading.

"Ya, need to let me pass. Ya?" she said softly as she tried to walk around them.

They persisted, and she started crying. The puns were funny. Everyone laughed, and I laughed right along with them. I thought it was funny. As she ran away from us, we kept laughing and high-fiving each other. I didn't realize how degrading this must have been for her. I had no thoughts about how this made her feel—not until it happened to me. When it does, racial slurs are not funny anymore.

As eighth graders, our lockers were assigned to us in the better part of the school. The lockers were located on the second floor of what was known as the eighth-grade hall. Many of us took pride in being the top dogs. Some of the teachers made us feel special. We were all grown up and enjoying the attention. For some reason, I got a locker next to some football jocks. They were rough and tough (at least they thought they were) boys who liked to push their weight around. On Fridays before a football game, the school made a big deal of showing its spirit by hanging up posters honoring the team. The football players wore their jerseys, flaunting their toughness. Cheerleaders went out of their way to show their school spirit by dressing up in blue and white, our school colors.

One day, I was standing near my locker, getting ready for my next class, when a group of white athletes walked down the hall. One of them pushed my locker door shut, barely missing my hand as I reached for a book. Frustrated by this reckless behavior, I turned toward them.

"You need to watch it!" I said to no one in particular.

One of the boys turned around and mimicked me. "Wash it. Wash it." He looked me straight in the eye, then added, "Why don't you Mexicans go back to Mexico!"

They all laughed and walked away. I felt humiliated by their bigoted taunting. I knew full well that I couldn't do anything about it. I'm not much for confrontation, but that day, I could feel the anger swelling up inside. I wanted to run up behind that kid and bash his head into the lockers. Funny how we remember the things people say when it makes us feel humiliated and embarrassed, but not the times when we humiliate and embarrass others.

That one remark made me second-guess myself. Self-consciously, I began to question whether I had said the word wrong. Did my remark sound like *wash* instead of *watch*? Did I not pronounce the word well enough? Was it my Spanish? Could I not pronounce words well enough for people to understand?

Learning from such experiences, no matter how demeaning, helped me understand myself. I was a "Mexican" kid who spoke two languages, and when the two merged, it revealed the real me. Thelma had a Minnesota accent not appreciated by the kids in her new environment. I now knew how she must have felt.

Thelma turned out to be a very popular girl in school and was very much admired because of her people skills and sense of humor. I envied her, and I never forgot the incident. Although I never apologized for being cruel to her, the experience did one thing for me. For the first time, it made me aware of the bigotry in my town.

But it would not be the last. At that moment, I began working on losing my accent—the first step in becoming an assimilated American. I was now questioning my appreciation for my own culture.

I wanted to be white.

A Musician

O ne afternoon after school, I was on the big screened-in porch that led to the kitchen. I blew out a few notes on my cornet. I couldn't play inside for fear of being ridiculed by the siblings. The porch was my sanctuary, where I practiced new tunes. The sound of my playing flowed rhythmically throughout the hood, and people could hear me a block away. Out of the corner of my eye, I saw an older kid listening to me play. He was standing a block away but was still visible from my vantage point. I would see him again several times as the days turned into weeks. One afternoon, he showed up at my house.

"I heard you playing your trumpet," he said. "How long have you been playing?"

I knew who he was, and although he only lived a block away, we'd never spoken. His name was Armando. He was a couple of years older than me, and he played the trumpet as well. Because he was in high school, I didn't really know him.

"I've only been playing for three years. Mine is not a trumpet. It's a cornet."

"You're pretty good! Have you ever considered playing in a band?"

"I will one of these days, but I'm still not good enough."

"You sound pretty good. Listen, my sister, brother, and I play in this band. We practice every Friday night. How would you like to come hear us practice?"

"Yeah. When?"

"Come by this Friday, and maybe you could join us in a song or two."

"Yeah. I'll ask. I think it will be fine."

"Then I'll see you Friday."

Then he left, crossing the alley back to his house.

I was curious. I wanted to see if this was really a band or just some group of neighborhood kids trying to be a band. So I showed up at their practice session that Friday—and then every Friday thereafter for the next few years.

After practicing with them for a few weeks, I became the trumpet player for Linda Sanchez and the Blue Notes, a real band that played on real stages for real people. I started with ten songs, learning them solely by ear. There were no music sheets to play from. We listened to the song on a small turntable, played the instrumental parts on our horns, then wrote down the letters of the notes on paper. As long as I could remember the melody, I could play without music sheets.

After a few practice sessions, the Sanchez parents came to my house to ask my parents for permission to take me on the road with them. Mother was hesitant at first. Her main issue was my age. How could I be allowed to enter bars and dance halls, where beer, whiskey, and wine were sold, and not get in trouble? Who would take care of me? How long would I be gone?

I'm fourteen years old. I don't need a babysitter, I thought. An agreement was finally reached when "La Vieja" (Mrs. Sanchez) assured Mother that I would be riding with them to every venue and not with the older boys. She promised to look after me.

For the next year, I played Tejano dance music, with some Top 40s mixed in. We played in surrounding towns for weddings, quinceañeras, birthdays, holidays, divorces, and graduations. We were in bars, town halls, warehouses, gymnasiums, and dance halls, and in summertime, we were outside under the stars. In Fort Stockton, we played at the Large Community Hall—which was not that large—until the county built the Pecos County Coliseum.

I was making anywhere between ten and twenty dollars playing on Saturday nights. During the holidays, we'd play several days in a row, making a total of fifty dollars! Big-time money. It all went to Mom. I usually kept five dollars to get me through the week. But it was not about the money for me. It was about playing music. I took joy in being on stage in front of people, something totally against my nature. Being a quiet, shy kid growing up didn't add to my confidence, but when I was on stage, I turned into Michael Jackson without the moves. We moved to the music, swaying back and forth like most band members did. We were performers, and the more we got into the moves, the more the girls smiled and clapped. I would have played for free. The money was the icing. The experience was the trophy. I loved the attention I got on stage from people I didn't even know. Especially the girls. Awesome!

This was the beginning of my music career. I was fourteen years old—an eighth grader—playing in a real live band to music I loved. For money! Fantastic!

I wanted to save enough to buy a trumpet. A real musician didn't play a cornet on stage. It was embarrassing. I wanted a trumpet like all the cool kids had. However, at this rate, it would take me a year to save enough, so I borrowed one from the school. It was an old banged-up thing and belonged to the director.

"Can I play the trumpet that's in your office, sir? I forgot my cornet at home," I lied.

He waved me off, which gave me the impression he didn't care. I went to his office, took the trumpet, and kept it for the remainder of the year. Once the school year was over, I had to return it. I don't know why I felt embarrassed playing the cornet at dances, but I did. I wanted a trumpet. It would be another five long years before I would finally get one.

Driving

Chuy called me over one Saturday morning.

"*Estás bastante grande y necesitas saber como manejar,*" he told me. ("You are big enough and need to learn how to drive.")

"*¿Yo? ¿Manejar?*" "(Me, driving?")" I was thrilled. I was going to learn how to drive! "When?" I asked.

"Now," he said.

We got into his '51 Chevy pickup. He tried to explain all the parts of the driving method as I sat on the passenger side, listening intently. He told me about the gas pedal, the brakes, the clutch pedal, and the shifting handle situated on the steering column.

"Now, you press the clutch pedal down, then shift the gear into first, like this," he said. He slowly let the pedal up, and used his right foot to press on the gas. "This has to be done right if the truck is to move forward. Look at me. I'm going to show you again."

With the left foot, he pressed the clutch pedal, put the gear in first, and slowly let out the pedal while pressing on the gas.

"Simple. Right?" he asked.

For a coordinated person, this looked easy. For someone who can't walk and spit at the same time, it was near impossible. But I wanted to try.

He parked the truck on the dirt street behind our house, a part of the barrio where you rarely saw any traffic. I got into the driver's seat, and he got on the passenger side, sitting close to me. With his foot and hands ready to take over if anything went wrong, he turned me loose.

Excitement meshed with panic created an exhilarating feeling. I was totally nervous. My body was mildly shaking. I was terrified, but I was going to learn how to drive! What a dad! Nervously, I pushed the left pedal down. Started the truck. I switched the handle on the wheel column to first gear like he'd shown me, then slowly released the pedal while pressing on the gas. The truck lurched forward, causing the back wheels to spin wildly and sending rocks and dust into the air! The truck engine died.

"You have to let the pedal out slowly," Chuy demanded. "Now, try it again. But this time, slowly let the pedal out. And don't press on the gas pedal too much. Take it easy."

"I don't know if I can do this," I said. "Maybe you can teach Nancy first. She wants to learn to drive really bad."

"No. You're the oldest, and you have to learn to drive before anyone else. So, try it again."

"I can't reach the pedals. How am I going to push all the way down?" I remarked. I was beginning to panic. I could feel the tears welling up inside. *I ain't gonna cry*, I told myself.

"Well then, sit up closer to the steering wheel."

"But if I do that, I can't see the road."

"Sit up higher!"

"I'm only fourteen. Is it legal to drive a car or truck at my age? What if the cops come by? Will we get in trouble?" I was nearing total, uncontrollable fear.

"Be quiet and get ready." Chuy grabbed my arm, explaining again how it was done. I sat up closer to the steering wheel and tried again. Then I started the truck, mentally playing out the sequence of right foot, left foot, left hand, right hand, shift up, shift down, look up, hold the wheel. This time, the transition between the pedals went smoother. However, the truck lurched forward again. But this time, the engine didn't die. We moved forward as I pressed on the gas pedal slowly, like instructed.

"Keep it steady and watch the road," Chuy said. "Don't look down! Watch the road! Now, press the left pedal, and push the lever up to second gear! Good. Now, press on the gas pedal. Slowly. Look up! Watch the road! Keep it straight and on your side of the road! Keep your hands on the steering wheel! Press on the left pedal again, and shift to third gear. Yes! Better. Now release the gas, and press on the brake. No!" he yelled.

"No?" I yelled.

"No!" we both yelled.

"The brake! Hit the brake!" he yelled. "The one on the right! The other one!" There was panic in his voice. Keep your head up! Watch where you are going! Hit the brake!"

The truck came to a complete stop right before we ran out of road. The engine died. Chuy was sweating. I was shaking. He jumped over to the driver's side and drove home.

"We can try this again tomorrow," he said.

I didn't want to learn any more. The last thing I wanted was to face Jesus Christ at the Pearly Gates and have to explain how I got us both killed.

We didn't try driving the next day. I think Chuy wanted to recover from the trauma I'd caused. I was hoping he would not give up on me. But I went out and sat in the truck. With the engine off, I practiced the moves he had taught me.

"I can do this," I told myself, knowing full well it was a lie. I still didn't have the confidence.

The following Saturday, we tried it again. It wasn't the smoothest drive, but at least the shouting stopped. Our hearts were not racing as much as the first time. Chuy was hopeful. So was I. It took several attempts before I got good enough to drive a standard transmission truck. I'd learned enough.

I took my driving test at the age of fifteen. I made a few mistakes during the driving test and barely scored a passing grade. But it was good enough, and that was all I needed. My driver's license came a few days later in the mail, making me an official driving machine. I didn't know it at the time, but Chuy's reasoning behind teaching me to drive was not so much that he thought I needed to learn. His idea centered around the thought that if we were left alone, like we were during our onion-picking trip to New Mexico, at least I could get us to the store or elsewhere.

Driving was a demanding task. I would always make the sign of the cross whenever I got behind the wheel. I didn't want to take any chances. I'd silently pray. "God, please don't let me crash this truck! Jesus, please tell God to watch over me and ask Him to keep people as far away as possible while I'm driving. Mary, mother of God, please look out for me and for anyone else thinking of crossing the road. Don't let anyone get in my way. Please."

I didn't need to crash that truck! Chuy would kill me.

A Big Change

The end of my eighth-grade year proved once again that I was promotion material. I still didn't have stellar end-of-year grades, but they were enough to get me promoted. I did have several satisfactory marks for things like attendance, behavior, PE, library, and sometimes band. This would keep Mother happy for the summer. Next stop, ninth grade! Imagine that. It meant high school! But getting through the summer months came first.

School was out the last Friday in May. I thought surely we were going onion picking again.

I was right. Chuy made the announcement on Saturday afternoon, sending panic tremors throughout the room, where we were all sitting watching TV.

I hated it. After what happened the summer before, I felt sure Mom wouldn't allow it. But when the time came, she relented and told him he could take the five oldest, but he had to bring us back every afternoon. No more out-of-town stints.

The picking went on for several weeks as we moved from onion field to onion field. When the last of the onions were picked, he landed a job picking watermelons. This was a new adventure for us. I thought this would be easier than picking onions all day, but after an all-day job of lifting, carrying, and setting down those heavy watermelons, my back was screaming for help. It was miserable. This job only lasted a week.

We lived through that summer, making enough money for new clothes for the next school year. I played every Saturday with the band and made a little money. By this time, I was allowed to keep most of it, though it wasn't much—just enough for whenever I'd go out with friends. I stopped begging my parents for money. I was earning it.

I was fifteen. It was July 29, 1966. The 1960s defined modern America with a generation of young people determined to be heard and seen. 1966 was the year that opened the floodgates to this new, mod age. The war in Vietnam was in full swing, and the number of deaths of young American men had tripled. Walter Cronkite, the anchor for *CBS Evening News*, began his report every night by revealing the number of deaths thus far. By the end of 1966, six thousand men had died, and another thirty thousand were wounded. In March, over two hundred thousand protesters against the Vietnam War attended rallies worldwide. That July, four thousand protesters in London demonstrated at the US Embassy, drawing attention to America's war. A 1966 Gallup poll revealed that American public support for the war had gone from 52 percent down to 37 percent, striking a severe blow to President Johnson's war. Most evenings, I watched the news. The announcer talked about the continuation of atrocities committed by soldiers on both sides and how they seemed to be multiplying. Many Vietnamese people were caught in the crossfire. Old men, women, and children suffered and died because of this political confrontation.

At home, America experienced its first-ever mass shooting when a sniper atop the University of Texas tower killed sixteen people and wounded thirty. The sniper, Charles Whitman, a former US Marine sharpshooter, climbed up the observation deck of the three-hundred-foot tower and started firing. For ninety-six minutes, bullets rained on students and people walking the campus. He was killed by two police officers.

Ronald Reagan, a movie star, became the governor of California, setting him on a course for an eventual Republican presidential nomination. NASA completed six Gemini space missions in a race against the Soviets to be the first to land a man on the moon. The first artificial heart implant was performed in a Houston hospital with some promising results. The same year, Frank Sinatra became the Grammys' top winner, while *The Sound of Music* won top honors at the Academy Awards. This was the end of the goody, feely, love-all era of the 1950s and early 1960s. It was now all about the counterculture and young people demanding change.

In music, four of the most iconic albums in rock n' roll made their debuts. The Beatles released their hard, pounding album called *Revolver*. The Beach Boys released *Pet Sounds*. Bob Dylan's *Blonde on Blonde* was hitting the charts, and The Doors' self-titled album broke the mold and set young music lovers on fire with a determination to be heard and not just seen. Marijuana became a drug of choice, particularly for the hippies.

For two years, a new TV series got me and many kids like me back to the screen. *Batman*, with Adam West as the title character, became a popular series. *Star Trek* also made its debut. It continued for three years until filmmakers created a long line of *Star Trek* movies instead. *How the Grinch Stole Christmas* became the most popular show for families during the 1966 holiday season.

In the world of sports, the Redskins beat the Giants with a score of 72 to 41, the highest-scoring game in football history. The Dallas Cowboys were in their seventh year as a team, finishing the regular season with ten wins, three losses, and one tie. This was their first winning record as a franchise and their first Eastern Conference title. Under Tom Landry, the Cowboys played the Packers that year for the NFL Championship title. They lost 27 to 34. Even though they lost, they were well on their way to becoming America's team!

The events of the world and country brought me closer to what was happening outside our little bubble. But nothing got my attention more than a fashion trend emerging from the upscale clothier in London. Mary Quant opened a clothes shop in Chelsea in London, showcasing her latest fashion—shorter skirts. Mary is credited with the popular miniskirt. By 1966, as its popularity grew among the younger generation, hemlines gradually moved up the thigh, revealing more leg than ever before. Of course, in Fort Stockton, they were forbidden in school. Bummer time for boys.

Fashion became an obsession for me. With the little money I made, I bought nicer shirts and pants. Jeans were the fashion. They weren't designer jeans—just Levi's. Everybody wore them. I had two pairs I could switch out with no one knowing the difference. Button-down shirts were more noticeable, so I tried to keep at least two or three I could wear over a colored T-shirt.

I knew I was cool. I was coming into my own with fashion and music. The feeling boosted my ego. Appearing on stage with the band also gave me the confidence I needed to speak to girls without stammering, stuttering, or making a fool of myself. I was now noticing girls and seeing them as possible girlfriends. Or so I thought.

My freshman year started with me driving Mom's car to school. I'd take the younger kids to their schools, then drive up to Fort Stockton High. The first week of school, as I was walking to my car, Gloria Mercado approached me. She asked if I would give her a ride home.

"I know your sister Nancy, and she asked me to ask you," Gloria said.

"Sure, get in," I replied. I drove her home, then went around to pick up my brothers and sisters. Gloria and I were in the same grade—both freshmen. I really didn't know her that well. She was short for a girl her age and had a determined look in her eye. She was studious, serious, and cautious of people.

By the end of the week, she approached me again. "My mom wants to meet you," she confided.

"Why?" I asked.

"She wants to talk to you about a job."

"What kind of job?"

"She'll tell you if you give me a ride home."

We drove to her house, and she invited me in. Her mother was sitting on the living room couch, watching TV. She turned it off when we walked in.

"Hello, please sit down," she said. "Gloria told me you gave her a ride home."

"Yes, ma'am." Reluctantly, I introduced myself. Why I felt uncomfortable, I couldn't say, but she looked at me with suspicion.

"Gloria tells me you have a car and can be trusted. You're not a bad driver, are you?

"No, ma'am."

"You don't drive fast, do you?"

"No, ma'am."

"I want to know if you will be so kind as to give my kids a ride to school. I can pay you five dollars a week."

I quickly realized Gloria's mother was single and raising all these kids by herself. She insisted I get paid five dollars per week. I accepted. She was a nice lady who never got up from her chair the whole time she spoke to me. I bid her a good afternoon, then left.

Monday morning, I dropped off my brothers and sisters first, then drove to the Mercados' house to pick them up. I parked outside and honked.

Out came Gloria, her younger sister, and her brother. Her sister was a year younger, in the eighth grade, and had beautiful eyes. She was taller than Gloria and much prettier. She wore glasses and walked with some self-assurance. Gloria introduced us.

"This is my sister, Franny, and my brother Joe. Sammy will be right out."

I caught only Franny's name.

It started innocently. I'd take my brothers and sisters to school, then pick up Gloria and her siblings. One day, I was running late, so instead of dropping off my family first, I picked up Gloria and her group too. I had eight kids in the car! Somehow, Franny slid in right next to me. I mean really close to me so everyone would fit. Having her sit that close made me tingly and nervous. I didn't quite understand the feelings, but they were there. It was the first time I felt emotionally nervous. I liked the way Franny made me feel. Every day thereafter, I longed for her to sit next to me.

We didn't start dating until the following year. It was 1967, and I was sixteen. Franny was fifteen. We were seeing each other, which meant we were boyfriend/girlfriend. I'd never had a real girlfriend before. This was new. Don't get me wrong, I liked it. We didn't see each other much at school, but everyone knew we were going out. I don't know where this going-out thing came from, since we never went anywhere together that first year. She was a freshman, and I was in the tenth grade.

Imagine that! I'd made it again!

Franny was now sitting next to me every time I picked up her and her siblings. Any chance I'd get, I'd try to be alone with her—just her and me—talking, laughing, and whispering nothings to each other.

We'd hold hands as we walked across the school parking lot. In time, the nervousness left me. As it did, I wanted to kiss her but didn't know how to approach it. I had seen people kissing in movies. It didn't look all that difficult.

How will she respond once I move my face close to hers? Will she know I want to kiss her? Will she back away, making me feel dejected with rejection? Will she kiss me back? All these thoughts ran through my mind. What if she didn't kiss? What would I do?

I wanted to kiss her. I wanted it to be a great kiss. So I practiced on my hand just like I had seen on a comedy TV show and wondered if that was what it would be like.

I kissed her on the mouth for the first time after six months of going out. It happened one day as she and I were headed to the car after school.

"Where's Gloria," I asked.

"She has to finish up with some work. She said she would be out in fifteen minutes. Can we wait for her?"

"Sure, but I have to pick up the kids."

"I'll go with you, then we can come back for her. Would that be alright?"

"Yeah," I said. "Let's go."

We left, picked up kids, and dropped them off. Franny went inside and told her mother we were going back for Gloria. Smiling, she got back in the car, and off we went. Sitting next to each other, we waited outside the school for what seemed like an eternity.

I was thinking this was the perfect time to make my move. I put my arm around her, gently squeezing her shoulder, and moved her closer to me. Then I turned my face and moved in for the killer kiss.

The surprise on her face told me she had never been kissed before. I tried talking softly, telling her I'd wanted to kiss her so many times but didn't know if she wanted me to.

After a few minutes, she moved closer, and we kissed. Our lips touched. I closed my eyes. She closed hers. I didn't feel a thing! That was all. There were no sighs, or moans, or any stirring feelings of love. Just the touching of the lips. All that practice! All that pent-up fear of everything going so badly. All those thoughts of rejection!

What's so special about kissing? What was I thinking? I could do without kissing, I told myself.

Or so I thought.

I was allowed to take Franny out for rides in my mother's car. By now, I was driving it all the time. I'd run errands, hang out with friends, cruise Dickenson Boulevard on Sundays, or just circle around Rooney Park. For all intents and purposes, it was my car. I loved it. By this time, Chuy had bought another, newer car—a 1964 Chevrolet four-door hardtop. It was maroon and much bigger than the Ford. I drove that '61 to school for four years. I'd cruise Dickenson Boulevard after school, thinking I was a big shot.

Franny and I would stop at Big Ben's for a soda before I took her home. When Gloria stayed after school, Franny and I would go out for a "drag down the boulevard." It was nice having a girlfriend who'd listen to me brag about my adventures playing music in different towns every weekend. She never tired of my talking. She'd just sit there, look at me with those beautiful eyes, and smile.

I loved this girl. At least I thought I did.

"Why don't you come to one of my gigs?" I said one day. "We're playing in town next week."

"I don't know. My mother won't let me go. She says I'm too young to be going to dances."

"Tell her you'll be with me."

"Robert, Mom doesn't know we're dating. If she was to find out, she'd never let me see you."

"What? She doesn't know?"

"No one knows except Gloria, and she isn't going to say anything."

Franny never came to see me play. But I was okay with that. There were plenty of girls there anyway. Not that I was interested in them like I was with Franny.

We continued like this for the rest of the year. Occasionally, I'd try the kiss thing again, but it just was not resonating with me. For the time being, I was content with holding hands and sitting close to her.

The Band

Ninth grade proved to be full of surprises. Analyzing decisions about girls, friends, and school consumed my thoughts. *Who am I going to associate with? Do I keep my present girlfriend? If not, will I have a difficult time finding another?* All my friends had girlfriends or at least pretended they did.

But I considered dropping Franny. She wasn't any fun. I'd known her for a while now, but it wasn't the real thing. We were not compatible at all. And it wasn't her. It was me. Playing with the band didn't afford me the luxury of attending Friday night activities. Most high schoolers would go to football games or some school dance. Or they'd just hang out with other kids on weekends. I didn't get the chance to go out with Franny. This caused problems. The band practiced every Friday. By the time we emerged from the garage, we were all too tired to do anything. On Saturdays, we played mostly out of town. The band members became my close friends even though they were all older than me. Music was my girlfriend every weekend. Although I felt I was missing out on social gatherings with those my age, playing music was my love.

Riding to all gigs with Linda's parents, I was missing out. I wanted to ride with the guys. I wanted to be treated like the older boys, not like someone who needed a babysitter. If I was going to give up my Friday and Saturday nights, then at least I could socialize with the older band members instead of always riding in the car with Linda's parents. I was old enough to go with them. So I approached El Viejo and La Vieja, Linda Sanchez's parents, with my desire to ride with the boys.

"I need to be going with the band members and not with you when we go out of town," I said. "They need my help."

"You'll have to speak to your parents," La Vieja said. "Especially your mother. If she says it's okay, then you can ride with them."

I said I would. But I didn't speak with Mom. I just pretended I had.

"Mom said I can ride with the boys next weekend," I reported. "She told me to tell you it is okay with her."

It was never questioned. The very next weekend, we were on our way to a wedding in Marfa, Texas. But riding in the van with the guys proved worthless. We slept all the way. They weren't fun at all.

We got to Marfa, set up our equipment, tested everything, ran over a couple of songs, then retired to the changing room for a quick bite.

The dance started with the Mexican wedding song. The married couple moved around the dance floor, with the bridesmaids and the groomsmen following. It was a sight to see. The place was packed. As soon as the celebratory introduction was over, we played a Mexican polka, and everyone joined in the fun.

After ninety minutes, we took a break. The couple's parents came over and invited us to share in some wedding cake and drinks. They didn't have to ask twice.

Out of the corner of my eye, I saw the drummer and the singer approach a group of girls standing by the foyer. They were talking and laughing, and they seemed to be flirting.

When our break was up, we were up again. The dance floor was rocking with couples dancing cumbias, boleros, and polkas. It was thrilling to watch the dancers enjoying our music. The place was big enough to give everyone plenty of dancing room. There must have been two hundred people there. Seemed like the whole town showed up.

During the second break, I followed the guys to the foyer, where the girls were waiting.

"Hello," I said to no one in particular.

The girls giggled.

"Oh, this is Robert. He plays the trumpet," Armando announced. I reached out to shake the hand of the first girl, but instead of shaking her hand, I brought it up to my lips and kissed it. What a Romeo!

"Oh, what a guy," one of the girls said as they all smiled and giggled at my daring escapade.

"He's got more balls than you," Armando said, laughing as he pushed the drummer's shoulder. I stood next to the girl whose hand I'd kissed. Her long black hair fell just short of her shoulders. Tall and stunning, she looked at me with beautiful light-brown eyes. I smiled. She giggled. I didn't know what to say. I got stuck.

"Are you here with your boyfriend?" I finally asked.

"I don't have one." Again, a slight giggle. She was there with her parents, she said, taking one hand to move her hair to one side. Our teenage conversation lasted no more than eight to ten minutes. Obviously, my eyes diverted to her physical appearance. She had to have been eighteen or so. She had this incredible smile with straight white teeth augmented by smooth red lips. She was so good-looking, and I couldn't believe she was talking to me! I didn't ask her name or how old she was. We just talked about music and the songs she liked.

At midnight, we played our last song. We broke down our equipment and were ready to load up when I saw her. She was still in the dance hall. Walking toward her, I interrupted her as she was talking to one of her friends.

"What's your name?" I asked boldly.

"I'm Natalia. My friends call me Lolly," she said, smiling. "When will you be back here again?" she asked.

"I don't know."

"Would you write to me? I want to know where you're playing next. If you play close by, maybe my parents will take me."

She gave me her address, and I was flattered.

Her friends kept telling her they had to leave. "Let's go, your parents are waiting," the friends said.

I wanted to kiss her but decided it would be a move I wasn't ready to make, since kissing was not my thing. Besides, I wasn't sure how she would react. I'd heard guys got slapped by girls when they tried to kiss them. I didn't want that to happen.

I had a girlfriend in Marfa! Not a girlfriend I went out with, but one I could say was my girlfriend if I needed bragging rights with my friends.

For her to ask me to write was not out of the ordinary. In those days, very few people had phones. Even if they did, long-distance calls were made only during emergencies, and then there had to be visible blood oozing from your body for that to even happen. Long-distance calls were exceedingly expensive. It was cheaper to slap a nickel stamp on an envelope than to call.

We left Marfa that night, arriving in Fort Stockton by two or three in the morning. I walked home from the Sanchez house, still thinking of the fun I'd had in Marfa. I plunked down on the sofa and tried to fall asleep. When sleep did overtake me, I was having vivid pictures of Lolly smiling and giggling. I would not forget her. I planned on seeing her again. We would write to each other for several weeks thereafter.

The band traveled in an old 1960s panel van. We removed two bench seats to fit some of the instruments, which gave us room for four guys. When playing at large venues, we pulled a trailer behind the van with all our equipment. It wasn't much, but it got us by.

One day, we were on our way to Crane, Texas, to play at a small venue called the Veterans of Foreign Wars Dance Hall. It wasn't far from Fort Stockton.

Oswaldo, who usually drove, handed me the keys when he realized I had a license.

"Why am I driving?" I asked.

"You and I are the only ones with a license. You drive there, and I drive back."

"Why don't the others have a license?"

"They're stupid and can't pass the written test," he said.

"Why? Can't they read?"

"Of course they can read. They just can't pass the test. Shut it and drive!"

The guys would talk about girls and the things they would do with them—kissing and petting and such. They'd cut up and tell stories about the girls they had befriended in various towns. Each girl from each town was their special girlfriend. Bragging on how many they had became a game of machismo.

I wasn't there yet, even though I'd just made my first female friend in Marfa. I listened and pretended not to notice. Enjoying the driving while the guys recanted their stories of love and excitement made me feel like a full-fledged member of the band. Most of the time, they'd just talk about music and the popular Tejano bands playing in cities like San Antonio, Dallas, or Houston. I imagined us doing the same at some point.

Saturday night gigs were awesome. We became known as the West Texas band to see and hear. We were gaining followers. I would see some of the same people at our dances in different towns we played in. Some were girls. They would come up to the front of the stage and watch us play. Their smiles made me feel like a real celebrity. With a twinkle in their eye, they'd write down a song request on a napkin, with their lipstick pressed on it. They'd dance and sway to the music as we performed dance moves of our own. How exciting.

When we took breaks, the girls would engage in small talk. Some of the guys would walk outside with a girl or two. On the way back, they would point at lipstick on their face or neck and smile. I knew what they were doing. I wasn't that naïve.

The night ended with people chanting, "One more, one more, one more!" We'd play to pacify, then unplug the speakers and run off the stage like real musicians. Once the van was loaded, we'd say goodbye to the girls, then drive back home at two in the morning.

The next weekend, we were headed to a rundown old building in McCamey, Texas. After the dance, Linda, the bandleader, and her parents drove off before the rest of us were ready. Once they were gone, Ernesto, the guitar player, walked back into the hall and walked out with a case of beer. They were old enough to drink. I think. Nevertheless, I drove back to Fort Stockton. They drank, sang, and laughed. By the time we arrived, not one of them could carry a tune or remember the words to a song.

No one drank before a night's performance, although a couple of guys would drop some "beanies" to help them through the night. I didn't care. I didn't know much about drugs other than what other kids in school would share. It was taboo to speak of such things.

"Beanies are only diet pills. They don't do much but help me relax before I play," remarked one player. At least that's what I was told. If they took too much, the pills made them jittery. That much I did notice. But other than the jittery facial movements, they acted normal—about as normal as a bunch of band members could act. In many ways, they were subtle about their drug experiences. They knew parents were always watching them.

Monahans, Odessa, Snyder, Abilene, Fort Davis, Balmorhea—these were some of the places we ventured to for our gigs. The VFW in Crane—a dive bar with enough room for about seventy-five people to dance—became one of my favorite places to play. It was cozy, clean, and popular with the surrounding townsfolk. Admirers would come from as far away as McCamey, Iraan, Imperial, Grandfalls, and sometimes Fort Stockton. They liked the music, and they liked to dance. Dancing, drinking, and raising hell was the norm. It was perfectly alright with me. I enjoyed playing for them.

This was my weekend routine for several years, even after high school.

First Real Date

Having friends in the high school band proved to be a disadvantage since I couldn't hang out with them on weekends. Although we did socialize during school hours, missing out on all those school activities left me out of the school culture. People thought I was a loner who didn't socialize or participate in much. I hate to admit it, but they were right. But there was one exception.

Band was always my first-period class. One day, an announcement went out regarding our yearly band dance. It was to take place in two weeks, and we were all encouraged to attend. The band hall was filled with excitement. Guys were talking about who they were going to ask to the dance.

"Robert, who are you asking?" Jimmy, another trumpet player, asked.

"No one. I'm coming stag," I said.

The word *stag* was used to describe a boy going without a date. If he took someone, then he was going drag. Don't ask me why. I could never figure that one out. In my attempt to analyze the wording, the only thing that made some sense was *drag* meant dragging a girl along when she didn't want to go. *Stag* meant you were brave enough to show up by yourself. Caveman shit.

"Why don't you ask, Delma?" one of my friends suggested.

"What? I don't even know her!" I said. "Besides, she's an upperclassman. She wouldn't go with me."

"Yes, she will. No one has asked her. Do it! Go ask her." The guys practically pushed me in her direction, but as soon as we got close to the door, I busted out of there.

"I don't think so!" I yelled back as I ran down the hallway, suspecting a trap.

The harassment lingered for the rest of the week. They were sure she'd say yes. I wasn't so sure. *Will she accept?* I wondered. *What if she says no? I would be devastated and ridiculed. What about my ego? My reputation?*

Why was I so worried? Asking an upperclassman was just not appropriate or justified. I could have asked Franny, but her mother wouldn't have allowed it. I agonized over the whole blasted thing.

Peer pressure.

Friday night was rapidly approaching, and I needed to decide. The guys were relentless. They prodded me time and time again, saying, "You've got to ask her."

So I finally ambled over to where she was sitting at the end of class. Delma was the first-chair flute player. She was very conservative, quiet, and, what seemed to me, a little shy. She wasn't the best-looking girl in the band, but she was better looking than me. She was tall with long dark hair that flipped outward at the ends. She didn't wear any makeup, but she did wear some light, almost invisible, lipstick that made her lips shiny and wet. The period came to an end, and we were dismissed. I approached her. I could tell my friends were watching from a distance. My hands were beginning to sweat, my confidence dwindling with every step I took. I had to ask her, or they would not leave me alone.

"Hi. Are you coming to the dance Friday?" I managed to ask.

371

"I haven't decided," she said, taking her flute apart and putting it in the case without making eye contact with me. "I don't have a date."

A date! I thought. *This is going to be a date? Oh my God!* I finally said, "Well. I was thinking. I haven't asked anyone, but would you come to the dance with me?"

How I found the balls—I mean, the courage—to ask is beyond me, but I did. Inside, I was shaking like a willow tree in March.

"Sure. I'll go with you," she said in a low, somewhat reluctant tone as she looked up and made eye contact for the first time. She had pretty, soft eyes. I smiled at her and walked away.

She said yes! But did she say yes because I was a handsome stud? Or a good-looking musician? Or a hunk she couldn't refuse?

In reality, I think the guys had conspired with her friends. Her friends had talked her into accepting because no one had asked her, and they hated for her not to go. I hadn't asked anyone, so they assumed this would be a great match. They must have threatened her or something to make her say yes. I still doubted her honest acceptance.

Is this even real? I wondered. *I'm going on a real date! My first real date! I asked a girl to go with me, and she said YES!*

I bounced in jubilation through the halls all day. What a Romeo! I had asked an upperclassman, and she was going on a date with me! Imagine that!

The day of the dance finally arrived. It must have been some holiday or perhaps a teacher training day because we were let out of school after lunch. When I got home, I told Mom I was taking a girl to the school dance. She just smiled and kept on folding laundry. I was expecting a reaction. Perhaps some advice.

"Did you get her a corsage?" she asked.

"What is that?"

"It's a flower you pin to her dress. Every girl going to this kind of dance has to have one."

How does she know that? I wondered. *She's never been to a dance like this in her life. How does she know?* I was always impressed with how smart my mother was, particularly on the subject of girls.

"Where am I going to get a flower? She doesn't need a flower. It's just a dance, Mom," I said.

"Yes. She'll need one." She got up, leaving her laundry, and grabbed her purse. "Now, here's some money. Go to the flower shop, and buy her a corsage."

She handed me five dollars, and off I went. I didn't think it would be difficult to buy a flower for a girl.

When I got to the florist's shop, I walked up to the counter. "I need a corsage for a girl I'm taking to a dance," I said to the lady working there.

"Do you know what color dress she's wearing?" she asked.

"No, ma'am. Why is that important?"

"Well, because we want a corsage that matches her dress. Don't we?"

"I suppose so. But I don't know what she's wearing."

"In that case, let's get her a white one that will match anything she wears." She pulled one out of the cooler behind her. "Here, how do you like this one?"

"How much is that?"

"This is three dollars and fifty cents."

"Okay."

"Do you want a boutonniere for you?"

"What is that?" I asked stupidly.

"It's a flower boys wear on the lapel of their coat. Is your girl getting one for you?"

What the hell? I wondered. *This is way too much for me to handle. Is she getting me one? How the hell should I know? She didn't say anything about a blasted bootynear. Why in the world would it be called that when it doesn't even go near your ass? What if I bought one and she did get me one? What do I do? Would this embarrass her? Would she be displeased? What should I do?*

Miraculously, the lady settled my mental argument when she said, "You should get a white one. It will match hers. Wouldn't that be nice?"

She strolled over to the counter and checked me out. I was short thirty-five cents, with taxes and all. I reached in my pocket and handed her two more quarters. I walked out of the store, thinking, *If I'd known this was going to be that difficult, maybe I should have just gone to Friday night practice.*

I spent the day washing and cleaning out the car. Picking her up at six thirty gave me plenty of time to really give the car a great detail job. I polished everything both inside and out. It took me three hours to get it looking not like a million bucks, but maybe a million pesos. But that was enough.

I ran inside, bathed, then put on my new outfit. Mom had bought me a light-blue jacket, a white shirt, and a matching tie. I slicked my hair back, brushed my teeth, looked in the mirror, and said, "What a good-looking guy you are!"

Then I was off to my first date.

The road to her house was mostly caliche—that white powdery dirt that attaches to everything, including your shoes. The house was in our barrio, but it was east of where I lived. It wasn't lavish, but it was nicely painted and very well-kept. A small white picket fence adorned the front entryway. I opened the screen door, took a deep breath, made the sign of the cross, and knocked. I was a little early. After what seemed a lifetime, her mother opened the door.

"Hello. Please come in," she said. "Delma is getting ready. Would you like something to drink?"

"No, ma'am. I'm fine." I said, hoping she hadn't noticed my shaking hands. My mouth was drying up, and I was finding it hard to swallow.

"Oh, how pretty. Delma will love it," she said as I handed her the corsage. I stood there paralyzed. Delma looked just like her mother. But younger.

Then Delma came out of a doorway and walked down the hall in a pretty blue dress. She smiled. Silky ruffles around her neck and shoulders accented her long hair. She looked wonderful. The light makeup gave her a glow I'd not seen before, especially when she smiled, which was not that often. She looked a little scared too. I wondered if she had ever been on a date.

I smiled at her and asked her mother if she would pin the corsage. I was so nervous that any attempt on my part would have caused severe hemorrhaging.

"Have fun, you two," her mother said as she walked us out the door.

I ran to the car's passenger side and opened the door for Delma. That's when I noticed white powdery dust all over the car. The wheels were full of mud. Three hours of labor, gone in an instant. I cautioned Delma about the dirt, hoping she wouldn't get any on her dress. Then I walked to the driver's side, got in, and started the car. And off we went.

"We are a little early," I said. "Want to pick up a Coke or something?"

"Yes. We are early. A Coke is fine."

That was all she said. There was no conversation from either of us. I drove. She sat motionless. I drove up Main Street, crossing the railroad tracks onto Dickenson Boulevard. Not far down was a local drive-in where girls came out and brought your drink without you having to get out of the car. I pulled in and ordered two Cokes.

There was not much to say between us. The silence was so thick that you could see it blindfolded. I didn't know what to say. Small talk was not something I was used to. She wasn't much of a talker either, so we just sat there. Thank God the radio worked.

The longer they took to bring us our drinks, the more nervous I became. Panic was setting in. Hands were shaking. I didn't know what to do. It wasn't a very pleasant outing.

When we got our drinks, I casually said, "Do you mind if we go back to my house? I forgot my wallet."

I hadn't forgotten my wallet. I didn't even have a wallet. But I had to come up with some reason to go home. The palms of my hands were sweaty. My head was sweaty. I could feel the trickle of sweat coming down my back. The air conditioning was on but not doing a good enough job of keeping me cool.

Exceeding the speed limit, I got home fairly quick. I wasn't thinking straight. My nerves were getting flustered, with my heart racing and all. I was having a panic attack.

"I'll just get my wallet. I'll be right back." I left the car running out in the street and went inside.

"Why are you here so soon?" Mom asked.

"Mom, I'm so nervous. I think I'm going to faint."

"What?" she asked as my distress level rose. She saw it in my eyes.

"Okay, now just sit down. Relax. You're going to be just fine." She turned and called down the hall, "Nancy! Nancy, *traigame las espirinas*." ("Bring the aspirin.")

Nancy walked in holding a small bottle of pills. Mom took a couple out and said to me, "Here, take these. It will help you calm down."

I slammed both aspirin with a glass of water.

"You don't have to be so nervous," she said.

"Well, she makes me nervous. I don't know why. She doesn't say much."

Baloney, Baloney, Baloney!

"In that case, you should tell her about the different places you've played in. She'll like that. You make conversation with her. Talk to her."

Several minutes passed. Mother talking to me in her reassuring voice gave me the confidence I needed to go back out there. I wiped my face with a washcloth, asking God to please keep me from making a fool of myself. I made the sign of the cross, then walked outside.

I opened the door and got back in the driver's seat. "I'm sorry it took so long. I couldn't find it. Anyway, I don't need it. I've got my license in my pocket," I lied.

When we arrived and walked into the school, we found that the band hall had been decorated in school colors. There were streamers and balloons all over the place. Her friends rushed up to her, and she walked away with them as they all chatted excitedly. I stayed with a couple of guys, talking bullshit, until one of her friends came over.

"Are you going to sit with Delma?" she asked.

"Ah, I guess so," I sheepishly whispered through a dry throat.

"Well, she's over there," she said, pointing to a dimly lit area.

I walked to where Delma was sitting. Next to her was her close friend Debra. Next to Debra was Debra's date—a senior who played basketball and was very good at it. His name was Larry. He was charming and talkative. Debra was also quite cheery. Very different from Delma.

I sat there while Delma had a conversation with the other couple. I was not included in their small talk. A slow song I recognized played. Debra and Larry got up to dance.

"Would you like to dance?" I asked, getting up off my chair and holding out my hand just like I was supposed to.

"Not now. Maybe later," Delma said.

I sat back down. The band took a break, signaling intermission. Students mingled around, talking to each other. Some walked outside.

"Would ya'll like to go outside?" Larry asked.

"Sure!" both Debra and Delma said at the same time.

They got up. I got up. We went outside toward his car. Delma and I got in the back seat, then Larry pulled out a six-pack of beer.

"Here!" he said after taking one for himself and one for his date.

I declined. So did Delma. By this time, I was wondering whether this date was worth the five dollars and thirty-five cents I'd spent. Not including the labor involved in cleaning the damn car.

We sat there for what seemed an eternity. Delma became animated and bubbly, carrying on simple chitchat with Larry and Debra.

Is she ignoring me? I wondered. *Is she embarrassed by me being a freshman while she and her friends are upperclassmen? Why will she not speak to me like she's speaking to them?*

All these feelings were beginning to surface, like I was being used and taken advantage of. I was being played. I didn't like it one bit, but I kept my mouth shut. Once the beer was gone, we went back inside.

I asked Delma again if she wanted to dance a slow song. She got up, and I held her hand as we moved toward the dance floor. She lifted her arms and placed her hands on my shoulders. I reluctantly placed mine on her hips. This was the first time I'd danced with a girl on a serious level. Dancing in public with Aunt Amy when I didn't even know how to shake my booty was better than this.

I'd seen kids on *American Bandstand*, so I did what I'd seen couples do. It wasn't hard. I moved slowly from side to side, shuffling my feet to the rhythm. We sat back down right before the song reached the end. We did not dance again. We just sat there watching everyone else have a good time.

Finally, the dance ended at eleven o'clock. I'd had enough. We walked back to the car, and I didn't bother to open the door for her. I just got in and started the car. I drove up to her house, stopped the car, and walked her to the front gate.

"Thank you for taking me," she said.

I didn't get any sincerity from the statement.

"You're welcome," I replied, reaching out my hand. She reached hers out, and we shook.

"Good night," she said.

I nodded.

What a freaking disappointment. As I walked back to the car, I decided that the night was not over for me. I went looking for Juan, my childhood neighbor I'd played baseball with. Since starting high school, we hadn't spent much time together. He'd gotten into sports, and I went in another direction. But I walked up to his front door and knocked. His brother Felix came out.

"Is Juan here?" I asked.

"No. But if you got gas in the car, we could go look for him. I'll be right out."

A few minutes later, he walked out the door with a six-pack of Coors. He offered me one, and I took it. We drank beer and rode around until we spotted Juan's car parked in front of a store along Dickenson Boulevard. The store was closed, so we just parked the cars side by side, sat on the hood, and drank beer as the last of the school crowd drove by. We talked until one in the morning.

This was so much better than a date with Delma. I don't know whether she was using me to get to the dance or simply wasn't pleased with me. But I blamed her for such a despicable time. I didn't have fun on the date. It would be several months, maybe years, before I'd ever ask another girl out. I was still seeing Franny anyway. Interesting that she never asked me about the date with Delma. Maybe she didn't know. I didn't tell her. I guess no one did.

Having to deal with the turbulence of a real date was not for me.

No More Picking

S chool ended. It was 1967, and my freshman year had gone by so quickly with my being so busy with school, band practice, music, and work. I still helped Mom on weekends, cleaning rooms at the Sands Motel. So I had very little time to concern myself with other matters—particularly when it came to girls.

That summer of '67 became a year of surprises. I was promoted to the tenth grade, which was a miracle in the making. Then I turned sixteen in July.

Since I was sixteen, going back to the onion fields was not going to work for me. I knew I had to find work without bringing about panic at home. Chuy had a good, honest friend who was a World War II veteran—Manuel Nunez, a gentleman who, for some odd reason, liked my dad. He managed a furniture store in town. He'd look after Dad and give him advice on how to do better for himself. They got along well. Knowing about their friendship, as soon as school ended, I went looking for him.

"Mr. Nunez, I'm looking for a job for the summer. Do you think you could use someone to help out at the store?" I asked.

"Don't know if we need anyone, but let me see what I can do. Come see me on Monday."

I used the weekend to convince both Chuy and Pino that I was out looking for a job and didn't want to work in the fields anymore.

"Look," I told them. "I can make more money working someplace else. I might have a chance to work at the furniture store. That, along with what I make playing with the band, puts me in a better position to help out."

I had to get that job, or I'd have no choice but to toil in the fields again. Mom sympathized with me. She didn't want any of her children going back out in the summer heat just to bring in a few measly dollars, even though it helped immensely.

When Chuy worked full-time, there was less stress and more food. As long as we still had bologna sandwiches for lunch— doused with mayo, lettuce, tomato, and an occasional jalapeño— we were doing fine. Coffee and biscuits for breakfast was ideal. Dinner promised tortillas, beans, and potatoes for sure.

We needed the money, and my job was to convince my parents that I was old enough to work in other places. I always got the same answer: "*Vamos a mirar que pasa.*" ("We'll see what happens.")

I got the job at the furniture store! I started that Monday, making a dollar fifty an hour. Imagine that! I was rich by the end of the first week. When I wasn't loading furniture to be delivered to customers, Mr. Nunez had me dusting furniture.

"Move those tables over there," he'd say. "Make sure you sweep the floors when you move furniture around. Clean those mirrors. Wipe that spill." There was always something to do.

One day, he asked me to go with him to replace an air conditioner. Most people living in the desert used water coolers, or "swamp coolers," during hot days. I didn't see a refrigerated one until much later in life. We didn't sell those.

Mr. Nunez showed me how to fit straw pads on the sides, how to replace the water pump, and how to set the water hose to provide a continual supply to the pads. That was what kept the indoors cool. I got pretty good at it.

We got back to the store, and right away, Mr. Nunez sent me to another house to replace the pads and water pump. This time, I was by myself. I got in the truck and headed out to the address he provided. I knocked on the door, and a small older woman answered.

"I'm here to fix your air conditioner," I said.

"It's right around the house. Are you from the furniture store?" she asked.

"Yes, ma'am."

I gathered my tools and headed around the house. Removing the pads revealed a broken water pump.

"Ma'am!" I shouted through the window. "Is the A/C off?"

"Yes. It's off!" she yelled back.

I replaced the pads with new straw, then attached the water hose. Piece of cake. I grabbed a new water pump from the truck and grabbed the wire cutters to cut the old one off. I took hold of the wire and pressed. The electric shock threw me on my ass a few feet from the A/C unit. It shocked the devil out of me! Damn!

Regaining my equilibrium, I slowly stood up. I could feel the anger rising within. "Stupid old bitch! She could have killed me!"

I went around to the front and knocked. Hard this time.

"Yes?" she said.

"Ma'am, you told me the A/C was off! It is not. It gave me a shock when I tried to cut it."

"Did you want me to unplug it?"

"Yes!"

"I'll unplug it for you," she said, then she went back in the house.

Again I yelled through the window, "Is it unplugged?"

I didn't trust her. I went inside and made sure it was. *Stupid old lady*, I thought.

I finished the job, then checked to see everything worked before leaving the place, still flustered and angry with her. Driving back to the furniture store, I was still shaking from either the shock or anger when it dawned on me. I should have asked her if the A/C unit was unplugged to begin with instead of asking her if it was off! I'd made the mistake. She hadn't.

Lesson learned. If you are dealing with electricity, make damn sure things are not plugged in.

I learned to love the work I did around the store. I even got a promotion after a month. Not monetarily—just in name. I was now a gofer for Mr. Nunez. I rode around in the truck, delivering furniture, moving things around, and cleaning. Not hard work, but certainly better than the onion fields. I liked working inside, where the sun was not bearing its ugly face down on me. I was also learning valuable lessons just from hanging around Mr. Nunez. He was polite and professional with customers. He was never angry. He whistled as he worked and was always in a good mood.

"Roberto," he said. "Your customers pay good money when they buy things here. You treat them with respect and honesty, and they will forever remain loyal."

He'd never raise his voice but politely listened. I didn't realize how important this lesson would become for me later in life.

A Mistake?

I met Luciano Moreno—"Lucio" for short—in our ninth-grade year. As sophomores, we were in the same science class. Sitting side by side, we partnered up on projects. We became good buddies. We shared stories about girls, sports, music, and cars. His father owned a grocery store in the northern end of town, which made it possible for Lucio to own his own car—a small Chevrolet Corvair. It was a new design, with the engine in the back and the trunk in the front. It was also a standard shift and a joy to drive. Oftentimes, he'd pick me up, and we'd go for a drag up and down the boulevard.

On one occasion, he brought his girlfriend along. Her parents were gone for the weekend, which gave Lucio and his girl "spend together" time. Isabella, his girlfriend, was the only girl in a group of brothers. A pretty girl with long blond hair, she was light complected with lovely light-brown eyes. Different for a Hispanic girl. Because she was one of the prettiest girls in her grade, she was quite popular. Her bubbly spirit added to her genuine personality. In her junior or senior year, she was crowned the Fiesta de San Juan queen. She was that beautiful and fun to be around. She was also talkative, not shy like Franny or quiet like Delma. They were opposite in almost every way. Isabella was spirited. Delma and Franny were reserved.

One beautiful, sunny Sunday afternoon, Lucio asked if Franny and I would join Isabella and him for a drive in the country. By this time, being with Franny had given me confidence. She was going into the ninth grade, and I liked her a lot. She and I had been seeing each other for nine months by this point.

Lucio picked us up in his little ol' Corvair. We drove off toward Belding Farms, a very small community southwest of town. It was a perfect afternoon.

We drove along an old country road. With the windows down, the air flowed through the car and kept us cool on the hot afternoon. The newly arrived spring heat didn't have a chance against that cool air. Lucio decided to park the car beside an old abandoned house.

"Let's go in and see what's in there," he said, getting out of the car with Isabella right after him.

"That's okay. You go. We'll stay here," I said.

I wanted some time alone with Franny. The smallness of the car forced us to sit really close to each other. I moved closer, turning my face toward her. Then I kissed her. It wasn't a passionate kiss. Just a plain and simple kiss.

She responded by kissing me back. Then it got passionate. I was sweating. I closed my eyes, enjoying the moment. With her eyes closed, she opened her mouth. I opened mine, and I kissed her again. Sparks started flying as the kisses lasted longer.

Then it happened.

I don't know what possessed me to think I could do the unthinkable. In the excitement of it all, I brought her in closer. Whether it was a male reaction or just me trying to see how far I could get, I reached over with my right hand and touched her breast. I'd never touched a female breast before. But it just seemed like the thing to do.

She quickly reached for my hand and grabbed it, removing it and practically shoving me away. She looked shocked. Mortified. She glared at me like I'd committed a mortal sin.

I was astonished and didn't know what to do. I moved away from her, offended by her reaction.

Two offended people was not good. She looked at me as if I had committed the crime of all crimes.

I'd only touched her breast. *Isn't that what boys do?* I wondered.

We sat in silence, looking away from each other.

"Go get them. I want to go home," Franny said in a voice filled with contempt.

"Why? I thought you liked me," I said.

"Just take me home."

Lucio and Isabella emerged from the house, laughing and hugging on each other.

"Lucio. We need to take Franny home," I said as he got in the car.

"Why? We just started. I was hoping we could go down to Comanche Pool afterward and hang out."

"I don't think she is in the mood. Let's just go home."

Franny and I sat in silence. We didn't say one word to each other.

If I can't touch her breast after nine months of buying her soft drinks and driving her around, then what the hell? I wondered. Other boys had bragged about touching breasts. Why couldn't I? I wanted to know what it felt like. *That's what boys are supposed to do? Right?* I told myself. *Don't I want the same?*

I tried to justify my actions by thinking just like a man. I gave her rides to school. I bought her lunch sometimes. I took her out for drives on Sundays. I was polite to her mother. I did, I did, I did. The more I thought about the incident, the more I began to resent her.

In the end, we broke up. Then I avoided her. We never spoke afterward. I still picked her and her siblings up for rides to school, but she sat in the back seat.

I wondered if this really was what guys were supposed to do at some point in a relationship. Perhaps this was not the right time for her. Perhaps this was not the right time for me. I was sixteen. She was fifteen.

Life moves on. Having a steady girlfriend was not in my immediate future. My experiences with both Delma and Franny had completely turned me off to dating altogether. I wanted no part of this "going steady" business. It wasn't worth the hassle.

Turning my focus and attention toward music and playing in the band gave me time to analyze relationships. Boys going steady with someone for long periods of time posed problems. Relationships were on today and off tomorrow, with each person wondering what had happened. I didn't have to deal with any of that if I kept from falling into the boyfriend/girlfriend trap.

Other boys would be with someone for a short period of time, then they were off with someone else days later. What was that all about? The girls were notorious for saying things like:

"Oh, she broke up with him because of that girl."

"He broke up with her because she was dating another guy."

"Don't they look good together?"

"Check out that two-timing slut."

"She broke his heart."

"I'm asking him out."

All this back-and-forth just created too much drama to deal with. So I remained a single guy committed to no one. That suited me just fine.

That was, until I met Barbara from Balmorhea, Mary from Fort Stockton, Adelida from Pecos, Karen from McCamey, Sophia from Sonora, Tricia from Grandfalls, and of course, the girl from Marfa—Lolly. They didn't all come into my life at the same time. I met them when I was playing in different towns.

Balmorhea was a small town some sixty-odd miles west of Fort Stockton. We played there off and on for several events. The place was an old, rundown warehouse with a small stage on the opposite end of the entryway. There were benches lined up against the wall, allowing plenty of room for dancers to get down. We always had a crowd at that place. People came from as far away as Pecos, Monahans, and Fort Stockton. Balmorhea, mostly a farming community, was hopping with farmers who came in to let their hair down. They wanted to forget, if for a few hours, their eighteen-hour workdays and seven-day workweeks. For a small fee at the door, folks would enjoy our covers of songs by recording artists like Little Joe Y La Familia, Sunny Ozuna Y Los Sunliners, and Agustin Ramirez Y La Revolucion Mexicana—all Tejano musicians.

The place didn't have a bar, so the customers could bring in whatever they wanted to drink. The more they drank, the better we sounded. I so enjoyed watching the audience swing to the music and having fun.

The second or third time we played there, I went out back during intermission. I thought some fresh air would reinvigorate me, since the crowded place got exceedingly warm. I was going over the second set in my mind, humming lyrics. We'd learned a new set of songs, and I wasn't up to par with a couple of them. The back of the dance hall was dark. One streetlight several yards away made it difficult to read my notes. A full moon sat motionless in a clear sky, offering some respite from the darkness. Most of the other band members were either talking to our loyal followers or fixing equipment.

"Hi there," came a voice from behind. It startled the crap out of me. I must have jumped three feet in the air. I never knew who would come up and surprise me. I just prayed it wasn't someone looking to harm me.

"I'm sorry. I didn't mean to scare you," said a female as she stepped out into the light.

"You didn't scare me," I said, swallowing hard.

She was smoking a cigarette. "Would you like one?" she asked.

"No thanks. I don't smoke."

"Well, I didn't smoke either until last year."

"What are you doing out here?" I asked.

"I came to listen to the band."

"Why aren't you inside?"

"Too many people. I don't like crowds. My name is Barbara, by the way. You're the trumpet player, right?" She came closer.

"Yes."

"I've been watching you. I watch you every time you come here to play. I live right over there," she said, pointing toward the darkness.

"Did you walk here?

"No. That's my car over by the tree."

I couldn't make out the brand in the dark, but it looked like a nice, decent car. Impressive.

"Well, Barbara, will you be going inside?"

"Nope. I'll just stay right here until you come back out again. I like talking to you. I like watching you dance on stage. You dance a lot."

"It's part of our routine. I'm not very good at it, but I'm trying," I said.

Someone opened the door to announce the start of our next set.

"I'll see you in an hour or so," she said. Then she walked back toward her car.

Barbara looked a year or two older than me. She was tall with dark wavy hair, which closely resembled an Afro—the kind worn by hippies out west. She had a slightly darker tone to her complexion. Big brown eyes coupled with long eyelashes gave her an exotic gypsy look. She was very confident and strikingly beautiful. She wore tight jeans and a halter top, exposing a trim waist and super body. I couldn't wait until the next intermission.

She was in her car smoking when I came out the second time.

"Come over here. Get in," she said.

I jumped in the passenger side of her car, and we resumed our conversation. We talked about music, the songs she liked, and what she did when not in school. She was a junior and couldn't wait to graduate so she could leave what she called a *triste* place. A sad place. She was so easy to talk to. The moonlight cast a glow against her pretty face. I couldn't help but stare at her like some kind of lunatic. I was fascinated by her.

When the dance ended, I went looking for her, but I didn't find her. It would be some time before I'd see her again.

Two months later, we were back in Balmorhea for a quinceañera. She saw me standing by the van and ran toward me. Then she jumped up and hugged me, and we both laughed. She kissed me smack on the lips. I kissed her back. We kissed. She kissed. I kissed.

"I like you," she said between kisses.

I was overwhelmed by her passion and beauty. "I like you too," I whispered.

I met Adelida through my friend's girlfriend, Sylvia. The girls were cousins.

My friend Edward lived in Coyanosa and went to school in Fort Stockton. He lived somewhat closer to Pecos, where he spent a lot of time hanging out. That was where he met this nice-looking girl. He had just enrolled in Stockton High, and, as fate would have it, he sat next to me in history class. We started talking, and before long, he invited me to his house. We became friends. One Sunday, after his mother fed us lunch, Edward asked me if I'd like to go to Pecos because his girlfriend had invited him over for the afternoon. I wasn't sure about going, since I had to get back home. But after some coaxing, I relented, and off we went to Pecos, Texas.

We stopped at Sylvia's house and casually walked in to find her sitting next to a small, pretty girl—Adelida. She was about our age and had short brown hair, a round face, and deep, thoughtful, kind eyes. She was somewhat tiny for someone her age and wasn't like any other girls I'd known. She presented herself as sophisticated and smart. Her makeup was perfectly applied, giving her a beauty only she could pull off.

The four of us rode around for a while, giving me time to get to know her. I started seeing Adelida whenever we played in Pecos or Monahans. She'd keep track of where we were playing, then make Edward take both her and Sylvia to the dance. If the band played a song I didn't have a part in, I'd walk off stage and ask her to dance. She never refused. It made me feel kind of special that someone as pretty as her would dance only with me when there were so many other guys who were free to dance with her all night.

It wasn't long before she became important to me. She was smart, kind, and pleasant to be around. When she looked at me with those big eyes, I'd smile. I really liked her. Nothing was going to stand in the way of our friendship. It was definitely becoming more like a courtship.

One day, La Vieja announced that we would be playing in Balmorhea in two weeks. A promoter was sponsoring the venue and promising a contract, which meant a little more money. I was excited. I was going to see Barbara again. When the day arrived, we got there early and quickly set up the equipment so we could run sound checks. Satisfied with the sound, we played a couple of songs to measure volume, then lingered around until start time. I spent every second I could outside at the back of the building, hoping to see Barbara before we started.

The crowd came in, and the band started playing at exactly seven. Toward the end of the first set, I saw Adelida walk in with Sylvia. We locked eyes, and she smiled.

Uh-oh. Why is she here? I wondered.

When the intermission started, I walked toward her. "Where's Edward?" I asked Sylvia.

"He didn't come. I drove us here," she replied.

Adelida smiled at me and said, "I wanted to come see you play. We can't stay long. Maybe just until you finish your next set."

"It's good to see you," I said, hugging her.

Then Sylvia went out the front door.

"Let's go outside, where we can talk without this noise," I said to Adelida.

We walked out the front door, and I glanced in the direction of the back door. We stood by Sylvia's car, talking. My mind was racing.

What am I going to do if Barbara shows up? I'm here in front, and Barbara is probably standing in the back, waiting for me. How the hell did this happen? I wondered. I had not been expecting Adelida. Never did I think two girls, who supposedly liked me and I them, would wind up in the same town, at the same event, at the same time! I didn't know what I was going to do if one of them saw me with the other. What a mess. How did I get into this? I certainly didn't want to hurt anyone's feelings, although it was rather flattering—and scary.

"I have to go back inside," I told Adelida.

"Will you dance with me when you aren't playing?"

"I don't know if that will be the case since we have a whole new set. I'll come by and talk with you next break."

Then I walked off, floundering for a solution.

"Robert! Hey, Robert! There's this girl in the back waiting to see you," shouted Jessie right before we were to start up.

"Is she still there?" I asked. "What did she say to you?"

I wasn't very comfortable with this. Now I was in a bind and searching for a way to keep the two girls away from each other. There was still time to talk to Barbara. So I walked out back, but she was gone.

Now, stay calm, I thought. *She must have seen me with Adelida. Oh, mercy. I'm in trouble.*

I was preoccupied with the situation, so when I got back to the stage, I didn't realize the guys in the band were gawking at me. Then I noticed their smiles and looks of "Oh, you're in holy hot shit now, boy."

Oswaldo motioned for a slow song. Fortunately, I didn't have a part in this one. The guys looked at me as if to say, "What are you going to do, you dumbshit?"

Those damn bastards, I thought. *They're doing this on purpose.*

Adelida saw me standing there, and I knew I had to ask her to dance. So I moved across the dance floor, grabbed her hand, and took her toward the front, where people would block the view of me from the back. I was sweating bullets. I was sure Barbara was watching me from the back door.

Shit, I'm in trouble, I thought. *I can't lose Barbara. I like her way too much.*

The song ended, and I walked Adelida to the bench. She hugged me and said, "We have to go. Sylvia's parents don't know we're here. She doesn't have permission. We have to go. Please write to me or call me. When will you be coming to Pecos again? Please call me." She leaned in and kissed me. "Call me," were her final words as she turned and left.

I walked back to the stage, smirking at the guys. Those damn excuses for musicians were laughing. They'd played that song intentionally. To teach me a lesson? Hell no. They did it to get a kick out of it. I knew that they would not let this die down anytime soon. I was to be the butt of their jokes for some time.

In some respects, I was glad Adelida had left. Now I had to deal with Barbara. Did she know?

The second set ended. I felt Barbara had seen me, and I feared a confrontation. I'd been looking forward to this time for two weeks! Now I braced myself for who knew what.

I walked outside and saw her standing by her car. I waited. Nothing. She looked up and came toward me.

Get ready for a slap, I thought. *Please don't kick me in the nuts. Please.*

She wrapped her arms around my shoulders and said, "I'm sorry I wasn't here for your first break. My parents didn't want to let me come. I waited until they fell asleep and crawled out the window. I had to see you."

She kissed me. Holding my hand, she took me back to her car, and we sat. How lucky can a guy get! She hadn't seen me with Adelida. Amazing! Was that a close call or what! I smiled at her and told her I'd missed her too.

"Look, we hardly have time for us. I really like you," I said. "What if I come see you some Sunday when I have more time?" It wasn't that far.

"I'd love that," she said, smiling and leaning in for another kiss. We chatted for a few more minutes. Then she said, "I have to go back home before my parents find out. Please come see me if you can."

She kissed me again and started up the car. Then she was gone.

Driving back home after our gig, I had plenty to think about. How could I have let myself get into this uncomfortable situation? I would have hurt two people I cared about, and I vowed not to let it happen again. I learned a valuable lesson that night: don't get involved with two girls at the same time, especially if they live close to each other.

It was valuable advice at the time. But why did this bother me so much? It wasn't as if I was either girl's boyfriend. We didn't have any commitments to one another. We were just friends. Well, kissing friends. That was all. I'd learned my lesson with Franny. There was no reaching for breasts. I kept my hands to myself. At least for the next two years. Lessons learned.

Two weeks later, I told Adelida I couldn't see her as much as I wanted. "Pecos is too far," I said. "I can't come see you as often as you'd like."

"I know," she said sadly. I'll be here if you ever come back to Pecos. Come see me. Okay?"

"Sure. I can do that," I lied. I felt terrible. Going to Pecos was something I didn't like to do. The guys there were jealous around outsiders. They protected their own. I considered them hoodlums and didn't want trouble. Guilt and inconsiderate feelings left me to write one last time to her.

I wrote, "I can't see you again. Please don't hate me. It hurts to say this, but I can't. Sorry."

I never heard back from her. It was the right thing to do. Between her and Barbara, I chose Barbara.

For some reason, I never went to see Barbara on Sunday. Or any Sunday, for that matter. By the time the band did go back to Balmorhea, I learned she'd left. She had graduated and disappeared. She never wrote to tell me where she had gone.

I missed her. And I missed Adelida.

Year of Learning

I was going into my sophomore year, and the world was opening up around me. I don't know whether it was because I was fascinated by modern history or simply because I was paying more attention to the evening news. Either way, I was more aware of what was happening in the world.

The Vietnam War was still raging on and getting deadlier by the day. Civil rights activists were taking too many chances trying to change the Southern mindset and getting killed or maimed when they ventured too far into Alabama, Georgia, Mississippi, and/or Texas. The race to the moon was in full swing as we tried to beat the Ruskies to be first there. The clothes were getting flashier, men's hair was getting longer, and girl's dresses shorter, just like the rock and rollers we'd seen on TV.

The Summer of Love started in 1967, when over a hundred thousand young people gathered for a rock festival in San Francisco's Haight-Ashbury neighborhood. They wore hippie fashions that coincided with public behaviors not so well-known by previous generations. The Summer of Love encompassed a different kind of music, hallucinogenic drugs, anti-war protests, and free-love scenes up and down both the East and West Coasts. Young men and women, called hippies by the general public, were also referred to as flower children. They were an eclectic group who were suspicious and untrusting of government, rejected consumerist values, and fiercely opposed the Vietnam War. Identifying with this group came easy for me, but the nature of small-town conservative thinking would not allow it. I believed in the hippies' views, but I didn't know how to speak out like they did. I still lived in a very isolated world.

I was fascinated by the relentless effort on the part of my friends to look chic. They imitated the hippie fashion of long hair held in place with bandanas, round glasses like those sported by John Lennon from The Beatles, bell-bottom pants, short skirts, vests, and more. I stuck to what I knew. Not flashy. Simple, so as not to attract too much attention.

I worked at the furniture store all summer, then used the money I made to help out with groceries, utilities, and sometimes rent. For once in my life, there was money in my pocket. It wasn't much, but it was enough to splurge on myself. It was okay for me to keep five to ten dollars in my wallet without having to give it all to the family kitty. This money was for things I wanted instead of things I needed, like new clothes for school when it started again.

I ventured into Odessa, running crazy in the downtown stores with my parents. I bought shoes, socks, underwear, a shirt or two, and more jeans. I picked what I wanted instead of what Mother thought I should have. The clothes were not designer at all—more like discount store stuff, but nice.

Without having to travel to distant farming fields, I got more time to spend with friends when I wasn't at the furniture store or playing on weekends. The Ford Fairlane, for all intents and purposes, was mine. Mother had bought herself another used car, and Chuy still drove the '51 Chevy truck.

The extra money also allowed me to pay my own way when I went out with friends. No more bumming from them. We'd hang out at Comanche Pool in the evenings, sitting on benches in the pavilion and looking down at the last of the die-hard swimmers. We'd cruise the drag from one end of Dickenson to the other, then back again. By this time, I was drinking beer—but not a lot, since it only took two or three for me to feel woozy. It was a very pleasant and happy time.

Then I met Mary.

It all started so innocently, or at least I thought it did. Every year, the school had a fundraiser called Slave Day. This fundraiser was a yearly event sponsored by the cheerleaders. Students were "sold" to the highest bidder, and for the day, sold students belonged to their "owners," doing what they were told, dressing as ordered, and performing work and tasks. It wasn't considered derogatory, racial, or offensive at the time. Fort Stockton had two or three Black families and only a handful of Black students. They mostly identified with the Hispanic group because they spoke pretty good Spanish and didn't question the idea of a Slave Day. There was no pressure to not call it a Slave Day like there was in other parts of the country.

"Hey, Robert. You going to volunteer for slave day?" Troy asked me one day shortly before the fundraiser.

"Nah. I'll go though," I said. "It's always fun to see which girl brings in the most money. Besides, we get to miss class!"

"You should volunteer. I am. So is José, Junior, and Sammy."

"Nah. Can't do it," I said as two girls we knew walked up to us.

"Robert, you are going to volunteer, right?" one of them asked.

"I don't think so. I might not be here."

"Come on. Do it! Mary Urrabazo is going to bid on you."

"Who? I don't even know a Mary U."

"Yes, you do. She's the one who flirts with you during passing period. Right before history. She's always flirting with you."

"Oh. Her," I said, realizing who she was talking about. "Nah, she's just kidding around. You know Mary. Besides, she's going out with Junior. They've been boyfriend/girlfriend since junior high."

"No, no," the girl said. "They broke up weeks ago. She likes you."

"I don't think so. I've gotta go, or I'll be late for class again."

"She likes you!" the other girl shouted as I ran down the hall.

Mary likes me? I thought. *When did that happen? She's never said a word to me. Yes, she does flirt with me, but she's taken. She's a senior, for heaven's sake, why me? Why would she consider someone younger? I'm a junior. I know what happens when you try to go out with older girls.*

My experience with Delma still lingered.

The days went by, with Slave Day just around the corner. One day, I was standing by my locker, getting a history book for my next class. Mary separated from her group, came up, and then leaned against the locker next to mine.

"Hi. I hear you are going to be a volunteer for Slave Day," she said.

"Nah. I'm not." I closed the locker door and looked her straight in the eye.

"Why? My friends and I would love to bid on you. If we win, I'd make you my slave."

What in the hell's name does that mean? I wondered. *Why would she bid on me? It's got to be a joke.* I was skeptical and very embarrassed. I thought I was being set up. *What if Junior comes down the hall and sees her talking to me?* I thought. *This could spell trouble.*

"Why would you do that?" I asked. "I thought you and Junior were going out."

"Oh, don't mention his name. We broke up. He's a squirrel."

"In any case, I don't think it's a good idea," I replied, then I walked across the hall to my class.

She followed.

Mary, a popular girl, hung out with other popular girls. I wasn't a popular guy. I'd never thought of myself as being popular at all. I didn't know what to make of it, but I was flattered yet cautious. I got this sensation of wonder and awe around her. I liked her flirtatiousness. She was good-looking, AND she always wore short skirts, exposing long brown legs. She was mystifying and flirty, giving me the impression I was important, good-looking, and debonair. She would hold eye contact, smiling at me as if I were the only person in the room.

Mary lived a few blocks east of me in a better part of the hood. My brain was insisting that I should avoid her like the plague.

Stay away from girls who like to woo guys then drop them like cow turds, I thought. *They laugh and mock boys who are deemed vulnerable. Why pretty girls show attention, then walk away is mysterious. Beware of such beauties*, I mentally noted.

"Why?" she asked, getting closer to me as we walked toward my class.

"Let me think about it," I said. "Okay? I've got to get to class."

She walked away, with her books close to her chest, and caught up with her girl gang. I walked to class. I was baffled by all the attention, but I didn't trust her or her friends. I thought her interest could be a joke. Besides, I was not convinced this was truly an honest attempt at getting me to volunteer for Slave Day.

The same thing happened the next day. She came around the hallway corner with her girly friends, laughing and chatting away like there wasn't a care in the world. Then the whole gang stopped and looked my way.

I was standing by my locker. Mary approached me while the rest of the gang made silly comments.

"Get him to say yes!"

"You can do it, Mary."

"Hey, girl, send him over here. I'll make him say yes!"

They laughed and disappeared around the next corner, leaving Mary and me alone.

"Will you sign up? Me and the girls want to bid on you," she said.

"Why me? I don't understand. There are plenty of guys around here who would jump at this. If you are really doing this to raise money, I'm not your guy. I wouldn't bring a dollar bid! That would be embarrassing. But why me?"

"Oh, come on. You're not afraid, are you?" She smiled and batted her long eyelashes, looking glamorously stunning. There were a couple of other girls who had also asked me if I was signing up. Just casual friends I shared classes with. The fundraiser was for a good cause, though they never told anyone where the money went. I was getting hit from both sides.

Reluctantly, that afternoon, I signed up.

The entire student body gathered in the gymnasium as cheerleaders called out names of volunteers. The agriculture teacher was the auctioneer for the event. Guys went first. They lined up, ready to mount the auction block. We were having an auction in an event called Slave Day, and no one thought it was humiliatingly inappropriate! This was Texas, for heaven's sake. We still believed we were part of the Confederacy.

They started with a few of the freshmen who were dumb and daring enough to participate. The auctioneer began with a one-dollar bid for this skinny white guy. He brought in five dollars. He moved on to the next, like the boys were livestock, until he reached juniors. My last name starts with an *A*, so I was one of the first ones up.

My name was called, and I ambled down the stands to the gym floor to some feeble applause. No cheers for bravery. Two cheerleaders locked arms with me as they escorted me to the torture box. There I stood, in full view of the entire student body. Why I wasn't shaking or peeing in my pants, I'll never know. But scared to death I was.

The auctioneer started the bid at two dollars. As he rambled on, I was looking at the floor, praying someone bid two dollars. I heard someone yell, "Two dollars!" I hesitated to look up, not wanting to know who it might be.

"Two fifty!" someone called out.

Then I heard "Three dollars!"

I could tell the bidding was coming from opposite sides of the stands. It eventually stopped. The auctioneer slammed his gavel and yelled, "Sold to that group over there for three dollars!"

Three dollars! I thought. *Is that all? Is that all I'm worth? How embarrassing! That skinny white kid got five dollars! I'm only worth three?*

I was led away from the floor by cheerleaders as the applause died down. The juniors and seniors brought in the most money—especially the athletes. By this time, the girls were up for sale. One went for as much as sixty-five dollars. The student body had forgotten about my measly three-dollar bid.

I came to find out that Mary and her bunch had the highest bid on me. I would be their slave on Friday.

That Friday, I looked like an idiot dressed in a pink floral dress, a matching head scarf, and someone's mother's white shoes, which bound and hurt my toes. The girls paraded me around the hallways, making me carry as many of their books as I could possibly handle. They threw insults at me, laughing and having the time of their lives.

I was okay with it all since I was not the only guy dressed so stupidly. At least the girls didn't dress me like an animal and pull me around by the collar. I managed to make it through the day without losing my dress. However, the shoes had to go by third period. I was actually having fun getting all the attention from a gang of girls who were also having fun. I didn't have much of a choice, so why not enjoy it?

Finally, the bell rang at the end of the last period of the day. Thinking the bell signaled the finality of this odd event, I felt relief. Then Mary walked up to me and whispered in my ear, "It's not over yet. You have to take me out tonight."

The date ended up being only her and me. Not the whole gang. That would have been costly and possibly deadly, knowing those girls.

I picked her up at her house at seven. We rode around, then settled on sodas from Big Jo's Drive-in. We talked. She flirted. At one point, she scooted over next to me, smiling. She wasn't intimidated by her actions. I was. But I liked it.

We rode up and down Dickenson until she asked if we could take a ride through Rooney Park. I parked the car under a sycamore tree. We sat and talked. Well, she did most of the talking. I listened. We had the music playing in the background with the windows down. She moved closer to me.

Small talk ensued. I wanted to know more about her, but I was careful not to share too much about me. I didn't have to. She'd already scoped me out and knew I was in a band. Before long, she leaned over to kiss me, and I closed my eyes just like I had seen in the movies. She knew how to kiss. She ran her tongue around my upper and lower teeth, then between my inner lips and gums. I'd never had that done before! I wondered if that was what they called French kissing.

The longer we kissed, the warmer it got. I kept my hands away from boobs and ass. I wasn't about to get slapped and dropped like hot coals.

We really got into it and slid down on the bench seat of the car. Things were getting hot and heavy. Right when I decided to go for a tit grab, I heard a car park right next to mine. It came out of nowhere, surprising us both. A group of girls I didn't know lowered their window and swung a bundle of carrots out while they laughed.

"Here, bunny, bunny. Come and get it!" they shouted.

Mary sat up, demanding that we drive away. The girls' car backed up and disappeared in the darkness.

"What was that all about?" I asked.

"Nothing. Let's just get out of here. Those girls are out to get me. I think Junior put them up to it."

I didn't understand the gesture. But our night ended abruptly. Although I was okay with that, the incident troubled me. Why would anyone hold a bunch of carrots and call her bunny? Why did she get so upset?

Mary stopped coming by my locker after that incident. I figured she'd probably made up with Junior and started dating him again. That was fine. Yet, for reasons I didn't understand, a bout of jealousy struck a nerve with me. I liked her a lot. I felt deflated. Defeated. Heartbroken. Dumped.

A week later, as I stood by my locker, I heard her voice. "Where have you been? You haven't spoken to me since that terrible night. Why? Are you trying to avoid me?"

"Mary, I've been here," I said. "Where have you been?"

We walked down the hall, me carrying her books.

"I'm sorry about that night," she said. "Those girls were just being stupid. I found out who they were. They won't do that again. So, can we continue to be friends?"

"Of course," I said, wondering why they would not do that again. *Did she have them beaten up? Did she get even? What was the yelling "Bunny, bunny" about?*

Mary and I didn't spend a lot of time together on weekends. I wasn't one of those teenagers who typically hung out. I practiced on Fridays and played on Saturdays, which made it very difficult for us. The flirting eventually stopped, and in a matter of days, she went back to Junior, dropping me without telling me.

I saw her coming down the hall one day. She was holding on to Junior's arm and giving him the same look she'd given me—flirty. Was she trying to make me jealous? Well, it was working. A year later, after I'd gone out with her once more, I found out why the girls mocked her by calling her "Bunny." Her two front teeth were separated, giving her an odd look, much like a rabbit or bunny. I found it rather attractive.

There was a problem with young people saying, "They're going out." If you fell into that category, your boyfriend/girlfriend's attitude was, "Keep your hands off my boyfriend/girlfriend." I knew that if I got into that situation, girls who might have an interest in me and girls I might have an interest in would not dare infringe on that relationship.

I met Imelda Lopez, who was a year behind me at school, during a party I attended. She was cute and had short hair and a skinny body. But her eyes were to die for. They were the most attractive side of her. She also had a beautiful smile that revealed perfect teeth. She was standing by herself in the kitchen during the party, holding a drink. The minute I saw her, I fell in love with her looks—her eyes.

"Hi," I said as I walked over to where she was standing.

"Hello," she said in a soft, quiet voice as if she was embarrassed to talk.

"Are you here by yourself?

"No, I'm with my friend Rebecca. She had to go to the bathroom.

"Oh. I've seen you before in school. Are you a sophomore?"

"No. I'm in the ninth grade. I've seen you before," she said. "You're in tenth, aren't you?

"Yes. I'll be going into my sophomore year."

Her friend Rebecca bounced toward us with a smile and grabbed Imelda's arm, taking her away to the patio. Imelda walked away, but she turned her head to look at me and smile.

I was hooked.

I tried hard to get a date with her, but I was rebuffed with, "You're going out with Mary."

I wasn't "going out" with anybody. Or was I? It wasn't like we were going steady or anything like that. To the girls, if a boy was going out, it meant he was untouchable.

When Imelda finally said yes, we met at Comanche Pool one evening, where we spent the time talking and laughing until someone came by and picked her up.

I really like her. I liked her style. She reminded me of Twiggy, the first international supermodel and fashion icon of the 1960s. She was that cute. But she was going to need some convincing if she was going to like me like I did her. Just the fact that she didn't talk much indicated a shyness. All she had to do was smile, and I could feel something unexplainable come over me. It made me feel special all over.

We went out a couple of times, but something was just not clicking. I talked music, she talked books. I talked cars, she talked school. I wanted to kiss, she wanted to hold hands.

By chance, as I was driving down Main Street one evening, I saw her in a billiard hall. I stopped the car, parked, and headed to the door. But just as I was about to enter, I saw her laughing and talking with a guy.

I hesitated. *I thought she liked me*, I thought. *What is she doing here with that guy? Should I go in there and talk to her? Maybe they're just friends.*

I was confused. I slowly moved away from the door, got in the car, sat, and watched her like some stalker dude. I saw the other guy whisper something in her ear. *Is she on a date with him?* I wondered. I was trying to make sense of this. She seemed to be having too much fun. It didn't take me long to realize that her demeanor and body language were very different with him than when she was with me.

For the next few days, I avoided her, or she avoided me. I questioned a serious relationship between her and me. That let-down feeling haunted me again, and a blow to the old ego sent me into a whirlwind of emotions. I would never go out with her again.

In the end, she married the guy.

I wasn't having too much luck with Fort Stockton girls. I don't know why, other than perhaps they did not want to be associated with a poor kid from the barrio. I'm sure there were girls who would have talked to me, but not the ones I liked.

Why are relationships so complicated? I'd wonder.

Nothing about having a girlfriend seemed serious. They came and went as if it was normal. I didn't think these romantic experiences were about love at all. They were about feelings. All the girls I dated were different, yet each one taught me to beware and safeguard my true feelings. I learned beauty doesn't necessarily come with smarts. Beware. Passion can be switched off and on in seconds. Girls can be finicky, rash, pleasant, high maintenance, clingy, bipolar, and even persuasive when it comes to teenage love.

Knocked Down

Toward the end of the school year, every student had to see the counselor to prepare schedules for the following year—that is, if they passed to the next grade. The visit called for the assumption that we would pass.

The time came when we were all talking about what kind of classes we would be taking as juniors. Mother beamed with pride when she found out I was going to see the counselor to schedule for my junior year. I was getting close to her expectations—graduate from high school, get a job, be a productive citizen of the community, and get out of the house. So far, if I didn't do anything stupid, I just might set an example for my siblings.

When the announcement came for us to be thinking of classes to take, I made a mental note to ask my buddies. Four or five guys talked about the kind of schedule best suited for us. Because I hadn't thought I'd make it that far, I hadn't given it much thought. I wanted to keep it simple. Somehow, somewhere, I'd picked up on what other people were saying. I must have been paying attention.

"I'm taking college prep courses next year," one of the guys said one day. Upon hearing this, the others chimed in with the same intentions.

What does that mean? I asked myself. *What's college prep?* All my friends were going to ask for college prep classes. I had to make a choice, but I didn't know the options, so I talked myself into it by asking myself, *What could it hurt?* I didn't want to be left out. The decision would put me in the same status as my friends, even though college was not in the cards for me.

The excitement from the group lifted my spirits. *I can do this,* I thought.

When the day came, I waited my turn to see Henry Ward, our class counselor. We were all quite nervous about our eleventh-grade year. I sat in the waiting room as student names were called. The five of us guys had signed up together as a force of support for each other. One by one, my friends emerged from the office with a pre-schedule, shouting, "I'm in for college prep!"

That excitement fueled my desire. I wasn't going to be left behind. I could feel it. I knew I was a shoo-in for college prep. I was just as smart as the other guys. I was going for it!

"Robert Alfaro," the loudspeaker above the counselor's office called out.

I stood up, walked into Ward's office, and sat right across from him, with his desk between us. He pulled out my transcript and reviewed it in front of me. Finally, after a few minutes, he looked up.

"So, what kind of courses do you want to take next year?" he asked.

"I want to take college prep courses."

"Do you think you can make it in college?"

"Yes, sir. I do."

"Let me tell you something," he said, taking off his glasses. "Your grades are not good enough to get you into college. I would be doing you an injustice if I placed you in college prep. I think the best thing for you is to take classes that will prepare you for a trade. Now, we have building trades, automotive, and welding. And cosmetology, which I don't think you'd like since it's mostly for girls." He scribbled down something on the schedule card.

My heart stopped. He didn't notice the devastation he'd created in my being. I felt like someone had punched me in the stomach. The shock was making breathing difficult. Those words blew away any hope I had of becoming something more.

"Mr. Ward, I know I can do it," I said. "I'll work hard."

"Your grades in math tell me you are not prepared for Algebra I, which you'll have to take your junior year. I don't see you taking any advanced classes. Your transcript shows only basic classes. You're not prepared. Take this, and discuss it with your parents. They will need to sign off on it. Thanks for coming in."

I was dismissed with a wave of the hand. Deflated emotionally, mentally, and spiritually, I walked out with my head hanging low, crushed and close to tears. My heart, saddened by his words, pulsated in my ears. I'd been knocked down several rungs and fell into an abyss, wondering if I would hit rock bottom. I walked out wanting to cry, feeling like I was not good enough to even think about going to college.

One of the guys was waiting for me, and I immediately snapped out of my black hole.

"Did you get college prep, man?" he asked.

"Of course!" I lied.

Then I rode around a bit after school, feeling humiliated until doubt set in. *Perhaps he's right*, I thought. *Maybe I am too stupid.* How could I explain what happened to my mother? I had to tell my parents, even though they wouldn't understand. *How did I get in this predicament?*

Doubt turned into a fool's dream. *Who is he to claim I'm not college material?* I wondered. *What makes him such an expert? Why wasn't I counseled about this? Isn't this their job? To help students understand the kinds of classes they need in order to get into college?* I didn't want to take trade classes. *I'm not going to do this*, I told myself. *I'm going back and argue with him.*

All these thoughts didn't make me feel any better. I knew I wasn't prepared. I knew I would struggle. I had to try and convince my parents to come to school and support me. But going to college wasn't remotely viable, so why was I so determined? What was I trying to prove?

One of my favorite shows on TV was about Perry Mason, a defense attorney who took on very difficult cases, helping those accused of crimes they didn't commit and saving them from injustice. What if I wanted to be an attorney just like Perry Mason? I could dream, couldn't I? If I couldn't get into college prep, then the establishment was saying, "You've reached your intellectual ability. You're not smart enough. This is as far as you get."

I went back and forth, trying to convince myself I could go to college while, at the same time, knowing I might not be academically prepared. By the time I got home, inspiration and determination were slowly abandoning me. The sound of "You're not good enough" throbbed in my mind like a bad headache.

That night, I sat at the kitchen table, sharing my schedule with Mom.

"He says I have to take one of these classes," I explained. "Building trades, welding, or auto mechanics. I don't want to take any of these classes. I want to take advanced classes like the other kids. You need to come to school with me tomorrow and help him understand."

"What's wrong with these classes?" she asked. "If he says you need these, then he must be right."

"No, Mom. He doesn't know. He thinks I can't do this."

"Do you not like any of these other classes? Look, you could learn something that will help you get a job."

"I don't want to do this."

Apparently, Chuy was listening to the conversation from the bedroom. He came into the kitchen and said, "You need to take auto mechanics. Do you know how much money those guys make? Some are making seven dollars an hour! That's big money! You take mechanics."

That was the end of the discussion.

I avoided turning in my pre-schedule for days and almost missed the deadline. Mom had signed it, but I had yet to turn it in with auto mechanics taking up two full periods of the day. I was stuck. My friends were going in a different direction, and only the morons were going into vocational classes.

I was one of them.

The summer of '68 found me still working at the furniture store. I'd be seventeen in July. Getting my summer job back helped me forget about the next school year. I was super glad. My onion-picking days were over! I could sleep a little later and still make it to the store in plenty of time.

Before work started, I'd sit and visit with the older men, sharing their coffee, listening, and enjoying their conversation. They talked about politics, business, Vietnam, LBJ, Social Security, upcoming elections, and a whole lot more. Over coffee and biscuits, I listened to them scrutinize everything, including what they called "those hippies from California." They would ask me questions regarding school and what I was learning. I told them about college, and they all agreed it was a good thing. I didn't have the heart to tell them I wasn't going.

The conversations ended as soon as the owner of the furniture store showed up. He was a short, balding white man with a pot belly. He was always mad at the world and complaining about school taxes, city taxes, and all government taxes. He believed the school board was going to run him out of business.

"They keep raising my taxes. How's a man going to make any money if all they want is more blood?" he'd moan.

I was learning about local politics through the eyes, mouths, and ears of these older men. Then it hit me. Maybe this auto mechanic stuff wasn't so bad. I could start my own business. I started thinking more about mechanic work and less about the cockamamie idea of college. I was going to make this work.

As my spirits rose, the summer became bearable.

Recording Artist?

The band got better the longer we played together. Contracts for weddings, quinceañeras, birthday parties, and the like were coming in more often. Our talents were expanding beyond our regular two-hundred-mile radius. No longer were small venues paying us a percentage of what was collected at the door. We experimented with music other than Tejano, even though it was still very popular with our audiences. We branched out to country and western, rock and roll, and Top 40 music. There was talk of recording some of our original songs. A daring concept, yet seemingly possible. We'd be taking a great risk.

"We can do this," one of the band members said. This comment set us on a long road toward creative thinking. Ecstatic yet fearful of failure, we started writing our own music. Mostly Tejano.

Douglas, our bass player, kept bringing it up.

"We have enough original music. We can fill an album," he said one Friday. He was sure we were ready. A respected musician from Alpine, Texas, he believed it was time, and his confidence permeated our thoughts. It didn't take much to convince us.

That summer, we hunkered down and cleaned enough songs for an album. We modified some cover songs, but for the most part, we had originals our followers liked. Someone found a recording studio in San Antonio the following year that would lease us time to record. It was the first time I ventured that far from Fort Stockton and my first trip to a large city.

San Antonio's cultural love of music filled the streets. I was in awe over the river walk, the people, the friendliness, and the beauty of the place. It was amazing. It went beyond what I had imagined it would be. I was enthralled with San Antonio. I wanted to live there. I loved it.

Walking into the studio, with its sophisticated recording equipment, made me feel like a rock star. The place was not fancy at all. It was small, with soundproof rooms, recording equipment, and a large window separating the musicians from the man mixing the recordings. I could not believe a group of kids from a small hick town were about to record music in a real-life studio! Most people dream of such things. We were doing it!

Recording in a studio was very different from what I thought it would be. The drums were in a place enclosed with plexiglass, while the bass, guitar, and keyboard players were in another. They were the first to record the rhythm and beat. When they finished, the trumpets and saxophones were next. We wore headphones, listening to the beat from the first group. Then the voices recorded their part. The audio mixer then synchronized all three parts, producing a full song. He played the first one back to us. A technological miracle! It sounded great! At least it did to me.

This went on for the better part of the day until it was time for a break. We listened to our progress. There were a couple of songs that were just not coming out the way we wanted, which forced us to struggle through several takes. Exhaustion set in by the end of the day, and we weren't finished. Time meant money, and we weren't through. I wanted to explore the city at night, but we were all too tired from an exhausting day. The wonders of San Antonio were going to have to wait.

Beers from an all-night convenience store were brought into our cheap hotel room. The older guys drank. I went to bed.

The recordings were finished early the next day. We headed back home, missing the opportunity to immerse ourselves in the great Hispanic culture San Antonio was known for. I swore I would be back.

The recording tape was taken to a studio in Midland to further mix the sounds before it went off to be produced into a full-fledged album. It would be several weeks before it would be released. In the meantime, Linda sat with several pictures of us taken at different events until she settled on the one she wanted for the cover. It was a picture of her in a long yellow gown with a ribbon around her waist. She was holding her saxophone. Behind her was a handsome young man of seventeen cradling his trumpet and looking to one side.

When I saw her choice, I just smiled. I was going to be on the cover! The white shirt with the black vest I wore brought out that smile. I couldn't believe that tall, dark, and handsome guy was me! Why she chose this picture was never divulged.

I was surprised when the first few albums landed in our practice garage. We were on top of the world. We made plans to promote the album by going on tour the next summer.

Playing on weekends was something I looked forward to. I got a chance to meet many more girls. Nothing ever serious— just fun times. As my confidence on stage improved, so did my daring. I asked to be considered for singing a song or two. Pretending to be someone else on stage, I found it easy to sing some love songs. Because I had a high voice, I was asked to try a John Lennon song called "Imagine." A slow song that was popular with the young crowd, it brought about smiles on their faces. However, my solo singing career ended as fast as it started.

Our popularity was taking us to bigger and better venues in Odessa and Midland. Linda Sanchez and the Blue Notes were being broadcast on radio stations around our area. I was a recording artist! Not fully understanding the significance of it all, I remained indifferent. I didn't feel any better having my face plastered on the cover of the album. I didn't treat my friends any differently, and they didn't treat me differently either. There was a lot of hoopla when the album came out, but it didn't affect me. Once off the stage, I was still a kid from the barrio like everyone else who lived there.

A Junior!

W hen I was not on stage playing before large crowds, the reality of small-town life set in. Once school started, I was back to reconnecting with friends. I'd spent the whole summer working or playing music, which gave me very little time to socialize.

I was a junior now, and most of my classes were filled with some of the same basic-level students—except English III. It was a literature class taught by a veteran teacher who must have been there since they built the school. She took great pride in her work and demanded we do too. The class had a mix of students, from the real smart advanced type to the not so advanced. How this class showed up in my schedule, I didn't know. It had to have been a mistake. Stepping inside the classroom, I saw mostly white students. As strange as it was being in such a class, this was where all the good-looking people were. *So, this is what a true heterogeneously grouped class is supposed to look like, huh?* I thought.

I took a liking to the class and the students there. If I'd been treated differently by the system, perhaps this would've been an incentive for me to ask for advanced classes from the very beginning. How was I to know? Yet, at the same time, I found it boring and trivial. Nothing made sense. Shakespeare, Christopher Marlowe, John Fletcher, and Francis Beaumont were the teacher's focus, along with some American writers, like Mark Twain, William Faulkner, Washington Irving, and Edgar Allan Poe.

Our biggest assignment was to read one of their books and report on it. It wasn't a report in writing but a report given to her in person, face-to-face. She'd made it clear in the beginning that we were expected to read at least three books or a total of so many pages.

It seemed insurmountable. Impossible! *Maybe I don't belong here,* I thought. *I'm still not much of a reader. I know my limits. But I don't want to leave this class.*

For the first time in my school life, I felt like I belonged. The students around me gave me an incentive to learn. To take it seriously. To pay attention. To be part of something.

Charles, the smartest boy in class, was going to be a doctor. He knew what he wanted to be! I found that astounding. Paula was going to be a teacher. Patrick, a policeman. Jackie, a lawyer. These students had their futures planned out. They were very different from the students I'd been attending classes with. Up to this point, I'd just wanted to pass so I could get out of there.

I opted to go with a book containing a tremendous number of pages. I'd heard of such books but never opened one. Seven hundred pages seemed outrageous. I picked it off the library shelf a week before I was up to present. The cover made it look appealing.

I speed-read the book, meaning I scanned it, thinking I could get away with the gist of it by glossing over it.

It didn't work.

The day of my report, I sat next to her desk and handed her the book.

"How did you like it?" she asked.

"I thought it was interesting."

"What was it about?"

I rambled something I'd read while she flipped pages.

"This book is not on the list. Did you know that when you picked it?

"No, ma'am."

As she scanned the book, she asked me about the characters, naming specific ones from the book. Of course, I didn't know them all. Like I said, the book had seven hundred pages. Who in their right mind could remember all the characters?

"This book has some parts not very appropriate for anyone your age," she said. "I suggest you go back and pick another book."

I looked at her quizzically. I couldn't understand her remarks.

"And, Robert." she said. Read it."

"Yes, ma'am."

Lesson learned. Don't try to trick some old English teacher who has probably read every book in the library. Second, don't cheat on an assignment, thinking you are smarter than older people who read for a living. I'm glad the assignment was face-to-face. In a whisper, I got an ass-kicking. It would have been a death sentence if the others had heard her. Embarrassing if I'd had to answer questions in front of the whole class and made a total fool of myself.

I decided to read smaller books by English authors. Tom Sawyer became a favorite. It took me a lot longer than I expected since I had to stop every so often and think about what I had just read.

My conclusion? Reading sucks!

When I got to the auto mechanics class, I found the teacher had an excellent background in the workings of engines. He was an older man with thick glasses. Rather tall for a mechanic but still very knowledgeable. He had never been a teacher before, so this was all new to him, as it was for us.

On the first day, he laid out his plan for our education. We were to read about combustion engines, how they work, which part does what, the dangers of the business, and how we would be graded. There were about fifteen of us in this class. Some of the worst rabble-rousers in the school were there. I wasn't at all like them. At least I didn't think so. I was there to learn something. They were not.

After a few days in the shop, Talacho was sniffing a rag soaked in gasoline. On the days he did this a lot, his mouth was powdery white from gasoline. His lips were chapped, and his nose was runny.

Some of the others didn't fare any better. They snuck out the back when the old man was not watching, lighting up cigarettes and not caring whether there was a can of gasoline next to them.

At one point, El Pinacate tossed a lit cigarette butt into a can of gasoline, sending us all running for our lives. I was waiting for the explosion. It never came. Apparently, the gasoline snuffed out the cigarette. Miracle.

Some of those boys didn't care, and there was nothing anyone could do about it. I stayed away from them.

My first assignment, after a few weeks, was putting new brakes on a truck. After a few nicks and cuts, one smashed finger, brake fluid in my eye, and grease all over my clothes, I got the brakes on. To my surprise, they worked! The old man watched me, then winked in approval. It was not long before he made me his go-to student. If he wanted anything done, it was, "Robert, please check out the tools."

"Robert, please make sure everyone has his assignment."

"Robert, take the roll and mark who's absent."

All this attention made it difficult to get along with the other students. I didn't want them to think I was the teacher's pet. So I protested.

"Sir," I said. "Why doesn't Roy do some of this? He doesn't do anything!"

Roy didn't like being singled out because he was also sniffing gas. But I went along with the teacher's directives, complaining under my breath to no one in particular. No one cared.

At the end of the first hour of class, we'd get a break and go into the halls during the passing period to mingle with friends. We wore our greasy coveralls, not bothering to take them off when wandering the halls. Eventually, "grease monkey" became synonymous with our crew. That included me. It was not hard to spot one of us. Our fingernails were always black with grease, grime, and dirt.

I'd accepted my future as a mechanic. Seven dollars an hour seemed like a good living wage when others were only making a dollar seventy-five working in restaurants. Like many other jobs around there, the pay would never make someone rich. But at seven bucks an hour, perhaps I would retire with some money.

By the end of the first semester, I was making an A in the class. This was the first A I'd ever made in a class. (PE and library didn't count.) By the middle of the second semester, I had learned how to tear down an engine and put it back together. I might have a few nuts, screws, or bolts left over, but when I was done, it ran.

Chuy bought himself a newer truck—an automatic. He was proud of it. The old '51 Chevy was parked in the yard, forgotten and disintegrating in the elements. One day, he asked me if I'd learned enough to overhaul the engine on it. He told me it didn't work but that it was too expensive to have a mechanic work on it.

"I'll need parts for the truck if you want me to fix it," I said. "Where am I going to get parts for it?"

"Get what you need at NAPA," he said. "Tell the owner, John, that I sent you."

"How am I going to pay for it? I just can't walk in there and ask him for parts," I responded, hoping he'd change his mind.

"Just go. I'll take care of it."

I didn't know how he was going to take care of it. He shot me a disturbing look and walked away.

During a break from school, I started on the engine. Removing the hood gave me enough room to crawl on top and work from the top down. I knew what parts I needed. When I entered NAPA with a list of the numerous parts needed, John set up an account in my name, giving me access to everything. I was seventeen years old, and I had an account at NAPA? Someone certainly trusted me.

It took over a month of working afternoons and weekends to get the truck disassembled. I'd accumulated a pretty good bill at NAPA, but John never complained. He knew he'd get paid.

I finished putting the engine parts back together, then I was ready to try out my work. I turned the ignition and held my breath. It cranked, but nothing happened.

I went through a process of elimination, just like I've been taught: this is connected to that, this goes into this, this plugs into this ... Everything seemed to be in order, but it wouldn't start. It turned over, which told me there was something mechanical missing. I checked again. Everything seemed to be in order.

I was baffled. *What a disgrace if this thing doesn't start*, I thought. *Wait a darn minute! Gas! It doesn't have gas!*

I grabbed the container, poured gasoline down the tank, gave the gas pedal a few pumps, and turned on the ignition. The engine sputtered. I held my breath and tried again. The darn thing came to life!

"I did it! I did it! I'm a mechanic, I'm a mechanic!" I sang to myself.

Chuy was as happy as I'd ever seen him. He slapped me on the back and said, "I knew you could do it." He took the keys and drove off.

Two days later, I saw him towing a V8 truck into the yard. It was a few years newer than the '51.

"Where's the old truck?" I asked.

"Sold it."

"What? I thought I could use it."

"Nope. Fix this one."

My account at NAPA was paid off when he sold the truck. It all made sense. I then realized why Chuy had wanted me to take auto mechanics: I would provide free labor while he made money buying and selling trucks.

I did this not for seven bucks an hour. I did it for room and board. I worked on a few of his trucks and cars until my senior year. I kind of enjoyed working on trucks and an occasional car. I didn't like black fingernails though.

I'd learned something my junior year.

The Summer of '69

School ended the last day of May 1969. I'd be eighteen years old in July.

The job at the furniture store was no more. Edward Casillas, my buddy from Coyanosa, told me about an ammonia tank company looking for a couple of guys interested in sandblasting older sunbaked ammonia tanks and asked me if I was interested. I really didn't understand what sandblasting was, but I said I'd do it.

"Have you ever used a sandblasting machine?" the man asked me during the interview.

"Of course," I lied. Anything was better than picking onions for a living.

I would have to travel from Fort Stockton every day if I was lucky enough to get the job. Coyanosa, a farming community thirty-five minutes northwest, posed an economic challenge. Gas was twenty-five cents a gallon. Not having that kind of money would cost me. Nevertheless, I'd have to figure something out if I got the job.

"I don't know if I can travel back and forth every day. My parents will loan me the car, but I have to pay for gas," I told Edward, coming clean with my dilemma.

"You don't have to. My sister is graduating and leaving for California immediately after. You can stay in her room until the job ends."

After I talked to Mom, she agreed to let me. She didn't want me traveling back and forth every day anyway. Problem solved. Now I needed to get the job.

And that I did. We started a week after school let out for the summer. We arrived at the ammonia plant to find a fenced area that held a sea of white tanks. Spreading ammonia over the fields somehow helped produce better-quality food. Over the years, with the sun beating down on them, the tanks were showing signs of decay. Once we took the old paint off them, they would eventually be painted white again.

An older employee showed us how the equipment worked. After our thirty minutes of orientation, he warned, "Make sure you put that canvas hood and the gloves on before you start blasting these tanks. The sand coming out of that machine will cut your fingers right off if you are not careful. Second, never get too close to that tank over there. It leaks, and if you inhale the mist, it could damage your lungs. Get it? Now, go to work."

I wasn't worried about the dangers of sandblasting. I was a few days shy of eighteen years old. Who fears anything at eighteen? Not me. I was glad I got the job.

We worked throughout the summer as temperatures reached over a hundred degrees. With the thick canvas hood covering my body, it felt like an oven set on high. Sweat flowed freely from the top of my head to my waist. The hood had a scrotum protector, much like the thing you see baseball catchers wearing. I figured it was designed to protect the goods from accidental sandblasting as grains of sand ricocheted off the tanks.

With a small opening made of double durable glass affixed to the front, I could see. It wasn't a big area, but it was big enough for me to see what I was doing. Sweat would blind me when it rolled off my forehead and into my eyes, forcing me to stop every so many minutes to wipe it off. The last thing I wanted was to blast my friend, who was doing the tank next to me. And I certainly didn't want him blasting me. The old man's words, "It can cut your hand right off," swirled around in my head as I worked.

The blaster was extremely powerful. It blasted the paint right off those tanks with a pressure exceeding 1,000 psi, or pounds per square inch. It was enough to remove anything on steel tanks, including pieces of our bodies if we were not careful. The worst part was sand ricocheting off the tanks and hitting my legs. Jeans did not provide enough protection. By the end of the day, my legs were redder than a sunburn. Every hour or so, we'd stop, turn off the blaster, fill it back up with one-hundred-pound bags of sand, and continue the blasting. It was excruciating, painful work. At night, as I lay in bed, I could feel the sand pricking my body. I could feel the particles stinging my legs. It took almost a week for the sand nightmares to finally wear off.

After a long, hot workday, we'd go back to the trailer completely exhausted. Edward's mother would have dinner ready. Nothing fancy, but it was filling. After dinner, I'd help her clean up the kitchen. It was the least I could do since I was staying there for free.

We had no TV reception. We were cut off from the world. There was nothing to do but look at each other. Edward and I would go outside, disengage from the tiring day, and just rock back and forth on rockers his parents had. I'd stare at the night sky and revel in the brilliance of millions of stars.

In the darkness, with the sounds of nature filling the void, I'd contemplate my future. Would I be working like a horse for a dollar twenty-five an hour all my life? Was this my destiny? Could I change the path from poverty to riches? Why couldn't I get out of this miserable life and see the world?

Edward and I would engage in small talk, but nothing important. Lights went off at nine. I'd sit in my room and stare at the ceiling, wondering what my own family was doing. They weren't going to bed at nine, that was for sure. I was lonely. It was too quiet. There were no kids running around, crying, pushing each other, screaming, or fighting. I wasn't used to this quiet environment. But it gave me time to think about what I was going to do with my life. I really hadn't thought much about it, but I was getting close to being on my own. I'd be turning eighteen in a few days. I knew I was going to move out as soon as I could. Yet, after a month of living in the middle of nowhere, I was ready to go home even though the job wasn't finished.

I looked forward to the weekends. On Fridays after work, I'd get in the car, drive back to Fort Stockton, say hello to Mom and the kids, then head out to the Sanchez house for band practice. With the album out, our music was catching on. One day, I was sitting at the kitchen table, having a conversation with Mom about the work I was doing, when I heard Fred Dutchover, the radio announcer for "The Spanish/Tejano Hour," say, "And now, our very own, Linda Sanchez and the Blue Notes with their latest hit!

I jumped up, yelling, "That's us!" I scared the bejesus out of Mom. "That's Linda Sanchez and the Blue Notes! We're on the radio! We are on the radio!" I was dancing around the kitchen, smiling, laughing, and imitating dancers.

Mom just stared and smiled. "Is that really you?"

"Yes. That's our song!"

I was on the radio! The band was now seriously talking about going on tour and promoting the album. I never thought we'd make it this far. Excited as I was, I wasn't sure exactly what *touring* meant. But if it was anything like I'd seen on TV, I was looking forward to traveling to distant places.

A promoter was setting up the tour for the summer. It would take us to New Mexico, Arizona, California, and, of course, places in Texas we'd never been. It would require us being on the road until school started back up in September. I looked forward to the opportunity to live the life of a true professional musician.

In the music business, bands promoted themselves as better or the best. One such band was from Pecos. They were actually pretty good. People bragged about how good they were, so they became our competition for big events. When our album came out, they were bold enough to challenge us to a music duel of sorts.

One day, when we were practicing, someone called into the room, "We just heard on the radio that the band from Pecos has called us out to a challenge."

"They've been saying that for some time now. I think they're bluffing," commented the drummer.

"No, they said it on the radio," the first person said. "They announced they are a better band, and they can prove it. They challenged Linda Sanchez and the Blue Notes to a 'battle of the bands' event to be held in Pecos within three weeks. The audience will vote on who the better band is, and they're sure they can beat us."

"There's no damn way! Those idiots can't beat us!" someone shrilled.

"They don't even have a complete horn section!" said another.

"*Son una bola de pendejos*," chimed a third. ("They are a bunch of idiots!")

We accepted the challenge during an interview with Fred at the radio station. The date was set for the "battle." Arrogant, egotistical, and sure of ourselves, we were ready to take them on. We had a record album, and they did not. We were ready.

At about the same time, Edward and I were having delusional talks about going to California after the tank job was over. He spoke of interesting places we would see and things we would do. I thought it would be wonderful to be on *American Bandstand*! I wanted to be one of the dancers.

My mind raced with ideas of being part of the hippie scene, protesting like them, visiting Disneyland, going to the beach, and attending the play *Hair*. I'd never seen the Pacific Ocean. How amazing it would be to walk the beach during the day. I could swim in the ocean waters. I dreamed of going to Warner Brothers Studios and seeing movie stars like John Wayne. The more we talked about California, the more I wanted to go. Edward talked about us staying with his aunt and uncle.

"We can have so much fun with my cousins," he said. "They know of every place we could go and meet girls. Think about it. It will be fun."

There wasn't much thinking to be done. I wanted to go. I felt the excitement in my belly. I could see us in the place we only saw on TV. But I had to convince my parents. The job ended the middle of July. I had saved enough money for this trip. If I could convince my mom, it would be a go.

"I've worked all summer. I really want to go," I told her. "We are staying with Edward's family in Los Angeles."

"How are you going to get there?" she asked. "You think that car will make it? *Ay, no se*," she said, looking exhausted.

"Mom, it's a dream come true for me. I really want to do this. I'll be careful. The car works just fine. If anything happens to it, you know I can fix it."

"Chuy is talking about going to Mexico in a week. He's decided to visit his hometown and find his family, who he hasn't seen in over twenty-five years. I can't have you gone while we are gone. Who is going to take care of the kids?"

"Mom, they're not kids anymore. Nancy can look after them. She's been doing it since she was six!"

"I don't know. Let me talk to your dad."

Sunny California

I was home the day my parents set out on a thousand-mile journey into Mexico. This was 1969! Dad was looking forward to this and wasn't too concerned about my request. Mom didn't pursue my notion of going to California. She was spending too much time thinking about the Mexico trip. If anything was worrying her, it was that. She just didn't know if going to Mexico was a good idea, but she wanted to be supportive of Dad. In not so many words, she didn't put up a fight when I asked again if I could go.

"*Bueno, pero tienes que regresar antes que se comience la escuela.*" ("Okay, but you have to be back before school starts.")

It was going to be my senior year. If I was lucky, I would be the first to graduate from high school! A promise to my mother was a promise to God. I agreed to be back before school started.

That night, the band drove to Crane, Texas, to play at the VFW dance hall. I did not tell the band members my plan. I knew I was going to leave them in a bind if I wasn't there for the battle-of-the-bands event. I also knew I was not going on the tour. That really bothered me. How could I let them down? Was I being selfish? Why was I so scared of telling them about my plans? Was I afraid they'd talk me out of it? Was I doing the right thing? As band members, we just didn't do this to each other. I was regretting the idea of leaving, but at the same time, I really needed to go.

"I need this," I whispered to myself. After the show, we packed up the van and headed back to Fort Stockton. I couldn't sleep. Guilt consumed me.

On a Sunday, I left for Coyanosa with the little clothing I had. Edward was ready, and his parents offered their blessings for a safe trip. They'd bought us a road map with the highway marked from their house all the way to Los Angeles.

Happy days, here I come! I thought.

We stopped briefly in Pecos. Edward wanted to say goodbye to his girlfriend. Thinking Adelida might be there, I was reluctant to even show up. I couldn't face her. After a brief goodbye, we drove off in the '61 Ford, smiling as we sped down the highway. I was smiling, thinking of how exhilarating and wonderful this whole trip was going to be.

We weren't too far outside Pecos on Interstate 10 when I heard the sirens. What luck!

I pulled the car over to the side, looked at Edward, and said, "I wasn't speeding. Why are they stopping us then? Are you sure?"

I was nervous, thinking I must have done something wrong. I stayed in the car until the highway patrolman came over to my side. I rolled down the window and kept my hands on the steering wheel.

"Where you two going?" asked the officer.

"We're on our way to California, sir."

"Let me see your driver's license and car registration." Just like in the movies! "Why are you going to California?"

"We are going on vacation," I replied.

"You there," he said, talking to Edward. "Where's your driver's license."

Edward gave it to him.

"Do your parents know you are going?"

"Yes, sir," we said simultaneously.

"Wait in the car," he said. Then he went back to his car. It felt like he was gone for an eternity. The longer he took, the more scared I became. He finally came back, handed us our licenses, and, without telling us why he'd stopped us, said, "Make sure you drive safe." Then, to our surprise, he walked back to his car.

Edward's parents would later tell us the police called them to make sure we had permission to go on the trip and weren't just a couple of Mexican runaways. Racial profiling was not a thing yet. I still wonder why the white patrolman pulled us over.

We took turns driving and stopped only for gas or drinks. Edward's mother had made sandwiches, so we'd stop to buy something to drink, making sure we didn't spend money needlessly. If it had been my mother, she would have made us some bologna tacos, which I would've preferred.

Windows rolled down, we did sixty miles an hour, not wanting to push the eight-year-old car's engine too hard. We covered some distance the first day and talked about how enjoyable it would be to spend time on the beach, soaking in the sun.

"What about the girls?" I asked.

"There's lots of them," he said. "There's blond blued-eyed girls, redheads, brunettes, even girls with dark-black hair! There are girls from every country in the world. The best-looking ones are from California. You'd like them."

I was caught up in the moment. *Would they be interested in me?* I wondered. I'd always thought, for whatever reason, that California girls were all white. I'd never imagined girls from different backgrounds, cultures, and countries being there. The anticipation was overwhelming. I so wanted to get there as fast as I could, forgetting everything I'd learned from dating girls back home.

At the end of the first day, we reached Tucson, Arizona. Pulling into a roadside park, we stopped in the darkness, hoping to get some sleep before setting out again. But noise from the traffic didn't allow for much rest. Besides, it was so hot that we slept with the windows open, and I worried someone would come by and try taking what little we had.

When the light of an early dawn sprinkled on my face, I was relieved and reenergized. The roadside park did not have any bathrooms—just a table with a canopy that offered very little protection from the hot Arizona sun. There was no one else there but us. After taking a leak close to the car, we were off again.

As we crossed the mountain range separating the California valley from the coast, I could feel the ocean breeze. A few miles into California, the salty smell of the ocean sent visions of bikini-clad, blond, blue-eyed girls. A new world was showing itself to me, allowing my imagination to run free from the mundane life I'd lived and into a world of adventure. The beauty of the countryside was overwhelmingly seductive, inspiring me and taking hold.

As we got closer to the big city, the amount of traffic on the road surprised me. I'd never seen so many vehicles on a highway. The sheer number was enough to scare even the most cautious driver.

On the outskirts of Los Angeles, from high above the valley, I couldn't see the city through the thick smog—that yellowish haze that enveloped the mighty skyscrapers hovering in the clouds and the low-lying businesses and neighborhoods. The smog made it difficult to make out the immensity of the city, which only added to my curiosity. It was not at all how I had envisioned it.

We weaved in and out of traffic, moving slowly through the beast. The stop-and-go driving went on for miles, or so it seemed. It took so much time just to cover a couple of miles because of traffic moving ever so slowly. It was exhausting, infuriating, yet exhilarating at the same time.

In the northwest part of the city, not far from downtown Los Angeles, we reached our destination. Parking on a hilly street where modest homes lined both sides, I secretly made the sign of the cross, thanking God we'd made it. The wood frame house, weathered by years of sun, water, and whatever chemicals the thousands of cars and trucks pumped into the air, was old but modest—much larger than houses I'd lived in growing up.

We climbed the concrete stairs to the front door, and the family welcomed the two from Texas. Leslie, Edward's sister, was the first to run and hug us both. We'd done it!

I was introduced to the aunt, uncle, cousins, neighbors, visitors, and so many other people that I would never remember either their faces or their names. Peppered by questions about Texas, I answered nonchalantly.

Was I a cowboy? Did I live on a ranch? Did I have a horse? How did I get to school on a horse? Had I ridden in a wagon before? Who the hell did these people think I was? A Mexican John Wayne?

Once the dust settled, one of the two cousins—who were boys about our age, maybe older—showed us to our room. We were to share a bedroom, it being large enough to accommodate three regular-sized beds. The cousins shared a bed while Edward and I took the smaller beds. Perfect accommodations.

The cousins, doing who knows what, left every morning at about the same time each day and returned at around three in the afternoon. While they were gone, Edward and I would get in the car and ride around the city, eventually making it down to Santa Monica, which became one of my favorite places. Spending hours on the beach, swimming in the cold Pacific waters, was indeed invigorating. I would lie on the beach, soaking up the sun as it forced itself through the smog. I loved it!

The first weekend, the cousins asked us to join them for a party downtown. I had the car, so I drove. We wound up in some neighborhood about forty minutes away. I don't know what part of town we were in, but the houses were smaller and crowded together. There were twenty-five to thirty people there, all representing some minority group. No gringos. The young men were dressed rather shabbily, while the girls' dresses were a bit risqué. They had teased hair reaching upward at least half a foot, eyelashes longer than most, blouses that revealed more cleavage than the Santa Elena Canyon, very short shorts or skirts, and enough makeup to cover a bedroom wall. Quite revealing! Very strange. Not wanting to stare, I kept close to the door in case one of them challenged my stupid look. The entire environment signaled, "Danger, danger!"

Where are all the blue-eyed blonds? I asked myself. Just about everyone was either drinking or smoking or both. Some were smoking pot. Others were taking pills. I didn't feel comfortable. No one acknowledged us when we came in, leaving me to suspect whether we'd really been invited. I was drinking Budweiser, the "King of Beers." It was strikingly different from what I was used to, but when it was handed to me, I didn't say no.

A Marlboro cigarette dangling from my lips gave the impression I knew what I was doing. The decision to try smoking when I turned fifteen had turned into a habit. I didn't really like it, but after some time, I got used to it even though the Federal Cigarette Labeling and Advertising Act of 1965 required that the warning "Caution: Cigarette smoking may be hazardous to your health" be placed on one side of cigarette packages. I didn't pay too much attention to the government. By 1969, Congress had updated the packaging by changing the language to "Warning: The Surgeon General has determined that cigarette smoking is dangerous to your health." The law also prohibited cigarette advertising on TV and radio. Did anyone pay attention to this warning? Everybody smoked, so why couldn't I?

Music in the house continued to play in the background as people gathered in small groups, debating topics of no significance. After a few minutes, it was obvious none of us, including the cousins, knew anyone from the party. How we were allowed to enter a loud, private party where no one seemed to mind strangers was a mystery. After an hour or so, we left.

The next party was in a much better neighborhood. The houses were not as close. The neighborhood was very well-manicured, and light from the street illuminated the walkways. A very modest area, it made me less cautious of those around me. Young people there were very different from the first group—mostly Hispanic with a smattering of white teens. Well-dressed, they sported the fashion of the time—bell-bottom pants, polyester shirts or blouses with leather vests, and shoes with high soles and round toes. The girls were prettier. They looked smart and talked smart. It was all about politics, movies, music, and Hollywood.

After two or three more Budweiser tall boys, I was confident enough to join a group talking about music. Time stood still as I listened to the discussion. I made eye contact with a couple of the girls who didn't seem to be accompanied by some guy. One smiled. I smiled. I was feeling good. About the time I'd built the courage to walk over and introduce myself, one of the cousins pulled me over.

"We are going to the beach," he said.

We left around midnight. The beach was peaceful at that time of the night, apart from a few young people sitting around a campfire, playing guitar, and singing. I strolled over. Invited to join them, I rather reluctantly sat down on a blanket with my legs crossed. The others decided to go swimming. Someone passed around a joint as freely as they passed around beer. The singing continued. The light of a full moon, delicately shining in the sky, shimmered off the ocean waves. The western winds blew the smog west, away from the city, and the beach gave me my first glimpse of the stars gleaming brightly.

Lying back, I stared at the night sky, feeling happy. The waves from the ocean pounded the beach, creating a soothing sound that brought a sense of peacefulness. After a few more beers, I rocked back and forth to the sounds of the guitar, wanting so desperately to be back on stage.

More marijuana passed hands as more people joined the group. Not knowing what weed would do to me, I was still reluctant to try. I stuck to beer. The laughter, music, and sound of the ocean waves brought weariness.

The sun coming up over the mountains, with its first rays of light reaching the beach, slowly woke me up. I felt a hand on my shoulder.

"We better get out of here before the police come," one of the cousins said. "No telling how much weed these guys have." He pointed at some long-haired dudes still asleep.

I got up and tried to shake the sand out of every crevice known to man. Then I walked toward the ocean and dove in. The cold water brought back life. I wasn't ready to leave. I wanted to stay and swim. What a great night!

The next day, we hopped on a bus heading into downtown Los Angeles. I wanted to feel the drumbeat and vibrancy of its heart and revel in the noise rising up into the tall buildings. We wound up on Broadway, a street cluttered with shops selling just about anything you wanted. I bought a pair of round-toe shoes to go with my new bell-bottom jeans. When I stepped out of the store, I lit a cigarette. On my first puff, a long-haired, shoeless, skinny guy came up to me.

"Can I bum a cigarette from you, man?" he said.

I opened the box and pulled one for him. Edward and I had walked a block down the street when another guy bummed another cigarette off me. I gave him one. This went on for several blocks until I was left with half a pack.

"What the hell?" I said to no one in particular. "If I keep smoking in public, I'll be out of cigarettes before I walk another block!"

I snuffed it out and hid what was left in my jeans pocket. "Let's get out of here," I said. "These bums are going to leave me with no cigarettes before we get to the end of this street."

Bumming was casually accepted in downtown Los Angeles. Besides cigarettes, some would come ask for money. I'd never encountered this kind of mooching from people before. They were good at it. An older gentleman came up to me and said, "You're a good-looking kid. Are you the one dating my daughter?"

"No, sir," I replied.

"Well, you should. She is beautiful, and I bet she'd like you."

Of course, I was flattered.

"I'm trying to get home," the man said. "You wouldn't happen to have a quarter on you, would you? That's all I need to catch the bus."

I gave him a quarter.

Bums came in all shapes and sizes. All colors. All types of demeanor. Some beggars, some not. There were so many bums that I learned to avoid eye contact and just keep moving. Edward hadn't mastered the technique, and he was going to pay for it.

We managed to get to Long Beach one afternoon. We'd heard of a circus/carnival happening there and wanted to see it. It was set up beyond an enormous parking lot, and the bus dropped us off several blocks away. The music and the noise of the crowd flowed over the pavement. Halfway up the street stood an older Black man, a bit taller than us. He was scraggly looking and dirty. He stopped in front of us.

"Hey, you got some change you can spare?" he asked us both.

"No," I said forcefully and kept walking.

"How 'bout you?" he asked Edward.

"No, I don't have change."

"Well, how 'bout a dollar?" the man said.

"No, you're not touching those," Edward responded.

It happened so fast. I was stunned. The man grabbed Edward by the arm and put his other hand behind his shirt.

"I have a knife," the guy said. "You don't give me a dollar, I's gonna stab you."

I stood motionless, not knowing whether he was serious or not. Did he have a knife? Would he use it? I didn't want to find out. Edward and the man were having a staring contest. I looked over at Edward.

"*Yo lo empujo, y corremos,*" I told Edward. ("I'll push him, and we'll run.") He and the man stood staring at each other, motionless. I ran across the lot and found two policemen. I told them we were being threatened by a Black guy with a knife. Neither too concerned nor in a great hurry to do anything, they walked with me in the direction of the incident. They walked! It was over by the time we got there.

"What happened?" I asked Edward.

"I had to give him a dollar. He wouldn't let me go."

The police walked up to us. "Are you okay?" one asked.

"Yes, sir," Edward replied.

"Good. Enjoy the carnival," the other said. Then they turned around and walked back to where they'd been standing. I was appalled at the nonchalant attitude toward an incident that could have gone horribly wrong. Why would two police officers take this incident so casually? Why didn't they see fear or apprehension in my eyes and voice when I approached them? Or in my demeanor? Did they not care? This one boggled my mind. It would not be the last time I would deal with cops in Los Angeles.

Shortly after, the cousins asked us to attend another party. Attending parties was their favorite pastime. This time it was at one of the cousins' girlfriend's house. We got all dressed up, me sporting my new round-toe shoes, bell-bottom jeans, and an orange windbreaker. No shirt underneath. My hair was growing. It had never been that long. It was over my ears and down to my neck. If I pulled it back, I looked more and more like an Indian. Or, should I say, a Native American. The ocean air mixed with the sun had brought out a golden dark tan, separating me from a true Native American. My natural color gave way to a tan without the need for tanning lotion or sunscreen. I did not know such a thing existed.

The bus dropped us off in a neighborhood somewhere near Culver City. Several people mingled around. A cousin introduced us to a guy from Morocco who spoke English with an accent. Impeccably dressed in the up-end style, he looked smart and debonair. A Black kid from Compton, also well-dressed in the latest fashion, joined our conversation. A third kid was indeed a Native American who belonged to some tribe in Northern California. The five of us talked for some time about what was important to us—girls, music, theatre, the beach, traveling, and movies.

It was an amazing, eclectic group of young people. Most my age were smart, articulate, and well-mannered. Dressed not like hippies but in a more stylish polyester fashion, they were not like us poor kids from Texas, who wore cotton. Nevertheless, we fit in. It was the kind of style you'd see on *American Bandstand*. The group displayed an aura of intellectual respect and spoke in awkward dialects that reflected their culture. I was impressed.

Growing up in a town where half the students were Hispanic and the other half white, aside from skin color, we hardly noticed our varying differences even though there weren't many. However, the Hispanics stuck to their own, and the whites did the same. We remained segregated by choice. Most knew full well that the two races intermingling was frowned upon, mostly by the white population. Whereas the parents of Latino kids didn't care one way or the other. I had many acquaintances who were white, including girls. However, my real friends all looked like me.

I'd never heard of or seen a white boy or girl dating a Hispanic. If they did, it was done in secrecy, and when confronted, it was denied, denied, denied. I always thought the white girls were much prettier than the Hispanic girls, with the exception of Isabella, who was just simply a 100 percent knockout! In school, the two ethnic groups talked to one another, but we knew our limitations. But in Los Angeles, we were integrating with global races and cultures, and, surprisingly, no one cared. No one saw the other as better or worse. They were all friendly and respectful of each other. Totally different world.

The Moroccan suggested we hit a nightclub. He built it up to be more entertaining and exclusive. He suggested we take his car and not bother with public transportation. We agreed. Four of us were standing on the sidewalk, waiting for him to bring the car around, when a small—I mean, really small—old convertible semi-sports car pulled up.

He opened the door and said, "Get in!"

"Whoa! We can't all fit in that car!" I said.

"Yes, we can! Just make yourself small. I've done it before! Come on, let's go!"

Reluctantly, we all piled into what had to be the smallest car I'd ever seen. Scrunched up, we managed to get five young men in that thing. He drove southwest down side streets and alleys. We must have traveled about ten minutes through the neighborhood when the lights of a police car shined through the back window.

Oh my God! I thought. *We're going to jail.* I didn't know if these guys had any kind of drugs on them. I made the sign of the cross and closed my eyes, hoping this wouldn't turn into jail time. Miraculously, drugs were not to be the problem.

"Do any of you have weed?" the Moroccan shouted.

"No, no, no, no," came the replies.

"If you do, get rid of it before I stop."

The windows were rolled down, but nothing went flying out. The Moroccan pulled over to the side of a deserted street. We all waited, crunched up against one another. Two white officers got out of their car. One walked toward the driver's side. The other went toward the passenger side, staying a few feet away from the car with his hand on his pistol.

I knew I was going to jail. How was I going to explain this? I was terrified, shaking uncontrollably. I'd had two beers. *Am I drunk enough to see the inside of a cell?* I wondered. *I'm a descendant of a Mexican father. Will they think of me as a Mexican? Will they try to deport me?* Terrified was not how I felt. It was more like scared shitless!

"Let me see your license," the first officer said to the driver while the second officer shined his flashlight into the car, never taking his hand off his pistol. The police officers showed no expression. They were playing a cautious game. I knew they were about to arrest some juveniles.

"Where are you going?" the first officer asked the Moroccan.

"We are going to a party, sir."

"Where," he said, not asking. He shined his flashlight into the car.

"In Culver City, sir."

"You boys got any drugs? Weed? Alcohol?"

"No, sir. We don't do that."

"Wait here," the officer said, moving back toward his car after giving the Moroccan a smirk.

The minutes felt like hours. *Why is he taking so long?* I wondered. *This is not good.* In a few minutes, another patrol car showed up with two more cops.

Uh-oh.

"We're in trouble," someone whispered to the rest of us.

Now I was actually praying the Our Father. In Spanish. Why? I'd always felt the Spanish version sounded more desperate. Perhaps God would hear the desperation in my voice.

"Get out of the car," the first officer said. He opened the door on the passenger side. We started piling out.

"How many of you are in there?" the second officer asked, laughing. Then he said, "Get up against that wall and place your hands where I can see them." He didn't take his right hand off his pistol. "I want to see those hands up on the wall. Take a step back. You, there! Step back and look at the wall!"

This time, he said it in a loud, gruff voice. I took two steps back, keeping my hands on the wall. Five kids were up against the wall—five distinctly minority kids. The officers were white. All of them. The two new officers patted each one of us down. I turned my face slightly to watch the Native American kid on my left getting frisked.

"I said, face and stare at the wall!" an officer shouted at me. "You don't want me to shoot you, do you?" he yelled.

By now, I was having a hard time breathing. Hysteria overwhelmed my insides. I wanted to throw up. I had a hard time keeping the tears of fear at bay. I wanted to cry like a baby. I wanted my mommy. *Will he really shoot me?* I wondered while staring at the wall. My legs were shaking, and I was fearful of falling.

The officers went through every inch of the car. They pulled out a coat the Moroccan had in the back. They looked under the seats, under the light panel, around the carpet, in the glove box. They looked everywhere while we were being patted down.

Am I in the movies, or is this for real? I wondered. *We ARE near Hollywood.* I was still scared.

After about thirty minutes, and not having found anything, one of the officers told us to turn around and put our butts against the wall with our feet spread apart.

"There's nothing, sir," said the second officer to the first.

"Okay, now. You boys don't move until we are out of sight. If we see any one of you move, we're coming back. And I swear, I will shoot you. Understand?"

We all nodded.

"DO YOU UNDERSTAND?"

"Yes, sir!" we all shouted in unison. No one made a move.

Once they were gone out of sight, the Black kid shouted, "You're just a bunch of racist pigs! We didn't do anything! What gives you the right to stop us!" All of a sudden, we all grew some balls.

"Yeah, those pigs are racist."

"They're a bunch of idiots. Pigs!"

"Let them come back. I'll say it to their faces! Pigs!"

"*¡Pinches, putos! ¡No valen madre!*"

We drove to Culver City. As soon as we got there, I told Edward, "Let's just take the bus and go home. I've had enough excitement for one day."

I needed a change of underwear.

Hollywood

t least once while in Cali, I was determined to attend the studio where *American Bandstand* was being filmed. The show was first filmed in Philadelphia in 1952. It went national in 1957 and was filmed in a place called the Starlight Ballroom in Wildwood, New Jersey. The producers eventually moved the filming to LA's Stage 5 of the ABC Television Studios in 1964. It was so close, I could practically walk there. If I couldn't be one of the dancers, I'd settle for being in the audience.

Inquiring about showtimes, when the show was filmed, and what a person needed to do to get on the show took time. Using the yellow pages phone book, I called the studio, but I could never get anyone to answer the phone. I had to go there in person.

Using a paper map of Los Angeles and the surrounding areas, I finally located the studios. It was so heavily guarded that I couldn't get in. Disappointed after weeks of trying, I gave up. My chance to be on TV was not going to happen.

Hollywood Boulevard at night was hopping, and I wanted to see it. We got off the bus not too far from Whiskey a Go Go, a well-known chic Parisian discotheque frequented by the hippie crowds. The billboard touted music by The Doors, The Byrds,

Buffalo Springfield, and a mixed-race band headed by a guy named Jimi Hendrix.

The bouncer would not let us in, claiming we weren't old enough. Our driver's licenses would prove he was right. We walked past theatres—like the Pussycat and the Vogue—restaurants, delicatessens, bakeries, novelty shops, and places the rich and famous frequented. The streets were crowded with a mix of people, many richly dressed. Every effort was made to avoid the poorly dressed homeless peasants who walked by. They were bums.

Music blared from all sides, much of it coming from expensive Mercedes convertibles, Porches, Mustangs, Audis, and so many more. This was Hollywood at its finest, and I was in the middle of it all.

We managed to swing around to Sunset Boulevard, where the sidewalks were even more crowded with longhairs meandering from storefront to storefront, not really buying anything but pausing to light their marijuana cigarettes from someone else's. Bearded young men wearing jeans and cutoffs with oversized green military jackets reminded us of the war. The girls sported striped bell-bottom pants and bikini tops, showing their contoured abs. Everyone had long hair, including us.

As I was standing by a store window, lingering like the crowd, I heard someone yelling.

"You can't push me like that! We're not doing anything wrong!" A long-haired blond girl of about nineteen was yelling at two white police officers. They were big and burly, with scowls on their faces, as they pushed people forward.

"You motherfucker!" someone shouted at them, getting no reaction from either of the two.

"Pigs, you got no right!" yelled another. The obscenities continued as police pushed the bystanders with billy clubs held in front of them at arm's length. They walked arm in arm, pushing people forward. The same thing was happening on the other side of the street.

"Oh, crap!" I shouted over the noise. "Here we go again."

We didn't move. We had nothing to hide. We weren't doing anything wrong. As soon as the cops cleared the sidewalk, the same people who'd moved just circled back and got in right behind them.

"Move along, people! You can't stand here! You have to keep moving!" The police were now shouting with visible anger on their faces. Their voices got louder as they pushed people, some of whom were going off the curb and into the street. Within minutes, the cops walked right up to us, swinging their billy clubs from side to side. In the middle of a throng of humanity, we tried desperately to get out of the police officers' way.

Around store doorways, bottlenecks hampered movement. Those simply browsing were inundated by those trying to buy something. The stores were overflowing with young people, some trying to get in while others were hoping to escape the crowd. We moved with the crowd. I was taking it all in, observing the circus of humanity, many high on whatever their drug of choice was.

With this many people on overcrowded sidewalks, someone was going to get hurt. I could feel the tensions mounting. Something was going to happen. But what? I wasn't sure, but it didn't look good. The crowd moved scornfully along, looking meaner by the second. The young men and women continued to harass the cops with obscenities and offensive gestures that just wouldn't stop.

"We need to get out of here before a fight breaks out," Edward's cousin said, sounding alarmed. Without a word, we crossed the busy street at an intersection and walked back to the bus stop, leaving the masses to deal with the inevitable drama that was bound to ensue.

A few days later, I found out that the longhairs—or hippies, as they were called by the media—had fought a series of bloody battles with police.

Los Angeles was a city of celebrities. Artists abhorred the police's handling of young people who were just hanging out, not only on the Sunset Strip but also in other parts of the city. This moved music artists like Sonny and Cher to march in solidarity with protesters, seeking to end police harassment on the Strip. The environment reeked of trouble. I feared that a cop, who might feel threatened, would pull out his gun and create a riot.

The scene in Hollywood and other parts of the city became great fodder for musicians. Stephen Stills, from a vocal music group called Crosby, Stills, Nash and Young, wrote a song that soared to the top of the music charts. "For What It's Worth," sung by Buffalo Springfield, spoke to the drama unfolding in California. Experiencing the brutality up close made me question how civility could have gone awry. I got caught up in the drama playing out. Imagine that: a skinny guy from Fort Stockton, Texas, in the middle of a compelling scene in American history— the battle for human rights. Stephen Stills's song resonated with us young hippies because it described not only how we felt but also how the country felt.

Those lyrics still resonate so clearly, causing me to sing along when I hear them. It brings back memories of a time when this country was at odds with a younger, liberal generation who longed for peace in the world, equality among citizens, and justice for all. It was a time when the country was at odds with itself, and I was absorbed by it all.

It wasn't all bad. I did enjoy myself. Many a time, I would sit on the beach, directly on the sand, with cutoff jean shorts, no shirt, no shoes, and a bandana wrapped around my head like the real hippies wore them. Listening to the waves gave me a sense of calm. The sound enveloped me with a peaceful humility. During these times sitting alone, I'd contemplate my purpose.

Who am I, and what am I doing here? What am I supposed to be doing? Is this the place for me? Am I part of some revolution, like The Beatles song suggests? At what point do I become a contributing member of society? Is it now? Am I in it? Will I go back home or stay in this wonderful, idiotic, crazy city? What does this all mean? What is my purpose, and when will I know?

Why this mattered to me at this time, I wasn't sure. These questions would consume me as I'd lie basking in the morning California sun. I was a man now. I was eighteen, and in the eyes of "the man," I was an adult. I was now eligible to go to war, get a real job, pay taxes, buy a home, and pay more taxes. I'd be able to buy alcohol in two years. Yet all this seemed so far away from my young mind. I saw what was happening all around me, and I didn't care for it. Somehow, my mind floated, asking, *Do I care for my country? Is this why I'm feeling troubled?*

For the meantime, I was determined to find out as much about life as I could. I needed some time to reflect. Most importantly, I needed to have fun while doing it.

Drugs and Disneyland

I'd always been an early riser, so the quiet in the household of several people changed my sleeping habits. I wouldn't get up until much later in the day. At night, I'd stay up long hours with the cousins and Edward.

On one particular evening, there was little to do since it was a workday. So we sat in my car, drinking beer and listening to music while the others lit a joint.

"I've not been to Disneyland," I said. "I want to do that this weekend. How about it, guys?"

"I think Disneyland is a riot, man. We should do it!" one of the cousins exclaimed. "We can meet girls there," he said, slurring his words. He motioned, with his hands, the shape of a female as he puffed on the slim marijuana cigarette, then burst out laughing.

"We're out of Zig-Zag!" someone said.

"I'll go. I need beer," I replied. Then I walked down to the corner store and picked up some rolling paper and a six-pack of Budweiser. As I approached the car, I noticed the windows were up, which made the inside look like the Cheech and Chong van. Smoke everywhere!

"Come on, man. Take a hit," one cousin said, pushing the joint toward me.

"Nah. Thanks, man. I'd rather drink beer."

I wasn't too keen on starting a habit that I thought, or had been told, was the doorway to harder drugs, like cocaine, LSD, and heroin. I wasn't about to start a habit I could not afford. Truthfully, I was scared of what it would do to me. Too many commercials about drugs prevailed. I'd heard it in the hallways at school, but mostly from one of my favorite science teachers, Mr. McKenzie. He said marijuana only led to harder drugs and eventually death from overdoses. I wasn't about to do that to myself, so I stayed away from the stuff.

By the time I was into my second Bud, my head started spinning and I was feeling nauseous. The guys were laughing up a storm. Anything anyone said would start a series of hacking laughter. I didn't see anything funny about anything being said. We'd been sitting in the car for a while now. The marijuana smoke floated out the window when I rolled it down to breathe fresh air.

"Roll the window back up, man! You're letting out the smoke!" There was more laughter.

"I can't breathe, shithead," I replied.

"No, no, don't let out the smoke!" one of them yelled.

I rolled up the window and held my face toward the roof. That didn't help. I was feeling woozy. I opened the door, letting smoke curl out like a cloud, and got out to stand outside as the laughter continued. I felt wobbly, and my head was spinning.

Then, it all came out.

I leaned over the bumper of the car and started puking my guts out. Beer, beans, corn tortillas, and everything I'd had that day. With beer gushing out my nose and my eyes watering, I could not stop. I left the guys in the car and took the keys, just in case they got any ridiculous ideas, then went inside.

On the bed, I could feel the ceiling swirling, round and round like a merry-go-round, until I fell asleep. Or passed out.

That was my first experience with pot, weed, Mary Jane. It was at that moment, before passing out, that I promised myself I would never indulge in such stupidity. I'd stick to beer.

Or so I thought.

Thursday night was a good day of the week to get the fun started. It was suggested we all go down to Whittier Boulevard. It was in an older neighborhood, where people gathered to see some of the fanciest low-rider cars drive up and down the street. The boulevard had four lanes of bumper-to-bumper cars, all sporting incredible paint jobs, fancy wheels, splendid interiors, and hydraulics that made the cars bounce up and down. The drivers wore bandanas, oversized khaki pants, Converse shoes, and white sleeveless undershirts.

The girls were beautiful—even the plump ones. They all wore short-shorts, high heels, and bikini tops. With their hair held back with varying-colored bandanas, they looked every bit like the girls in the movies. Their lips shone bright red, giving them the look of seductive beauty. I was amazed at how good-looking the Mexican girls were. Like a child at a candy store, I was captivated by their exuberance. I waved at one who was sitting on the passenger side of a low-rider car. As she rode past, she looked at me with that quizzical look, like, "Do I know you?" I started to wave at her again, but as I raised my hand to do so, one of the cousins reached over and slammed my hand down.

"Look away, dummy," he said.

"Why? I think she likes me."

"Not here. You don't mess with the girls here. A gesture like that could land you in the morgue. Guys get beat up for less around here. Since we are here with you, we'll all get beat up. These guys don't take too kindly to strangers coming around and taking their girls. Men have been shot just because they looked at a girl." He spoke sternly to me.

"Come on, man. I was just waving."

"Keep moving, and don't wave. Don't look. Don't smile at the girls. It's not worth the beating we all could get!"

"Then why are we here?"

"To see the sparks coming from beneath the cars when they let the air out of the pistons. Look at the cars. Not the girls."

Strange. Such good-looking girls, and I couldn't flirt with any. We left after an hour or so. I was disappointed that I hadn't met a girl I could become friends with.

We headed to the bus stop and took it to Anaheim, farther south of Los Angeles, where Disneyland Park was located. The bus ride was a lot cheaper than taking my car. Paying a mere quarter to get to different places suited me just fine. This way, I wouldn't have to concentrate on driving. Driving in that congested city made me nervous. The bus rides gave me the chance to view the city through open windows. No one else knew how to drive a standard, so I wound up driving everywhere we went. I didn't know the city that well, so taking the bus made sense.

We got to Disneyland at nine, which was early for us. The price of admission was 50 percent less then. As soon as we arrived, I noticed a group of girls standing a few feet away. A blond girl about a year younger than me approached us. Looking at me with bright-blue eyes, she smiled.

She couldn't be looking at me, I thought. She was surrounded by a light that made her look stunningly beautiful, so I looked again.

She wore jeans cut off at the ankles and brown platform shoes. Colored suspenders, which she didn't need, accented a see-through blouse that revealed a dark-blue bra. Her blond curls framed her tanned face, creating the appearance of innocence and despair. I was mesmerized by the look.

"Are you going in?" She was talking to me.

"Yes, we are," I said, smiling.

"Can we come with you? We were waiting for some friends, but they didn't show up."

There were three of them. I found it rather strange that a group of girls would just come out of nowhere and ask if they could join us. That would never happen in Texas. Or anywhere else, for that matter.

"I guess that would be fine," I said, looking back at my three partners, who also showed startled faces. Edward, the last one off the bus, was asking, "What did she want?"

"They want to join us."

"Why?"

"I don't know, and I don't care. They want to go in with us. I love it!"

We walked into the park, got our tickets quickly, and walked down a pathway illuminated by bright, colorful lights that lured us toward the park entrance. With big permanently affixed smiles on their cartoonish faces, Micky and Minnie Mouse greeted us. Dumbo, Goofy, Donald Duck, and Snow White were all posing for pictures with children who held on to the adults' hands. Their faces showed looks of concern over whether these creatures were friendly or evil.

Enchanting music blared all around us. Lights everywhere glistened with untold brightness that overshadowed the light of the moon. I was in heaven! I loved this place. Amazement over the scenery of this magnificent place made me forget, if for a moment, the girl walking next to me. It was only when she took my hand in hers that I really looked into her eyes for the first time. I smiled at her.

"What's your name?" I asked boldly.

"I'm Heather. Those two are Sherry and Lilly. We're friends. It's boring to ride by ourselves. Which ride do you like the best?"

"This is my first time here," I said, wondering if she was truly talking to me.

"Then you must ride the monster. Come on!" She hooked her arm into mine, and off we went, leaving the others to fend for themselves.

"Wait! We're coming with you!" cried one of the cousins.

We went into the bowels of the enormous park, smiling like little kids, wide-eyed and marveling at such a wondrous place. We rode every roller-coaster ride, not just once but several times, circling back quickly to get in line again. Time simply slipped away without notice.

"Let's go here!"

"Let's go there!"

"Let's ride this one!"

"Let's go in here!"

I just couldn't get enough of it. I looked up and, for the first time, saw the Milky Way—a series of stars floating in the night sky. An amazing sight. It wasn't like downtown Los Angeles, where the smog lingered like a thick yellow cloud that smothered the stars at night.

I was standing there gawking in amazement when I felt Heather pulling me over to the side. My heart erupted in throbs of joy. She was a beautiful and charming girl. I liked her.

"Let's go to the tunnel," she said.

"What's the tunnel?"

"Come on. You'll see."

We were standing in line, ready to catch another ride, when she grabbed my hand and pulled me under the barricades.

"Where are you going?" yelled Lilly.

"Let's all meet at the entrance at eleven before the park closes! Robert and I are going to ride another ride!" hollered Heather as we rushed to get away. Astonishingly, they didn't follow.

We rode a log boat on the water through a series of tunnels where all the characters from the different Disney movies were either dancing, singing, or just waving at the passengers floating by. We rode alone. Possessed with unbelievable happiness, I smiled at her. With her arm locked in mine, she smiled back, showing a perfect row of gleaming white teeth. The first time we went through the tunnel, we whispered nothings and pointed at the characters. The boat moved slowly, from dark to dim.

"Where are you from?" she asked, not taking her eyes away from mine.

I looked away, slightly embarrassed. "I'm from Texas."

"You don't have a Texas accent like Edward."

"Is that good or bad?"

"No, I love the way you talk. You just don't have that Texas drawl."

"I didn't know there was such a thing."

"Well, there is, silly."

"Where are you from?" I asked.

"I'm from Long Beach. I was born and raised here."

The boat floated slowly. We talked about her school, her friends, her ambitions, but mostly about her ability to study people's demeanor. She was into deciphering people's characteristics, translating that into whether people were good and kindhearted or simply boring, frustrated, and selfish. She went on and on about how she could identify kind people and those not so kind.

"So, what am I?" I asked.

"You are gentle and kind. I knew it as soon as you walked off the bus."

And with that, she leaned over and kissed me. On the lips! I was caught off guard, fumbling with what to do with my lips. I'd not been kissed like that before. Such a soft, gentle kiss. We held each other until we came out of the tunnel and into the park's bright lights.

"I want to ride it again!" she said with a smile.

Then she pulled me back toward the entrance. The park was becoming devoid of parents and children. As tired families worked themselves toward the exit and the sidewalks emptied out, I felt we were the only ones there. Just Heather and me.

We jumped back on the boat and headed into the tunnel once again. I could feel the closeness of her body as she scooted up right next to me. She turned her face toward me and kissed my quivering lips again. Who knows if this was meant to happen or whether it was just a coincidence. I was fully captivated by her—absorbed by her jubilance, her beauty, her smile, and, above all, her seemingly complete happiness at being with me. I'd not known this kind of affection from anyone. If this was love, then I was fully immersed in it. If it was something else, then I wanted to have this wonderful experience engraved in my brain for the rest of my life.

"I want to see you again, if that's okay with you," I told her as we walked hand in hand to the exit.

"I'd like that, but how?"

"How about we meet back here next Saturday? I really like this place. Maybe we could find other rides we didn't have time to enjoy. What do you think?"

"I'd love that. Let's get here earlier. Say, five?"

"Five is good. I'll meet you at the entrance."

I leaned over and kissed her once more before she boarded the bus. As I stood there watching the bus move away, she leaned out the window and waved goodbye.

I saw her again the next Saturday and the Saturday after that. Each time we spent the day together, we shared more of ourselves—our likes and dislikes, our favorite music, our dreams, and our individual plans for the future. Mine didn't amount to much compared to her dream of attending UCLA and becoming a journalist.

"I'll be lucky if I can make it out of high school," I said. That didn't seem to bother her, which made it easier to talk about myself. I shared with her my love of music and my dream of making it big in the business. I talked and joked about my family, making her laugh at all the silly things we did. I was comfortable sharing my thoughts about being on *American Bandstand*. She smiled.

Unfortunately, our continued rendezvous options were becoming difficult to sustain. In the following weeks, I saw less and less of her.

It was too good to last, I thought.

I didn't see Heather again. Yet for a long time, I could see her smiling face whenever the moon shone bright on warm summer nights. With time, as with anything else, the memory of youthful love fades, but it is not forgotten. Time erases dreams and thoughts of a first love.

Leaving

W e had been out one Saturday night and got back to
our neighborhood late. It being the weekend, we
headed down the hill to the corner store. Although
it was closed now, a food wagon would set up next to the store.
Don Juan was an illegal immigrant from Mexico who made
some of the best corn tacos twenty-five cents could buy. He also
made hamburgers and hot dogs for those bored with tacos.

"I'll take one of your delicious hamburgers, Don Juan," I
said, taking in the aroma rising from the hot skillet as he threw
on a patty. As soon as he was finished, I dished out one dollar
and grabbed the burger with both hands, biting off a chunk of
delicious flavor that exploded in my mouth. "I really like your
hamburgers, Don Juan. What's the secret?"

"No secret. Just fresh meat, tomatoes, and clean lettuce.
Remember, clean lettuce."

"That was it?" I mumbled to no one in particular as I took
another bite.

"Well, these are the best!"

The area was well lit by the only streetlight the kids hadn't
broken yet. He had a small radio blaring music, which energized
and provoked the younger children to dance. Don Juan would
be there until the last customer was fed or he ran out of food,

which could be as late as two in the morning. I would dish out one dollar for one of his hamburgers every time I came strolling in after nights of partying. Just being around a few people late at night on the corner of the neighborhood street felt like being back home. People gathered around, eating, drinking, and having conversations with one another made me a little homesick. Yet I didn't want to go home. I wanted to be there in Los Angeles.

As I gobbled the remnants of the burger, a song came over the radio, putting me in somewhat of a spiritual trance. "My Cherie Amour," by Stevie Wonder, triggered a soulful joy in me. The song just grabbed me. This would be the song that would remain on my mind forever more. For years, this song would bring back memories of a time when, as a teenager, I was experiencing a love for life. It would remind me of the glorious days of California dreaming.

Money was getting low. I had spent practically every penny allocated for the trip. So I asked one of the cousins if he knew where I could get a job. He mentioned a restaurant nearby that was always looking for dishwashers or busboys.

"I'm a musician. I can get a job at any nightclub. Let's see if we can find a place where I can make some money," I told one of the cousins.

"What kind of music can you play?"

"All sorts. But I'm mostly familiar with Tejano music."

"What's that?"

"It's polka dancing music. Everyone in Texas loves this kind of music."

"That's not happening here," he said. "However, there is a place down on Broadway where they play live music. I don't think we'd be able to get into the local bars in Hollywood. Let's go to the one on Broadway."

"I'm ready," I told the cousins. One of them said he had other plans, so the three who were left piled into a friend's car, and we took off. I was in the back seat, listening to music blaring from the radio.

"Hey, you want one of these?" the friend of one of the cousins asked, holding out his hand with some pills in it.

"What is it?"

"It's a downer. It'll help you relax when you get on that stage. That is, if they let you. Here, take it with a beer."

I swallowed a small blue pill with a long chug of beer. We moved slowly through traffic, heading into downtown. The sounds coming from the car radio filled the air. "Bad Moon Rising," by Creedence Clearwater Revival, came on.

"Turn it up, turn it up!" I shouted from the back seat. It was followed by "Good Golly, Ms. Molly." I was getting into the music, my head nodding as I sang at the top of my lungs. I felt relaxed. Overly relaxed. The music pounded loudly in my ears. I bobbed my head to the rhythm, my eyes closed.

We stopped at a filling station to buy more beer. I needed bladder relief. So I got out of the car and headed to the restroom inside the convenience store. I was feeling woozy. It wasn't more than fifteen steps to the door, but my eyesight was not very clear. My limbs were not responding to my brain's directions. There was a curb that required one step up before I entered the store. I was asking my feet to move, but nothing happened. The curb looked higher than a regular curb, but it really wasn't. My legs were not responding. But my bladder was saying, "I'm ready to release!" I just couldn't lift my leg to take that one step up. I was standing there, staring at the curb and not moving.

I'm going to pee right here! I thought. *I can feel it!* Turning around, I moved to the side of the building where there were no steps, and my piss flew against the wall. Holding on to the side of the building with the other hand, I was not seeing straight. I peed all over my shoes, but by some miracle, I missed my pant legs.

My hand was wet, so I dried it on my pants. I zipped up, making sure the thing was carefully tucked in. I forgot where I was.

"Hey, guys! Can you come help me get in the car?" I heard myself calling out.

"Hey, dude. You're high!" someone said.

"My legs won't move, man!"

"I should've given you half of that pill." He laughed as he guided me back to the car. Another Creedence song came on. I rested my hand over the car seat, using my ring finger to tap on what I thought was a drum. In my mind, it was a drum. It turned out the drum was a bottle of Hai Karate, a cologne popular at the time. Imitating the beat of the drum, I was hitting the bottle so hard that the bottle broke. The liquid released a fragrance so powerful that it quickly engulfed the entire car.

"What the hell?" yelled the cousin, who quickly rolled down his window.

"Roll down the windows! That bottle back there must have spilled! Roll down the window!" the driver yelled.

My hand was smothered in Hai Karate. I couldn't clean it off fast enough. The bottle had been half full, and it spilled all over the headrest, down the back seat, and into the side of my pants. I smelled like a whore sitting on the front bench of a Southern Evangelical Church!

"I'm sorry, you guys, but I'm going to have to go home," I pleaded. "I'm not feeling very good."

I closed my eyes and rocked back and forth as the car weaved through traffic. I couldn't keep my mouth closed. My lower lip drooped, allowing drool to flow slowly and freely, soaking my shirt with tasteless spit.

When we got back to the house, the guys carried me inside and dropped me on one of the beds, leaving me to fend for myself.

"He'll sleep it off. Let's go to the beach," Edward suggested.

Getting to the nightclub for a potential job was out. There went that idea. As I lay there still conscious, the room began to spin. A nauseating feeling overwhelmed me. I couldn't control the movements happening in my head. The room spun repeatedly, making it difficult to stand up. It wouldn't have mattered. I wouldn't have been able to get up anyway.

In the morning, still wearing the same clothes I'd had on the night before, including my shoes, I opened my eyes and quietly tiptoed to the bathroom.

"How was the club?" Edward's sister, Leslie, asked, looking up from the newspaper while sipping on a cup of coffee.

"We didn't make it."

"Oh?" She looked up at me. "That kind of party, huh."

"Any more coffee?" I asked.

"Yes. Help yourself," she said, not looking up from her reading.

I managed to pour it without spilling much. I could still feel the effects of the pill. I wondered what I'd taken.

Note to Robert the Idiot, I thought. *Let that be a lesson. This is what happens when you take pills not prescribed by doctors! Future drug use must be avoided! Stay away from them.* And with that piece of self-advice, I did.

Meanwhile, the summer was coming to an end, and we had very little money left for any kind of entertainment.

"Let's get a job and stay," was all I said to Edward one morning.

"I can't stay. My parents want me back."

"Well then, I'll stay. Do you think your aunt and uncle will let me stay here until I get a job? I can help out once I start making money."

"How am I supposed to get back?"

"Take the bus."

"I can't take the bus. I don't know if it will take me all the way back to Coyanosa."

I didn't want to go back, but I realized that staying could be troublesome. I knew I could become a professional musician there. But my promise to finish school surfaced in my head. If I stayed, found a job, and made money, I would not go back to school. I also missed my family.

By week's end, the decision was made to go back to Texas. We left on a Monday morning in the middle of September. I talked to Mom on the phone the previous Sunday, letting her know we were heading back. She and Dad had returned from Sahuayo, Mexico, with stories she couldn't wait to share with me.

Two days later, we were back. Good ol' Texas. There was nothing spectacular between El Paso and Fort Stockton. Just desert and dry heat. Even Interstate 10 was devoid of the kind of traffic I'd gotten used to in California. After dropping off Edward in Coyanosa, I was glad to be heading home.

Mom and Dad had some very interesting stories to tell about their visit, giving me little time to tell them about my trip. We had dinner like always. I grabbed a plate and found a place to sit. I was back to my dull, mundane life.

The next morning, I was awakened by yelling coming from the kitchen. Dad was saying something to Mom, and he didn't sound happy.

"This is marijuana. I knew it! We shouldn't have let him go. I told you they were up to no good!"

I walked into the kitchen. Dad was holding a ball of aluminum foil in his hand.

"What is this? Is this marijuana?" he asked.

"It's not mine. Where did you find it?"

"In the car's air conditioner. Did you put it there?"

"I don't know what you're talking about," I said. "Where in the A/C?"

He showed me the vent that had been pulled out to create a space for the pot.

"That's not mine. It's Edward's. I don't do that." I looked at Mom for some support.

"I'd better not catch you doing anything like this," Chuy said. "You understand?"

I knew he wanted to slap or just hit me, but he restrained himself. His face, red with rage, showed he wasn't happy. He paced back and forth, holding the ball of aluminum with the weed still in it.

"What if the police had stopped you?" he kept yelling. "Do you know you could go to prison? Is that where you want to be? In prison? You can't be caught with this. You tell your friend he is not coming here anymore. Stay away from him!" And with that, he turned and left.

I never saw or heard about the pot after that. Did Chuy sell it? Did he smoke it with friends? I always wondered what he did with it. I'm sure it was put to good use.

I had a couple of weeks before school started, and I just couldn't see myself standing around doing nothing. I had to get a job and get out of the house. Dad kept hounding me about my long hair. He believed I had turned into a hippie, and he didn't like it. It was time to avoid criticism. I came to realize criticism was not coming just from home. Eventually, it would catch up with me in other places too.

I found a job working for my uncle at a filling station doing odd jobs. Since I had some mechanical experience, he had me do minor tune-ups and brake jobs, wash cars, and do anything else he thought would bring in some extra money. He didn't pay much, but the few dollars I made I kept for myself. I didn't let anyone know I was back in town. But it wasn't long before Juan came by as soon as he found out I was home. So did Luciano. With my work, I had very little time to talk about my California adventures.

Late in the evening a couple of weeks before school started, I was driving through Rooney Park when I saw flashing lights come up behind me. Not cop lights. Just car lights flashing me to stop. I pulled over by some picnic tables and got out. The car following me pulled up behind me, and Armando, the saxophone player with the Blue Notes, got out and rushed over to me. I thought he was going to punch me because I'd left the band in a bind when I left for California. I could see the anger lines on his face. I prepared myself. If he swung, I'd have to swing back. Although I wasn't one to engage in a dogfight, I was not going to let him intimidate me either.

"Do you know you cost us the battle of the bands! Did you know we could have won if you'd been there?" he yelled as he walked toward me. "Why didn't you tell us you were leaving instead of hiding?" He took the last few steps, and I braced myself for the hit. It never came. Instead, he grabbed me in a bear hug and swung me around.

"I was hoping to catch up with you, you little piece of shit! What's this?" he asked, slightly pulling my hair, which was now shoulder length. "You think you're some kind of hippie?"

"Nah. Just letting it grow for the summer. How could ya'll have lost the battle? No other band can play better than the Blue Notes! What the hell happened?"

"It was all a set-up. The judges were from Pecos. We should have taken the challenge at a neutral site instead of going to Pecos. We were outnumbered. They had a bigger crowd supporting them."

We talked for an hour, catching up on what had been going on in my absence. He told me of the tour the band took to promote the album. He talked about playing in different venues, some better than others. He made it sound like they'd had some fun. The sun was setting, and I had not been home yet, so I told him I needed to get going.

"Hey. Wanna come back to the band?" he asked.

"What will Linda say? You think she'll let me back in after ditching you guys?"

"Why don't you come by on Friday for practice, and we'll find out."

After I promised to show up on Friday, we said our goodbyes.

Friday came, and I was reluctant to go by the practice garage. *Will they accept me back?* I wondered. *Will they tell me to get lost?* But something inside me wanted to get back to playing with the group. After standing outside the garage, I mustered enough courage to walk inside. Everything went silent when I walked in. All seven members of the band looked at me and smiled.

"'Bout time you showed up!" someone shouted.

"How was California?" someone else asked.

It was like I had never left. The guys were happy to see me and called me *indio*, or Indian, because of my long hair.

A Dropout

The band director sent out a letter letting everyone know they had to show up for practice two weeks before school officially started.

I arrived late. The band was already on the practice field. I got there just in time to hear the band director give instructions on the new routine for halftime, which would be performed during the first football game of the season. He looked at me but didn't say anything.

Did I see a smirk on his face? I wondered. Mr. Hanna, a mean man whose demeanor rested on the precipice of evil, liked to yell at students. When mistakes were made, he'd grab their instruments out of their mouths, get in their face, and yell at them.

"That's the wrong note!"

"Hold up your horn!"

"Move left! No, your other left!"

Things had to be perfect with no mistakes. We all understood his foul mood swings. If someone made a mistake, he'd stop everything, get in the face of whoever he thought wasn't listening, and totally embarrass them. Some of the younger girls would silently hold back a tear or two because of the humiliation they experienced from his insolent ways. No one said anything about his demeaning behavior. Not the parents. Not the administration. Not the students. Fear drove his agenda.

A cold snap had rolled in that morning, making most of the students shiver as the wind blew in from the north. There was nothing to hold it back or shield students from it. Mr. Hanna held a mic attached to a megaphone, which some freshman kid carried, following him around wherever he went. He barked instructions as we stood at attention in the biting cold.

"This line is not straight! Watch the person next to you. See? You can't be that blind!" His orders pierced the air like the cold wind. At that moment, he came toward me, looked directly at me, and shouted, "Hold that horn up!" He pushed the bell of my trumpet up in such a rough manner that the mouthpiece hit my cold lips. "Hold it up, I said."

What happened next was so sudden that it surprised me. Without thinking about my actions, I pulled the horn away from my lips and looked at him.

"I've had enough of your bullying!" I said. Then I walked off the practice field.

"Get back here!" he yelled. "If you walk away, you might as well change your schedule 'cause you ain't coming back! You hear me?"

I kept walking. He kept yelling. I was fuming mad. I suppose he was too. I was a senior, and this man was not going to treat me like a child. I walked into the band hall and grabbed my trumpet case, determined not to come back. Then I walked into the counselor's office. Without question, he changed my schedule, adding some dumb course I didn't need. Later, I ran into a couple of my buddies from band period who told me two other students had walked out as well.

"You really gonna quit?" asked one of them.

"This is our senior year, man," the other one said. "You can't quit. We're going to district this year and win it all! You have to be part of this!"

"I'm done with that dirty old man," I said, still showing signs of disgust at the way he treated kids. "I don't need this. Besides, I just don't care about band anymore. It's a waste of time."

I walked away, leaving them gaping at my rebellious attitude. I had some regrets about leaving, but my mental anguish was stronger, making me somewhat relieved at the fact that I didn't have to go back to that abuse.

It took a couple of days to get over the decision, which, in the long run, was the best decision I'd ever make. I was happy with myself. But I didn't know that abuse by old white men was just the beginning of a terrible ending to the next terrible few days.

It was Monday of the first week of school. I'd cut my hair short and shaved the little facial hair from my upper lip. I was ready for school. This would be my last year. Thank God. I was ready to get this over with, find a real job, and make real money. I was still working at my uncle's garage in the early mornings and late afternoons, but I'd left work early enough that day to make it to school on time.

Running to catch up with a couple of the guys from the hood, I yelled, "Hey, wait for me!" We talked nonsense about what we were going to do to freshmen this year.

"I'm going to kill some of them!" remarked one of the guys.

"I'm making them hold my books. If they drop them, I'm doing wedges on their ass," the other said.

We entered the building, laughing and joking about the teachers we had for our classes. The first bell took us by surprise. Or at least it did me.

"I'm going to be late!" I yelled over my shoulder as I jogged down the hall. I was jogging past the front office when the principal, Joe Moring, came out of the door and into the hall.

"Hey, you! Stop running!" he yelled.

I slowed down, still walking fast in order to get to my first-period class before the tardy bell rang.

"Hey! Stop!"

I stopped and turned around. Moring was coming toward me. Joe was a tall man who sported really short hair called a crew cut. And he didn't look too happy. He must have been in the military at one time because he acted like the kind who yelled and insulted young cadets.

"You know you're not supposed to be running in the hallways," he said. "I'm making an exception today, but if I see you running again, you're coming into my office!"

I knew what that meant.

"Sorry, sir. I was just trying to get to class on time," I said respectfully.

"Let me see. Turn around." He grabbed me by the shoulders and spun me around. I did as he asked, a bit startled by this odd request.

"Your hair is too long," he stated. "You can't have your hair touching your ears. Get it cut! You hear me?" he boomed as he towered over me, a little too close for comfort.

"Yes, sir. I just haven't had time since I work late."

"I don't care what your excuse is. Get it cut!" Again, he barked orders right in my face.

I walked away knowing I'd be late for my first-period class. By the time I got to that class, all the back seats were taken, so I had to sit up front—a place reserved for smart students. I was not in the right chair, the right row, or the right class. I'd forgotten that my schedule had changed. After apologizing for being late, I told the teacher I was in the wrong class and walked out. I eventually found my class—a homemaking class attended mostly by girls. This was the class I didn't need.

On Tuesday, I was getting acclimated to my new classes. Wednesday arrived without incident. Or I thought so.

The last period of the day was history with Joe Primera, a veteran teacher who happened to be the only token Hispanic male teacher in the school. He was a short, odd-looking man who always wore a sweater no matter what the temperature was. He had an accent, which very few students noticed. He wasn't a mean character, but he wasn't a nice one either. He was married to a teacher who was definitely odd but nicer than he was.

This was the third day of school, and I'd already been yelled at by the band director. I'd been yelled at by the principal. And I'd heard that bad things happen in threes.

José, Troy, and I walked into Primera's noisy, chaotic class. Lanky José sat on one side of me, and shorty Troy sat on the other. Once Primera checked the roll, he asked the three of us to meet him outside his classroom door. We got up and went out into the hallway. I wondered why.

"Why did he say we needed to go outside?" I asked the guys, feeling perplexed and confused.

"I don't know. He's dumb and stupid," barked José.

"Did we do anything wrong?" I asked.

"No, he just wants us to help him bring books or something," said Troy without stammering.

No more than two minutes went by before the principal, Joe Moring, came around the corner. Walking up to us, he asked, "What are you doing in the hallway? Why are you not in class?"

I hadn't had time to get a haircut, so I tried to stand behind José, who was a lot taller than me.

"I don't know. Mr. Primera asked us to wait for him out here," I said meekly.

Joe Moring opened the door and waved Primera out. "Why are these boys outside instead of in class?" Moring asked.

"Well, you see, yesterday, at the end of the class, one of these boys walked out and slammed the door so hard that it almost fell off its hinges. I was going to ask them who had done it. They didn't have to slam the door that hard. They could have damaged school property." As he said this, he stood with his hands on his hips, trying to look imposing and concerned about a door.

"Who slammed the door?" asked Moring.

"I didn't slam a door," I said.

"I didn't slam the door," José said.

"I– I– I– didn't do– do– do it," shorty Troy replied.

"Now, listen here, boys. One of you slammed that door, and I want to know who." Moring was getting frustrated.

"I didn't do it," I repeated.

José and Troy said together, "I didn't do it."

Joe Moring stepped up closer. "I'll ask you again. Who slammed the door? One of you did it, and I want to know who!" he said, looking right at me.

I looked at him and replied, "Sir, I had nothing to do with the door being slammed, and I don't like being called a liar."

In retrospect, perhaps I should not have used those exact terms, but he was clearly blaming me for the incident. Immediately, the man turned a turnip color and began shaking from head to toe in visible anger.

"Go inside and get me a paddle!" he yelled at Primera.

Primera jumped at his command, went inside, then returned immediately with a board the size of a baseball bat.

"You bend over, son!" Moring yelled, still visibly shaken by my remarks. He grabbed my arm and tried to turn me around.

I pulled away from him, looked him straight in the eyes, and said, "I'm not getting hit for something I didn't do!" I pulled back some more. I could tell that if I relented, he would beat me without restraint. I was not about to let him do that. I didn't care if he was the principal.

"Then you get out of here, and don't come back to this school again!" he yelled.

I walked away. José, Troy, and Primera stood there, shocked at what had just happened.

I got in my car and drove around, retracing the incident in my mind. *Did I approach this correctly? Was I wrong in how I handled this incident? Is he not going to let me come back? What am I going to say to Mom?*

When I got home, Mom was sitting at the kitchen table, reading some pamphlet a Jehovah's Witness had given her.

"What are you doing home so early?" she asked. "Aren't you going to work?"

"Mom, I'm quitting school. I'm not going back there."

"*Por qué?* What happened?"

"The principal wanted to hit me with a paddle for something I didn't do! I told him I didn't do what I was being accused of, and he got mad at me. I'm not going back there!"

"Oh, *mijo*. You have to. If the man was wrong, then we have to tell him he was wrong."

"Mom, he was mad, and I don't think he will listen. I didn't do anything. It had to have been José."

"What did he do?" she asked.

"The teacher said someone slammed the door yesterday and almost knocked it off the hinges."

"Then you have to go back there and tell him."

"I can't do that. He will beat all of us."

At this point, Mom was so concerned that she started to cry. "You have to go back. You must graduate. Your life will be ruined if you don't. You have to graduate," she said as more tears found their way down her cheeks.

I was at a crossroads and didn't know how to resolve this. I was mad. She was sobbing. I was hurt—not from being kicked out, but from seeing her cry.

After a few minutes, she said, "We'll go see the superintendent. He is a nice man. He will know what to do."

"Mom, I don't think the superintendent can help me."

"Yes, he can. Get your keys. We're going to see the superintendent."

I drove us to the district office. We walked in, and in her choppy English, she managed to convince the secretary to let us see Mr. Huckaby, the superintendent.

An older man, he was wearing a charcoal suit and leaning back in his oversized chair. He looked up as the secretary announced us.

"These folks are here to see you, Mr. Huckaby," she noted, rolling her eyes.

"What can I help you with?" he asked. "Here, sit down." He never left his chair, but he did sit up behind his desk as I recounted the incident with the principal and Primera. He listened. After a few minutes, he leaned back in his chair.

"You must go back and explain to Mr. Moring your side of the story. You have to be a man about this and take whatever punishment he thinks you deserve. I know you don't think this is the right thing to do, but you have to face up to what he thinks is right."

He stood up, repeating his statement about being a man and facing the consequences.

I knew this was not going to solve the issue, but Mom was insistent.

"You see, the superintendent is right. You have to go back and talk to the principal. You have to go back and speak to him," she pleaded.

We got in the car. I could see her shedding tears once again.

I knew she was right. I had to face the consequences of my words, but I was not going to apologize for standing up to the man. He wanted to beat me for something I didn't do.

After dropping Mother off at the house, I drove back to the high school and went inside. As much as I hated and resented having to do this, I had to do it for my mother.

"May I see Mr. Moring?" I asked the secretary.

"Let me see if he has time. What is this about?"

"I have to talk to him about an incident that happened this afternoon."

She walked to his office, opened the door, and whispered, "This boy wants to speak with you." Then she waved me over.

Before Joe Moring could say a word, I said, "Mr. Moring. I'm sorry for what happened this afternoon. I was out of line, and I should not have said what I said. I want you to know that I didn't slam the door to Mr. Primera's room. I had nothing to do with that. I'm here to apologize for my behavior, and I'm ready to take my punishment like a man."

He walked from behind his desk and stood over me.

I got up, thinking I was going to have to grab the desk by the edges if and when he decided to beat me with his paddle. Texas law allowed corporal punishment in schools as a means of disciplining students. In our schools, it had been used hundreds of times to punish students for misbehaving. In some states, it is still legal to discipline students by hitting them. In the South, the Southwest, and the Midwest—including Alabama, Arizona, Arkansas, Colorado, Florida, Georgia, Idaho, Indiana, Iowa, Kansas, Kentucky, Louisiana, Mississippi, Missouri, North Carolina, South Carolina, Tennessee, Texas, and Wyoming—it is legal to paddle students with a wooden board. While it was much worse several years ago, it is appalling that in the twenty-first century, the richest nation in the world still has nineteen states that permit an adult to spank a child in school. In the most recent year for which data is available, more than one thousand Texas schools used beating a student with a wooden board as a disciplinary action.

Joe Moring stood still, contemplating his next move.

"I want to thank you for coming back and apologizing," he said. "I know you didn't slam that door. As soon as you left, the little guy, Troy, admitted he'd done it. Thank you for coming back and admitting that you were wrong and are willing to take your punishment. You can go now."

He turned around and walked back to his desk.

I was shocked. I wasn't getting a beating! How lucky can one get?

As I left his office, something came over me—something that brought clarity about fairness. On one side was the whole idea of teachers being cruel to students over insignificant things, and on the other was the issue of adults letting emotion get the best of them and taking it out on kids. In that instant, I knew José had slammed the door and not Troy. I knew Primera had let this get out of hand. He should have intervened and played out the incident as a mistake.

I walked down the hall to Primera's class, hoping to pick up books I'd left there. He was sitting behind his desk.

"Because of you, I'm quitting school," I said. "This incident should never have happened. The wrong kid was beaten because of you. You should have stood up to the principal and defended your students. If anyone should have done this, it should have been you. You are Mexican, just like us."

I turned and walked out of his class.

"Wait, Robert," he said. "You can't quit school. You need this! It wasn't your fault. You can't quit."

Not looking back, I walked to my locker, got all my books and personal belongings, then went back to the office.

"Here are my books. I need to check out of school," I told the secretary.

"You'll need your parent's permission to do that."

"No, I don't. I'm old enough. I don't need anyone's permission."

I signed my name on the checkout sheet and walked out of Fort Stockton High School, the home of the Panthers. I didn't know what I was going to do, but I could not tell my mother what I'd done.

Instead, I lied.

Buena Vista High

I went home that afternoon with what little I had from the few days of my senior year. When I walked in the door, Mom was waiting for me, sitting at the kitchen table and reading the same pamphlet.

"The principal did not spank me. He told me I was a man to come back and take my punishment. He said Troy confessed, and he got the beating. I'm good. He told me I could come back to school. Thanks, Mom."

We didn't say another word about the incident. And I didn't go back to school for the next two days. I went to work at the garage in the morning and just drove around until it was time to head home. Saturday, I called Edward and shared with him the decision I'd made. He wasn't surprised.

"Why not come to school in Imperial? Buena Vista High School will accept you. They don't care, and the people there are certainly not bigots like they are in Fort Stockton."

"I don't know. I can't drive to Imperial every day. I couldn't afford it. Besides, don't you have to live there for them to let you in?"

"You can come live with me. You can have Leslie's room. She's not coming back. I'll talk to my parents. Call me tomorrow."

With that, I walked around, trying to figure out how I was going to convince Mom to let me attend a high school several miles away. I knew she wanted me to graduate. In her mind, this was the most important task all her children had to do. She was determined to see all seven of us graduate from high school because she believed that such an accomplishment would improve our lives forever.

"You are graduating from high school. It is all you'll ever need to be successful in this country," she would continuously remind us, especially me. I think it was because I was the oldest, and if I did it, then the others would follow suit.

She worked so hard to keep us focused on school. Her eyes would light up when we came home with some award as evidence of how hard we worked. We could tell by the way she looked at us whenever comments on the report card showed we were on the right track. The pride in her voice and in her cuddling embrace reminded each of us how important this was to her.

I did not want to disappoint her. In her mind, once we graduated, finding a job that would help us out of poverty would come easily for all of us. She truly believed this.

There was no talk about going to college. In our little barrio, graduation from high school was the ultimate goal. Knowing how much this meant to her, I planned my approach carefully. I was determined to convince her. If she approved, Dad would not stand in the way. When it came to our education, he had very little to say.

On Saturday, Chuy would be out of the house. This would be the perfect time to bring forth my plan. I prayed it would work.

"Mom. I've been thinking," I said. "The way I was treated by the principal and Mr. Primera this past week was not right. I don't want to go back there. They embarrassed me, threatened me, insulted me. And for no reason at all, they wanted to punish me. Why? Because Primera blamed some stupid door slamming on me? I don't want to go back."

"You have to!" she cried.

"Mom, I can graduate. I'm willing to do that. But not here."

"Where? Where will you go?" she asked, almost on the verge of tears again. This must have been agonizing for her.

"Buena Vista High School in Imperial will take me. I spoke to Edward about it. He left Fort Stockton and is much happier there. I think I can register on Monday without missing any school, but only if you let me go."

"I don't know. You can't drive there every day. If the car breaks down, how can you make it every day? It's too dangerous."

"Edward spoke to his parents, and I can live with them in Coyanosa. They're in the Imperial school zone. I can graduate from there. We will both be seniors, and his parents want us to go to school together. Mom, I can graduate from there! Who cares where I graduate from as long as I get a diploma!" I was trying to sound excited and convincing.

"I'll need to speak to his parents. If they think it is okay, then you can go. They have to agree. Do you know how much they are going to charge you for living there?" she asked, shaking her head. She still seemed to not be sure I was doing the right thing.

"I don't know. We didn't talk about that."

On Sunday morning after church—which she made me go to so I could pray that we were making the right choice—I left and, with a few belongings, drove to Coyanosa, Texas. Edward's parents were glad to see me. In the early morning of my first day of school, I boarded a bus for Buena Vista High School. I showed up with hair touching my ears, a pair of striped bell-bottom pants, a light-blue sweater, and my trusted brown platform shoes.

The front office had windows to the front entrance, giving every student coming into the building a clear look at the new kid.

"Where is that hippie from?"

"What's he wearing?"

"Is he coming to school here?"

"Look at how he's dressed."

Those totally audible comments rang in my ears. I ignored them. *Will I fit in?* I wondered. *Did I make the right decision?*

These kids didn't look like me. They were not the best dressers. At best, they looked like regular students from a small hick town. The simplicity of dress told me they were not in touch with the outside world. But who cared? I was there to graduate and nothing more.

Students and teachers alike stopped just long enough to stare at the oddity in the office. Some of the girls looked at each other and giggled. They bumped shoulders like children making comments about who they thought I was.

I was the new kid in town.

The entire student body was housed in one building, with major walls separating the elementary kids from the junior high kids, and them from the high school kids. The school was the center of the Imperial universe. All things in the community revolved around the school. There wasn't anything else to do but participate in school events. I had gone from a high school whose graduating class in 1970 was almost 150 students to one whose senior class was made up of only twenty students. The students I had gone to school with for seventeen years were replaced by strangers.

I was beginning to doubt this whole stupid idea. *What have I done?* I wondered. *How am I going to survive here on my own?* I only knew Edward, and he was off to class.

The high school principal/teacher provided me with a schedule of classes I needed. I had to have English IV, history, math, and at least one science class. The rest of my day was filled with band, PE, journalism, and Spanish. As I roamed the tiny high school, looking for my classes, I got more stares from students.

The classes were easy enough, and the teachers seemed friendly. I soon settled into a routine, focusing on getting better grades. With time, I was somewhat accepted by my senior classmates. One of these students was a tennis player named Louie Jimenez. There wasn't much to do after school, so I'd spend my time learning how to play tennis. That's how I came to know Louie. He would eventually become one of my best friends. He lived with his grandmother, drove a nice car, and dated a senior girl, whom he eventually married right after high school.

After a few weeks with Edward's family, I felt like I had overstayed my welcome. Those little things that are felt but not said caused me concern. Nothing needs to be said when body language speaks volumes. And their body language told me it was time to move on.

One weekend, I drove to Imperial, looking for a place to live. I needed an affordable place to sleep and keep my meager things. I had stayed with Louie a few times, but his house was small, and a third person made it quite crowded. His grandmother didn't have a lot of money, and I didn't want to take advantage of her hospitality. Louie had mentioned that there were some rooms above one of the only two filling stations in town.

"Ask the owner of the gas station," Louie said when I got to his house that weekend. "I know of one older man who lives upstairs. I bet he would rent you a room."

"Do you know the owner?" I asked.

"Yeah. I'll go with you."

We got in his car and headed to the gas station. The owner was an older man who looked at me rather suspiciously.

"Hello, Mr. Canton," said Louie. "This is my friend Robert, and he is looking for a place to rent."

Mr. Canton pulled his reading glasses down to the tip of his nose and looked up at me without saying a word.

"Hello, sir. My name is Robert, and I'm a senior this year. I moved here from Fort Stockton, and I really need a place to rent for the year until I graduate. Would you be interested in renting one of your rooms upstairs to me?"

"Why are you going to school here?" he asked. "I thought Fort Stockton had a good education program. I'm told it's better than here. What do you think?"

"Fort Stockton is a good school, but I like going to school here. Sir, I'm very comfortable going to school here. I like the school, but if I can't find a place to stay, I'm going to have to go back, and I don't think they want me back."

"Why? What did you do?"

"I stood up to the principal when he decided to intimidate me with his bravado."

"Bravado, huh? I don't rightly rent to strangers, but since you are in school, I might have room for you. Old Man Jenkins lives up there, you know. He's been living here for some years. I don't know if he will be okay with others living there."

We walked up some rickety old wooden stairs on the south side of the building and entered a long hallway. There were four doors, which I assumed led into rooms.

"It's only a room, you know," Mr. Canton said. "There's a bathroom at the end of the hall that you'll have to share with Jenkins."

He showed me the room. It was in the corner of the building, facing the only blinking traffic light the town had. The room was small, with a bed on one end and a small chest of drawers on the other. That was it. Three windows faced the street. The garage roof obscured everything below. The red blinking traffic light was at eye level with the room. There was no air conditioning and no heating.

"You can't have people up here. Only you. Mr. Jenkins is an old man, and he don't take too kindly to visitors."

"No, sir. No other people. Just me."

"Okay, then. Let's go downstairs, and I'll get you a key. When you think of moving in?"

"I'd like to move in on Sunday if that's okay with you. I have to be in school on Monday."

We walked back downstairs. He handed me a key and said, "You can't have too much noise up there, understand?"

"Yes, sir. How much is the rent? Maybe I should have asked you first because I don't have a lot of money."

"I charge sixteen dollars a week. Can you afford that?"

"Yes, sir. I think I can."

"Good then. I'll see you Monday."

And with that, at eighteen years of age, I was living by myself above a gas station, with a bathroom at the end of the hall, which I shared with a Mr. Jenkins.

The year went by fast. I'd get to Imperial on Sunday, early enough to finish any kind of homework that needed to be done before Monday. I'd leave town on Friday right after school, returning to Fort Stockton in time to practice with the band. I barely made enough money to pay rent and buy gas and whatever meals I needed, which wasn't much since there wasn't a grocery store anywhere for miles.

I bought a Styrofoam ice chest made of flimsy material to keep slices of bologna from a meat market in Stockton. Many a night, bologna sandwiches were dinner. I could live on cool bologna sandwiched between two slices of bread. That was enough for me. To make it last longer, I'd ration, and it could last up to three days. On those quiet, lonely nights, I'd relish the comfort bologna gave me.

I was down to 129 pounds, and Mom seemed concerned. She bought a small electric cooking stove, which I used to heat up cans of soup. This presented me with a delicious discovery—I found that a bologna sandwich and a bowl of soup were great together. That was living! Not able to afford much else, I stayed on this diet not because I wanted to but because I had to.

When Louie would invite me over to dinner with his grandmother, she'd shower us with freshly made tortillas, complemented by fideo mixed in with potatoes and ground beef. This was by far some of the best meals I had. Simple but delicious. I never turned those invitations down. No, sir. Not ever.

Since I was living on my own, I applied for free and reduced meals in the cafeteria, and I ate for free. It was embarrassing in the beginning, but as I looked around, I found that very few students paid for their food. No one noticed or cared whether I got a free meal or not. If I didn't have something to eat the night before, those meals in the cafeteria were lifesavers. Embarrassing as it might have seemed at the time, it was a free cooked meal. Why not take advantage?

There were times when some of the guys would invite me out for a burger in Grandfalls, eleven miles west; in Crane, twenty-five miles north; or in McCamey, thirty miles east. When I was short on money, I'd make up excuses as to why I couldn't go. Money was tight, and I didn't want them to know I was too poor to indulge in such luxuries.

At the end of the day, it was do homework, heat up soup, take a shower, and sleep. I had no TV or radio. Only the passing of cars, with the little noise they made, broke the silence. Mr. Jenkins never stirred. I wondered whether there was a real Mr. Jenkins living two doors down.

The quiet gave me time to think about what I was going to do when school was over. I wanted to graduate and immediately look for a job that paid me good money. No summer heat and picking onions. Just thinking of those laborious, hot, ugly days gave me the inspiration I needed to dream about jobs inside a building where I didn't have to be in the sun anymore. I dreamed of being self-sufficient, not relying on anyone for anything.

The nights were long, being by myself, and I could feel the clamps of loneliness swelling up inside. I didn't cry, but I came close several times. The promise of what a diploma would do for me drove my efforts. So many adults promised me that this was the key to success. Besides, I owed it to Mom. I needed to show her I was old enough to take care of myself without her having to worry. I was the oldest, and she expected me to set the example for the rest of the kids. I was on a mission to succeed.

"You have good common sense, Robe," my mother said. "Jesus blessed you with it. You need to pray and thank him for all he does for you. Now, don't waste it on frivolities. That will not get you anywhere. Think before you jump, and don't ever let the world close in on you." Fine words that were meaningless to a kid who had just turned eighteen and was living on his own. I didn't realize those same words would save my hide many times over.

In the end, I had all the credits I needed for graduation. Easy.

Graduation came on a Friday, with the ceremonies held outside in the football stadium. Nineteen out of twenty seniors graduated that day. The ceremonies were quick and painless. By graduating from high school, I was honoring my mother, who had spent eighteen years waiting for this occasion.

When my name was called to receive the diploma, I swelled. It was a proud moment for me. I took a deep breath, made the sign of the cross, and walked across the stage, holding my head up for the world to see. To have made grades that allowed me to reach this point was a miracle. All those years of blood, sweat, and tears culminated in one event.

When the superintendent handed me the diploma, I looked up at the stands, searching for my mother. I saw her smiling face, then I walked across the stage with the diploma in hand, proudly waving it in the air. I wanted her to know I had done what she had wanted me to do all those years.

When I looked up at her, I was looking for a sign of acknowledged pride. I saw it when she wiped a tear from her face. A joyful tear. I had accomplished the impossible. It was time to venture out into the world and become a man.

I opened the diploma. Inside was a wallet-size version of the real thing. I would carry that smaller version in my wallet like a trophy everywhere I'd go, proving to the world, and mostly to myself, that I had made it.

After the Party

The after-party was held in a small venue two blocks from the school. The Blue Notes played for a couple of hours, and we sang and danced the night away. When the celebrations were over, Louie and I got into his car and drove out to the Imperial Reservoir, a small man-made lake in the middle of nowhere and not far from town.

Enjoying the moment, we sat around a fire with beers in hand. I'd been living on my own for most of my senior year and survived. We shared dreams and aspirations about our future. Now that we had earned high school diplomas, we could do anything. We spoke of new adventures—of things we'd always aspired to do. I was going into the world of work, hoping to make serious money for the first time in my life and planning to buy a new car. He was moving to New Mexico to rejoin his mother, hoping to find a job in construction. I fell into an exhausted slumber from the day's activities, dreaming of my future.

The morning sun crept over the bush-like trees surrounding the lake as it cast shadows far into the water. I was ready to start my new life. Louie and I drove back to Imperial, said our goodbyes, and promised to stay in touch. As we went our separate ways, I had no idea that it would be over thirty years before our paths would cross once again.

Back in Fort Stockton, I spent the next two days recounting my graduation for the younger ones. Sitting at the kitchen table with Mom, I told her I was going to look for a job come Monday morning.

"I've got my diploma in my wallet. I'm going to apply everywhere. I'll have a job that pays me money, and then I can move out."

"I'm glad. You should have no problem finding a job now that you have graduated. Make sure to show them your diploma," she stated proudly.

On Monday—a bright, sunny day—I put on my best outfit: regular clean jeans, a nice button-down shirt, and the black shoes Mom had bought me for graduation. I looked employable. With a cup of coffee in my hand, I reached for the keys to the Ford Fairlane and walked out the door, smiling with confidence and a sense of purpose. I just knew I was going to find a job. A job that paid well. I was a high school graduate with a wallet-size diploma to prove it, for heaven's sake.

Before Walmart was created, we had a Gibson's Discount Store. It had everything anyone needed—clothes, school supplies, groceries, cleaning products. This was the first place I tried. Taking a deep breath, I squared my shoulders, then walked inside.

"You hiring?" I asked the lady at the checkout counter.

"Go check over there," she said, pointing to a section of the store in the back that was cordoned off by a wall with a small window.

I rang the little courtesy bell, and the manager appeared from behind.

"I'm looking for a job. Do you have an application I can fill out?"

"We're not hiring at the moment."

"But I have my diploma," I said, pulling it out of my wallet and showing her proof. She didn't even look at it.

"We don't need anybody now. We are fully staffed."

"But I just graduated, and I need a job. Can I fill out the application?"

"No. We're not hiring," she intoned, giving me a slightly frustrated look.

I'd been expecting to get hired right away. I was told all I needed was a high school diploma. I had it. Why wasn't she willing to give me a job? I picked up my diploma and walked out the door in total disappointment.

I moved on to the furniture store where I'd worked before. They were not hiring. I went to two filling stations. They weren't hiring. No one cared whether I had a diploma or not. *Why?* I kept asking myself. But I was determined to find a job no matter what. I had a diploma, for God's sake.

I went to more places. No luck. I was losing hope fast. My shoulders slouched, and a frustrated expression was on my face. Finally, with my head down, I walked into a huge warehouse that looked like a barn. It was an onion processing plant.

People were standing on platforms overlooking this large rubbery belt as it moved onions from one end of the building to the other. Onion sacks straight from the onion fields were being fed onto the belt while people on both sides picked out onions according to size and color. White onions went down one side while the yellow ones were pushed to another belt. Each belt carried the differing onions and deposited them into red sacks held open by workers. These workers tied the tops of the bags when they were filled and placed them on wooden pallets. Once the pallets were four or five sacks high, they were loaded onto eighteen-wheeler trailers bound for different markets.

The sun bearing down on the metal roof and walls contributed to a stifling environment. The place was steaming hot. Even with the large barn doors open, the air circulated inside the place like a small tornado going nowhere. The place had an overpowering stink of rotting onions.

"Hey!" I shouted over the noise. "Who's the manager?"

"I think that's him over there," replied a skinny Mexican kid. He had a bandana covering his nose and mouth, which made it hard to understand him. He pointed in the direction of a small office at the end of the barn.

I opened the office door, letting cool refrigerated air leak out.

"Close the door, will you?" said the white man sitting behind an aluminum office desk. "Why aren't you working?"

"I'm here to ask for a job."

"Oh, I thought you already worked here. Go see Fred. He's that tall guy over there." He motioned toward a tall Hispanic guy standing over the belt with the other workers, barking directions over the noise.

I went over to Fred and said, "The guy in the office told me to talk to you about a job."

"Yeah. Just a minute," he replied. He continued to show people how to separate the good onions from the bad ones. "Have you worked here before?" he asked.

"No, sir. Someone told me you were hiring. I worked the onion fields before, so I know about onions."

"You can start over there," he said, pointing toward one of the belts as it deposited the onions into the red bags. "We need someone to tie those bags and place them on the pallets so the forklift can put them in the trailer. Think you can do that?"

"Yes, sir."

So, in my nice, employable outfit, I started my first full-time job with my diploma in my wallet. The diploma no one cared about. The diploma this onion business didn't even ask for. The diploma that was supposed to open up vast job opportunities for me was entombed in my wallet.

Nobody cared.

Rolling up my sleeves, I grabbed the red bags and filled them to capacity. I had no gloves, so after a couple of hours, my fingers were blistering from tying bags. My back was hollering for relief from the pain caused by bending over and picking up thirty-pound bags of onions and strategically placing them on pallets. Careful placement of the bags was necessary to prevent the top ones from falling over when the forklift picked them up.

By the end of the day, my nice clothes smelled of onion. My hands were raw, smelling of onion. My hair smelled of onion. My whole body stunk of onion. Even my sweat came out smelling of onion. I was back to my dreadful relationship with onions, something I'd promised myself I would never get into again.

I hated onions.

I hated the wallet-size diploma.

I worked at the onion barn for six weeks, making three dollars an hour for eight hours a day, six days a week. After taxes, I took home a little over a hundred dollars a week. It was the most money I had ever made by myself.

I dreaded and hated going to work every day. I kept telling myself the adults had not been truthful with me. At this rate, I was never going to be self-sufficient. I wasn't going to make enough money to buy a car. I was never going to have money to spend on nice things. I was never, never, never. I was mad at the world. I was mad at life, work, parents, adults, and myself. I felt defeated. Discouraged.

I suffered through the summer. The only thing that made me happy was playing music with the band. Every year in the third week of July, there were two events we all looked forward to— the Water Carnival and the Fiesta De San Juan. The band had been hired to play on Saturday night right after the big Water Carnival show at Comanche Springs swimming pool. This event was the culmination of weeks of preparation and the last day of the event, when Miss Fort Stockton would be crowned. Whoever won this title would move on to compete in the Miss Texas pageant.

Once the Water Carnival was over, most of the people ventured out to the tennis courts, where we would play for the evening dance. During one of our intermissions, the new Miss Fort Stockton would be paraded around for the crowd to observe. The Fiesta de San Juan queen, sponsored by the local Catholic church, would also be announced. The previous year's queen would crown the new one at our show. The two most beautiful girls would be at our dance! I was looking forward to seeing them up close.

When the new Fiesta de San Juan queen was announced, Lucio's girlfriend, Isabella, walked toward the stage. It caught me by surprise, forcing me to take a step back. I hadn't seen her in over a year. She looked stunning in her long white gown. She was just as beautiful as the day I'd met her. Too bad she was my friend's girlfriend.

She walked up to the microphone, and, for a split moment, we locked eyes. She smiled, turned toward the mic, and announced the runners-up for this year's crown. When she announced the new queen, she took her crown and placed it on the head of the new one.

I could not stop staring at her. There she was. I looked around the crowd for her boyfriend but couldn't find him. During the second intermission, Isabella walked over to where I was standing.

"Hi, Robert."

Those two words shook me to my core. I tried to say, "Hi," but not a word came out of my mouth. I couldn't take my eyes away from her. She was so beautiful. Remarkably stunning. As she smiled, her lips parted in a way only she could manage. Seductive, special, alluring. She made me smile too. She was that good-looking. The light sparkled in her eyes and gleamed with brilliance. I was amazed she was even talking to me! I smiled again.

Hoping to not spit on her, I managed a weak reply. "Hello. It's so good to see you. Where's Lucio?" I asked rather shyly, looking around and hoping he wasn't close. I wanted uninterrupted time with her.

"I don't know. Lucio and I broke up some time ago."

"Oh. I didn't know that," I said politely. Secretly I was glad. "When did that happen? I haven't seen you guys in some time." Inside, I was jumping with joy.

"It just wasn't working out, you know. We have grown apart."

"You want to sit down? I have a few minutes before our second set." I motioned toward a couple of empty chairs sitting not far from the stage. "I've missed all my friends from high school," I said as I sat down.

"I heard you had moved to Imperial. What was that like? Did you like it?"

"It was okay. I managed to graduate. That was important. You know I almost quit high school."

"Why?"

"There was a problem with the principal and Mr. Primera."

"Nobody likes him. I heard what he did. Is that why you left?"

"I couldn't stand the demeaning attitude of the teachers and administrators. Well, not all of them. But most of them. I don't know why they teach. They don't like kids."

We talked like we'd seen each other just the day before. She made me feel important and special. After a few minutes, I was experiencing an incredible desire to touch her.

"Hey, I'm so glad to see you," I said. "I need to get back. I think we're starting our last set. I hope to see you again." I put my hand on her shoulder.

We finished our last song. Some people were dancing to the last slow song, and others were walking out of the park. I looked up and saw her standing with one of her friends as I was tearing down our equipment. She approached my side of the stage.

"My parents will be here in a few minutes," she said. "Do you have time to talk with me? I have something to share with you."

We walked over to my car, which was parked several feet away, obstructed from view by several trees. I opened the door, and she got in.

"I don't think he is for me," she said. "It was hard breaking up, but I'm over him. Do you think I should have stuck it out?"

I could tell she was having second thoughts. I thought, *There is only one way to find out.*

I leaned over and kissed her.

She kissed me back.

As she wrapped her arms around my shoulders and neck, I could feel the warmth of her touch. Her hair, her eyes, her cheeks, her entire body filled me with a passion I'd never felt before. *Am I falling in love with this girl?* I wondered. My hands automatically wrapped around her waist, pulling her closer to me. Our lips parted briefly, then she kissed me again, this time with serious affection. My head swirled in fear this would end.

"I'd better go," she finally said. "Robert, I'm glad you're back."

And with that, she opened the door and walked briskly back to the parking lot, where her parents were waiting.

A joyful feeling shook the world that absorbed me. In a few short moments, I'd fallen in love. Her radiance and beauty filled me with happiness. But as soon as it started, that feeling went away, bringing me back to a realization that I could not understand.

What's a beautiful girl like her doing with a guy like me? I'm a poor onion worker who can't buy a portion of the lipstick she is wearing. My parents don't own a convenience store. I'm poor. I'm an onion man.

She was too good for me. I knew it.

Two weeks later, as I was standing at a filling station, I saw them in Lucio's car on Dickenson Boulevard. Lucio was driving. Isabella sat right next to him. They didn't see me. I turned away and smiled. I knew it! I wasn't the person she wanted. I didn't have the money or the status. I closed my eyes and wiped a tear out of the corner of my eye. Disappointment settled in my heart.

"I suppose it was inevitable," I said to myself.

I didn't want to see or speak to anyone after that. I drove around aimlessly. At Rooney Park, I drove up to the front of Comanche Pool. Sitting on one of the benches, watching a kaleidoscope of light bounce off the water, I questioned my love life. Swirls of light rocked my thoughts. It was a warm, lovely evening. I sat alone, contemplating and wondering where I'd made a wrong turn in my life. I needed time to think—to think about my future as a young man who was determined to succeed no matter what. But how?

I was in a dark mood and feeling sorry for myself when the headlights of another car caught my attention. It was a small Chevy Corvair. When it stopped, I recognized the girl who got out. It was Samantha. Two years older than me, she was tall and dark-skinned, with a simple yet adorable smile. She looked in my direction. Then I saw her from the corner of my eye walking toward me.

"Didn't know if it was you. What are you doing?" she asked.

"I was waiting for you. What do you think?" I replied.

"That's funny. Are you here by yourself?"

"Yes. What are you doing?"

"I'm here for the summer. I'll be starting my third year in college in a few days. I got bored, so I came out here."

We talked for thirty minutes about nothing in particular, but her comment about starting back to college in a few days caught my interest.

"Is it hard?" I asked.

"Is what hard?"

"College?"

"Not really. It's like high school all over again. I'm taking the same classes I took in high school, with professors who talk all period long. I do like the freedom it gives me though. I get a lot of time to study for classes since I don't go to each class every day. I take some classes on Mondays, Wednesdays, and Fridays. And on Tuesdays and Thursdays, I take other classes. I like it. Now, don't get me wrong, it can be overwhelming if you don't stay up with your classes. Hey, you want to take a ride with me in my new car?"

We drove around in her light-green Corvair. She cranked up the engine as we sped down the boulevard, and I realized she could drive a stick shift. We stopped at Jim's for a Coke, went around the Sonic Burger joint, then circled back around toward the park. When she parked, I got out of the car.

"I love your car," I said. "One of these days, I'm buying me one. Not like this one, but maybe a sportier car. Like a '68 Chevelle Super Sport."

"I think you have the motivation to do anything you want and buy anything you desire," were the last words she said to me before she drove off into the night. She stuck her hand out the driver's-side window and waved.

I watched her until she disappeared from view, leaving me with different thoughts about my future.

The Right Decision

R ichard Nixon, a Republican, was voted in as the thirty-seventh president of the United States in 1970. He promised to end the war in Vietnam and bring peace to the world stage.

It didn't happen right away. What happened instead was the Vietnam draft lottery of 1969, a method the federal government used to replace the young men being killed or wounded in the war. It focused on nineteen-year-old men. This brought the war closer to home.

I'd heard many of the older boys who graduated that year talking about joining the military as opposed to being drafted. The scuttlebutt created tension and anxiety among students. However, the national tension was playing out in very dangerous forms in the bigger cities.

The 1969 draft lottery didn't affect me, but it encouraged resentment toward the Vietnam War and the drafting of young Americans. The nightly news showed pictures of people decrying discrimination by the draft system. They raged on about how the system was focused against low-educated, low-income, underprivileged members of society.

That clearly included me.

The evening news kept America apprised of the reckless symptoms of war. Between August 5, 1964, and May 7, 1975, over 9 million military personnel served on active duty. Nearly 3 million were men and women in uniform. Of those, five men were only sixteen years old. Of those fighting in Vietnam, 58,000 were killed, 75,000 were severely disabled, 23,214 were 100 percent disabled, 5,283 lost limbs, 61 percent were younger than twenty-one, and 11,465 of the 58,000 who were killed were younger than twenty.

Inside, I struggled with the damage this was imposing on America's youth.

On December 1, 1969, I was tossing a football around with Jesse and Waldo as the national TV stations were showing the draft lottery taking place that day. This particular lottery, which was held when I was a senior, covered 1951 birthdays, meaning those young men born in 1951 would be inducted into the military to fight in Vietnam the following year. The way I understood it, on December 1, the drawing date, 366 capsules representing 365 days of the year, plus one more for leap year, would be pulled from a large rotating clear drum. A second drum would also have capsules with 366 numbers. A representative from the Selective Service System would pull a capsule from the drum and announce the birthday, then pull from the second drum, announcing the number. If they pulled June 20, and the number was 165, all those kids born on June 20, 1951, were assigned draft number 165. If they pulled a July 10 birthdate, with the second number being 1, all those born on that day would probably be the first to be called in for duty.

That was why I was out playing football with my brothers instead of worrying about whether I would be one of the ones to be drafted. Chances were slim, and I wasn't worried. Should I have been?

One of my sisters ran outside, yelling, "Your birthday was the seventh pulled from the drum!"

Holy shit! What are the odds? I thought. *This Nixon fellow has talked about ending the war. Perhaps when my day comes, it will be over.* I silently prayed that night, asking Jesus to look out for me. I wouldn't be eligible for the draft until I finished high school, so I set it aside. However, as seniors, we talked about the draft in every class. One teacher even told us that the military was making exceptions for those going to college.

"It's called a student deferral," she said.

"How does that work?" one student asked.

"If you go to college, you get a deferment. Meaning, they won't take you. However, as soon as you graduate, you'll be drafted."

Going to college was not one of my options at the time. Henry Ward had told me I was not college material. Why should I spend time worrying about this?

I was young and naïve, that's why. It wasn't affecting me, so why should I worry? Right?

I was home from work, still contemplating what Samantha had told me about college life. With the war still looming, I had to make some serious decisions. Could I go to college and succeed? Could I avoid the draft until after college? Did I have the grades? I started investigating the possibilities.

"I want to go to college," I told my mother on the last day of my job at the onion barn.

"I don't have the money to send you to college," she said. "You know that."

"I've been talking to people who are going, and they tell me it's not that hard. They told me about loans and grants. Grants are dollars you don't have to pay back, from what I understand. The government also loans you money that you can pay back when you get out of college. I want to try and see if I can do it."

"Just know that we don't have the money for you to go," Mom said solemnly.

I knew she was right. But I was not going to be an onion worker for the rest of my life. I was determined to leave that kind of employment behind, having learned very quickly that a high school diploma was not enough to land me the kind of job I wanted and needed. Problem was, I didn't know how to get started. The counselor had never explained college entrance exams, college tuition, or college life. He hadn't explained college, period.

I found out that Sul Ross State University in Alpine, Texas, sixty-seven miles away heading southwest, was enrolling students for the fall semester. So, on a Monday morning, I drove to Alpine. The university stood halfway up a mountain and overlooked the city. It was a beautiful place, with large brownstone buildings shimmering in the sun. I parked the car and headed toward a building where several other students were headed.

"Hey. Where do you register for school?" I asked a boy my age who seemed as lost as I was.

"It's that building," he said, pointing toward a monolithic four-story red brick structure.

"Thanks."

I walked into a long corridor with tables set up alongside the walls. Registrars were talking to those registering for classes. The long line of students talking and waiting their turn stretched beyond the corridor. After forty-five minutes or so, my turn came up.

"Are you registering?" asked a young woman without looking up from her papers.

"Yes."

"Where's your paperwork?" She looked up at me with a quizzical sigh.

"What kind of paperwork do I need?"

"You need an application. A transcript. A letter of recommendation from your counselor or principal. You'll also need to fill out any financial information if you are applying for assistance." She checked off each box as she told me what I needed, then added, "You have until the end of the week to get these things in, or you'll be charged extra for late registration. If you wait until then, you might not get into the classes you need."

My head was spinning. Where and how was I going to get all these things in time?

"You need to go over there, to that office, and ask for an application and a financial assistance packet," she said. "Ask for Rosie."

I waited another full hour before I could talk to Rosie. Noting the look of despair and frustration on my face, she graciously offered to help me get started.

"It's going to take some time, but if you hurry, you might be able to get in," she said, handing me a large envelope with several documents in it. I was completely lost. Rosie could sense my anxiety as she walked me through every step. I had four days to get this done if I was to attend college.

I drove around the campus, thrilled by the openness of such a large place. Seeing students walking around, smiling, and talking to one another inspired me. I wanted to be there. I had to be there.

I drove back to Fort Stockton and went directly to the high school. The secretary showed me to the student affairs office, where the transcripts were kept. It cost two dollars. I paid. He handed me a copy of my transcript.

"Is this an official transcript? I need an official one."

"Nope. This is a copy. If you want an official, you'll have to come back tomorrow. The counselor will be here. She will have to sign an official one for you. Oh, and bring two dollars for that one."

I went home, read over the financial packet, and tried to decipher the instructions. They needed my parents' income tax statements, a copy of their latest payroll checks, signatures, family history, siblings' ages, and their names. It seemed so insurmountable.

I went to the high school the next morning and waited for the counselor. After an hour, she came in and asked me to follow her. I was glad Mr. Ward wasn't there anymore.

"I need some help with this financial packet. I'll need an official transcript, and I need some help with this application."

"I can help you with the financial assistance package and the application, but since you did not graduate from here, you'll have to go to, let me see here, Buena Vista for your transcript."

"I went here for three years. Here is my transcript from my years here. Will that help?"

"Why didn't anyone help you if you knew you wanted to go to college? All this should have been done months ago," the counselor said, annoyed.

"The counselor at that time told me I was not college material. I'm trying to prove him wrong."

It took me all of four days to complete everything. I drove back to Sul Ross the last day before early registration ended, waited in line for what seemed hours, then approached the girl registering students.

"Who is your advisor?" she asked.

"What's an advisor?"

"The person who is supposed to help you with your schedule. What is your major? Minor?"

"I don't have an advisor. I don't have a major. I don't have a minor." I said robotically, emphasizing the *don't* part.

"Then you have to see Dr. Baiza. He is the undecided advisor."

"Where do I find him?"

"In the 300 Building." She turned to a woman sitting nearby. "Janie, will you walk this freshman to Dr. Baiza's office?"

Janie walked me to another building that had similar hallways and was devoid of human beings. Dr. Baiza's office was in the basement. He motioned for me to sit down, then went over the particulars of an undecided schedule. Once it was completed, I ran back to the registration table and waited for another few minutes while the same girl looked over my paperwork.

"That class is full. You'll have to take this one on Tuesday/Thursday. This one is okay. You can't take this history class. It's full. You need to take it on Monday/Wednesday/Friday."

By the time the agony was over, only one of the classes Dr. Baiza recommended was left intact. I had a full schedule with sixteen hours' worth of classes. English, math, science, history, PE, and music.

Next, I was sent to the financial office for a review of my application. The high school counselor recommended that I apply for a Pell Grant—money from the government that I would not have to pay back if I finished and got a degree from the university.

I was hoping I had correctly done all the things asked of me. Until I got a letter from the university, I would not know if I'd been accepted. I drove home at the end of the day exhausted.

I waited for a letter from the school letting me know whether I was in or not. I waited. Nothing.

The days went by slowly. I prayed to all of Jesus's family for a miracle. The counselor's words, "You are not college material," haunted me. "I'd be doing you a disservice if I put you in college prep classes." The words kept resonating in my head. *What if he's right? What if I don't belong there? What if I don't have the background? What if I fail? What if …*

Finally, the envelope arrived. Slowly, with shaking hands, I tore the end of it. Making the sign of the cross for strength, I asked Jesus to look out for me. I asked Mary, mother of Jesus, the Holy Ghost, God, Joseph, and all the apostles to help me. I opened my eyes and read.

"Dear Mr. Alfaro, we would like to congratulate you for being accepted ..."

I cried. I literally cried uncontrollably for several minutes. I had never been so happy in my life. I was going to college! The first in one of the poorest families in Texas was going to college!

The first semester, I made the dean's list of academic achievement. I didn't stop going to school. I didn't stop working. I didn't stop playing music. I didn't stop until I graduated in three years with a Bachelor of Science degree in political science from Sul Ross University.

Then I pulled away from the campus. My next stop: Texas Tech Law School, in Lubbock.

I was on my way to that better future!

Or so I thought.

Epilogue

On my birthday in July 2020, one of my grandsons sent me a fill-in-the-blank book entitled *Tell Me Your Story*. I called him and asked why he'd sent me that particular book, and he stated that he and his brothers didn't know much about my childhood other than what they knew of me as an adult. He wanted to know how I got to where I am today.

Sitting at my desk in the middle of the COVID pandemic, I looked at the book and started filling in the blanks. Setting it aside, I decided to tell them about my childhood via stories I remembered growing up. I wanted them to know about my parents and my siblings, whom they knew very little about. I wanted them to know how similar my life growing up in the barrio—other than living in poverty and having trouble with the English language—was to theirs. I wanted them to know where I came from, where I'd been, and how I got there.

Hence, this book.

As I wrote, I was surprised at how much I remembered about growing up in a Hispanic household with an American mother and a Mexican father. How the two cultures, not being very different, intermingled to reveal how poor families were able to survive in the early 1950s and 1960s, a time when America and the world were changing dramatically—when things were difficult for many and time stood still for those living in small Texas towns like ours. The stories were intended for my children and grandchildren, who, when I mentioned what I was doing, inspired me to tell it all.

I had my wife read the first draft of the manuscript. Once finished, she told me these were stories that needed to be shared with families other than my own. I laughed, and when she gave me the "look," she proceeded to defend her position.

"There are many young parents today who are raising children and having the same trials and tribulations your family experienced," she said. "Your stories are filled with life recipes and anecdotes closely similar to what many experience. And they show how your family's religious upbringing helped you deal with difficulties. I think you should have it published."

And with that, I decided to share my stories with you.

My editor, Kristy Phillips, suggested I include an epilogue that summarizes what happened after I graduated from college. She said there were so many unanswered questions that would leave the reader with the inevitable question: "What happened next?"

I'd always wanted to be a lawyer, and in the back of my mind, I thought I could become one. When the time came to decide my major and minor in college, I chose political science and history. After graduation, I took the LSAT exam, which opened the window of opportunity. I applied to several law schools but chose Texas Tech because it was the closest to home and cheaper. Plus, it had a reputation for graduating some of the top lawyers in Texas.

But I missed the registration deadline and had no choice but to wait until the spring. I was married and had a son. So I needed to find a job to sustain us until I could get into law school.

In the hallway of the administration building, a bulletin board showed vacancies for various jobs around the state. I stopped to look for something that was close to Lubbock and found a teaching position in Plainview, Texas. I called, and the principal asked me if I knew Spanish.

"Of course," was my reply.

He sent me an application, and in a matter of days, I got a call saying I had the job. This would put me in the right place until I heard from Texas Tech.

I taught English as a second language to seventh- and eighth-grade non-English speakers. In November of 1973, I got my acceptance letter for law school. However, because I needed to provide for my family, I made the decision to postpone law school until the following year.

Before the end of the school year, the high school principal came by to see me. He asked me if I would be interested in teaching high school government and history, and I quickly jumped at the opportunity because it paid a little more money—something I needed.

I fell in love with teaching and didn't apply to law school in the spring of 1974.

Teaching young adults was my calling, and I found it purposeful. I loved teaching high school students. I soon settled into believing that this was the right decision for me. I could talk to students about the world's problems and how their generation would change things for the better. Instead of defending adults who had already committed an alleged wrong, I figured, why not teach students to think about how they could, through a good-quality education, bring harmony into a divided country? I wanted to give every child a chance to succeed regardless of where they came from, what color their skin was, or how poor they were. I dedicated myself to working in mostly poor, minority school districts. I taught middle school and high school for eleven years.

In 1984, I earned a master's degree in educational administration and was appointed principal of Comanche Elementary School in my hometown of Fort Stockton. It was here that I started breaking down traditional educational practices that hurt the poor and non-English speakers. The school moved from homogeneously grouping kids based on intelligence tests to heterogeneously grouping them, much to the dismay of teachers. No more basic, average, or advanced classes. Instead, every child had an opportunity to learn in classes that research showed was a better system.

But I knew I could do more.

From an elementary school principal's position in Seguin, Texas, I was appointed superintendent in South Texas—a poor, mostly Hispanic community. After three years, I moved to San Antonio, Texas, to work as assistant superintendent of an urban school district. Again, it was a largely minority and poor area. In 2005, after completing what was known as Broad Superintendents Academy, I became a regional superintendent in the Clark County School District in Las Vegas, Nevada—the fifth-largest school district in the country.

Mom was right. Education was the key to a better future. She saw every one of her seven children graduate from high school. Three went on to college, earning degrees in education, business, and counseling. Two went into the military, one became a successful businessman right out of high school, and one went into the medical field.

Mom would have been proud.

If you'd like Robert to speak at an event or if you'd like him to help transform your school or district into a world class institution supporting students of all walks of life, please contact him at the information below. He is also available to coach, mentor and assist educational administrators and aspiring superintendents.

Contact Information for Robert Alfaro:
https://www.linkedin.com/in/robert-alfaro-22363836?lipi=urn
%3Ali%3Apage%3Ad_flagship3_profile_view_base_contact_
details%3B4UaPAIFrRjGTU9QGUzU4kQ%3D%3D

Robalfaro1951@gmail.com

www.ingramcontent.com/pod-product-compliance
Lightning Source LLC
Chambersburg PA
CBHW021500090426
42739CB00007B/390